Charity in Islamic Societies

Muslim beliefs have inspired charitable giving for over fourteen centuries, yet Islamic history has rarely been examined from this perspective. In *Charity in Islamic Societies*, Amy Singer explains the basic concepts and institutions of Muslim charity, including the obligation to give on an annual basis, as well as an array of voluntary activities undertaken at every level of society and across the span of individual lifetimes. Charitable endowments – bestowed by rulers, wealthy individuals, and even those of more modest means – shaped Muslim societies and cultures in every era. This book demonstrates how historical circumstances, social status, gender, age, and other factors interacted with religious ideals to create a rich variety of charitable practices, from the beginnings of Islam to the present day. Using written texts, buildings, images, and objects to anchor the discussions in each chapter, the author explores the motivations for charity, its impact on the rich and the poor, and the politicization of charity, arguing that the study of philanthropy affords a unique prism through which to examine the past. This lucidly written and accessible book will capture the attention of anyone who is interested in the nature of Islamic society and the role of philanthropy throughout history.

AMY SINGER is professor of Ottoman History in the Department of Middle Eastern and African History at Tel Aviv University, Israel. Her recent publications include *Palestinian Peasants and Ottoman Officials* (Cambridge, 1994), *Constructing Ottoman Beneficence: An Imperial Soup Kitchen in Jerusalem* (2002), *Poverty and Charity in Middle Eastern Contexts* (ed., 2003), and *Feeding People, Feeding Power: Imarets in the Ottoman Empire* (ed., 2007).

THEMES IN ISLAMIC HISTORY comprises a range of titles exploring different aspects of Islamic history, society and culture by leading scholars in the field. Books are thematic in approach, offering a comprehensive and accessible overview of the subject. Generally, surveys treat Islamic history from its origins to the demise of the Ottoman Empire, although some offer a more developed analysis of a particular period, or project into the present, depending on the subject-matter. All the books are written to interpret and illuminate the past, as gateways to a deeper understanding of Islamic civilization and its peoples.

Editorial adviser:
Patricia Crone, *Institute for Advanced Study, Princeton University*

Already published:
Chase F. Robinson, *Islamic Historiography*

Jonathan P. Berkey, *The Formation of Islam: Religion and Society in the Near East, 600–1800*

Michael Cook, *Forbidding Wrong in Islam: An Introduction*

David Cook, *Martyrdom in Islam*

Charity in Islamic Societies

Amy Singer

Tel Aviv University

CAMBRIDGE UNIVERSITY PRESS
Cambridge, New York, Melbourne, Madrid, Cape Town, Singapore, São Paulo, Delhi

Cambridge University Press
The Edinburgh Building, Cambridge CB2 8RU, UK

Published in the United States of America by Cambridge University Press, New York

www.cambridge.org
Information on this title: www.cambridge.org/9780521529129

First published 2008

Printed in the United Kingdom at the University Press, Cambridge

A catalogue record for this publication is available from the British Library

ISBN 978-0-521-82164-3 hardback
ISBN 978-0-521-52912-9 paperback

To the memory of Mine An Ener (1965–2003),
friend and colleague

Contents

Illustrations

Cover *Emperor Jahangir weighing his son Khurram in gold*, attributed to
Manohar, *c*.1615.

Acknowledgments

I began this book convinced that the study of charity and philanthropy offers profound insights into the nature of human societies and historical change. At its conclusion, I remain equally persuaded that this is the case. In 1994, Michael Bonner, Mine Ener, and I began a partnership to organize a first panel on charity in Middle Eastern societies at the Middle East Studies Association annual meeting. Other panels followed that one and our joint efforts culminated in a National Endowment for the Humanities (USA) conference on Poverty and Charity in Middle Eastern Contexts held at the University of Michigan in 2000, and published under the same title in 2003. Our conversations, the papers of scholars at all those meetings, and new research since then have inspired the present study.

The research and writing of this book have stretched over many years and benefited from the financial, intellectual, and emotional support of several institutions, and countless colleagues and friends. This research was supported by The Israel Science Foundation (grants no. 888/01 and 730/04). It has also benefited from the support of the American Research Institute in Turkey and the Research Center for Anatolian Civilizations at Koç University, Istanbul. Final revisions of the manuscript were accomplished during a year as a senior research fellow at RCAC-Koç during the 2006–2007 academic year. I would like to thank in particular the director, Professor Scott Redford, for his collegial welcome and to acknowledge how much I have learned from him. My fellow fellows and the RCAC-Koç staff created a most supportive and congenial intellectual community. I would also like to thank the staffs of the Sorasky Library at Tel Aviv University, the library of the İslam Araştırmaları Merkezi (Istanbul), the Başbakanlık Arşivi, Topkapı Sarayı Arşivi, and Duygu Kızılaslan at the RCAC-Koç Library.

For a decade, I have taught undergraduate and graduate seminars on different aspects of charity in the Department of Middle Eastern and African History at Tel Aviv University. My students in those courses have been an important part of this project, contributing immeasurably to my work with their questions and their papers, and by sharing from their own experiences. You are too numerous to name here but I extend my sincere thanks to you for your hard work and your insistent calls for clarifications and answers. In particular, I extend my thanks to Isa Amin, Ateret Aharon, and Liran Yadgar. During this same decade, I was fortunate to have dedicated research assistants who contributed their own thoughts and critiques on the topic of this book, as well as their research skills: Guy Burak, Shuki Ecker, Gali Genossar, Liat Kozma, Tsameret Levi-Dafni, Yochai Primak, and Avner Wishnitzer.

My colleagues in the Department of Middle Eastern and African History at Tel Aviv University, as well as student and faculty audiences at Bilkent, Boğaziçi, Hacettepe, İstanbul Bilgi, and Sabancı Universities in Turkey, heard preliminary versions of parts of this book at different times, and contributed their comments to help me hone my own thinking.

During the years of research and writing, I have incurred innumerable debts and would like to recognize a variety of contributions. For their careful critical readings of all or parts of the manuscript at different stages in its completion: Patricia Crone, Ilana Krausman-Ben Amos, Tsameret Levi-Dafni, Daniel M. Singer, and anonymous readers. For their assistance, comments, critiques, and willingness to share their expertise or experience: Mark Cohen, Müge Göçek, İştar Gözaydin, Michal Hacham Dallal, Hamid Haji, Ekrem Işın, Cemal Kafadar, Billie Melman, Gülru Necipoğlu, Nadir Özbek, Sait Özervarlı, Leslie Peirce, Uri Rubin, Housni Alkhateeb Shehada, and Deborah Tor. For their particular help with preparing the illustrations: Patricia Barbor, Halenur Çalışkan, Dana Katz, and Ilana Katz.

Marigold Acland of Cambridge University Press has been a firm believer in the possibility and worth of this project even when my own determination wavered. It has been a pleasure to work with her and the Cambridge University Press staff in the production of this book.

David Katz has never faltered as a companion and critical reader. As long as we continue to finish our manuscripts by turns and not simultaneously, our partnership is safe.

Mine Ener has continued to be a source of inspiration even after her death, as her enthusiasm echoes through her own writings and my memories of our conversations. Her direct contribution to this manuscript is missing, and her absence too great for words.

Note on spellings and foreign words

Non-English words have been written in the most familiar form, to the extent possible, for example: Qur'an, qadi, Mecca. Arabic words have been transliterated without diacritics above and below the letters. However, the 'ayn character (') has been retained. Turkish words have been written as they are written in Turkish; where possible, they have been written in familiar forms (for example, pasha). In some cases, they retain Turkish characters, including c (like the j in jam), ç (like the ch in cheese), ğ (silent), ş (like the sh in ship), ı (like the u in cushion), ö (like a German ö), ü (like the French ü). Only the first occurrence of a foreign word is italicized. Brief definitions will appear at the first use of a word and in the index.

Abbreviations

d.	died
EI	*Encyclopaedia of Islam*, 1st edition, 4 vols. (Leiden: E. J. Brill, 1913–1936)
EI²	*Encyclopaedia of Islam*, new edition, 11 vols. plus supplements (Leiden, London: E. J. Brill, 1954–2003)
İA	*İslâm Ansiklopedisi*, 13 vols. (Istanbul: Milli Eğitim Basimevi, 1945–88)
TDVİA	*Türkiye Diyanet Vakfı İslam Ansiklopedisi* (Istanbul: Türkiye Diyanet Vakfı İslam Ansiklopedisi Genel Müdürlüğü, 1988–)
USC-MSA	University of Southern California, Muslim Students Association

Introduction

In the Name of God, the Compassionate the Caring
Do you see him who calls the [day of] reckoning a lie?
   He is the one who casts the orphan away
   who fails to urge the feeding of one in need.
Cursed are those who perform the prayer unmindful of how they pray
who make of themselves a display but hold back charity.

Qur'an 107[1]

In the summer of 2005, Tariq Fischer was killed in a car accident. His parents pledged a generous gift in memory of their son to Swarthmore College, the Pennsylvania school in the United States where Tariq had just completed his first year of study. Describing their donation, his parents wrote: "It is not often that a college is given the responsibility to invest the inheritance of one of its young students, and we consider this a special and serious commitment. Tariq loved his friends at Swarthmore. He loved his involvement in sports. He loved writing for *The Phoenix* [the college newspaper]. And he loved Islam. We will have some peace if his inheritance is invested by Swarthmore to honor these things that he loved." Most of the Fischers' gift was directed to support the new Islamic Studies program at the college. As Tariq's mother, a physician originally from Pakistan, explained: "There is a tradition in Islam called Sadaqa-e Jariya, where Muslims are encouraged to set up educational facilities or programs that will continue to benefit people even after the donors are gone ... We hope this endowment will continue to benefit students, many of whom will become future leaders, in understanding Islam and Muslims and bring harmony between the people of the world."[2]

On the face of it, the Fischers' gift fits seamlessly into US philanthropic traditions rooted in Judeo-Christian ethics and American history, traditions that have inspired generations of donors to support public and private education, medicine, poverty relief, religious buildings and services, the arts, literature,

---

[1] Qur'an verses in this book are cited mainly from Arthur J. Arberry, trans., *The Koran Interpreted* (New York: Macmillan, 1955), unless otherwise indicated. The translation here is that of Michael Sells, *Approaching the Qur'ān: The Early Revelations* (Ashland, OR: White Cloud Press, 1999), 124, except for the word "charity," for which he prefers "small kindness."

[2] Http://www.swarthmore.edu/news/releases/05/fischer.html (accessed 6 February 2006).

and a host of civic societies and endeavors ranging from veterans associations to the protection of animals, from local town initiatives to nationwide and transnational organizations. Yet the Fischers framed their donation within another tradition as well, that of Muslim beliefs and practices, which have likewise inspired charitable giving throughout the fourteen centuries of Islamic history. For example, almost five hundred years before the Fischers, the Ottoman Sultan Süleyman I and his wife, Hurrem Sultan, sponsored the construction of a mosque, *madrasa* (college), public kitchen, and tomb in memory of their favorite son and heir, Prince Mehmed (1521–1543), who died of an illness at almost the same age as Tariq Fischer.[3] Until today, the buildings of this Ottoman complex, known as Şehzade ("son of the ruler"), remain a vibrant part of life in the center of Istanbul.

From approximately the early 1990s, Muslim charity has attracted growing attention, much of it not in academic circles, and since September 11, 2001, it has received some very bad press, with analysts and observers frequently emphasizing the links between charity and extremist violence. The headline "Defining Hamas: Roots in Charity and Branches of Violence" was a typical one for newspaper stories in the early twenty-first century.[4] Yet with all the negative ink spilled on the subject by government officials, journalists, pundits, and others, few have stopped long to consider why it is that the discourse and practice of charity are so prominent in Muslim communities, historically and today, except to give passing lip service to the fact that almsgiving is one of the five basic obligations of every Muslim. In the post-9/11 world, where fear of highly visible political Islam represented by radical minorities runs high, one of the challenges for scholars is to examine Islamic societies without feeling compelled either to condemn or to glorify them. Such a critical examination of history strives to discover the particular and the universal within one or more societies in order to understand the commonalities and specificities of diverse peoples and in so doing to appreciate more fully the entire human experience.

Throughout history, the responsibility for social welfare has been distributed variously among individuals, families, governments, and associations of many types. Not all of their efforts might be called charity by everyone, and indeed "charity" has become, and is used here to describe, a wide variety of behaviors. Yet the historical investigation of giving in this broadest sense – whether

---

[3] On Prince Mehmed, see Leslie P. Peirce, *The Imperial Harem: Women and Sovereignty in the Ottoman Empire* (New York: Oxford University Press, 1993), 60, 67, 80. Peirce believes that Mehmed died of natural causes, probably smallpox. On the founding of this complex of buildings, see Gülru Necipoğlu, *The Age of Sinan: Architectural Culture in the Ottoman Empire*, photographs and drawings by Arben N. Arapi and Reha Günay (Princeton: Princeton University Press, 2005), 191–207.

[4] Ian Fisher, "Defining Hamas: Roots in Charity and Branches of Violence," *The New York Times* (June 16, 2003), A8.

beneficence, philanthropy, welfare, or aid – is integral to interpreting any society or culture. To understand the history of charity means also to understand how notions of entitlement and obligation evolved in societies, creating the networks of responsibility and dependence in which we live today. Without an appreciation of the ways in which states and societies develop effective forms of relief for dependent individuals and groups, one can scarcely comprehend much of contemporary political and economic discourse and culture. The same is true of the past.

The religion of Islam is more than 1,400 years old and its adherents around the world number in excess of one billion people at the beginning of the twenty-first century. Within a century of his death in 632 the followers of the Prophet Muhammad had traveled as preachers, merchants, and conquerors from their first home in the Arabian peninsula to the lands of Asia, Africa, and Europe. Today, Muslims live in most countries of the world, in some as the majority population, in others as minority communities. They are united by a common adherence to the Qur'an as a sacred text which provides the basis for religious belief and the correct way to conduct one's life.

The present work asks what comprises charity in Islamic societies and explores the multiplicity of roles it has played, beginning from its recitation, analysis, and imitation from the teachings and practices of Muhammad, to its reinforcement as the Islamic community (*umma*) expanded and as interpretation and historical experience divided the community into separate polities and distinctive cultures. To be sure, practices have varied tremendously across time and space as they were affected by factors such as class, gender, education, and the environment. Charity in Islamic societies constitutes a rich field of investigation in and of itself, and the study of charitable ideals and practices provides significant insights into the histories and cultures of Muslims. At the same time, however, this study assumes charity to be a universal phenomenon, such that the insights gained in this particular context also provide insights into the experiences of human history in general. This book thus presents a constructive alternative approach to what had been posited so destructively since 9/11 as a nexus between charity and violence among Muslims. It decouples the connection by contextualizing charity within Islamic societies historically. As such, charity becomes not an act that is stigmatized by its association with Muslims but a social practice that travels the globe.

Until very recently, the ideals and practices of charity have been virtually absent from historical discussions of Islamic societies, despite the fact that they permeate the experience of Muslims past and present. While ideologically associated with religious belief, practice, and fundamental notions of social justice, these same ideals and practices have worked historically in as complex and even problematic ways as does charity everywhere. This book is thus conceived as a starting point for further research and thinking about charity, setting out a basic conceptual framework and analyzing a broad range of examples. My intention is to introduce readers to the rich possibilities offered by reconsidering history through the prism of charity.

What is charity?

A sense of the complexity of ideas implicated in the notion of charity can be gleaned by exploring some of the vocabulary related to charity in other languages and religions. Two relevant points of comparison for Islam are Judaism and Christianity, which preceded Islam and contributed directly and indirectly to its initial formation. The Hebrew term *ṣedāḳā* is cognate with Arabic *ṣadaqa* and the two are related to the Semitic root /ṣdḳ/ meaning "right," "privilege," "grant," or "gift," and to the idea of giving a stipulated gift as an appropriate course of action. On the other hand, an Aramaic cognate of the Hebrew had a meaning of giving charity or alms. Arabic *sadaqa* thus derived its meaning directly from the Semitic root or else it absorbed the term as a loan translation. *Ṣedāḳā* in Hebrew had primarily a moral sense, meaning "justice" or "righteousness." Scholars understood both justice and righteousness to be acts of religious merit, such that the two became synonymous, expressed simultaneously in the single word. As the Jewish and Aramaic concepts began to fuse in the sixth century BC, the Hebrew also came to refer to concrete, material assistance, "the charity which a Jew is required by law to give to the poor." In the fifth century BC, the term referred to sums levied for the common welfare and then more specifically for the poor as a result of the circumstances provoked by the Babylonian exile (586 BC). In addition to *ṣedāḳā*, Hebrew used the word *hesed* (graciousness) to talk about the manner of extending hospitality and aid to the needy.[5]

Both the moral and religious explanations of charity and the philological discussion consider charity from two perspectives, that of the donor and that of the recipient. On the one hand, charity is a gift or grant required by law; on the other hand, charity represents a right of the poor or a just claim on the community. This duality in charity relationships is important to remember because charitable actions are shaped by the motivations and expectations of both donors and recipients, although the relative influence of either side varies enormously from one charitable occasion or undertaking to the next.

The early Christians evolved general principles concerning charity, which emphasized mutual love and the love of God, together with warnings against the attachment to money and material things. In addition to a communal ethic, Christianity also evolved an emphasis on individual charity and asceticism,

---

[5] Franz Rosenthal, "Ṣedaḳa, Charity," *Hebrew Union College Annual* 23 (1950–51): 411–30.

which, among other things, ultimately influenced the creation of monasteries. Monasteries were inseparably linked to charity, subsisting at least in part on charitable contributions while, at the same time, dispensing charity in one form or another to the poor and deserving.[6] These basic attributes of charity in early Jewish and Christian communities provide points of comparison for our discussion of charity in Islamic societies, and make it clear that charity in Islamic texts and practices derived partly from a prior history of beneficent practice. A full discussion of Jewish and Christian practices and ideas, however, is not the purpose of this book. Moreover, if this book were an investigation into the origins of Islamic charity, it would also be appropriate to explore extensively the contributions of Greek, Roman, Sassanid, Byzantine, and pre-Islamic Arabian cultures to the formation of early Islamic societies.[7]

The words we use to talk about charity are not neutral, and because we are using English here to represent ideas and experiences created in other languages, it is worth taking a moment to consider their meanings. English-language dictionary definitions of charity include both a material aspect, that is, giving substantive assistance to those in need, and a more emotional or philosophical component, namely the love of humankind. The latter aspect derives most immediately from traditional Christian ideas related to the Latin word *caritas*. Actually, the central position of charity in modern Christian thought, at least in the English-speaking world, paradoxically derived from a mistranslation in the King James Bible, first published in 1611. In the New Testament, St. Paul named faith, hope, and love as the three chief virtues, subsequently called the three theological virtues by the Church Fathers in the

---

[6] Frederick B. Bird, "Comparative Study of the Works of Charity in Christianity and Judaism," *Journal of Religious Ethics* 10 (1982): 162.

[7] For a recent general discussion of the early period of Islamic history, see Jonathan P. Berkey, *The Formation of Islam: Religion and Society in the Near East, 600–1800* (Cambridge, UK: Cambridge University Press, 2003). For discussions of charity in Judaism, see Ephraim Frisch, *An Historical Survey of Jewish Philanthropy* (New York: The Macmillan Company, 1924; repr. 1969); Abraham Cronbach, "The Maimonidean Code of Benevolence," *Hebrew Union College Annual* 20 (1947): 471–540; Mark R. Cohen, *Poverty and Charity in the Jewish Community of Medieval Egypt* (Princeton: Princeton University Press, 2005), 288. For charity in the classical world, see Paul Veyne, *Bread and Circuses: Historical Sociology and Political Pluralism*, introd. by Oswyn Murray, trans. Brian Pearce (London: Allen Lane, 1976; repr. 1990); A. R. Hands, *Charities and Social Aid in Greece and Rome*, Aspects of Greek and Roman Life (Ithaca: Cornell University Press, 1968); Peter Brown, *Poverty and Leadership in the Later Roman Empire* (Hanover, NH: University Press of New England, 2002); Maria Macuch, "Charitable Foundations in the Sasanian Period," *Encyclopaedia Iranica*, V: 139–42. On Byzantine charity, see Demetrios J. Constantelos, *Byzantine Philanthropy and Social Welfare*, Rutgers Byzantine Series (New Brunswick: Rutgers University Press, 1968); Judith Herrin, "Ideals of Charity, Realities of Welfare: The Philanthropic Activity of the Byzantine Church," in *Church and People in Byzantium*, ed. Rosemary Morris, Society for the Promotion of Byzantine Studies, Manchester Twentieth Spring Symposium of Byzantine Studies, 1986 (Birmingham: Centre for Byzantine, Ottoman and Modern Greek Studies, University of Birmingham, 1990), 151–64.

fourth and fifth centuries.[8] "Love" in the New Testament was the Greek *agape*, God's love, or "the nature of God himself."[9] Agape came into Latin as *caritas*, which also described God's love for humankind. The King James Bible translation committee rendered "caritas" into English by "charity" with the result that the translation actually changed the meaning of the original Greek to focus on the love shown by humans for each other, and so to God, through beneficent acts.[10] With the translation into English, "charity" in the modern sense took on a higher place than before in God's perceived agenda for people.

Philanthropy, literally "love of man", is probably the English word most commonly used as a synonym for charity. However, some authors insist on drawing a precise dividing line between the two as distinct phenomena. Charity is then seen as deriving from spiritual or religious motivations while philanthropy describes the nineteenth- and twentieth-century realm of rational, professionalized, secular action. Perhaps this attempt at a distinction arises from the Greek origins of the word "philanthropy" and its place in classical as opposed to Christian texts. A more useful contrast between charity and philanthropy might be found in definitions of charity as relief or "acts of mercy to relieve suffering" and of philanthropy as development or "acts of community to enhance the quality of life and to insure a better future."[11] However, even a brief tour through historical and sociological writings on charity and philanthropy makes clear that distinctions between the two are not universally adopted and are, in any case, unhelpfully rigid. It is not always an easy task to separate "acts of mercy" from "acts of community," especially when the terms of the discussion are in (or originated from) another language, one which frames these acts differently. Nor is it always possible to untangle religious and secular inspirations in any one place or time or in any one person, since religious teachings are a fundamental aspect of ethical education in many parts of the world, delivered in a variety of devotional contexts, even where schools are organized with a secular and rational outlook. Moreover, the importance of family and community socialization to generous behavior is probably at least as important as any formal instruction. At the same time, projects articulated in

---

[8] I Corinthians 13:13. Chapter 13 is the famous passage from the New Testament which begins: "Though I speak with the tongues of men and of angels, and have not charity ..." where "charity" throughout the chapter was translated from *caritas* or *agape*.

[9] Bernard Hamilton, *Religion in the Medieval West* (London: Edward Arnold, 1986), 132.

[10] F. L. Cross and E. A. Livingstone, eds., *Oxford Dictionary of the Christian Church*, 3rd edn. (Oxford: Oxford University Press, 1997).

[11] Robert Payton, "Philanthropy in Action," in *Philanthropy: Four Views*, Robert Payton *et al.* (New Brunswick: Transaction, 1988), 1. See also the discussion in Robert A. Gross, "Giving in America: From Charity to Philanthropy," in *Charity, Philanthropy, and Civility in American History*, ed. Lawrence J. Friedman and Mark D. McGarvie (Cambridge, UK: Cambridge University Press, 2003), 29–48, which describes a chronological development of philanthropy in the course of the nineteenth century.

religious language may be motivated by forces not even remotely religious. Some preference seems to be retained in current American usage for choosing "philanthropy" when talking about the donations of wealthy individuals, referred to as philanthropists, in particular when referring to cultural projects in contrast to efforts to ensure basic human welfare, especially those effected through faith-based organizations. Yet in the UK it is the "Charities Commission" that oversees all philanthropic contributions and organizations.[12]

Many other words exist in English as partial or whole synonyms to the word charity, like altruism, beneficence, benevolence, or munificence. This list might be expanded to other languages to include the original Hebrew, Greek, and Arabic of the Bible, New Testament, and Qur'an, not to mention the languages of other holy texts. Modern secular terms used by governments and non-governmental organizations (NGOs) alike add words to the vocabulary of beneficent giving: aid, development, relief, support, welfare. These words are not fully congruent and each word also carries with it lexical nuances and built-in references to time, place, ideology, and policy, as well as a specific range of meanings that depart from the sense of charity. Ultimately, as we will see, there is no definitive solution to the problem of how to talk about beneficent giving in Islamic societies using the English language. However, it is necessary at the outset to articulate the complex range of terms and meanings that adhere to or intersect with the word charity. In this book charity, beneficence, and philanthropy will be used interchangeably.

After reviewing some of the vocabulary associated with charity, it is worth considering the meaning of charity. In one sense, "charity" or "philanthropy" is an answer to the larger question: what are the proper uses of wealth? That is, different belief systems respond in distinct ways to the accumulation and spending of material wealth. Some encourage charitable giving by both condemning wealth and praising giving, others by emphasizing the plight of the needy and the responsibility of the rich. It is frequently the case that people are encouraged for religious reasons to divest themselves of property, in part or in full, for the benefit of others. Meanwhile, some pagan belief systems hold that objects have their own essence and must be passed on to prevent them working against their owners.

While this book does not cover the economic histories of Islamic societies or even the more limited contemporary field of "Islamic economics," it contributes in some measure to each of these fields. At some level, discussions of charity in

---

[12] For the meanings and etymologies of "philanthropy," see *Oxford English Dictionary* (online edition). See the discussion of terms and meanings in W. Ilchman, S. N. Katz, and E. L. Queen, eds, *Philanthropy in the World's Traditions* (Bloomington: Indiana University Press, 1998), x and Kevin C. Robbins, "Philanthropy," in *New Dictionary of the History of Ideas*, vol. IV, ed. Maryanne Cline Horowitz (New York: Charles Scribner's Sons, 2005), 1757–58.

all societies are about economics, because they explain how people have come to define acceptable uses of wealth acquired and held by individuals. Most obviously in the contemporary world, capitalism advocates the private accumulation of wealth and different national legal systems make laws requiring people to share their wealth (for example, through direct taxation) or provide inducements for them to distribute it (for example, by allowing tax deductions for philanthropic giving). Today, varying tax rates reflect, among other things, where responsibility is assigned for social welfare. Higher tax rates, such as in Scandinavia, are typical of states with a highly centralized and developed public service and social welfare sector. Lower tax rates, such as in the United States, partly result from the belief that citizens with means (larger and smaller), who believe it is important to fund one endeavor or another, will do so from their own monies and with the cooperation of like-minded individuals, thus strengthening civil society through the proliferation of non-governmental organizations. In an era when market forces seem to rule economic decision-making at the micro and macro levels, a study of charity pauses to examine what appears to be a prevalent, non-market factor influencing economic decisions. At the same time, it may reveal to what extent charity has also become a marketable commodity.

What else does charity mean? One useful definition is "voluntary action for the public good."[13] *Action* includes an individual giving money or material goods or rendering services in the form of donated time and expertise, as well as the formation of associations that both collect and disburse these same commodities. Understood in this broad sense, we can identify similar kinds of actions across time and space around the globe. *Public good*, in contemporary western terms, defines a sphere of action outside the family. Similarly, in Islamic thought the key idea of *maslaha* is usually translated as "public interest" or "public welfare" and reaches beyond the immediate family to include extended family, neighbors, fellow subjects or citizens, and the Muslim umma altogether.[14]

It is important to recognize that beneficence is not benign, either in its motivations or in its effects. Countless endeavors owe their existence to donations from individuals inspired by love and honor for a beloved family member, by the memory of hardships overcome, or by dedication to ideas and causes. Yet the less generous motivations of self-promotion and economic self-interest are also prominent factors in motivating beneficence. Charity may be an act to be admired and praised but at the same time cogent critiques exist about what

---

[13] Robert Payton, as cited in Ilchman *et al.*, *Philanthropy in the World's Traditions*, x.

[14] See Madjid Khadduri, "maṣlaḥa," in *EI²*, VI:738–40; Charles Tripp, *Islam and the Moral Economy: The Challenge of Capitalism* (Cambridge, UK: Cambridge University Press, 2006), 24–26, 49–51, 68–76.

charity is, what it achieves, and how harmful it can be. Thus the study of charity is not only about well-meaning assistance offered to people in need; it also explores how charity is used for personal gains of power and status, and how givers manipulate recipients, and, in turn, are themselves manipulated.[15] A question related to that of motivations for giving is the ability of any charity to achieve its stated goals. Critiques of donations squandered owing to misconceived projects and mismanaged resources appear repeatedly in historical sources. Among the critical themes in these sources that resonate even in the present is the problem of money diverted before it reaches its targets, as well as the problem of donations promoting further dependence among recipients. As a component of human endeavor, charity is susceptible to the best and worst impulses and foibles of human beings, as well as the unintentional corruption of well-intentioned projects.

Ideas about giving

Muslim law makes a clear distinction between charity and gifts. However, the immediate context of any single act together with the status of the giver and recipient may influence more the way an action is perceived as well as its impact. Thus the practical line between charity and gifts is blurred, even if a legal separation exists in theory. This means that the ideas of the sociologist Marcel Mauss (1872–1950) about gifts are important when we consider the significance of charity. Based on his own observations of Pacific Island societies and those of Pacific Northwest America, Mauss posited that all giving is obligatory and reciprocal. Gifts of all kinds are signs of status and convey the assertion of superiority, the recognition of parity, or an acknowledgment of inferiority or subservience. According to Mauss, it is the continuous exchange of gifts between individuals that creates social order and stability, while an interruption or distortion of gift-giving signals a challenge to or breakdown in the established system.[16]

From Mauss' perspective, then, what we identify as charitable giving in Muslim contexts really belongs to the pervasive, ongoing gift exchanges that make societies cohere. Different belief systems refer to giving with a variety of names and compel believers to give within the context of distinct theologies.

---

[15] An interesting discussion of the motivations for charity can be found in S. Cavallo, "The Motivations of Benefactors: An Overview of Approaches to the Study of Charity," in *Medicine and Charity before the Welfare State*, ed. J. Barry and C. Jones (London: Routledge, 1991), 46–62. For a thoughtful critique of the motivations that steer contemporary aid and development organizations, see Tony Vaux, *The Selfish Altruist: Relief Work in Famine and War* (London: Earthscan, 2001).

[16] Marcel Mauss, *The Gift: The Form and Reason for Exchange in Archaic Societies*, trans. W. D. Halls, foreword by Mary Douglas (London: Routledge, 1990), originally published 1925.

However, giving also constitutes a universal of human behavior. Almsgiving, for Mauss, is a special case of his general theory of gift. He posited that alms appeared at a specific moment in the history of a society, when the "ancient morality of the gift" became a "principle of justice" such that people with a surplus of wealth and good fortune were obliged to be generous and share what they have. What had previously been destroyed in sacrifices to the gods and spirits was now given to serve the poor and children.[17] Mauss' discussion of almsgiving refers to shifts from potlatch-like destruction to almsgiving that occurred repeatedly in human history, one stage in the development of societies. Potlatch as destructive sacrifice was transformed to large-scale philanthropy.[18] Altogether, Mauss offered a sociological explanation for the existence and power of charitable giving. And he presented a sociologist's answer to the question: why does charity exist?

Altruism is another idea that overlaps with charity, sometimes even used as its synonym. The *Oxford Concise English Dictionary* defines altruism as "self-less concern for the wellbeing of others" or "behaviour of an animal that benefits another at its own expense," thus emphasizing the aspect of self-sacrifice or risk entailed by a specific donation. Some, however, will question the extent to which any behavior that appears selfless, precarious, or even harmful to a donor really is so. Cynics are quick to raise an eyebrow at the notion of altruism. Here, the "handicap principle," an idea from the world of biology, explains altruism in a way that merges usefully with Mauss' ideas about the role of gift-giving in human societies.

Biologist Amotz Zahavi coined the phrase "handicap principle" to describe his hypothesis about why animals engage in risky behavior or have extravagant physical features. Examples include the peacock's large and colorful tail, the stotting of gazelles (when they first leap up into the air when threatened by cheetahs instead of immediately running away), and the giving away of food. Zahavi suggests that dangerous, flamboyant, or altruistic behavior in animals is a means to signal strength and claim status and prestige; thus ultimately, these features or behaviors are "cost-effective" in terms of immediate survival or perpetuation of a species and they may entail no real sacrifice at all.[19] Zahavi studied babblers, a kind of bird that lives in communal groups in the Israeli and

---

[17] Mauss, *The Gift*, 17–18.

[18] *Potlatch* is an Indian word from the American Pacific Northwest used to describe a traditional ceremony or event at which the host lavished gifts of many kinds on his guests, differing in quantity and quality according to the status of each guest. These occasions sometimes entailed even the destruction of goods, as a way to demonstrate the wealth and power of the host. Mauss was one of the first anthropologists to discuss this phenomenon: see the discussion in *The Gift*, viii–ix, 6–7, 8, 18, 38–39.

[19] Amotz and Avishag Zahavi, *The Handicap Principle: A Missing Piece of Darwin's Puzzle* (Oxford: Oxford University Press, 1997), xv–xvi; Richard Conniff, "Why We Take Risks," *Discover* 22 (2001): 62–67.

Jordanian Arava desert. Decades of bird observations underlie Zahavi's thesis that "the altruist's investment in the altruistic act offers a reliable, concrete index of that individual's ability. Altruistic acts," he said,

have another benefit: they prove the giver's interest in the receiver, even while they proclaim the giver's dominance. By investing in the good of the group, the dominant male [among the babblers] shows off both his superiority and his willingness to give to his subordinates. This makes these subordinates less likely to leave and thus helps the dominant bird remain at the head of a large, strong group … In short, a babbler's altruistic acts are an investment in its prestige, and that prestige has real, concrete value. The difficulty – the cost, or handicap – of this altruistic advertising, whether food sacrificed or danger incurred, is what makes it a reliable indicator of the ability of the advertiser.[20]

In Zahavi's eyes, altruistic acts constitute a largely non-violent field of competition in which hierarchies are established, contested, preserved, and lost. In human contexts, philanthropy creates benefits for the whole society, reinforcing order and the ties that bind different groups, or defining a changed order with new rulers, be they secular or religious, political or social. Donations which appear to be large, perhaps testing the means of the donor, actually represent no loss for the donors because what is given away is in fact an investment in status and power. For the recipients, the gains are clear, as long as they willingly acknowledge the authority of the giver. Examples of this idea readily come to mind from human societies, whether it is in the sumptuous public feasts of sultans or the donations of famous super-philanthropists like Andrew Carnegie or Bill Gates.[21]

Writing charity into history

As a field of historical research, the study of charity developed out of and alongside the rise of social history in western historiography following the Second World War. The first studies focused primarily on the societies of Western Europe and the United States, but rapidly extended to include Asia, Africa, and Latin America. Before charity was investigated as a historical phenomenon, one that experienced and explained change in human societies, it was a subject that came up for discussion and analysis more often in the fields of religion, philosophy, and ethics, or as the subject of political analysis and public policy discussions in the context of emergency assistance, the welfare state, development aid, and the role of NGOs.

---

[20] Zahavi, *The Handicap Principle*, 142, 144.
[21] On Carnegie, see Andrew Carnegie, "The Gospel of Wealth," *North American Review* 148 and 149 (June–December 1889): 1–36 and David Nasaw, *Andrew Carnegie* (New York: Penguin, 2006). On Bill Gates, see *The Economist*, July 1–7, 2006, pp. 11, 65–67 and Amanda Ripley, "From Rags to Riches," *Time*, December 26, 2005.

In an early article published in 1957 in the *American Historical Review*, philanthropy was identified as one of the major culture segments left unexamined by social historians. The author claimed that the topic deserved more attention in the framework of American history because of how important "relatively disinterested benevolence [has] been in giving expression to, and in promoting at home and abroad, a major American value – human welfare," and he suggested "that philanthropy has been one of the major aspects of and keys to American social and cultural development."[22] The self-consciously American focus of the historical study of philanthropy continued in *American Philanthropy*, a book that was ultimately criticized for not studying philanthropy as an organic and evolving practice, one affected and informed by its social, economic, and political contexts.[23]

One of the driving forces in the early investigation of western philanthropy was the Ford Foundation, which commissioned a study by David Owen on British philanthropy. Owen himself observed that the topic of philanthropy had until then held little appeal for historians, although by the time his book was published, a series of major works on charity by W. K. Jordan, historian of early modern England, had already appeared.[24] Owen claimed that his study was intended "to serve as a background for more detailed investigations of the American experience." This focus and the very existence of the Ford Foundation also pointed to an important feature of philanthropy and its study: by the mid-twentieth century, the special tradition of philanthropy and volunteerism in the United States was a popular, well-rooted assumption in the American imagination and identity. These studies evoked Alexis de Tocqueville's early nineteenth-century claim that widespread philanthropic endeavor was a particular characteristic of American culture and an integral aspect of American democracy.[25] Moreover, the United States was becoming a center for what we now call third-sector activity as well as its study.

Owen's early conclusions about charity highlighted the achievements and shortcomings of private charity, which became a major theme in the research that followed. Owen pointed to "this dual importance of private charity – on the

---

[22] Merle Curti, "The History of American Philanthropy as a Field of Research," *American Historical Review* 62 (1957): 352–63, quote from p. 352.

[23] Robert Bremner, *American Philanthropy* (Chicago: Chicago University Press, 1960; rev. 1988); Friedman, and McGarvie, *Charity, Philanthropy, and Civility in American History*.

[24] David Owen, *British Philanthropy, 1660–1960* (Cambridge, MA: Harvard University Press, 1964); W. K. Jordan, *Philanthropy in England, 1480–1660: A Study of the Changing Pattern of English Social Aspirations* (New York: Allen and Unwin, 1959); W. K. Jordan, *The Charities of London, 1480–1660* (London: Allen and Unwin, 1960); W. K. Jordan, *The Charities of Rural England, 1480–1660* (New York: The Russell Sage Foundation, 1961).

[25] Alexis de Tocqueville, *Democracy in America*, ed. Gertrude Himmelfarb, trans. Arthur Goldhammer (New York: Library of America, 2004), 595, originally published 1835–40.

one hand its role as a pioneering force, pointing the way to action by the State, and, on the other, its ultimate inadequacy when measured against the requirements of industrial urban society."[26] By the 1960s, welfare states had been in place long enough to reveal their strengths and their inadequacies, inspiring citizens of various countries – including historians – to question how the role played by charitable giving had evolved historically so as to understand better the separate dynamics of and interactions between individual giving and the support provided by states.

The titles of early historical studies spoke of charity, wealth, munificence, piety, philanthropy, and social aid, and signaled that their emphasis was on the donors, whether individuals or associations. A basic assumption of these studies was that charity was a response to need or poverty. Yet the objects of charity were largely absent from their pages except as the passive recipients of largesse. Even as the methodologies of social history and subaltern history became increasingly refined, it remained easier to access the lives of the haves than those of the have-nots. Meanwhile, the history of charity continues to demonstrate the degree to which decisions about donations are determined by factors other than the recipients of the donations. A second and not uncommon flawed assumption about charitable giving concerns the beneficiaries: they were not and are not necessarily indigents, though all have been defined in some way as needy and also deserving of the benefits offered. Moreover, they are not necessarily passive beneficiaries, but rather may have a more formative influence on the character of charitable endeavors.

Brian Pullan's book, *Rich and Poor in Renaissance Venice* (1971), put the poor on stage with the rich, and also highlighted an ongoing discussion among historians, more theological than social, comparing Catholic and Protestant charity efforts. The debate posited that Catholic and Protestant societies developed different kinds of poor relief as a result of doctrinal differences. Yet Pullan's own work, and that of other scholars like Natalie Zemon Davis, showed that common economic and demographic factors of the sixteenth century prompted similar responses in Catholic and Protestant societies. Individual Catholics and Protestants may have understood the meaning of their charitable endeavors in different ways, but they evolved similar forms of relief, and the discussions and decisions about who deserved help given limited resources, as well as the activism of municipal and national governors in establishing legal boundaries for relief, all reflected the challenges facing Europe in general.[27] As the study of charity in Islamic societies continues, it may be interesting to compare the historical changes in forms of relief and

---

[26] Owen, *British Philanthropy, 1660–1960*, 6.
[27] Brian Pullan, *Rich and Poor in Renaissance Venice: The Social Institutions of a Catholic State, to 1620* (Oxford: Basil Blackwell, 1971); Natalie Zemon Davis, "Poor Relief, Humanism and

assistance with those in Christian and other societies, to understand more fully what factors induce change and to what extent religious identity may be a factor in shaping the changes.

The historical study of philanthropy was also profoundly affected by the emergence of the economic and social history methodologies that flourished under the historiographical influence of the French *Annales* school, including its emphasis on quantification, and the beginning of "history from below." These approaches produced a long list of works focusing on single towns or regions based on local archival research. Geography and methodology were the backdrop to questions about the identity of givers and recipients, such as: Who gave? Who received? Who were the deserving and the undeserving poor? What was offered to the poor and under what conditions or restrictions? Class analysis strongly affected how the behavior of rich and poor was interpreted, as well as their interactions. In addition to studies on early modern and modern Europe and the United States, the history of charity in ancient Greece, Rome, and the Byzantine Empire attracted significant attention.[28]

By 1980, the publication of F. K. Prochaska's *Women and Philanthropy in Nineteenth-Century England* heralded another development in the study of philanthropy and echoed trends in historical research generally. Historians were turning the spotlight onto women, reflecting the rise of feminist consciousness and women's activism generally. Prochaska rather apologetically opened his book by saying: "My research springs from an interest in philanthropy rather than in feminism ... but I would like to think that it has developed into a contribution to the history of the emancipation of women as well."[29] Prochaska's work reflected no obviously feminist agenda; however, it pointed to one key avenue by which women were brought back into history.

Ten years later, the work of Lori Ginzberg demonstrated how important the study of benevolence had become for the study of women and for the project of understanding how and where women affected the worlds they inhabited even when they were absent from the grand stage of political, military, and economic leadership. The belief (held by men and women) that women were particularly benevolent by nature and that their rightful role was one of nurturers and caregivers had long legitimized benevolent work as a field for women, historically giving them freedoms to act publicly in ways that were otherwise denied them in the realms of both private and public life. Gender as a category of

Heresy," in *Society and Culture in Early Modern France* (Stanford: Stanford University Press, 1968; repr. 1975), 17–64; Maureen Flynn, *Sacred Charity: Confraternities and Social Welfare in Spain, 1400–1700* (Ithaca: Cornell University Press, 1989).

[28] Hands, *Charities and Social Aid in Greece and Rome*; Constantelos, *Byzantine Philanthropy and Social Welfare*; Veyne, *Bread and Circuses*; and Evelyne Patlagean, *Pauvreté économique et pauvreté sociale à Byzance 4e–7e siècles* (Paris: Mouton, 1977).

[29] F. K. Prochaska, *Women and Philanthropy in Nineteenth-Century England* (Oxford: Oxford University Press, 1980), vii.

analysis has since contributed much to the study of history in general and philanthropy in particular, since philanthropy was a field of activity where both men and women were active as givers and as recipients, and where both men's and women's activities left historical records. The politics of gender in every era come through clearly in philanthropic endeavors. Hence the prism of gender offers a powerful lens through which to understand how societies assign roles to givers and how they define deserving recipients; the way in which laws about property rights affect men and women differently, particularly their individual access to wealth; the origins and concentration of wealth; and how the choice of beneficent projects is coded to publicize and legitimize the distinct roles of women and men, roles they assumed or that were imposed on them by a broader social ethos.[30]

Overlapping the growing impact of women and gender studies on the history of philanthropy was the influence of philosopher Michel Foucault. In his works on imprisonment and madness, Foucault raised questions about how societies come to define and control normality, confining or excluding those who fall outside its boundaries. While Foucault wrote specifically about criminals and the insane, his work was also relevant for considering the way women, children, the elderly, religious minorities, groups with different racial, ethnic, or sexual identities, and other people were measured against adult, white, male norms. Among the excluded in certain periods and places were those whose crimes or madness were defined by their poverty or by conditions induced by the physical weakness or social exclusion that accompanied poverty. Historians incorporated Foucault's ideas in analyzing the history of poverty as well as the programs of legal and charity reform that reorganized the lives of indigents in industrializing and colonized societies.[31]

Thus, by the last decade of the twentieth century, the historical study of philanthropy was expanding rapidly in terms of the number of works published and the subjects, regions, and periods being researched, as well as in terms of the theoretical and methodological appartus available. Under the influence of cultural studies and under the self-critical eye of historians of charity, subjects proliferated and the frameworks of analysis shifted from the how and what, the who and how much, to questions of meaning. Another scholarly trend was the move away from analyzing charity according to dichotomies dividing donor

---

[30] Lori D. Ginzberg, *Women and the Work of Benevolence: Morality, Politics, and Class in the Nineteenth-Century United States* (New Haven: Yale University Press, 1990); Kathleen McCarthy, ed., *Lady Bountiful Revisited: Women, Philanthropy, and Power* (New Brunswick: Rutgers University Press, 1990); Kathleen McCarthy, ed., *Women, Philanthropy, and Civil Society* (Bloomington: Indiana University Press, 2001).

[31] Michel Foucault, *Madness and Civilization: A History of Insanity in the Age of Reason*, trans. Richard Howard (New York: Vintage Books, 1965); Michel Foucault, *Discipline and Punish: The Birth of the Prison*, trans. Alan Sheridan (New York: Random House, 1975).

and recipient, public and private giving, poverty and wealth, volunteerism and obligation, and individual and corporate activities. By abandoning an essential association of giving with wealth and receipt with poverty, historians are acknowledging the presence of donors and beneficiaries throughout society. Further, by questioning dichotomies, historians naturally move to disaggregate the groups "givers" and "recipients" into their more natural diversity, where motivations and strategies are multiple and complex.[32]

The move away from dichotomies also induced a reassessment of previous assumptions about the linear progress of charitable giving from private to public over time, including the introduction of state-sponsored welfare services and the rise of independent welfare and relief organizations. State power and capability, the icons of modernity, fostered a belief in the increased efficacy of government systems and the shrinking role for private and non-governmental initiatives. Yet the flaws in and insufficiencies of governmental agencies are among the factors that have spurred activity by private individuals and NGOs as well as prompting the increased interest in the study of charity. Meanwhile, more studies investigated the history of welfare states and of domestic and international third-sector activities, prompted perhaps by the crises in welfare states around the world and the proliferation of international aid agencies, governmental and private, together with repeated emergencies testing states' capacities and expanding the debate around the ethical dilemmas of giving. By integrating private, individual, state, and corporate giving into discussions of a single historical period, the competitive and cooperative relationships between givers become more evident, highlighting the tensions and negotiations that take place as each stakes out a space in the giving game.[33]

Entirely unexamined in writing the history of charity, however, is the role of the people who, whether wealthy or not, did *not* give and those who did *not* receive, for whatever reason. They have all been mostly ignored, except as statistics. And yet it can only enrich our understanding of the dynamics of philanthropy to identify who did not give and why, and what were the sanctions or benefits they enjoyed as a result. Equally important is to consider the means

---

[32] Colin Jones, "Some Recent Trends in the History of Charity," in *Charity, Self-Interest and Welfare in the English Past*, ed. Martin Daunton (London: UCL Press, 1996), 51–63; Sandra Cavallo, *Charity and Power in Early Modern Italy: Benefactors and their Motives in Turin, 1541–1789* (Cambridge, UK: Cambridge University Press, 1995); Peregrine Horden and Richard Smith, eds., *The Locus of Care: Families, Communities, Institutions, and the Provision of Welfare since Antiquity* (New York: Routledge, 1998); Jean Quataert, *Staging Philanthropy: Patriotic Women and the National Imagination in Dynastic Germany, 1813–1916* (Ann Arbor: University of Michigan Press, 2001).

[33] Michael B. Katz and Christoph Sachsse, *The Mixed Economy of Social Welfare: Public/Private Relations in England, Germany and the United States, the 1870s to the 1930s* (Baden-Baden: Nomos Verlagsgesellschaft, 1996); Friedman and McGarvie, *Charity, Philanthropy and Civility*.

of and reasons for excluding people from the benefits of charitable giving. These two additional perspectives may be especially important when examining another long-ignored phenomenon: people who were sometimes donors and sometimes recipients, sometimes both, sometimes neither, and how they negotiated the line dividing recipients and givers, and its margins. Thus the entire subject of charity, and not only charity in Islamic societies, is one that calls for additional historical and analytic study.

Writing about charity in Islamic societies

I initially came to the study of charity through my research on a public kitchen (*imaret*) built by Süleyman I's wife, Hurrem Sultan (d. 1558). This kitchen was established as an endowment (*waqf*) in mid-sixteenth-century Jerusalem. It was probably the largest single Ottoman endowment in southern Syria throughout the period of Ottoman rule, and certainly among the most enduring. Yet in the context of Ottoman imperial endowments, the *takiyya* (public kitchen, hospice) of Hasseki Sultan (as it came to be known) was not exceptional in its size or purpose, since public kitchens were often included among the economic, social, and cultural institutions in endowed Ottoman building complexes.[34] Originally, I was preoccupied with the *Ottoman* aspects of this endeavor: why and how this kitchen came to be, how it operated, and what it revealed about similar public kitchens, about the nature of large imperial endowments, and about Ottoman charity in general. These questions led to more general ones: What was the charitable nature of such an undertaking? Why have Muslim endowments always been classified as charitable? Can we understand them as charity in the same way that we appreciate similar endeavors in other cultures? Is charity really ubiquitous in Islamic societies? What are the different ways in which it is organized and what insights can be gained by approaching specific historical topics from this perspective?

If, as has been suggested, social history is at least partly about the relationship between power and wealth, then it is curious that charity, a key expression of this relationship, has, until recently, been largely omitted from the study of Islamic societies.[35] Western scholars of Islam and the history of Islamic societies long ago took note of the discussions of zakat and sadaqa in theological literature. They studied them as religious practices and legal categories, or noted the individual actions of wealthy benefactors, but did not consider charity as a

---

[34] Amy Singer, *Constructing Ottoman Beneficence: An Imperial Soup Kitchen in Jerusalem* (Albany: State University of New York Press, 2002). On public kitchens, see Nina Ergin, Christoph K. Neumann, and Amy Singer, eds., *Feeding People, Feeding Power: Imarets in the Ottoman Empire* (Istanbul: Eren, 2007).

[35] Albert Hourani, "How Should We Write the History of the Middle East?" *International Journal of Middle East Studies* 23 (1991): 134–35.

framework for historical analysis. Yet charitable giving has been and continues to be a universal, life-long obligation for Muslims, one that permeates Islamic societies both as a religious ideal and as a social practice. The religious ideal assumes the existence of a relationship between individuals and God, one that prompts people to act in a pious and just manner. At the same time, this ideal inspires everyday behaviors that shape relationships between human beings. Since the beginnings of Islam in the early seventh century and over the ensuing fourteen centuries across the Muslim world, the command to beneficence has been translated into concrete practices that have taken countless forms, each act deriving from and acquiring a distinct significance in its particular context.

Muslims worldwide look for guidance to the Qur'an, the text which the Prophet Muhammad recited as the revelation of God. Commanded in the Qur'an, giving alms (*zakat*) is one of the five acts incumbent on all Muslims. In addition to obligatory alms, the Qur'an also repeatedly recommends voluntary beneficent giving (*sadaqa*). *Sura* (chapter) 107 of the Qur'an, quoted at the opening of this chapter, presents the orphan as the paradigmatic needy figure and food as the most fundamental form of assistance. Juxtaposed to these is prayer (*salat*), the most obvious external sign of adherence to Islam. Yet prayer is worthless without giving, and giving, here, appears as a *sine qua non* of belief. In many suras, zakat and salat appear together repeatedly, in variations on the rhymed phrase: "*wa-aqama al-salat wa-ata al-zakat*," as the core of Islamic belief (Fig. 1).[36] Noteworthy as well in Sura 107 is the absence of any reference to wealth or property as a condition of giving. Rather, the title, *ma'un* – translated variously as "small kindness," "neighborly assistance," "charity," and "alms" – seems to refer to something that could be given by anyone, possibly a gesture, or the loan of household utensils.[37] In addition to the Qur'an, many traditions about the Prophet (*hadith*) discuss zakat and sadaqa, giving examples from his life and those of his family and his early companions. From these basic texts, Muslim theologians and jurists have further elaborated laws for the correct practice of charity.

This book is a study of shared texts and divergent practices of charity in the history of Islamic societies. Its goal is to understand the exhortations and

---

[36] For example, Qur'an 2:43, 2:177, 9:18, 19:31, 58:13. The same commandment is recalled in the Qur'an as being at the heart of God's commandments to the Jews and to Jesus.

[37] The translations cited are, respectively, from Sells, *Approaching the Qur'ān*; M. M. Pickthall, *The Meaning of the Glorious Koran* (New York: New American Library, 1980); Abdullah Yusuf Ali, *The Holy Quran* (Ware, Hertfordshire: Wordsworth Editions, 2000); Arberry, *The Koran Interpreted*; N. J. Dawood, *The Koran* (London: Penguin, 1956). See also *The Qur'an*, Hebrew version, trans. and ed. Uri Rubin (Tel Aviv: Tel Aviv University Press, 2005), 538. The suras of the Qur'an are usually described as belonging to the early revelations of Muhammad at Mecca, or to those revealed at Medina after Muhammad left Mecca with his followers in the year 622. Sura 107 is often ascribed to the Meccan period, and it seems to fit with the brief and more general suras of that time.

Fig. 1. A pair of wooden doors from the Beyhekim Mosque (thirteenth century) bearing the Qur'anic verse (9:18): "Pray and give alms" (*Wa-aqama al-salat wa-ata al-zakat*). İnceminare Taş ve Ahşap Eserler Müzesi (İnceminare Stone and Wood Works Museum), Konya. With the permission of the Konya Museum Directorate. Author's photo.

admonitions of basic religious texts, on the one hand, and on the other, to explore how the charitable impulse was expressed in different historical settings, and the roles it played in shaping Islamic societies. Focusing on charity highlights a key shared aspect of Islamic societies while at the same time it offers a greater appreciation of the diversity of individual Muslim histories. Defining the scope of this book as "Islamic societies" highlights two key assumptions. The first ("Islamic") is that the Qur'an and hadith provide a common core of textual references for all Muslims, in which charity is repeatedly praised and recommended to the believers. The second assumption ("societies" in the plural) is that the interpretations of these texts and their translations into action are enormously diverse. Although shared, the textual references have not necessarily inspired identical practices of charity throughout the Muslim world or in Muslim societies of different eras. At the same time, the doctrinal differences between Sunni and Shi'i Muslims, differences between the Sunni schools of law and the different Shi'i groups, and the emergence of the numerous Muslim mystical orders known as *sufi tariqa*s, together with the various syncretic accretions to Islam from other faiths, influenced the evolution of charitable practices. No less important have been local historical experience, culture, language, ecology, politics, economics, and other factors that affected how individuals chose to act and to use their wealth.[38]

This book uses the Arabic words *zakat* and *sadaqa*, and translates the first as "obligatory alms" and the second as either "charity," "philanthropy," or "beneficence." Words and names are transliterated from Arabic if they were originally Arabic, although Muslims have used and still use many different languages in their daily lives, so that their pronunciations and transliterations of basic Qur'anic concepts differ somewhat from place to place. In addition to introducing new words, this book also faces the problem that the use of specific words changed over time and space. Throughout the lands and communities of the Muslim world, the terms *zakat* and *sadaqa* have been used for some 1,400 years. While both were used in the Qur'an, they have older histories, on the one hand, and, on the other, have been used to describe a variety of Muslim institutions and practices since the seventh century. "Sadaqa" even has negative connotations sometimes, in much the same way that "charity" may be used in a condescending or negative tone in English.

Charity in Islam has a complex texture and is linked to several other ideas. In pre-Islamic Arabic writings, generosity (*karama*) and hospitality (*diyafa*) were important and valued characteristics. *Karama* encompassed an ideal behavior, part of a code of chivalry. In pre-Islamic poetry, the hero (*karim*) is the generous one. According to the scholar Franz Rosenthal, Aristotelian ideas from classical

---

[38] See the discussion of "Islamic society" in Albert Hourani, "Islam in European Thought" (1990), 276–77, www.tannerlectures.utah.edu/lectures/hourani90.pdf (accessed September 22, 2006).

Greek philosophy that tied generosity to moderation in the context of balancing income and expenditure had a restraining influence on such pre-Islamic traditions. Generosity was emphasized in the Qur'an from the earliest suras and Muslim traditions further shaped ideas about generosity by emphasizing charity, that is, generosity shown to the needy, as a praiseworthy characteristic.[39] Hospitality was one of the main expressions of generosity among the pre-Islamic Arabs and Muslim hospitality remains a source of pride in many places today. Some of the pre-Islamic traditions of hospitality took on an extreme expression when exaggerated demonstrations of generosity resulted in the wholesale slaughter of camels, a practice reminiscent of potlatch in other contexts. Hospitality in Muslim societies, as in Judaism and Christianity, was exemplified by the key figure of Abraham, and the building of hostels by Muslim rulers and governors as part of the obligations of office seems to have begun relatively early and become widespread. The tenth-century historian al-Tabari ascribed these words to the Caliph 'Umar b. 'Abd al-'Aziz (d. 720):

> establish inns (*khanat*) in your lands so that whenever a Muslim passes by, you will put him up for a day and a night and take care of his animals; if he is sick, provide him with hospitality for two days and two nights; and if he has used up all of his provisions and is unable to continue, supply him with whatever he needs to reach his hometown.[40]

In the Qur'an, poetic expressions of generosity replaced its earlier manifestations in camel sacrifice, great feasts, and losing one's life in battle. Generosity in the holy book emphasized human beings, promoting social justice, caring for the weak and poor, and performing just deeds (*salihat*). Since the Qur'an also stresses that all wealth comes from God and is ultimately God's, generosity consists in giving from what is given by God, the most generous; *karim*, now meaning especially "the generous one," is one of the ninety-nine names of God. Generosity ultimately became codified as one of the fundamental values and obligations of Islam, articulated into two separate categories of obligatory zakat and recommended sadaqa in post-Quranic times.[41]

Patronage is a companion idea to generosity and hospitality, and may intersect with or overlap charity in different ways. Like charitable giving, patronage creates or reflects vertical relationships, whether the patron provides protection, work, social status, or material support. Historical writings about Islamic states from the time of the Abbasids (750–1258) onward analyze the impact of

---

[39] Franz Rosenthal et al., "hiba," in *EI²*, III:343.

[40] D. S. Powers, trans., *The History of al-Ṭabarī*, vol. XXIV (Albany: State University of New York Press, 1989), 94. See also Olivia Remie Constable, *Housing the Stranger in the Mediterranean World: Lodging, Trade, and Travel in Late Antiquity and the Middle Ages* (Cambridge, UK: Cambridge University Press, 2003), 48–51.

[41] Suliman Bashear, "On the Origins and Development of the Meaning of Zakāt in Early Islam," *Arabica* 40 (1993): 84–113; Sells, *Approaching the Qur'ān*.

patronage on political and social organization as well as on the production of culture generally. Patronage, a word covering rather different and distinct relationships, came to play a key role in all forms of military promotions, government appointments, and even in the establishment of business and commercial ties. It is usually discussed as a phenomenon unconnected to beneficence and generosity, yet the distinction may not be so clear. Consider, for example, the world of a high-ranking Ottoman official: he maintained a large household of salaried or otherwise-compensated retainers, who fulfilled military, bureaucratic, and service functions. Maintaining these people included feeding some or all of them on a regular basis, as well as finding positions for them and their sons, and perhaps ensuring suitable marriages for their daughters. The official himself was probably a regular guest in the houses of people more powerful than himself and sometimes at the table of someone subordinate who chose to honor him. Moreover, daily leftovers from the official's table were distributed to relatives or needy people in the neighborhood of the official residence, while on holidays, feasts and gifts were given to the entire household as well as to local needy people.

In each case, such distributions marked and affirmed a power gradient in which a weaker person received from a stronger one, and tacitly or overtly acknowledged the claim of the stronger to loyalty or service in return. Generally, historians call only the distributions to poor people "charity," and the rest are labeled "patronage," "hospitality," or "generosity." Yet in reality, all these words describe dynamic relationships that create, signal, or reaffirm gradients of power, and ties of patron and client, and imply uneven reciprocity.[42] It may be more accurate to describe them as different expressions of obligation and entitlement, each of which derives legitimacy from a specific relationship or interaction. Some entitlements were anchored in law. *Nafaqa*, for example, was the obligatory provision of food, clothing, and shelter as the basic necessities of life, which resulted from formal relationships of kinship, ownership, and marriage.[43] Yet entitlements were also established informally, if no less concretely, as the result of social, political, and cultural ties and obligations, experiences and expectations. These obligation–entitlement relationships were social building blocks. Obligation entailed responsibility; entitlement created obligation.

In contrast to the relative lack of scholarship, sources for the study of charity in Islamic societies are plentiful. There is no real need to discover new primary

[42] On patronage, for example, see D. Fairchild Ruggles, ed., *Women, Patronage, and Self-Representation in Islamic Societies* (Albany: State University of New York Press, 2000).

[43] Rudolph Peters, "*nafaqa*," in *EI*², 2nd edn. Supplement, 643–44; Ingrid Mattson, "Status-Based Definitions of Need in Early Islamic *Zakat* and Maintenance Laws," in *Poverty and Charity in Middle Eastern Contexts*, ed. Michael Bonner, Mine Ener, and Amy Singer (Albany: State University of New York Press, 2003), 31–52.

materials; rather, familiar texts of many different types – legal, literary, documentary, devotional, aesthetic, structural, and material – can be re-examined and studied with an eye to exploring the profusion of charitable practices. Examples are common, found in religious texts, stories, poems, travel narratives, buildings, ceramics, woodwork, paintings, administrative correspondence, financial accounts, historical chronicles, and biographies. Figurative depictions and instrumental objects testify to how charity has permeated the textures of everyday life and material culture. The ubiquity of sources mirrors the ubiquity of practice, making it all the more curious that so little has been written on the topic.

The study of charity enjoys the same advantages and is subject to the same limitations affecting the general field of Islamic history with respect to the availability of sources. Accordingly, sources become gradually more plentiful and more varied over the centuries, with a quantitative change remarkable from the fifteenth century, directly linked to the Ottoman Empire and the preservation of its official archives, literary collections, and material culture, and also owing to the advent of new forms of literary production.[44] Non-Muslim sources – those written by non-Muslims who lived permanently in or visited Islamic societies – add valuable observations in the form of diplomatic correspondence, commercial records, travel accounts, diaries, and illustrations. Foreigners experienced the societies through which they moved with greater or lesser sensitivity and insight, so that their texts may also be infused with bias or hyperbole aimed at persuading the reader of the inherent value or flaws in Muslim charity.

Since this book will focus on Islamic societies and point out historiographic developments throughout its discussions, only a few words on the subject are offered here. The first western scholarly writings on charity in Islamic societies focused on scripture and law as did much early western study of Muslims and Muslim societies in general. This perspective effectively flattened charitable practice into lists of dogma, rules, donors, and their gifts. The terminology of charitable endeavor in Islamic societies was studied relatively early on by western scholars, part of the general philological tradition of European Islamic studies in the nineteenth century. Such studies, focusing primarily on ideas related to Islamic belief, were not an historical record or analysis of philanthropic practice. Definitions and etymologies of words – like zakat, sadaqa, waqf, and *faqir* (poor) – appeared in the first edition of the *Encyclopaedia of Islam*, published between 1913 and 1936. Though the entries offered valuable information, and in the later edition (1954–2003) even

---

[44] For a thorough discussion of this, see R. Stephen Humphreys, *Islamic History: A Framework for Inquiry*, rev. edn. (Princeton: Princeton University Press, 1991), 25–65; Suraiya Faroqhi, *Approaching Ottoman History: An Introduction to the sources* (Cambridge, UK: Cambridge University Press, 1999), 46–81.

included extensive discussions about the history of these terms as reflected in institutions and practices, the entries still lacked any deliberate analytic consideration of charity as a subject in its own right.[45]

Even as we emphasize that charity constitutes a rich field of investigation, and that the study of its various expressions in Islamic societies would expand our understanding of these societies, as well as our appreciation of charity in general, it is noteworthy that relatively little has been written about the subject in English or other western languages for scholars, students, and interested readers who are not seeking guidance as practicing Muslims. General books on Islam and Islamic societies, recent and otherwise, mostly devote little space to the topic, treating "charity" and "alms" as transparent concepts presenting few problems of explanation or interpretation. This is true in books about Islamic culture and history written for general audiences as well as those aimed at specialists. One exceptional and excellent pamphlet entitled *Charity and Philanthropy in Islam* by the historian Robert McChesney provides a brief introduction.[46] Otherwise, no book-length general work exists on the subject and general books on Islam usually contain at most a few sentences. The review of one recent general book on Islam noted that "the chapter on ritual deals with the duty of almsgiving in less than a line but spends six pages expounding the far less important duty of pilgrimage to Jerusalem."[47] Specialized scholarly works go somewhat farther to give details of charitable practices and discuss their possible origins in Arabian and Judeo-Christian influences.[48] Yet few works undertake to explore at length the ideals of charity for Muslims and the specific practices they inspired throughout the history of Islamic societies, to say nothing of their broader political, economic, social, and cultural implications.

This situation is all the more strange when one remembers that zakat is one of the five fundamental obligations (the "pillars") of all Muslims. The other four comprise the declaration of faith (*shahada*), prayer (*salat*), annual fasting during the holy month of Ramadan (*sawm*), and the once-in-a-lifetime pilgrimage to Mecca (*hajj*). Together, these acts of worship (*ibadat*) are the core of Muslim belief and practice, the duties of the faithful. On these grounds alone, the

---

[45] Rosenthal, "Ṣedaḳa, Charity." Also see s.v. in both editions of the *Encyclopaedia of Islam*.

[46] Indianapolis: Indiana University Center on Philanthropy, 1995.

[47] Tim Winter on F. E. Peters, *Islam: A Guide for Jews and Christians* (Princeton, 2003), in *Times Literary Supplement*, January 30, 2004. For some examples of the discussion in general works, see, for example, John L. Esposito, ed., *Oxford History of Islam* (Oxford: Oxford University Press, 2000); Frederick Mathewson Denny, *An Introduction to Islam*, 2nd edn. (New York: Macmillan, 1994); David Waines, *An Introduction to Islam*, 2nd edn. (Cambridge, UK: Cambridge University Press, 2003); Andrew Rippin, *Muslims: Their Religious Beliefs and Practices* (New York: Routledge, 2005).

[48] For example, see C. Snouck Hurgronje, "La Zakāt," in *Oeuvres Choisies*, eds. G.-H. Bousquet and J. Schacht (Leiden: Brill, 1957), 150–70.

theological, ritual, and social aspects of almsgiving merit focused consideration in historical and contemporary contexts alike. It is worth stopping a moment to consider this lacuna, why it is that in all the scholarly literature written about Islam as a religion and on the historical, social, economic, cultural, and political aspects of Islamic societies, there is a comparative lack of study about Muslim ideas and practices of charity. The concepts and practices are familiar, particularly in the Judeo-Christian societies that dominate western scholarship and popular writing. Jews and Christians have ready comparisons in their respective practices. Perhaps scholars did not investigate almsgiving because they assumed they understood it. Compared with the other obligations for Muslims, zakat may seem straightforward and familiar, another form of the tithing recommended in Judaism and Christianity, another kind of wealth tax. Yet McChesney, writing for an American audience, hinted at other factors when he wrote: "the subjects of charity and philanthropy are not necessarily the features one is most likely to associate with the Islamic religion and its moral universe ... While Christian teachings stress love for humankind, compassion, mercy and self-sacrifice, Western writing on Islam seems unable to locate similar concerns and teachings."[49] Perhaps this is because the authors are unfamiliar with Muslim teachings or because they are not predisposed to emphasize positive cognate features in Islamic societies when they encounter them. Biases of culture and politics have constructed obstacles for non-Muslims studying Islamic societies.

Another possible explanation for the dearth of literature about charity in Islamic societies is that many Muslim practices of charity were not as visible to foreign eyes and ears as were the affirmation of the faith, the daily prayers, the month of fasting, and the annual pilgrimage. Short-term visitors to Muslim communities over the centuries could hear the muezzin's call to prayer which repeated the affirmation, observe the prostrations of Muslims praying, search for food during the daylight hours of Ramadan, hear the drumbeat or the cannon fired to punctuate the beginning and end of fasting each day, watch the caravans gathering in Cairo and Damascus for the long trip through the desert to Mecca and Medina, and see the houses painted and the celebrations to welcome returning pilgrims. Yet it required considerably more familiarity with one local society, its customs, and its language to be able to discern and understand the contributions and distributions that constituted charity. Long-term foreign visitors like the English lexicographer E. W. Lane, a resident of Cairo in the nineteenth century, were better placed to take note of local beneficence, as Lane remarked: "Benevolence and charity to the poor are virtues which the Egyptians possess in an eminent degree, and which are instilled into their hearts by

---

[49] Robert D. McChesney, *Charity and Philanthropy in Islam: Institutionalizing the Call to Do Good* (Indianapolis: Indiana University Center on Philanthropy, 1995), 1.

religion ... "[50] In general, zakat, and sadaqa for that matter, do not draw much attention *not* because they do not exist, but because these acts often were meant to be and were performed discreetly. In addition, the formal and official apparatus of zakat-paying, which seems to have functioned in Muhammad's day and in the early Muslim polity, did not exist everywhere continually. Zakat given directly from payer to recipient was mostly an invisible performance and likewise left no trace in historical records; the same was true for countless informal acts of voluntary charity. In contrast, monumental buildings and extravagant distributions, generally carried out by the very wealthy, were more immediately evident and these did attract some observers.

As with many themes in the history of Middle Eastern and Islamic societies, the study of philanthropy grew under the influence of trends in American and European history, and certainly the theoretical literature of reference emerged largely in those fields. The study of charity as a problematized and historicized phenomenon in Islamic societies had to wait until the 1970s. Among the first to write on the subject was Norman Stillman, who observed that "Arabic, Persian, and Turkish literature abound with scattered references to philanthropic individuals and institutions, but these have yet to be thoroughly gleaned and synthesized. Thus the historian of Islamic philanthropy and social services is still in the rudimentary stages of extracting needles from haystacks."[51] From this early observation, the study of charity in Islamic societies has progressed to the point where it is possible to write the present book as a first attempt at synthesis. Yet there remain many more needles to be extracted.

The chapters

This study attempts to convey a sense of the diversity of Muslim culture across time and space. Yet any one person would be hard pressed to explore the more than fourteen centuries of Islamic history. The source materials of Ottoman history alone present considerable paleographic, linguistic, and methodological challenges; the obstacles facing scholars in each subfield of Islamic history, no matter what the period, are equally difficult. Thus, this book makes no pretense of being comprehensive in covering topics, sources, places, or analytic approaches. Where necessary it relies on translations, secondary literature, and the generous help of colleagues to include a broad spectrum of historical examples. Inevitably, a certain bias toward Ottoman history and sources exists, as I am most familiar with these. Moreover, the study is not entirely systematic, but suggests where further systematic inquiry is possible and what types of

---

[50] Edward W. Lane, *An Account of the Manners and Customs of the Modern Egyptians* (London, 1836), 285–86.
[51] Norman A. Stillman, "Charity and Social Service in Medieval Islam," *Societas* 5 (1975): 105.

questions might usefully be investigated. Of course, even these suggestions are not exhaustive and they aim, in part, to prompt or provoke scholars and students in new directions. Because this book is intended as an introduction to the subject, it is obvious that others will have to fill the many gaps remaining. Specific references are provided for sources cited, but the notes and bibliography are not exhaustive with respect to published scholarly literature. They generally cite sources that are accurate and accessible, and include recent works that will help interested readers find their way into the larger body of scholarship. This is equally the case for references to Islamic history and to other histories.

This book is not a linear history and its chapters are topical. The discussion has begun in this introduction with a consideration of ideas about charity and how it has been studied as an historical subject. The following chapters focus more specifically on ideas and examples from Islamic history. Inevitably, some readers may protest that I did not provide a thick enough historical description, an extensive enough historical analysis, or a sufficient exploration of a theoretical idea. Obviously, a book of the present size cannot offer an exhaustive historical survey, and such is not its aim. It may serve, rather, as an introduction to the study of charity for scholars and students of Islamic societies and at the same time as an introduction to this aspect of Islamic societies for scholars and students of charity. Where they find gaps or believe that there are more examples or discussions possible, I invite them to share their expertise by publishing further on these topics.

Chapter 1 looks closely at zakat. Concrete examples of zakat payment and collection in history demonstrate the changing place of this religious tax in the context of other taxes and state impositions, as well as the variety of payments that came to be considered as zakat or associated with it. The reality of zakat payment reveals some of the problems inherent in obligatory donations, whether in the early Islamic era or as revived today in some places. While zakat is the formal duty of all Muslims, voluntary acts of charity were encouraged and widespread. Under the general heading of sadaqa, they seem to have surpassed zakat payments in volume and popularity, perhaps even at an early date. Zakat and sadaqa are discussed in separate chapters in order to clarify the theological premise of each and the distinct practices that evolved. Chapter 2 opens with a composite calendar of the occasions for voluntary charitable giving that punctuated the lives of Muslims; if not universal, these occasions were at least widely observed. This calendar aims to impart a sense of how pervasive was the practice of voluntary giving. The chapter also discusses the institution called waqf, a legal device for establishing pious endowments. Waqfs were probably the most obvious and prominent form of voluntary giving throughout the Muslim world, over many centuries. As a result of their extensive documentation, they offer a window into the identities of donors and beneficiaries alike.

Individuals replace institutions as the focus of chapter 3. The study of charity has in large part focused on those who give and not on those who receive. This is not surprising, particularly when one recognizes that there are far more historical sources, in almost every culture, for the lives of the wealthy than for those of the indigent or even the middle class. Indeed, much research has focused on the givers of charity to understand how they make decisions about what to give, to whom, how much, when, and, of course, why. Moreover, the study of charity is necessarily more involved with the givers than the recipients, since the actions of the givers often derive more from their own lives and their own perceptions and intentions with respect to charity, than from the lives of the recipients.[52] Even new methodologies cannot change the quantitative bias of sources toward the rich and powerful. However, the recipients often, but not always, constitute a crucial part of the relationship between givers and their donations. Beneficiaries of charity draw our interest as we try to understand their role in shaping donations and to assess the impact of philanthropic action. Chapter 4 considers the meaning of poverty, and looks especially at the poor and needy, perhaps the largest group of recipients numerically.

In addition to individuals as donors, two other actors need to be examined: the state and non-governmental organizations or private associations. To the extent that there is a chronological shape to the book it may be found in the deferring of the discussion of state and association involvements in social welfare to chapter 5. For the most part, the establishment of state social welfare agencies began in the nineteenth century, and their history has been part of that of the modern bureaucratic nation state, which is the welfare state. Obviously, however, state rulers and official authorities have affected the social welfare of their populations directly or indirectly ever since states came into existence. Also in the nineteenth and twentieth centuries, non-governmental social welfare organizations emerged to become more numerous and more prominent in the public sphere, a trend sometimes attributed to the strengthening of civil society and the growth of the middle class. Where once there were local and then national organizations, today there are also international and transnational associations, able to take advantage of modern communications, banking, and transportation together with economic globalization in pursuing charitable goals.

Giving to others is a universal practice and the relationships established by giving are fundamental to most human societies. Although this book is framed as a study of Islamic societies, it suggests that any one example of charitable giving may have as much to do with immediate historical circumstances or environmental factors other than religious belief or adherence. As varied as are

---

[52] Bronislaw Geremek, *Poverty: A History* (Cambridge, MA: Blackwell, 1994), 25.

human beings, so are their ways of and reasons for giving to others. Charitable giving may be obligatory or voluntary, carried out with consideration or meanness; it may be unrestricted or conditional, expansive or stingy, individual or communal, organized or haphazard, predictable or spontaneous, ritualistic or informal, anonymous or attributed. Motivations besides religious belief affect decisions to make donations: individual character, personal ambition, political legitimacy, financial concerns, social expectations, or cultural norms.

Re-reading the history of Islamic societies through the prism of charity offers a new perspective on the role of government and governors, the nature of individual social responsibility, the force of religious precept, the structure and functioning of the family and of extended households, the links between relatives, neighbors, and strangers, the impact of gender on individual roles and status, and attitudes toward the proper uses of wealth, to name only a few. This re-reading also provides a rich basis for comparative historical and cross-cultural study.

1 Pray and pay alms

> Only he shall inhabit God's places of worship who believes in God and the Last Day, and performs the prayer, and pays the alms (zakat), and fears none but God alone.
>
> Qur'an 9:18

Read the Qur'an. Talk to Muslims about their religion. Surf the World Wide Web for sites that explain Islam. In every case, you will encounter zakat, obligatory almsgiving. Normative Islamic legal texts describe the rules that govern zakat and there is no shortage of such texts from different eras of Islamic history, since zakat is one of the five canonical obligations of Muslims. One straightforward project for an historian would be to trace changes in the attitudes of the jurists toward zakat in order to write its intellectual and legal history. In comparison, however, the role that zakat has played in the social, economic, or political history of Islamic societies is much more difficult to discover. Historical evidence is not so readily available for the social organization of obligatory almsgiving, the economic importance of sums transferred, or the political implications of maintaining zakat collection and distribution, as examples of topics one might investigate. This chapter begins with an anthropologist's account from Morocco in the 1970s, which provides a rare description of zakat as interpreted by one family. We will then consider what is referred to in the story as "zakat as in the Prophet's time" and some examples from the fourteen centuries that separate the two. These examples, however, are insufficient to explain the dynamics of historical change; rather they provide indications of the challenges facing the implementation of obligatory almsgiving, the different ways it could be interpreted by individuals and governments, and the potential role or relative importance of zakat in Islamic societies.

A story

Abu Illya, the father of my friend Illya Muhammad, is the baker for the Moroccan town of Bou Jad. Each morning he rises at 3:30 a.m. and begins work at the bakery at 4:00 a.m. He and his second oldest son, Abdul Latif, mix, knead, and bake hundreds of loaves of bread in large hot ovens set in the walls of the bakery ... [The author usually sat with Abu

Illya in the family living room after lunch.] He smoked and I read books and generally tried to make sense of all I saw in Bou Jad.

One afternoon a knock at the door shattered our quiet and the rest of the family's siesta. Illya's sister, Khadija, ran to the door and admitted a woman dressed in a shabby gray caftan. They held a whispered conference and then Khadija came into the salon to consult her father. He reached for his wallet, pulled out several bills, and handed them to Khadija, who ran back to the entryway and pressed them into the woman's hand. The woman called out thanks to Abu Illya and faded back into the alleyway.

That evening I asked Illya and Abdul Latif about the woman. They answered in an off-hand fashion that it must have been Lalla Fatiha needing something for her son's schooling since autumn classes had just begun. Who was Lalla Fatiha? No, she isn't a relative; she is our neighbor. Down the *derb* (alley), the doorway on the right. The one painted orange for her daughter's wedding. You've seen her younger children playing soldiers and soccer in the street. She is a widow. My father pays his *zakat* to her.

Zakat? No it isn't zakat as in the Prophet's time when it was paid as a tax to the community coffers. We don't have any collection of zakat in Morocco now. Instead we pay income tax to the government. And then we give alms to the poor. Most people don't pay zakat regularly, just give alms during Ramadan or perhaps support a particular beggar, although Bou Jad has far fewer beggars than Marrakesh or Casablanca Medina.

Abu Illya, it seemed, believed in the responsibility of Muslims to pay zakat whether or not it duplicated income tax. He also believed that one should pay zakat as it says in the Qur'an, that Muslims should know their neighbor's situation and look after their welfare without being asked for help.

Abu Illya had known Lalla Fatiha and her husband, Si Mukhtar, since he was a boy. Si Mukhtar had been a clerk in the super caid's [district chief] office making a low but sufficient wage. After he had fathered seven children, two of whom died before they reached one year of age, he developed unexplained pains in his stomach, was treated by a variety of doctors from Bou Jad to Kenifra, but died within the year. A horde of relatives descended upon Lalla Fatiha to mourn her husband's death, but within a week they had all left for their homes having eaten enough food to feed her children for three months.

Lalla Fatiha quietly went about her life. Gradually her children's clothes grew shabbier; the older boys stayed in school, but each year Lalla Fatiha looked more worn as she struggled to buy them shoes and books from the small savings her husband left. Finally, Um Illya, Illya's mother, in conversation with Lalla Fatiha about an upcoming feast, discovered that she was not planning to sacrifice a sheep but to purchase a little meat for brochettes instead. In Morocco, failing to buy a sheep for sacrifice on 'Id al-Adha [the sacrifice festival during the month of the hajj pilgrimage to Mecca] is a sure sign of financial insolvency. Um Illya rushed home to consult with Abu Illya, and the next day Illya and Abdul Latif delivered a small sheep to Lalla Fatiha's door. That began the systematic zakat.

From then on, Lalla Fatiha and her children could hardly make a move without Abu Illya, his wife, or his children knowing. When money was short for the coming school term, an envelope was delivered to the orange door. When the oldest married daughter fell ill during the final months of her pregnancy and needed special food and medicine her husband couldn't afford, Abu Illya set up a credit line at the pharmacist. When the second youngest daughter discussed leaving school to apprentice herself as a maid, Um Illya was sent to speak to Lalla Fatiha about the need for her daughter's education in the fast-changing world that was modern Morocco. Each week, Abu Illya deposits sacks of flour at the orange door on his way home from the bakery. Illya's sister Khadija tutors the little girls in mathematics; Khalid, the youngest brother, tutors the children in English, his best subject.

After a few years of help, Lalla Fatiha reconciled herself to the omnipresence of Abu Illya's zakat after she tired of the lectures she received when he realized that she had not sent word to him when she lacked for anything. Again and again he told her: "This is only temporary. When your Abdul Rahman finishes the Bac [high-school diploma] then he can be responsible for you. If he or his brothers don't get an education, how can they support you or the little girls on an errand boy's or a dustman's wages? Little ventured, little gained. We must be willing to invest if we want a return. What would Si Mukhtar say if he knew you thought of sacrificing the children's education?" Weary Lalla Fatiha would nod her head, try to kiss Abu Illya's hand, and be brusquely told to get back to her work.

"But what about Lalla Fatiha?" I asked. "Doesn't she resent all the charity? Always taking from others?" Illya was astonished at the question. "This isn't charity," he retorted. "This is zakat. Our honor is to proffer zakat, her honor is to use the zakat. All is provided by God, not by us. This time we have sufficient for our needs; later it may be Lalla Fatiha's turn to provide for us when her children are educated and work as doctors and engineers, and Abdul Latif and I are worn out from working in the bakery. God provides for us; he gives us our wherewithal, our brains, our health with which we work. If we have enough, then we share with our neighbor. If we lack, our neighbor is to share with us. Lalla Fatiha helps us be better Muslims, and in turn is a good Muslim herself. Isn't this the way Islam is to be lived?"[1]

This chapter considers the ideal and the meaning of zakat in order to understand the role assigned to obligatory giving in Islam, both in constructing the relationship between believers and God, and in regulating the relationships of believers among themselves and with the material world. Some might wonder why zakat, an obligatory payment, is included in a book on charity, which is generally understood to be voluntary giving. And indeed, Illya's indignation at the attempt to identify zakat with charity confirms that a real distinction exists in the eyes of Muslims between zakat and voluntary charitable giving. Payment of zakat is first and foremost a reflection of belief in God and obedience to a divine commandment, and not an expression of beneficent feeling or obligation toward other people. As Illya emphasizes, zakat is *not* charity, that is, *not* a handout, a one-sided transaction. Rather, each party participates with honor. "Lalla Fatiha helps us to be better Muslims," he says.

Our understanding of zakat begins from the Qur'an and hadith, texts commonly known and revered by Muslims around the world regardless of their sectarian identity. As on many subjects, the Qur'an has little to offer by way of

---

[1] Donna Lee Bowen, "Abu Illya and Zakat," in *Everyday Life in the Muslim Middle East*, ed. Donna Lee Bowen and Evelyn A. Early (Bloomington: Indiana University Press, 1993), 218–21. Cited with the permission of Indiana University Press.

practical instructions for paying and distributing zakat. These guidelines cohered after Muhammad's death, articulated in hadith and in the works of *fiqh* and *tafsir* (respectively, jurisprudence and interpretation) that proliferated as scholars and jurists produced an expanding corpus of legal writings.[2] Throughout the long history of Islam since the seventh century, diverse practitioners and their communities have continually expanded the commentaries on canonical Islamic texts as well as creating variant practices of zakat, even as the obligation persists across the Muslim world. Because Muslims, like Jews, are not governed by a central ecclesiastical hierarchy in matters of faith and religious obligation, there have always been multiple authorities and opinions on the details of religious belief, law, and practice. The Sunni schools of law vary among themselves concerning some details of zakat assessment and payment, but agree in seeing zakat as a payment due to the Prophet as the leader of the Muslim state and to those who succeeded him as caliphs. The Shi'is (or more properly Shi'at 'Ali, the party of 'Ali) believe that Muhammad's spiritual authority devolved on a chain of successors distinct from the one followed by the Sunnis. These leaders, or *imams*, disappeared after several generations, and their temporary representatives on earth are the *fuqaha* (sing. *faqih*) or religious scholars.[3]

In addition to the story of Abu Illya, this chapter will refer to the jurist Abu Hamid Muhammad al-Ghazali (d. 1111). Al-Ghazali was one of the most prominent medieval Muslim thinkers – a theologian, jurist, philosopher, and mystic. His most important work, the *Ihya' 'ulum al-din* (The Revival of Religious Sciences), aimed to be a comprehensive guide to a Muslim religious life and was written while al-Ghazali was in his forties, having turned away from his career as a jurist and theologian to live as a sufi mystic, to write, and ultimately to return to teaching the truth of prophetic knowledge. In one section of the *Ihya'* called *Kitāb asrār al-zakāh* or *The Mysteries of Almsgiving*, al-Ghazali focused on zakat and questions surrounding charitable giving, explaining each point carefully to provide guidance to believers. As a learned and thoughtful man, his main goal seems to have been to ensure that people would perform all their obligations as correctly as possible, and not invalidate them through some thoughtless act or omission. He thus stressed the correct

---

[2] Each of these disciplines comprises an extensive literature. For an introduction, see Berkey, *The Formation of Islam*, 145–49; Humphreys, *Islamic History: A Framework for Inquiry*, 21–23; I. Goldziher and J. Schacht, "fiḵh," in *EI²*, II:886–91; and J. Robson, "ḥadîth," in *EI²*, III:23–29.

[3] Shi'is divide into groups depending on who they believe was the last of the imams; the English terms refer to the name or number of the imam in the line of succession. The main groups are thus known as Zaydi or "Fivers," Isma'ili or "Seveners," and Imami or "Twelvers." The last are the most numerous; see S. H. Nasr, "Ithnā 'Ashariyya," in *EI²*, IV:277–79 and W. Madelung, "Shī'a," in *EI²*, IX:420–24. On the Sunni madhhabs, see Editor, "madhhab," in *EI²*, Supplement, 551, and the recent bibliography there.

performance of zakat, both its mechanics and the necessary intellectual and spiritual preparations for paying. What he wrote echoed and amplified the Qur'anic message to fulfill God's commandments, all the while recognizing the human foibles that make it difficult for people to do so. Specifically with respect to paying zakat and to giving charity in general, al-Ghazali touched on some of the broadest themes and problems connected to charitable giving: personal ambition, cultural conventions, and economic concerns. His text is cited here extensively since it offers a detailed discussion by one of the key thinkers of Islamic history, well-known and successful in his own time and studied thereafter.[4]

What is zakat?

As Illya explained, zakat is an obligation of Muslims to God and not the result of a sympathetic or altruistic impulse. However, the obligation is realized through people, by virtue of their interaction, and not by an individual facing God alone, as in prayer. The material and social impact of paying and receiving zakat has much in common with voluntary charitable giving, reinforcing a sense of Muslim identity and community, as well as providing concrete material assistance. Both zakat and sadaqa are directed toward God in intent, yet each affects people immediately. And even though one is an obligation and the other a choice, in practice the responsibility to carry out both seems to have been left often to individual initiative throughout much of Islamic history. As Illya said, there are no official zakat collectors in Morocco today; rather his father decided to pay zakat to Lalla Fatiha in what looked like a voluntary gesture when he recognized her need. We do not know who preceded Lalla Fatiha as a recipient of Abu Illya's zakat, nor what happened to that person or persons when he began giving to Lalla Fatiha.

Although zakat and sadaqa are not always distinguished from each other in the Qur'an, certain verses clearly imply two kinds of donations. "True piety is this: to believe in God, and the Last Day, the angels, the Book, and the Prophets,

---

[4] For al-Ghazali's Arabic text see: Muḥammad b. Muḥammad Al-Ghazālī, *Iḥyā 'Ulūm al-Dīn: Kitāb Asrār al-Zakāh* (Cairo: Mu'assassat al-Ḥalabī, 1387/1967–68), 274–303. An English translation is found in Nabih Amin Faris, *The Mysteries of Almsgiving: A Translation from the Arabic with Notes of the* Kitāb Asrār al-Zakāh *of Al-Ghazzālī's Iḥyā 'Ulūm al-Dīn* (Beirut: Centennial Publications, American University of Beirut, 1966). (Subsequent references will cite the Arabic and then the English.) Al-Ghazali also wrote a chapter in the *Ihya'* entitled "The Book of Poverty and Asceticism," which discusses pious poverty and its role in bringing the believing Muslim mystic closer to knowledge of God. On this chapter and on al-Ghazali in his contemporary context, see the discussion in Adam Sabra, *Poverty and Charity in Medieval Islam: Mamluk Egypt 1250–1517* (Cambridge, UK: Cambridge University Press, 2000), 17–31. On al-Ghazali in general, see W. Montgomery Watt, "Al-Ghazālī," in *EI²*, II:1038–41 and Eric Ormsby, *Ghazali*, Makers of the Muslim World (Oxford: Oneworld Publications, 2007).

to give of one's property (*mal*), however cherished, to kinsmen, and orphans, the needy, the traveller, beggars, and to ransom the slave, to perform the prayer, to pay the alms (*zakat*)." (2:177) In defining true piety, this verse first mentions giving away money or material things in general, and then stipulates zakat as a specific duty. Two different kinds of giving are again mentioned in 58:12–13, which recommends giving sadaqa as a specific act before a private audience with the Prophet, and then refers to the familiar obligation to pray and give alms.

Zakat and sadaqa evolved as part of a specifically Islamic theology, and as typically Islamic practices of obligatory and voluntary giving, but they were not invented *ex nihilo* by Muslims. There is evidence, mostly ideological, to be gleaned from pre-Islamic Arabic poetry, as well as from the Old and New Testaments belonging to the Jews and the Christians of Medina where Muhammad spent his years after the *hijra* (the migration of Muslims to Medina from Mecca in 622) as head of the nascent community of Muslims. No clear lines connect zakat with what may have been its antecedents from the *jahiliyya* (the pre-Islamic pagan period in Arabia).[5] Still, the Qur'an verses that were intended to guide Muslims do explain the role envisaged for obligatory alms and voluntary giving.

The historian Michael Bonner, who has given much thought to poverty and charity in the early Muslim community, stresses that the study of poverty, charity, and generosity in early texts is important for understanding the transition from the jahiliyya and the formation of early Islamic society. Pre-Islamic values of generosity became institutionalized in zakat and sadaqa. In the jahiliyya, wealth was demonstrated by the slaughter of camels and distribution of meat, and was a means to attract and hold loyal followers. Surplus wealth was thus not sold or traded, but spent or given away in pursuit of power. Bonner posits a necessary connection between the redistributive practices of the pre-Islamic era and those of Islam. The pre-Islamic idea that any property contains a surplus, which its owner must give away, finds a companion notion in the Qur'an verses 70:24 and 51:19, which assert that the poor have a just claim (*haqq*) to a share in wealth. Both of these ideas also find an echo in Mauss' understanding of the transformation of gift into alms based on the obligation of those with a surplus to share their riches. While the Qur'anic revelation sanctifies giving alms, there are social implications that derive from the claims of the poor to the surplus of the wealthy. Were these a factor in creating patterns of patron–client linkage in the early Islamic period?[6]

---

[5] Berkey, *The Formation of Islam*, 143.
[6] Michael Bonner, "Poverty and Charity in the Rise of Islam," in *Poverty and Charity in Middle Eastern Contexts*, ed. Michael Bonner, Mine Ener, and Amy Singer (Albany: State University of New York Press, 2003), 16–18; Mauss, *The Gift*, 17–18.

Islam is often explained as a religion that requires its adherents to believe and to act in equal parts. Passages from the Qur'an repeat this idea and it is inescapable since the Qur'an is the text of reference for all Muslims and the first thing children traditionally have studied throughout the Muslim world. Verse 2:25 promises paradise to "those who have believed and have done good works" (*alladhina amanu wa-'amalu al-salihat*) and verse 2:110 enjoins the believers: "perform the prayer, and pay the alms; whatever good (*khayr*) you shall put forward to your souls' account, you shall find it with God; assuredly God sees the things you do." Throughout the Qur'an, belief and good works, prayer and zakat, occur as partners. Illya, too, stressed that zakat is part of the active, lived experience of Islam.

Qur'anic usage illustrates that the function of zakat was, as its root Arabic meaning suggests, both "to purify" and "to increase." Purification is one of the general aims of believers, who seek to make themselves as fit as possible for the Day of Judgment. Paying zakat is intended to purify the wealth on which it is calculated, legitimizing personal gain by reserving part of it for community benefit; by giving up one part, the owner can enjoy the blessing of what remains. The Qur'an makes abundantly clear God's dislike of avarice and the greedy accumulation of wealth for its own sake (though it does not censure wealth or the wealthy indiscriminately). Those who do not pay zakat are condemned to harsh sufferings on the Day of Judgment because of their unwillingness to obey God's commandment.[7] Among the most frequently cited with respect to zakat, verse 9:103 amplifies the notion of purification to include the idea that zakat is a donation of repentence. "Take of their wealth a freewill offering (sadaqa), to purify them and to cleanse them thereby, and pray for them; thy prayers are a comfort for them; God is All-hearing, All-knowing." Despite the fact that the word used for alms is "sadaqa" and not "zakat," this verse has been understood as an order to pay zakat regularly. At the same time, the verse highlights the Qur'anic ambiguity regarding zakat and sadaqa. One role of the jurists who came after Muhammad was to resolve such ambiguities, to ensure that the Qur'an could function as the basis for organizing and guiding the Muslim community.[8]

The other meaning of zakat, growth, is expressed in the promise of God to the beneficent that their generosity will be reimbursed many times over. Paying zakat is compared to the regular pruning of a thriving garden, so that what is paid out serves to increase what remains. More than one Qur'an verse articulates

---

[7] Qur'an 9:34–35; Hurgronje, "La Zakāt," 150.

[8] Jørgen Baek Simonsen, *Studies in the Genesis and Early Development of the Caliphal Taxation System* (Copenhagen: Akademisk Forlag, 1988), 30–31. Rubin says that some interpret 9:103 to refer to those who confess to sin, while others interpret the verse as referring to all the believers, and that "sadaqa" here means "zakat"; see *The Qur'an*, 9:103 (p. 165, note). See also T. H. Weir and A. Zysow, "ṣadaḳa," in *EI²*, VIII:709.

this idea, for example: "The likeness of those who expend their wealth in the way of God is as the likeness of a grain of corn that sprouts seven ears, in every ear a hundred grains. So God multiplies unto whom He will; God is All-embracing, All-knowing." (2:261) Or: "And what you give in usury that it may increase upon the people's wealth, increases not with God; but what you give in alms, desiring God's Face, those–they receive recompense manifold." (30:39) According to these verses, prosperity adheres to the conscientious zakat payer, increasing personal wealth and so the amount of zakat to be paid as well as the capacity for additional generous acts. Yet the real recompense for zakat paid is not prosperity in this life, but rather a greater chance of God's favorable judgment and a place in Paradise.[9]

One explanation of the combined spiritual and material purification achieved through zakat payment is offered by Nasir-i Khusraw, an eleventh-century Isma'ili-Shi'i intellectual and author.

With God's guidance, we say that giving *zakāt* purifies the believer while also benefiting his soul, since the purification of his soul depends on the purification of his body, the purification of the body depends on the purification of food, and the purification of food depends on making one's wealth *ḥalāl* [lawful], which depends on setting aside God's rightful share.[10]

In theory, zakat is a tax, one of five recognized by Muslim jurists. While zakat is a manifestation of belief, the other taxes all derive their legitimacy from the theory of holy war. Historically, the poll-tax (*jizya*), assessed at rates of high, medium, and low depending on the status of the taxpayer, was paid by non-Muslims living under Muslim rule. The tithe (*'ushr*) was a tax of 10 percent on agricultural produce from lands allocated to Muslims from conquered territory, while tribute (*kharaj*) was the tax, usually fixed at a higher rate than the tithe, imposed on agricultural produce from conquered lands that were left in the hands of non-Muslims. The fifth (*khums*) is the percentage taken from move-able goods captured in war.[11] These different taxes are relevant to a discussion of zakat because they demonstrate how the jurists envisaged the total financial demands of temporal rule and spiritual leadership.

For Sunnis, the khums was a one-fifth share of booty acquired in war, of which the four-fifths share belonged to the warriors. Shi'is interpreted khums more generally as a one-fifth share on gain from specific categories of goods,

[9] Bashear, "On the Origins and Development of the Meaning of Zakāt," 86–87.
[10] Nāṣir-i Khusraw, *Wajh-i dīn*, ed. G.-R. Aavani (Tehran, 1977), pt. 1, p. 206, as cited in Norman Calder, Jawid Mojaddedi, and Andrew Rippin, eds. and trans., *Classical Islam: A Sourcebook of Religious Literature* (London: Routledge, 2003), 224. On the Isma'ilis, see Farhad Daftary, *The Ismā'īlīs: Their History and their Doctrines* (Cambridge: Cambridge University Press, 1990).
[11] Colin Imber, *Ebus's-Su'ud: The Islamic Legal Tradition* (Stanford: Stanford University Press, 1997), 69.

although exactly which goods is disputed. The reward for paying khums, like zakat, is a greater chance of salvation on the Day of Judgment, but the khums is not considered to be of the same rank of obligation as zakat, and so the penalties for failing to pay are less. Like zakat, khums was assigned to fixed categories of people deemed worthy to receive beneficent support. The khums was divided into six parts, according to the Qur'an verse: "Know that, whatever booty you take, the fifth of it is God's, and the Messenger's, and the near kinsman's, and the orphans', and for the needy, and the traveller." (8:41) Sunnis and Shi'is generally considered that the first three parts belonged to the Prophet, and he received this to sustain himself and his family since they were ineligible to receive zakat. In practice, among most Shi'is, the first three parts belong to the imam (or the faqih in his place), while the other three are to be distributed among the descendants of the Prophet. The Shi'i faqih, therefore, became the recipient of both zakat and khums payments, and control over these revenues contributed substantially to strengthening the position of the Shi'i jurists in their communities.[12]

Zakat has important social implications for the community, even though its most specific definition and realization are religious and focused on the individual and on God. Whether one believes that the original intention was a radical recirculation of wealth or a conservative gesture of assistance, zakat was one means to sustain the poor and needy members of the community. It provided a mechanism for collecting and redistributing wealth and obliged Muslims to acknowledge a responsibility for other members of their confessional group. The contemporary Muslim scholar Fazlur Rahman (1911–88) emphasized this aspect of zakat in his explanation that belief (*iman*) is intended to produce action and so real good works must result from faith. Islam, literally "surrender to God's law," is the concrete expression of faith and is demonstrated by good works. Rahman added that Islam "is the overt, concrete and organized working out of *iman* through a normative community." Good deeds are not acts isolated in a void, but play a fundamental role in the Muslim community, which is, he said, a "social order" based on belief, surrender, and piety.[13]

Calculating zakat

Most broadly stated, every free Muslim (and only Muslims) must pay zakat on specific kinds of property and revenue, provided that the property and revenue

---

[12] Norman Calder, "Khums in Imami Shi'i Jurisprudence, from the Tenth to the Sixteenth Century," *Bulletin of the School of Oriental and African Studies* 45, no. 1 (1982): 39–47; R. Gleave, "khums," in *EI²*, Supplement, 533.

[13] Fazlur Rahman, "Some Key Ethical Concepts of the Qur'ān," *Journal of Religious Ethics* 11, no. 2 (1983): 170–85.

meet or exceed stated minimum amounts (*nisab*). Interpretations differ regarding the property of minors, incapacitated people, and slaves, but generally either they or their legal guardians or owners were required to pay. Even endowed properties (to be discussed in chapter 2) could be subject to zakat when their beneficiaries were individuals rather than public institutions or the poor. Sultans, too, were liable for zakat on their personal wealth, although the property of the state was not subject to zakat.[14] This personal obligation was emphasized, for example, in an anonymous twelfth-century Syrian "Mirror for Princes," a form of advice literature adopted into the Muslim world from Persian traditions of producing manuals of statecraft for rulers, part of an extensive literature of political theory:

Know that kings and rulers have lawful wealth, but more that is unlawful. If someone says that *zakat* is not required of kings and rulers because they have no property, that is a grave error, because *zakat*, pilgrimage, and charity are (all) required of them ... He who does not pay *zakat* on his wealth has no faith, and he who does not pay *zakat* on his position has no honor.[15]

This text reminded the medieval Muslim ruler for whom it was composed that he was an individual bound to fulfill his canonical obligations like anyone else, because his ultimate reckoning would be based on his standing as a Muslim and not as a king.

The famous Ottoman jurist Ebu's-Su'ud Efendi (*c.*1490–1574), who served as *mufti* of Istanbul and *shaykh al-Islam*, also stressed the ruler's obligation to pay zakat. In replying to a query from the Khan of Crimea, Ebu's-Su'ud said: "The performance of acts of worship whether physical or financial is a binding decree and obligatory order imposed on all individuals." However, the wealth raised from the other canonical taxes is "a claim of the Muslim public, which is at the disposal of Sultans, the income and expenditure of which is entrusted to their sound judgement."[16] Clearly the status of a ruler's wealth was an ongoing topic of discussion, and the distinction between the imperial purse and the state budget was relevant not only to the material well-being of his subjects but also to his personal spiritual standing.

Zakat is due annually on property that experiences growth in value, whether through its actual physical expansion or through the increase in its value while

---

[14] Al-Ghazālī, *Kitāb Asrār al-Zakāh*, 275; Faris, *Mysteries of Almsgiving*, 5; A. Zysow, "zakāt," in *EI²*, XI:414.

[15] Julie Scott Meisami, trans. from the Persian, ed. and annotated, *The Sea of Precious Virtues* (Baḥr al-Favā'id): *A Medieval Islamic Mirror for Princes* (Salt Lake City: University of Utah Press, 1991), 140–41. On the "mirrors for princes" genre of literature, see Ira M. Lapidus, *A History of Islamic Societies* (Cambridge: Cambridge University Press, 1988), 181, 184–87 and Humphreys, *Islamic History*, 163–65,

[16] The shaykh al-Islam was the highest ranking figure in the Ottoman religious hierarchy of judges and scholars. Imber, *Ebus's-Su'ud*, 82.

being held for later use or sale. Traditionally, zakat was calculated on five sources of wealth: animal husbandry, agricultural crops, gold and silver, mines, and merchandise. A minimum holding period (*hawl*) of one year exists before goods are liable for zakat. The nisab is fixed for each commodity, although the values of things like gold and silver may be combined in some cases. In addition, once in the entire period of their possession, the owners of gold and silver (including jewelry) and buried treasure must pay zakat on these objects.[17]

Zakat rates and methods for calculating payments appear to have been set so that the tax would not result in unjust or relatively uneven tax burdens. The rules of payment take into account the changing values of animals based on their age, sex, whether they graze or eat purchased fodder, and whether they are put to work. Likewise, different rates exist for crops grown on irrigated and unirrigated fields, young and mature trees, basic storable subsistence crops, and immediate consumables. These principles for the calculation of zakat have produced complexities worthy of any modern tax system, as well as differences of interpretation between the schools of Muslim law. Altogether, the topic of zakat fills many pages in the books of hadith and Muslim jurisprudence. Reading the rules (and the variants) may produce the same vertigo as that induced by studying a page of the US Internal Revenue Code or the guidelines of any national tax authority. Like all such systems, the rules have their own logic and history, and experts in the law stand ready to advise the perplexed, but well-intentioned payer.

A few examples will suffice to illustrate the zakat laws. One summary of how to calculate zakat on cattle reflects the precise assessment of values that depend on animal ages:

No *zakah* is due on less than thirty bulls and cows, on which is levied a calf in the second year of its age. On forty bulls and cows a cow in the third year of its age is levied, and on sixty bulls and cows two calves in the second year of their age. Beyond that the scale becomes fixed: for every forty bulls and cows a cow in the third year of its age is levied, and for every thirty bulls and cows a calf in the second year of its age.[18]

The following passage illustrates how specific points of law might differ between the schools of law:

The *nisab* for cattle is thirty. The rate of *zakat* is one cow or bull in its second year (*tabiʿ*) for every thirty head and one cow in its third year (*musinna, thaniyya*) for every forty. The Malikis understand the animals required to be in their third and fourth years respectively. The Shafiʿis, Malikis and Hanbalis impose this rate on multiples of thirty and forty, and according to them one *tabiʿ* is due for from 40 to 59 head of cattle. The Hanafis impose *zakat* at the rate of one-fortieth of the value of a *musinna* for each

---

[17] Al-Ghazālī, *Kitāb Asrār al-Zakāh*, 275–78; Faris, *Mysteries of Almsgiving*, 5–13.
[18] Al-Ghazālī, *Kitāb Asrār al-Zakāh*, 276; Faris, *Mysteries of Almsgiving*, 7–8. Different conventions hold in transliterating Arabic to English. Here, "zakah" is a variant on "zakat."

additional head from 40 to 59. For Ibadis, the *zakat* for cattle emulates that for camels, and they impose one sheep or goat for each five head of cattle to twenty-four and thereafter for each *nisab* substitute cattle of the required age for the corresponding camels ...[19]

These zakat laws were originally formulated in a society where animal husbandry was a familiar occupation and where there were agreed-upon values for animals of different sexes and ages as well as accepted "conversion rates" for translating the value of one species (or breed) into another. Regional differences in breeds, climate, pasturage, water, and other natural conditions probably affected the way different jurists interpreted the precise requirements of zakat and these interpretations produced the variations in calculations described above just as comparable differences produced varying rates for cultivated crops.

Zakat on gold and silver is levied at a rate of 2.5 percent, with the nisab usually set at approximately 85 grams of gold and 593 grams of silver. The same rates apply to the yields of mines and buried treasure, as well as to merchandise of all kinds, and the value of merchandise may be combined with that of gold and silver in order to assess the nisab. Differences between schools exist regarding the assessments on traders as compared with investors, as well as with regard to determining the status of merchandise like animals held for sale.[20] Today, 2.5 percent or one-fortieth is usually cited as the general rate for zakat. Equivalent values in gold are used as a standard for calculating the total value of different properties in order to measure the nisab. Examples of how these calculations are carried out may be found easily today on the websites of some large Islamic charities and other organizations, offering accessible assistance to Muslims who wish to calculate the zakat they owe. For example, the international organization Islamic Relief, established in 1984 and registered with the United Kingdom Charities Commission, provides a "zakat calculator" which includes a form to be filled out as well as hypertext links to detailed explanations and examples of what to include and how to calculate values.[21]

Altogether, zakat regulations reveal a legal culture that invested considerable energy in constructing a taxation system to fit the principles of Muslim faith, and, to a certain extent, attuned to the character of local economies, historically

[19] Zysow, "zakāt," XI:412.
[20] Zysow, "zakāt," XI:413; Al-Ghazālī, *Kitāb Asrār al-Zakāh*, 277–78; Faris, *Mysteries of Almsgiving*, 10–12.
[21] The Islamic Relief site is www.islamic-relief.com/uk/index.htm# (accessed December 7, 2006), and the zakat calculator linked to it is www.ramadhanzone.com (accessed December 7, 2006). The 2.5 percent rate is cited on the US-based English-language site www.islamicity.com/mosque/zakat (accessed July 14, 2005). See the site for its zakat calculator as well, where it is possible to calculate one's zakat, and pay online with a credit card, directing the zakat to a particular organization selected from the list provided. See also the website of the Qatar Zakah Fund, an independent public authority: http://www.zf.org.qa/english/Calc/money1.asp (accessed September 12, 2007).

emphasizing agrarian cultivation and animal husbandry practices. The legal details reflect attempts to be fair. However, some kinds of wealth were harder to assess than others and, like taxation systems elsewhere, this one seems not to have been immune to pressures from special interest groups. The third caliph, 'Uthman (644–55), is credited with the decision that the official collectors could take zakat only on apparent (*zahir*) property, that is livestock and crops. The remainder, including gold, silver, and merchandise, was defined as hidden (*batin*). Zakat on hidden property was to be paid on the owner's initiative, either to the collectors or directly to recipients with no intermediary. The reason given for the change was the increasing reputation of collectors as greedy and unjust in their assessments, though it also may have resulted from the impracticality of chasing after wealth that was more easily concealed from the assessors. While the government's claim to zakat from agricultural produce and animal husbandry was thus maintained, payment of zakat from other forms of wealth came to depend on the honesty and commitment of individual Muslims. Changes in zakat laws were probably not the result of unilateral policy decisions, or only effected in response to reported irregularities by tax collectors. Groups like merchants or the scholars ('*ulama*), who wielded social, economic, or political power and were able to secure changes to their own advantage, probably were able to influence decisions about the nature of zakat collection. Clearly, merchants benefited far more from the changes described above than would shepherds or the mass of peasant farmers. Although these changes were justified as protecting subjects from extortion, they also revealed how political concerns and the relative power of government as compared with that of commercial or juristic groups could influence the organization and collection of zakat.[22]

The jurists found ample fare for legal disputes in the zakat rules and individuals have continually sought clarifications about zakat calculation and payment. The resulting discussions are found in prescriptive literature and in *fatwa*s, the responses of jurists to specific legal queries. Fatwas do not cite actual personal names (only the fictitious Zeyd, Amr, and Hind), nor do they specifically situate any one incident. However, since they are often collected and grouped by author, fatwas can be located generally in time and space. One example of a straightforward query to Ebu's-Su'ud Efendi reads: "If Zeyd has at his disposal 800 akça [silver coins] more than [what is required for his] basic provisions, is zakat required on it after a year has passed?" The answer: "It is, being 40 [akça, i.e. 5 percent]." This fatwa may have been the product of an actual query or of theoretical legal discussions, or have been issued as a general reminder to people to pay zakat. Other questions articulated what sound like local, quotidian

[22] Zysow, "zakāt," XI:409.

concerns that people had regarding ritual and everyday behavior in specific circumstances. For example, Ebu's-Su'ud was asked whether money contributed by a believer to fund the imperial Ottoman navy could be considered as zakat, to which the answer was "yes." This fatwa may have been issued after the famous destruction of the navy at the battle of Lepanto in 1571, to encourage Ottoman subjects to assist in rebuilding the lost ships.[23]

The practice of issuing fatwas thrives, and today numerous websites also post fatwas to assist Muslims in calculating their zakat. The al-Islam.com website sponsored by the Ministry of Islamic Affairs, Endowments, Da'wah (Preaching) and Guidance of Saudi Arabia, offers its readers information in seven languages – Arabic, English, French, Malay, Indonesian, German, and Turkish – with a detailed section on all aspects of zakat. The contents include fatwas that illustrate some continuities of uncertainty from earlier eras as well as more contemporary concerns. For example, the general question is posed: "How can a Muslim estimate the amount of Zakah payable on his salary, or on his profit from businesses, gifts or other means of income?" The reply is detailed but still leaves many points to be clarified:

A Fatwa was issued at the First Conference on Zakah held in Kuwait [1984] to the effect that: The worker's wages, employees' salaries, earnings from other professions such as physicians and engineers, and the like, are all considered income gained from one's work. The majority of the conference participants observed that such a gain is not counted for Zakah when first received. However, if there are savings from it, it [sic: they] should be added to other properties counted for Zakah. Then, Zakah is to be paid at the end of a full year. The full year is to be considered from the time the wealth reaches the minimum amount countable for Zakah. On the other hand, any savings attained from one's work are to be added to the total amount of wealth, even though they have not remained in the possession of the owner for a full year.[24]

A conscientious person might ask for further clarifications, regarding, for example, which professions are included in "the like" and what the "other properties" are.

Over the centuries, one of the challenges for jurists has been to decide how new forms of income and wealth, which did not exist in the time of the Prophet and the initial elaboration of shari'a (Muslim laws and codes), should be

[23] M. Ertuğrul Düzdağ, Şeyhülislâm Ebussuûd Efendi Fetvaları Işığında 16. Asır Türk Hayatı (Istanbul: Enderun Kitabevi, 1983), 63–64. On fatwas generally see E. Tyan and J. R. Walsh, "fatwa," in EI², II: 866–67 and Humphreys, Islamic History, 217–18. On the battle of Lepanto, see A. Hess, "The Battle of Lepanto and its Place in Mediterranean History," Past and Present 57 (1972): 53–73.
[24] Http://zakat.al-islam.com/def/default.asp?l=eng&filename=Quest/desc/item7/item3/desc1 (accessed January 5, 2007). Kuwait has sponsored the very active Kuwait Zakat House as a government organization: www.zakathouse.org.kw (accessed January 5, 2007). See also Proceedings of the First International Conference, Bayt al-zakah in the State of Kuwait (Kuwait, 1984).

considered for the purposes of zakat. In answering the question of how to calculate zakat on shares of stock, for example, one authority says:

If the shareholder invests his shares in trade, the amount of Zakah will be 2.5%, according to the market price of the shares at the time the Zakah becomes due. However, if the shares are invested to obtain annual earnings, Zakah is to be paid in the following way: If the shareholder knows the value of every share as opposed to the assets owned by the company, he may pay Zakah according to this value. But if he does not know, it is sufficient for him to simply add the earnings of his shares to the total sum of his wealth countable for Zakah and pay a rate of 2.5% when a full year passes since the wealth has reached the minimum amount counted for Zakah.[25]

What is consistent here with the early Muslim era is a 2.5 percent rate on cash or specie (although Ebu's-Su'ud had calculated 5 percent) and the principle that wealth be held for a year before being subject to zakat. At the same time, the fatwas cited above acknowledge that to make zakat an effective tax, new forms of wealth and revenue need to be included in its calculation. This suggests that fatwas might usefully be studied to understand changing forms of and attitudes toward wealth and its liability for zakat.

Payment and distribution

While stating only generally that everyone with a minimum qualification should pay zakat, the Qur'an is somewhat more explicit about who should receive it. *Ayat al-sadaqa* (the verse of sadaqa), quoted below, is the one most frequently cited as defining zakat recipients, despite the use of the term *sadaqat* (here in the plural).

The freewill offerings (sadaqat) are for the poor and needy, those who work to collect them, those whose hearts are brought together, the ransoming of slaves, debtors, in God's way, and the traveller. (9:60)

On closer examination, each of the eight categories of zakat recipients turns out to be broad and flexible, perhaps intentionally so. Explicitly excluded from receiving zakat are wealthy people, non-Muslims, and slaves. Zakat cannot be paid to ascendant or descendant relatives, husbands may not pay to wives, and many hold that wives may not pay to husbands. Relatives are excluded because they already deserve routine support (nafaqa), as do slaves; zakat is meant to extend help to others in the community beyond immediate familial obligations. Minors and the insane can receive zakat, though they must have a legal guardian to accept it for them. For Shi'is, the fuqaha, the experts in Muslim law, are the proper recipients of zakat. People who are descendants of the Prophet

---

[25] Http://zakat.al-islam.com/def/default.asp?l=eng&filename=Quest/desc/item7/item3/desc1 (accessed January 5, 2007).

(the Banu Hashim and the *ashraf*) or formal clients of his family are also ineligible to receive zakat because it is essentially tainted money, paid in order to purify the use of what remains in the hands of the one paying. As such it would be inappropriate for the Prophet and his family to have any contact with it. People who claim to be poor may receive zakat without any of the usual obligations of proof defined in Muslim law, that is, either taking an oath or providing witnesses.[26]

Many practical issues about payment and distribution of zakat had to be worked out in the early Muslim community so that Muslims could carry out their obligations properly. As with zakat assessment, hadith and legal commentaries offer specific guidance about zakat distribution where the Qur'an provides only general principles. The poor and needy were the most materially deprived and the most numerous among the potential recipients of zakat. For this reason, they are discussed at length in chapter 5 together with more general ideas about poverty. The six additional groups of recipients are discussed below. Together, the eight groups illustrate what zakat was originally intended to achieve in the Muslim community.

The inclusion of zakat collectors (*'amilun*) among the zakat recipients in the Qur'an is evidence that a formal office was meant to be responsible for collection, part of an official system that presumably included distributions. Muslim histories recount that zakat was collected during Muhammad's own lifetime, although institutionalized only some time after the hijra to Medina. This may account for some of the ambiguous language concerning zakat and sadaqa in the Qur'an. It was one of three components that formed the tax system of the early Islamic state. Zakat was paid by the settled Muslims, jizya by non-Muslims, and sadaqa by nomadic tribesmen.[27] While a required tax, zakat may actually have constituted an improvement over pre-Islamic taxation in that it was more carefully regulated and more limited in the extent of its burden. Moreover, the Qur'anic listing of legitimate recipients of both zakat and sadaqa may have been intended to mitigate earlier tax abuses by rabbis and priests as well.[28]

After Muhammad's death, zakat collections sometimes provoked disputes, and the contest to enforce collection was depicted as a factor in the struggles of the young community to establish and maintain its authority over new adherents to Islam as well as over conquered subjects. The authority of the first caliph, Abu Bakr (632–34), was challenged by some of the tribes that had joined the

---

[26] Al-Ghazālī, *Kitāb Asrār al-Zakāh*, 291; Faris, *Mysteries of Almsgiving*, 53; Zysow, "zakāt," XI:415–16.

[27] Fred M. Donner, *The Early Islamic Conquests* (Princeton: Princeton University Press, 1981), 252, 265.

[28] Donner, *The Early Islamic Conquests*, 70–71.

Muslims under the Prophet. One sign of this challenge was their refusal to pay zakat, which they claimed was promised as a personal obligation to Muhammad. Zakat payment, however, was interpreted by the Muslims not only as a symbol of commitment to the religious obligations imposed by Islam, but also in recognition of the transfer of temporal political authority over the Muslim community from one leader to the next. The so-called *ridda* (apostasy) wars that ensued against the Arabian tribes who refused to pay zakat to Muhammad's successors were crucial to the definition of the fledgling Muslim authority in Medina, both spiritual and temporal.[29]

After Abu Bakr, the caliph ʿUmar (634–44) worked to establish an administrative framework for the growing Muslim state, which apparently included an expanded organization of zakat collectors and more assiduous collection, for example from Muslim merchants at stations along the roads. Some people questioned whether paying zakat to official collectors was proper given charges of corruption, yet the official collections continued, and it appears that the Umayyads in Damascus, the first dynasty of Muslim caliphs (661–750), invested further energy in organizing zakat collection, though they did not necessarily succeed in purging abuses.[30] The caliph ʿUmar b. ʿAbdul ʿAziz (717–20) implemented extensive tax reforms and toward the end of the Umayyad period a government Office of Zakat (*diwan al-sadaqa*) was created. A similar office existed under the successor dynasty of the ʿAbbasid caliphs (750–1258). The ʿAbbasid Office of Good Works and Zakat (*diwan al-birr wa'l-sadaqa*) managed the collection and distribution of zakat. Under this office was another one that oversaw the administration of endowments, though how this actually functioned is unclear. At the end of the eighth century, under the caliph Harun al-Rashid (786–809), there were reports again that zakat collection was corrupt and inefficient. One complaint was that zakat was sometimes collected together with other taxes like the ʿushr (tithe) and not accounted for separately. This is not so surprising in view of the fact that the zakat on some categories of agriculture was calculated at one-tenth. In such a situation the collection problems may well have made it difficult to distribute zakat reliably among the proper categories of recipients.[31]

---

[29] W. Montgomery Watt, "Abū Bakr," in *EI*², I:110–11. Azim Nanji, "Almsgiving," in *Encyclopaedia of the Qurʾān*, ed. Jane Dammen McAuliffe (Leiden: E. J. Brill, 2001), I:67; Fred M. Donner, trans. and annotated, *The History of Al-Ṭabarī, volume X: The Conquest of Arabia* (Albany: State University of New York Press, 1993), 40–45.

[30] Zysow, "zakāt," XI:409.

[31] Lapidus, *A History of Islamic Societies*, 64; Frede Løkkegaard, *Islamic Taxation in the Classic Period, with Special Reference to Circumstances in Iraq* (Copenhagen: Branner and Korch, 1950), 163. Løkkegaard's claim that zakat was distributed to the descendants of the Prophet and his family is problematic because they were not supposed to receive zakat because of the taint. Zysow, "zakāt," XI:409.

Problems with zakat collection did not originate only with the collectors. The Hanafi jurist al-Sarakhsi (d. 1106) discussed how a zakat collector should respond when confronted with someone who claimed to have paid zakat directly to the poor. In his discussion, al-Sarakhsi said that the poor do not have the right to demand zakat from the person paying, since the right of collection belongs to the governor and to the agent he appoints as collector. However, if the person who owed zakat decided on his own to pay it directly to the poor and the collector accepted his statement that he did so, then he did not have to pay a second time to the official collector, since the poor are allowed to receive zakat directly. In giving his answer, however, al-Sarakhsi emphasized the standing of the collector as someone deputized to implement what is due to God, and presented an alternative legal view that the person paying cannot take away the right of the governor to distribute zakat according to his own decisions.[32] Al-Sarakhsi's text emphasized once again that zakat payment was first and foremost a duty of faith between the payer and God, with the recipient playing a secondary role. The discussion also made it clear that distributing the zakat once it was collected was intended chiefly to be the task of the governor, though he could be circumvented if someone paid zakat directly to deserving recipients.

To put al-Sarakhsi's learned discussion into a broader perspective, we can cite his contemporary, al-Ghazali (d. 1111), who remarked that the collectors of zakat had, in fact, disappeared in most places. Differences between al-Sarakhsi and al-Ghazali may reflect distinct regional developments of zakat practices: al-Sarakhsi spent his life in Transoxania while al-Ghazali was born in the Iranian province of Khorasan and from there traveled mostly westward to Baghdad and Damascus. Al-Ghazali recommended that a person who distributed zakat (whether an official or an individual) should take care to give shares to each of the canonical categories of recipients who were present in a place, and within each category to at least three recipients. If categories became obsolete or irrelevant, then the sharing should be readjusted.[33] It is not clear how individual recipients were identified, but it may have been in consultation with or through the mediation of a local religious figure or other authority, like a *mukhtar* (village or neighborhood chief). As prominent members of the community who regularly had contact with a wide spectrum of local people they were likely to know who was in need of assistance.

Scattered evidence from medieval Egypt indicates that before the time of Saladin (d. 1193), people there had begun to pay their zakat directly to the needy and deserving. According to the historian Maqrizi (d. 845/1445) Saladin

---

[32] See Muhammad b. Ahmad al-Sarakhsi (d. 1106), in *Kitab al-mabsut* (Beirut, 1406/1986) (reprint of the Cairo 1324 edition), vol. II, pp. 161–62, as cited in Calder *et al.*, *Classical Islam*, 211.

[33] Al-Ghazālī, *Kitāb Asrār al-Zakāh*, 280–81; Faris, *Mysteries of Almsgiving*, 23.

initiated (or revived) the formal government collection of zakat in Egypt and opened an Office of Zakat. Among other things, government collection of zakat was a sign of the restoration of Sunni rule in Egypt, conquered by Saladin from the Shiʻi Fatimid dynasty. Under him, zakat money was distributed among four of the Qurʼanic categories of eligible recipients (poor, needy, debtors, travelers), while the state treasury (*bayt al-mal*) held the shares of the zakat collectors, new converts, fighters, and slaves seeking freedom. Ibn Jubayr (d. 614/1217), a historian who wrote shortly after the death of Saladin, complained that he himself had to pay zakat when arriving in Alexandria, and the fourteenth-century traveler Ibn Battuta noted the zakat pay-stations along the route of his journey. Among those between Cairo and Syria, he said, was a place called Qatya "where *zakat* is collected from the merchants, their goods are examined, and their baggage most rigorously searched." Other fourteenth-century sources recorded that merchants entering Egypt paid zakat on gold and silver at the rate of 5 percent, along with other duties. The state imposition of zakat seems an obvious attempt to increase public revenues, and it was levied on agricultural goods and commercial merchandise, but not always in accord with the require-ments of the one-year holding period or the canonical rates. The label "zakat," it seems, continued to be a convenient means to legitimize government extrac-tions, but may not have reflected a strict adherence to the canonical zakat.[34]

On a practical level one might ask how the collectors in Egyptian towns could assess the zakat payments of visitors or why these travelers did not pay in their home towns. Did the officials rely on declarations by the travelers as to whether or not they had paid zakat for the year preceding? Or was zakat in this instance more like a customs duty on the goods and wealth carried by the travelers? More serious was the problem of what to do when zakat was collected by abusive or rebel rulers. Jurists disagreed about whether people had to pay zakat twice, once at the demand of the tyrant and again to make sure that zakat reached its proper recipients, or whether once was sufficient, provided zakat was paid with the proper intention.[35] The very existence of the discussion, however, suggests that zakat (for these jurists at least) was not only a payment reflecting obedience to God's commandment but also a necessary part of the local economy.

Ibn Battuta made more than one observation about zakat collections, and the record of his travels provides a sense of fourteenth-century variations. In Morocco itself, he praised his patron Abu ʻInan for curbing abuses of the zakat collectors: "If the only instance of the benevolence of our master, God

---

[34] H. A. R. Gibb, trans. and ed., *The Travels of Ibn Baṭṭūṭa AD 1325–1354*, vol. I (Cambridge, UK: Cambridge University Press, 1958), 72; H. Rabie, *The Financial System of Egypt AH 576–741/ AD 1169–1341* (London: Oxford University Press, 1972), 96–100; Yaacov Lev, "Charity and Social Practice: Egypt and Syria in the Ninth–Twelfth Centuries," *Jerusalem Studies in Arabic and Islam* 24 (2000): 473–74.

[35] See the discussion by al-Sarakhsī (d. 1106), quoted in Calder *et al.*, *Classical Islam*, 213–14.

strengthen him, towards his subjects had been his abolition of the right of hospitality exercised upon them by the collectors of *zakat* and the provincial governors, that alone would be a manifest sign of his justice and a shining light of beneficence."[36] While the story was told to enhance Abu ʿInan's reputation, it revealed the kinds of problems that plagued state zakat collection. If his characterization was more literary topos than historical account, then it is possible that zakat collectors had become the stereotypical "bad guys" among public officials. As Ibn Battuta continued eastward, he added: "Two years after our arrival in India, the Sultan abolished these [other] duties and ordered that nothing should be taken from people except the alms tax (*zakat*) and the tenth [ʿushr]. This was at the time when he recognized the ʿAbbasid Caliph Abu'l-ʿAbbas."[37] Zakat in this instance became a symbol of closer adherence to caliphal authority, perhaps implying reform and heightened imperial piety. Yet reform could equally sweep zakat away. Two centuries later, in Mughal India, the Sultan Akbar (1556–1605) abolished the zakat as a tax on Muslims as part of a series of reforms he enacted toward the end of the first Muslim millennium (AH 1000 = 1591–92). While the state had ended its role, Muslims were still free to offer alms directly to the poor as they saw fit.[38]

Under the Ottomans (*c*.1300–1923), no official zakat office existed. Yet fifteenth-century Ottoman taxes on commercial commodities followed customary rates which were roughly the same as those of zakat.[39] And the sixteenth-century fatwas of Ebu's-Suʿud Efendi cited above demonstrated how various ordinary taxes and donations might be considered as zakat, depending on the intention of the donor at the time of payment. The question was put to him: "If the traders pay the akçes [silver coins] they give as customs and intend them as zakat, are they acceptable as zakat?" His answer, "They are acceptable," reflects the practical approach characteristic of Ebu's-Suʿud. It was not a matter of merging canonical and secular obligations, since no such separation really existed in the conceptualization of state authority in Islamic thought.

The Ottoman case demonstrates what seems to have occurred at least in some places and periods. Zakat rates resembled or became the basis for other taxes collected by a government. Jurists provided believers with a means to pay these taxes as zakat, thereby fulfilling their obligations and putting a more acceptable face on the official exactions. Or, perhaps similar to the way in which Abu Illya paid his income tax in Morocco, people paid the taxes demanded by the

---

[36] H. A. R. Gibb, trans. and ed., *The Travels of Ibn Baṭṭūṭa AD 1325–1354*, vol. IV (London: The Hakluyt Society, 1994), 930–33.

[37] H. A. R. Gibb, trans. and ed., *The Travels of Ibn Baṭṭūṭa AD 1325–1354*, vol. III (Cambridge, UK: Cambridge University Press, 1971), 604–5.

[38] Waines, *An Introduction to Islam*, 191.

[39] Halil Inalcik and Donald Quataert, eds., *An Economic and Social History of the Ottoman Empire, 1300–1914* (Cambridge, UK: Cambridge University Press, 1994), 198–99, 204–06.

government and then paid zakat directly in addition, without any official intermediary. This merging and separating of zakat and other state levies might also be considered in the context of debates about the relationship between *din* (divinely prescribed obligations of human beings) and *dunya* or *dawla* (the material world and government), which have been ongoing among Muslim thinkers for centuries. Together the pair express a unified notion of what today might be labeled "spiritual" and "temporal." Although distinct, they were inseparably linked historically because of the social reality of religion in a material world. Good government is good because a ruler adheres to his obligations as a believing Muslim and the governor and protector of a community of Muslims.[40]

At roughly the same time that Akbar eliminated the zakat and Ebu's-Su'ud was helping Ottoman believers to fulfill their obligations, zakat played a rather different role with respect to state power at the western edge of the Muslim world. In Morocco, zakat became a symbol of the relative strength of sufi *zawiyas* (hospices) vis-à-vis the central government of the Sa'di dynasty (*c*.1549–1659). Local peasants paid their zakat and made other contributions to the zawiyas of Dila in the Middle Atlas, Tit-n-fitr on the Atlantic coast, and Tamesluht near Marrakesh. In turn, the peasants enjoyed improvements to agriculture and local infrastructure initiated by the sufis, as well as better protection as a result of the presence of the zawiyas and increased commercial activity from the pilgrims who visited. By paying zakat, the peasants acknowledged the patronage of the local zawiya shaykhs, who were often more effective than the remote arm of dynastic power in offering physical and economic security, as well as spiritual guidance, despite the formal obligation that dynastic rulers should receive zakat. Payment of zakat essentially legitimized the political power of the sufi shaykh who received it.[41]

Five additional categories of zakat recipients remain to be discussed. "Those whose hearts are to be won over" (*al-muallafa qulubuhum*) included people recently converted to Islam or others whose ties to the Muslim community needed strengthening or reinforcement. Zakat served to recompense the converts for hardships they may have endured in losing family or community support as a result of their conversion. The disadvantages of belonging to a relatively small and weak minority community were more pronounced in the early Muslim era but lessened with the rapid expansion of Muslim rule from the second half of the seventh century, when the resources and political strength of the community increased exponentially. An eighth-century source already says that the category of *al-muallafa qulubuhum* no longer existed, and one from the

---

[40] A basic discussion of *din wa dawla* can be found in L. Gardet, "*dīn*" *EI²*, II:295.
[41] Francisco Rodriguez-Mañas, "Supplanting the Ruler: The Levying of Taxes by Sûfî Zâwiyas in the Maghrib," *Islamic Quarterly* 40 (1996): 188–99.

tenth century assigned the new converts' share of zakat to military pensioners and "to the destitute persons who visit mosques and have no pension nor a share in the spoils of war, but are not beggars."[42] According to al-Ghazali, the zakat collectors and "those whose hearts are to be won over" were rare among zakat recipients by the turn of the twelfth century.[43] However, this category, like others, can be interpreted to include groups of people in need who did not exist when the categories were first drawn up. Today in the Malaysian state of Selangor, for example, the category "*al-muallafa qulubuhum*" includes money for Muslims living as minorities or in conflict areas like Iraq and some African states.[44]

Slavery was common in Islamic societies as in much of the pre-modern world and was largely eliminated in the nineteenth and early twentieth centuries. In Muslim theology and law, the eventual manumission of a slave (*riqab*) was regarded as a charitable act and encouraged, often as part of the owner's final will and testament. For example, on his deathbed, Evliya Çelebi's patron, the former Ottoman grand vizier Melek Ahmed Pasha, freed 105 slave boys and gave each one a horse, equipment, and 100 gold pieces.[45] Freeing a slave, essentially donating his or her price to the slave, appears in one passage in the Qur'an (5:89) as the penalty for breaking an oath, an act of charity also equivalent to feeding or clothing ten needy men.[46] However, the specific term used by al-Ghazali and other jurists to discuss this category of recipients is *mukatabun*, which refers specifically to slaves who had contracted with their owners to purchase their freedom and not the more general Qur'anic term *riqab*. Zakat money could be given either directly to slaves seeking to buy their manumission, or to their owners for the same purpose. However, an owner could not pay zakat to his or her own slaves, since this would essentially be paying it to himself, which is forbidden.[47]

---

[42] A. Ben Shemesh, trans. and ed., *Qudāma b. Ja'far's Kitāb al-Kharāj*, vol. II of *Taxation in Islam*, (Leiden: E. J. Brill, 1965), 67.

[43] Al-Ghazālī, *Kitāb Asrār al-Zakāh*, 280; Faris, *Mysteries of Almsgiving*, 23.

[44] N.a. "The Efficiency of Zakat Distributions," posted in the publications section of http://www. iiu.edu.my/iaw (accessed March 2, 2006).

[45] Evliya Çelebi, *The Intimate Life of an Ottoman Statesman: Melek Ahmed Pasha (1588–1662)*, trans. and ed. Robert Dankoff, introd. by Rhoads Murphey (Albany: State University of New York Press, 1991), 264.

[46] See also Qur'an Sura 90.

[47] Al-Ghazālī, *Kitāb Asrār al-Zakāh*, 292; Faris, *Mysteries of Almsgiving*, 58. See Zysow, "zakāt," XI:415 on the differences between the schools of law regarding manumission in the context of zakat. There is a large literature on slaves and slavery in Islamic societies. Basic references and concepts may be found in R. Brunschwig, " 'abd," in *EI²*, I:24–40, and see also Y. Hakan Erdem, *Slavery in the Ottoman Empire and its Demise, 1800–1906* (Basingstoke, Hampshire: Macmillan, 1996); Bernard Lewis, *Race and Slavery in the Middle East: An Historical Enquiry* (New York: Oxford University Press, 1990); and J. R. Willis, ed., *Slaves and Slavery in Muslim Africa* (London, 1983).

Freeing a slave was essentially the donation of an asset and as such also had to be considered in the overall context of an individual's financial responsibilities. A hadith recounted that when the Prophet heard that a man had arranged for his slave to be freed after his death, he intervened and questioned the man about his resources. Upon discovering that the slave was the man's only property, the Prophet arranged that the slave be sold instead of manumitted. The money from the sale he then gave to the man, saying:

Start with your own self and spend it on yourself, and if anything is left, it should be spent on your family, and if anything is left (after meeting the needs of the family) it should be spent on relatives, and if anything is left from the family, it should be spent like this, like this. And he was saying: In front of you, on your right and on your left [i.e. giving it away].[48]

The hadith emphasized that charity exceeding the capacities of an individual is not recommended. In addition, a person's own needs and those of the family (nafaqa) should take priority and charity should not threaten their status or well-being such as to reduce them to begging.[49] This example demonstrates how exceptional was the behavior of saints and sufis (to be discussed in chapter 4), including the fact that they were not necessarily to be emulated. Thus, not all charitable actions were praiseworthy if they conflicted with prior obligations and responsibilities.

The Qur'an says that forgiving debts is a form of charity on the part of the lender (2:280). Debtors (gharimun) are eligible to receive zakat, whether they are poor or not, but only if the debt was incurred for legitimate reasons. A tenth-century legal text specified that debtors eligible for zakat included those who suffered "loss of property, influence and slaves for God's cause," and "those remaining behind, not participating in a battle and not in spoils of war who are poor and whose debts were not caused by irreligious activities."[50] For example, debts resulting from gambling or dealing in wine or pork – all forbidden activities according to Islamic law – would disqualify someone from receiving charitable assistance. However, if someone incurred disreputable debts but then sincerely repented, s/he was again eligible to receive zakat.[51] People in debt who nonetheless owned furnished houses and had servants and horses were not necessarily disqualified from receiving zakat. The same tenth-century source quoted above cited Caliph 'Umar b. 'Abd al-'Aziz as saying: "A Muslim cannot

---

[48] Muslim b. al-Ḥajjāj al-Nisābūrī, Al-Jāmiʿ al-Ṣaḥīḥ (Beirut: Al-Matkab al-Tijārī, n.d.), 5 (zakat), bab 6; Muslim, Ṣaḥīḥ Muslim, vol. II, trans. and ed. ʿAbdul Ḥamīd Ṣiddīqī (Lahore: Sh. Muhammad Ashraf, 1973), 479; USC-MSA, Muslim 5/2183.

[49] Muḥammad b. Ismāʿīl al-Bukhārī, Ṣaḥīḥ al-Bukhārī (Istanbul: Al-Maktaba al-Islami, 1979), 55 (wasaya), 2; Bukhari, USC-MSA, 51/0005. This hadith is repeated in different forms several times in Bukhari's collection.

[50] Ben Shemesh, Qudāma b. Jaʿfar's Kitāb al-Kharāj, 68.

[51] Frede Løkkegaard, "gharīm," in EI², II:1011.

exist without a house to live in, a servant to assist him with his work, a horse to fight his enemies and also some furniture in his home."[52] These few medieval examples do not offer details of any specific case. However, they do describe an attitude that did not privilege indigent poverty as a reason to receive beneficent distributions.

In addition to their other charitable distributions, rulers sponsored the release of debtors from prison to demonstrate pious gratitude for recovery from illness. Sultan Barquq (d. 1399) freed debtors and paid their debts during Ramadan. The Ottoman queen mother Kösem Sultan (d. 1651) went out incognito in Istanbul for the same purpose during the month of Rajab.[53] The redemption of debtors could also be carried out as part of a public spectacle and was another demonstration of imperial Ottoman beneficence at the circumcision festivities in 1582 for the sultan's sons, recorded in the magnificent album commemorating that occasion (Fig. 2). Whether people were released indiscriminately on such occasions or only after their debts were examined is not clear.

A companion to debt forgiveness was to encourage people to make interest-free loans to the needy. While not quite the same as an outright donation, such loans could ultimately be forgiven as well. In the meantime they spared the honor of the person receiving the loan by preserving the fiction of his or her independence. Muslim court records from the Ottoman period offer much evidence on the handling of debts, when creditors sought the intervention of a judge if a debtor could not pay. Yet a sampling of cases suggests that, where possible, debts could also be rescheduled rather than forgiven outright. Peasants with tax arrears came before Jerusalem's judges on a regular basis in the sixteenth century to acknowledge tax debts and promise to repay them. A judge in eighteenth-century Damascus heard the claims of several Muslim creditors against a Christian, Yusuf, son of Muhanna. In court, Yusuf declared that he was destitute, and four Muslim witnesses substantiated his claim. His creditor did not produce evidence to the contrary. The judge then ruled that Yusuf should pay his debts, stipulating a schedule that stretched over more than a decade. In another case, a *janissary* (Ottoman infantryman) acting as the chief of police for a village near Jerusalem claimed that ten of the villagers owed him money. They claimed they were poor and could not pay, and the janissary could not prove otherwise. The judge thereupon dismissed the case and ordered the janissary not to harass the villagers further.[54] Here, the debtors were Muslims

---

[52] Ben Shemesh, *Qudāma b. Ja'far's Kitāb al-Kharāj*, 66.

[53] Sabra, *Poverty and Charity*, 63–68; Peirce, *The Imperial Harem*, 209.

[54] Abdul-Karim Rafeq, "The Poor in Ottoman Damascus: A Socioeconomic and Political Study," in *Pauvreté et richesse dans le monde musulman méditerranéen/Poverty and Wealth in the Muslim Mediterranean World*, ed. Jean-Paul Pascual (Paris: Maisonneuve et Larose, 2003), 222–23; Amy Singer, *Palestinian Peasants and Ottoman Officials: Rural Administration around Sixteenth-Century Jerusalem* (Cambridge, UK: Cambridge University Press, 1994).

Fig.2. Release of debtors. Painting from the *Surname-i Hümâyûn*, an illustrated account of the celebrations for the circumcision of Prince Mehmed, son of Murad III (1576–95). People imprisoned for failing to pay their debts were brought in chains to the parade ground, from where they were released after the sultan paid what was owing to their creditors. *Surname-i Hümâyûn*, H.1344, f. 202a. With the permission of Topkapi Palace Museum, Istanbul.

and it seems they had to do no more than claim their insolvency in order to establish that they could not pay, similar to the statement cited above from al-Ghazali that there was no legal requirement that a person claiming to be poor should provide proof of this in order to receive zakat. The burden of proof was on the janissary. In the case of Yusuf in Damascus, above, his debt was not forgiven but only rescheduled, perhaps because he was a Christian or perhaps for other reasons related to his individual character or local practices. However, whether creditors could consider the unpaid debts as their zakat is not mentioned in the judicial protocols. This would have been a private matter, not one handled by a judge.

At first, the group intended by the category "in the path of God" (*fi sabil Allah*) were volunteer warriors in jihad, to whom the zakat contributed to living and equipment expenses. Within a generation following Muhammad's death, the Muslim empire had spread to include enormous resources and territory. Gradually, more funds became available from a variety of tax revenues and booty to support the military forces. Al-Ghazali observed that in his time the categories of "fi sabil Allah" and of slaves were found only in some places.[55] If it is unclear where or how long official zakat collections continued, it does seem that taxes collected under various names were used to fund the military expeditions of the Muslim states. Over time, Muslim states relied less on volunteers for jihad and more on the professional fighting forces that came to make up the greater parts of armies throughout the Muslim world. Participation in military campaigns, however, might also result in impoverishment because of injury, debt, or dislocation, such that those who fought "in the path of God" eventually qualified to receive zakat under other rubrics. In modern Malaysia, for example, the category also includes financing Islamic mass media and scholarships for talented Muslim students.[56]

Whether poor or well-off at home, a traveler (*ibn al-sabil*) was eligible to receive zakat if help was needed. Travelers might include merchants, migrants, soldiers, pilgrims, slaves, or sufis. Including travelers as a category of zakat recipients incorporated hospitality into the list of religious obligations incumbent on Muslims.[57] Zakat, however, was supposed to be given first to those

---

[55] Al-Ghazālī, *Kitāb Asrār al-Zakāh*, 280–81; Faris, *Mysteries of Almsgiving*, 23.

[56] Ben Shemesh, *Qudāma b. Ja'far's Kitāb al-Kharāj*, 68. The connection between alms and jihad received much international attention in the wake of the al-Qaida attacks on the World Trade Center buildings in New York City on September 11, 2001. For more on some of the late twentieth- and early twenty-first-century issues, see J. Millard Burr and Robert O. Collins, *Alms for Jihad: Charity and Terrorism in the Islamic World* (Cambridge, UK: Cambridge University Press, 2006). On Malaysia, see: n.a., "The Efficiency of Zakat Distributions," posted in the publications section of http://www.iiu.edu.my/iaw (accessed March 2, 2006).

[57] See Franz Rosenthal, "The Stranger in Medieval Islam," *Arabica* 44 (1997): 35–75; M. Montgomery Watt, "idjāra," in *EI²*, III:1017–18; and Constable, *Housing the Stranger*, 48–51, 83–88.

closest; adding travelers to the list seems to fly in the face of this condition. The same sentiment is echoed in Deuteronomy 15:7–8, which emphasized the assistance due to needy relatives. Related passages in Jewish law elaborated a hierarchy that stated: "My people take precedence over a Gentile. The poor take precedence over the rich. Your poor take precedence over the poor of your city. The poor of your city take precedence over the poor of another city."[58] This theoretical distinction was known and taken into account, at least in the medieval Jewish community of Cairo. Poor foreign Jews there used many different expressions to persuade the people reading their petitions for help that the authors should rightly be seen as "among the poor of your household" so that they could be considered more deserving of assistance.[59] Perhaps the inclusiveness of the zakat categories was meant to add a further measure of flexibility in distributions. In reality, someone cut off from the home context of family and friends – the people who would normally offer help in times of need – was relatively vulnerable and weak. Ideally, no Muslim would be considered a stranger to other Muslims.[60] The expression *dar al-Islam* (the abode of Islam) denotes the lands under Muslim rule and also conveys an inclusive self-perception of the Muslim community. The experiences of the first Muslim exiles and wandering sufis, as well as the economic realities of medieval merchant societies, all combined to give travelers a privileged place as recipients of individual hospitality and institutional charity in caravansarays, *hans* (large inns), and the like. Ibn Battuta related how he and his party were caught in a heavy rainstorm early in their journey, outside the town of Constantine (Algeria). Next day they met a local *sharif* (descendant of the Prophet's family) named Abu'l-Hasan, who treated them as follows:

Seeing my clothes, for they were all soiled by the rain, he gave orders that they should be washed at his house. The mantle which was amongst them was in rags, so he sent me in its place a mantle of fine Ba'albek cloth, in one of whose corners he had tied two gold dinars. This was the first alms which was bestowed upon me on my journey.[61]

Abu'l Hasan not only undertook to replace Ibn Battuta's tattered robe but also found a gracious way of giving him money for his journey. He was only the first of many whose generosity provided Ibn Battuta with the means to continue his travels.

---

[58] Mark R. Cohen, "The Foreign Jewish Poor in Medieval Egypt," in *Poverty and Charity*, ed. Michael Bonner *et al.* 57. Notably, it was Maimonides in the second half of the twelfth century who first codified the Jewish laws of charity. His seemingly normative text and the Geniza letters together document the theory and practice of medieval Jewish charity under Muslim rule, and provide a rare opportunity to make a close comparison of Muslim and Jewish worlds.
[59] Cohen, "The Foreign Jewish Poor in Medieval Egypt," 59.
[60] Rosenthal, "The Stranger in Medieval Islam."   [61] Gibb, *Ibn Battuta*, Vol. I, 12.

Travelers were also included among those who deserve sadaqa as well as zakat (Qur'an 4:36). Ibn Battuta's repeated descriptions as well as those of other renowned travel narrators like Evliya Çelebi left little doubt about the realities of hospitality offered to people of their learned or official rank in the Muslim world. Numerous institutions welcomed travelers of varying economic and social status. Hospitality and charity converged or overlapped in these accounts, ensuring not only food and shelter, but also protection, at least for the customary three-day period. Assistance to travelers was not limited to Muslims in Muslim societies, nor was it only dispensed by them. Ibn Battuta mentioned a monastery near Lattakiyya "known as Diar al-Farus, which is the largest monastery in Syria and Egypt. It is inhabited by monks, and Christians visit it from all quarters. Every Muslim who stops there is entertained by the Christians; their food is bread, cheese, olives, vinegar and capers."[62] Foreigners on the roads in Ottoman lands frequently noted the prevalence of caravansarays and hospices open free-of-charge to any traveler, and made a point of saying that they themselves were welcome, even in village guesthouses alongside Muslims and also people obviously of little means.[63]

Thus far, our discussion has not traced a coherent narrative of historical organization and change regarding zakat recipients. Rather, the examples presented point out the kinds of challenges governments faced in overseeing zakat collections and some interpretations of the categories of recipients. The diverse appearances of zakat illustrate how much local conditions affected the way zakat was or could be imposed by the state. Almost entirely absent from all of the preceding examples, however, are concrete instances of zakat payment.

Intentions and rewards

The Qur'an has much more to say on the manner and ethics of distributions than it has on how to calculate the division of zakat payments or the mechanics of distribution. In Islamic belief, the basis of all religious acts is intention *(niyya)* and without true intentions, actions like prayer or almsgiving are null and void. Niyya is the aim of performing an act well, in obedience to God's commandment, as a result of sincere belief. Just as *kavvana* is central to prayer and good deeds for Jews, niyya is a crucial aspect of any Muslim ritual or act regulated by shari'a, distinct and occurring prior to the act itself, emphasizing the constant presence of God as a witness to the acts of individuals. The ninth-century jurist al-Bukhari (d. 870), who compiled one of the great canonical collections of hadith, said at the beginning of his collection: "Works are only rendered

---

[62] Gibb, *Ibn Battuta*, Vol. I, 115.
[63] Louis Deshayes de Courmenin, *Voiage de Levant Fait par le Commandement du Roy en Lannée 1621 par Le Sr. D.C.* (Paris: Adrian Taupinart, 1624), 49–50.

efficacious by their intention" (*innama 'l-a'mal bi'l-niyya*).[64] Thus any benefit to the giver is canceled out if zakat is paid insincerely or begrudgingly, as a result of social pressure or concerns for personal salvation.

The fatwas issued by Ebu's-Su'ud Efendi have illustrated one role of niyya in connection with zakat. In yet another example, he was asked: "Can the money taken as taxes for the state from sheep on which zakat is owed be considered as the zakat on sheep?" His answer: "It may, if it was paid with that intention (*ol niyetle vericek olur*)."[65] Ebu's-Su'ud's answer enabled the well-intentioned sheep owner who may have posed this question to fulfill his religious duty. Yet the Qur'an gives the impression that even intention is not sufficient to ensure that zakat payments earn full benefits for the giver; rather intention includes more than just the inner, unseen attitude of the giver. A long section (2:261–81) in the second sura of the Qur'an discusses how people should give properly. Givers should neither boast of their acts of charity nor shame the recipients. Behavior of this kind voids the act of its worth, and demonstrates only that the giver does not truly believe in God. Obviously, this would apply equally to public bragging and private self-satisfaction, since God is "All-knowing." Yet even as it recognizes the risks of self-promotion and favors secret giving, the Qur'an also admits the merits of public donations. "If you publish your freewill offerings, it is excellent; but if you conceal them, and give them to the poor, that is better for you, and will acquit you of your evil deeds; God is aware of the things you do." (2:271) Furthermore, whatever is given should be "of the good things you have earned" and not from whatever a person would not keep for personal use. Charity is not meant to be a dumping ground for inferior or damaged goods.

The comparative merits of giving in secret and giving publicly preoccupied al-Ghazali, and he returned to weigh them several times during his discussion of zakat, and then again at length in the section on voluntary giving at the end of his *Mysteries of Almsgiving*. Giving in secret protected the identity of the recipient, so that the person was not shamed by receiving, laid open to reproach and doubt about his or her need, or forced to share what was received. Secret giving was better for the donor, since the Qur'an explicitly prefers that donors not reveal themselves to recipients. On the other hand, publicity has advantages,

---

[64] Al-Bukhārī, *Ṣaḥīḥ al-Bukhārī*, vol. I, p. 2; USC-MSA, Bukhari, 1/1; Denny, *An Introduction to Islam*, 118; J. Schacht, *An Introduction to Islamic Law* (Oxford: Oxford University Press, 1964), 116–17; A. J. Wensinck, "niyya," in *EI²*, VIII:66–67; Roy P. Mottahedeh, *Loyalty and Leadership in an Early Islamic Society* (Princeton: Princeton University Press, 1980), 65–66; Nasr Hamid Abu Zayd, "Intention," in *Encyclopaedia of the Qur'ān*, vol. II, ed. Jane Dammen McAuliffe (Leiden: Brill, 2002), 549–51; Zysow, "zakāt," XI:417; H. Elchanan Blumenthal, "kavvanah," *Encyclopaedia Judaica* (Jerusalem: Keter Publishing House, 1972) X:853–54.

[65] *Niyet* is the Turkish pronunciation of Arabic *niyya*. Düzdağ, *Ebussuûd Efendi Fetvaları*, 63, #217.

since the example may prompt other people to give as well, fostering sincerity while reducing arrogance and hypocrisy. If God is All-knowing, then secret giving can be a secret only from other people and will only remove an opportunity to display God's bounties. Ultimately, al-Ghazali concluded that the preference for secrecy or openness should depend on the character of the donor, and what would best minimize the donor's individual character flaws.[66]

To judge from al-Ghazali's further stipulations, he believed that fulfilling God's commandment to pay zakat demanded both spiritual and practical adherence, and could not be accomplished simply by paying out money. He said that a person paying zakat should be aware of external forms and also attain an intellectual understanding and spiritual consciousness, keeping in mind the following things: to pay with the proper intention; to pay promptly at the end of the year; to pay no substitutes for the things due (although the schools of law differ on this); not to transfer the zakat from the town in which it is collected; and to include all the eligible groups of beneficiaries. In addition to these conditions, one who paid had further obligations: to understand why zakat is obligatory; to pay at a good time of the year, preferably one of the months considered holy, like Muharram or Ramadan; not to nullify the zakat by paying it with any hurtful expression or scorn aimed at the recipient; to downplay the worth of the zakat paid as a safeguard against any vanity in the giver; to pay from good things and not choose the second-rate for zakat; and to make an effort to find worthy recipients.[67]

We can consider the discussions in the Qur'an and al-Ghazali alongside the contemporary Moroccan account that opened this chapter. Abu Illya appeared to adhere to many of the stipulations described in the Qur'an and discussed by al-Ghazali. He and his son both stressed the religious context of their actions toward Lalla Fatiha when she protested their help or neglected to ask for what she needed, perhaps to mitigate her embarrassment and discomfort at the extent of her dependence on them, and to caution themselves against a lack of humility. Illya concluded his explanation by putting his family and Lalla Fatiha's on a level spiritual footing because they played equally important roles in the performance of zakat and because one day her sons might be in a position to support him and his brother. Yet despite the religious gloss on their relationship, Abu Illya's zakat payments also existed in a framework of human social interaction, fraught with possibilities for insult and injury, as the Qur'an and other texts insistently point out. Face-to-face donations may be difficult to accept, and Lalla Fatiha was obliged to accept them on a long-term basis. One wonders whether she felt a spiritual equality with Abu Illya on a day-to-day basis. Unfortunately, in this episode as in much of recorded history, far less

---

[66] Al-Ghazālī, *Kitāb Asrār al-Zakāh*, 298–302; Faris, *Mysteries of Almsgiving*, 77–87 .
[67] Al-Ghazālī, *Kitāb Asrār al-Zakāh*, 279–91; Faris, *Mysteries of Almsgiving*, 17–52.

evidence exists to reveal the perspective of the poor or weaker people in such vertical relationships, whether the gradient between the stronger and weaker is based on wealth, gender, age, or social or political status.

Qur'anic injunctions, the hadith traditions, and the legal commentaries articulate the tensions produced between two opposing forces identified in human nature. On the one hand, a devout person may try sincerely to fulfill the letter and the spirit of God's commandment to give. On the other hand, human nature impels people to seek recognition for their actions, particularly those, like charity, that societies often admire and reward. In the context of Muslim theology, zakat is a duty to God, and the benefit to the community from zakat is a secondary, if intentional and welcome, byproduct. Any praise for zakat distributed ultimately belongs to God and not to those who pay. And while God may give the donor credit for paying zakat, a person who credits the donor overmuch runs the risk of associating that person with God (*shirk*), a sin of the most grievous nature, since it undermines the oneness of God.[68] Of course, stories praising generous people proliferate throughout Muslim literature, used as examples of praiseworthy and just behavior. As we will discuss further in chapter 3, in some cases human generosity is tempered with humility, yet in others it is an unabashed advertisement for the donor.

Muslim texts about zakat are essentially about the givers: their religious obligation, their wealth, their salvation, and the penalties they risk for not giving. Zakat is a spiritual matter, and the sole motivation for paying should be a desire to obey God that springs from profound belief. The Qur'an promises material gain as a reward to one who is sincerely devout and generous. Spiritual reward comes after death, with a justly earned place in Paradise, in part secured by a lifetime of honestly rendering zakat as due. At the same time, one cannot ignore the material impact of zakat on the recipients. It is the only one of the five pillars of Islam that engages the believer with the community, and makes belonging to a community a necessary condition for fulfilling the obligation. This message comes through clearly in the hadith: "O people! Give in charity as a time will come upon you when a person will wander about with his object of charity and will not find anybody to accept it, and one (who will be requested to take it) will say, 'If you had brought it yesterday, I would have taken it, but today I am not in need of it.'"[69] Ibn Battuta told a story echoing this hadith, about arriving in Zaytun (Quanzhou), a prosperous trading city on the Chinese coast. Of the Muslim traders living there, he said: "As these merchants live in infidel country they are delighted when a Muslim arrives among them. They say: 'He has come from the land of Islam,' and give him the legal alms due on their

[68] D. Gimaret, "shirk," in *EI²*, IX:484–86.
[69] Al-Bukhārī, *Ṣaḥīḥ al-Bukhārī*, 24 (zakat), bab 9; USC-MSA, Bukhari, 24/493.

property so that he becomes as rich as one of them." Otherwise, owing to the prosperity of the community, they had no proper object for their zakat.[70]

Both the Qur'an and the hadith contain lurid descriptions of the penalties that await those who fail to pay zakat. Temporal authorities do not enact these punishments. Rather, the things themselves on which zakat was not paid are said to return to torture the person who hoarded them. The Qur'an says:

Those who treasure up gold and silver, and do not expend them in the way of God – give them the good tidings of a painful chastisement, the day they shall be heated in the fires of Gehenna and therewith their foreheads and their sides and their backs shall be branded: "This is the thing you have treasured up for yourselves; therefore taste you now what you were treasuring!" (9:34–35)

In the same spirit, when asked about what would happen to the person who failed to pay zakat on his camels, the Prophet is reported to have replied:

If any owner of the camel does not pay what is due on him, and of his due in that (camel) is (also) to milk it on the day when it comes down to water, when the Day of Resurrection comes a soft sandy plain would be set for him, as extensive as possible, (he will find) that not a single young one is missing, and they will trample him with their hoofs and bite him with their mouths. As often as the first of them passes him, the last of them would be made to return during a day the extent of which would be fifty thousand years, until judgment is pronounced among servants and he sees whether his path is to take him to Paradise or to Hell.[71]

Belief in an afterlife, where accounts are drawn up for the deeds of a lifetime, is an integral component of Muslim eschatology. All the terrors described above – and similar ones involving sheep, cows, and other animals – are promised after death to those who failed to pay zakat or paid it insufficiently. As is so often emphasized in the Qur'an, even in life no action remains secret from God. How far this claim succeeded in prompting people to pay their zakat is something a historian cannot measure, particularly given the lack of sources as described in this chapter. Still, the hair-raising descriptions of promised penalties leave no doubt in the minds of believers as to how important almsgiving was originally intended to be in the divine reckoning of human fate.

The penalties for not paying zakat are severe because not to fulfill one of the five cardinal obligations is counted a grave sin (*kabira*), a sin that requires atonement and God's pardon. Moreover, to deny the obligation to pay zakat constitutes an act of unbelief (*kufr*), the worst kind of sin a Muslim can commit. On the other hand, those qualified to receive zakat must accept it as a collective obligation (*fard kifaya*), that is, one which can be fulfilled by a few individuals

---

[70] Gibb, *Ibn Battuta*, vol. IV, 895, 370, n.12.
[71] Muslim, *Ṣaḥīḥ Muslim*, 470–71, Book 5, #2161; USC-MSA, Muslim, 5/2161.

on behalf of the whole community.[72] Giving and receiving zakat, therefore, is a dynamic process built around a set of obligations between one individual and God, and between human beings, touching belief and community simultaneously. As Illya put it in explaining his father's relationship to Lalla Fatiha, "Our honor is to proffer zakat, her honor is to use the zakat. All is provided by God, not by us."[73]

Zakat al-fitr

Illya raised another important point. He said that most people do not pay zakat in any orderly fashion. Rather, they "just give alms during Ramadan or perhaps to support a particular beggar." Here, Illya may have intended the particular merit ascribed to paying zakat during Ramadan, or else he was referring to *zakat al-fitr*, a separate alms paid by all Muslims during the fasting month of Ramadan. The Qur'an does not mention zakat al-fitr. Instead, hadiths provide the authority for its payment. *Fitr* is the name of the meal eaten at sundown to break each daily fast. Not to be confused with the annual zakat payment, zakat al-fitr is paid before the beginning of the final holiday (*'id al-fitr*) celebrated at the end of the holy month. Zakat al-fitr is obligatory, although Muslim jurists classify its obligation at a lower level than zakat and define nonpayment of zakat al-fitr as a less severe omission than failing to pay zakat.[74]

Zakat al-fitr is calculated per person and not on property or revenue as is zakat. The minimum threshold of eligibility to pay is far lower than the nisab for zakat and the sum of the zakat al-fitr payment itself is also quite modest, since it has the immediate goal of enabling poor people to celebrate the festival. All Muslims must pay as long as they still have enough left over to feed their own households through the days of the holiday festival. Generally, every head of household is responsible for paying zakat al-fitr for each member of the household, even for non-Muslim members according to some madhhabs.[75] Traditionally, zakat al-fitr could be paid in cash but was usually described in kind, in the form of basic foods like wheat, barley, dates, and raisins, and could also include dairy products like yogurt or cheese: "Allah's apostle enjoined the payment of one *sa'* of dates or one *sa'* of barley as zakat ul-fitr on every Muslim, slave or free, male or female, young or old, and he ordered that it be paid before the people went out to offer the 'Id prayer."[76]

Today, zakat al-fitr is paid in cash or in kind, still focusing in some places on basic foodstuffs like rice, flour, oil, and sugar. Cash equivalents vary around the

---

[72] Weir and Zysow, "ṣadaḳa," XI:407.   [73] Bowen, "Abu Illya," 221.
[74] Zysow, "zakāt," XI:418; Hurgronje, "La zakāt," 70.   [75] Zysow, "zakāt," XI:418.
[76] Al-Bukhārī, *Ṣaḥīḥ al-Bukhārī*, 24 (al-zakat), bab 70; USC-MSA, al-Bukhari, 25/579; 1 *sāʿ* = 5 pints, on which see A. Bel, "sāʿ," *EI²*, VII:654.

world. In England, one source estimated that each person should pay approximately £3.[77] In 2006, as in previous years, the Qatari telecommunications firm Qtel enabled its customers to pay zakat al-fitr of 15 Qatari riyals (about US $4.10) to the Zakat Fund of Qatar by text message (SMS) from their cell phones to specially designated numbers, with Qtel contributing the cost of the message. During the month of Ramadan, Qtel customers could also make SMS donations to fund *iftar* (break fast) meals or to an ongoing charity initiative, the Sheikh Eid bin Muhammad al-Thani Charitable Association.[78]

Zakat al-fitr is due even if a person is not obligated to fast on Ramadan because of illness or pregnancy, for example. It is interesting that even some people who do not regularly observe the Ramadan fast do give zakat al-fitr scrupulously, emphasizing that the month is an occasion for beneficent gestures and philanthropic acts. The daughter of a wealthy Egyptian family remembered that her father, neither devout nor observant, never fasting, paid zakat regularly, built a mosque in his native village, and distributed clothes annually to the peasants there.[79] One hears the same from some Palestinian Muslims and also from Muslim Turks, who do not pray or fast on Ramadan, but claim always to pay zakat al-fitr.[80] A survey conducted in rural Egypt at the end of the twentieth century found that while only 20 percent of the farmers interviewed paid zakat on their crops, 76 percent claimed to pay zakat al-fitr.[81] It would seem that in the contemporary world at least, this religious practice has become an inseparable part of Muslim community culture and individual Muslim identity in some places, unrelated to personal ritual observance.

In comparison with detailed legal texts like that of al-Ghazali, we find limited evidence for the historical implementation of zakat, and only partial answers to the following questions are possible: How were zakat assessments, payments, and distributions actually organized? What kinds of local or state zakat institutions evolved to implement these processes? What kind of burden did zakat constitute relative to other taxes and impositions? Did zakat monies provide effective or sufficient assistance to their recipients? What were the political, economic, or social ramifications of the official organization of zakat? Where and when did official organization exist or disappear, and why did it not continue to be collected "as in the Prophet's time"?

---

[77] See http://www.cambridgemuslims.info/Eid/ZakatulFitr.htm (accessed January 3, 2007).

[78] Http://www.qtel.com.qa/NewsFull.do?News=1482 (accessed December 11, 2006).

[79] Interview with Afaf Lutfi al-Sayyid Marsot in Nancy Elizabeth Gallagher, *Approaches to the History of the Middle East: Interviews with Leading Middle East Historians* (Reading, UK: Ithaca Press, 1994), 96.

[80] These observations were shared in personal conversations with Palestinian and Turkish friends during the years when I have been writing this book.

[81] Zysow, "zakāt," XI:420.

Private or discreet individual zakat payment may have always been the most widespread practice. It is primarily through anecdotal evidence that we trip over zakat payments outside the context of prescriptive literature or official accounts. For instance, a seventeenth-century Ottoman architectural treatise noted that its main character gave zakat conscientiously from the money he made as a craftsman, praising him for paying zakat as soon as he received any fee.[82] Yet this is not the system as envisaged by the jurists. According to the lawbooks, zakat was due on wealth held for one year, presumably to ensure that people had enough to sustain themselves and their dependants through the natural fluctuations in income over the course of a year in a pre-modern society. Indeed, al-Ghazali's text contains an explicit warning to anyone who prepaid zakat that it would not be refunded in the event they suddenly became impoverished or suffered a decline in fortune.[83]

The story of Abu Illya, the Moroccan baker, with which this chapter began is equally full of practices that do not fit the canonical regulations for zakat. Nowhere in Abu Illya's story is there any mention of an annual calculation of revenues, of nisab, of a fixed amount to be paid, or of categories of recipients. No zakat collector appears and there is no pretense of anonymity on the part of the donor. All the formalities of zakat as described in the lawbooks are set aside here. Illya says quite clearly that this is not zakat as in the time of the Prophet. However, it *is* zakat in his eyes and Illya adamantly refused the label "charity" for his family's assistance to their neighbor.

While paying zakat is obviously an act of belief and of obedience, at the same time it shares with the wider world of philanthropy a universal aspect of self-interest. Those who pay stand a better chance of entering Paradise than those who do not (all other things being equal), and the latter will also endure horrible punishments. No one wants to be trampled by beasts or burned by coins for thousands of years while waiting to see if God will relent and admit the soul of a tortured body to eternal blessings. Yet while appealing to the self-interest of believers to pay, the Qur'an also makes clear that God distinguishes between those who are sincere in their belief and those who only go through the motions. What saves zakat paying from being a scenario of pure self-interest is the requirement that in order for zakat to be valid, anyone paying zakat should be guided only by the purest intentions springing from devotion to God.

Nothing replaces zakat as a ritual obligation for Muslims, and as such they are bound to continue to pay it. Yet, historically, payment of zakat seems to have devolved largely to the private sphere, and even if in some places state taxes

---

[82] Ca'fer Efendi, *Risāle-i Mi'māriyye. An Early-Seventeenth-Century Ottoman Treatise on Architecture*, Facsimile with translation and notes, ed. Howard Crane (Leiden: E. J. Brill, 1987), 42.

[83] Al-Ghazālī, *Kitāb Asrār al-Zakāh*, 279; Faris, *Mysteries of Almsgiving*, 18.

could be considered to constitute zakat, the responsibility for defining them in this way lay most often with the individual, not the government. It seems possible that, with the need for greater revenues and the creation of additional taxes, official zakat systems fell out of use in many places or were subsumed into state tax systems using other names. Historically, it would seem, zakat as an official institution could not weather the changes in the early Islamic polity, and rulers became more concerned to find effective means to tax their subjects than they were to preserve state control over zakat. Zakat, according to the historian Ulrich Haarmann, failed to evolve with the rest of the Muslim polity because it was not flexible enough in its regulations to accommodate changing economic realities. Moreover, it apparently did not prove an effective instrument for relieving need and redistributing wealth, as seems to have been part of the original intention.[84]

In trying to understand what happened to zakat over the centuries, it makes sense to look more closely at the evolution of other forms of giving in Muslim societies, since the Qur'an, hadith, and other literature insist on voluntary as well as obligatory giving. If the historical record of zakat has seemed to retreat from public view in this chapter, the following one discusses forms of giving that left more visible records and permanent monuments as a testimony to their sponsors' generosity.

---

[84] U. Haarmann, "Islamic Duties in History," *Muslim World* 68 (1978): 23; McChesney, *Charity and Philanthropy.*

Fig. 3. Inscription on a fountain of Hacıadlbey, at the south end of the Meriç Bridge in Edirne. "The best sadaqa is to provide water" (*Afdal al-sadaqa saqqa al-ma'*). Hadith attributed to Ibn Majah. Author's photo.

2 Even half a date

Guard yourselves against Hellfire even by giving half a date, and if you have none to give, speak a kindly word.[1]

A single *sadaqa* closes seventy gates of evil.[2]

The Prophet said, "Every Muslim has to give in charity."

The people asked, "O Allah's Prophet! If someone has nothing to give, what will he do?"

He said, "He should work with his hands and benefit himself and also give in charity (from what he earns)." The people further asked, "If he cannot do even that?"

He replied, "He should help the needy who appeal for help."

Then the people asked, "If he cannot do that?"

He replied, "Then he should perform good and keep away from evil and this will be regarded as charitable."[3]

Once charity becomes the focus of our attention, it seems to appear at every turn in sources for Islamic history, both those originating within Muslim communities and those authored by outside observers traveling or living in Muslim lands. Among the observers who encountered Islamic societies as a foreigner was the sixteenth-century French scholar, polymath, and mystic Guillaume Postel (1510–81). Postel traveled to the Ottoman Empire more than once, as translator for an official French embassy to the Ottoman sultan and again through many regions of the Middle East to collect manuscripts. His admiring passage about the variety of charitable good works and the diversity of benefactors he encountered conveys a sense of the ubiquity of charity as well as its visibility to the careful observer:

You find poor people who have nothing to give who understand that offering help to people consists not only of food and drink, but all kinds of needs: some spend their lifetime repairing bad roads by bringing stones, wood, filling holes and improving their surfaces; others arrange the course of streams and water sources, bringing water to the

---

[1] Al-Bukhārī, *Ṣaḥīḥ al-Bukhārī*, 24 (zakat), bab 10; USC-MSA, Bukhari, 24/498.
[2] Quoted in al-Ghazālī, *Kitāb Asrār al-Zakāh*, 297; Faris, *Mysteries of Almsgiving*, 72.
[3] Al-Bukhārī, *Ṣaḥīḥ al-Bukhārī*, 24 (zakat), bab 30; USC-MSA, Bukhari, 24/524.

roads; and some dig wells, or bring water to the road in a shed of some sort, and there invite [the passersby] to drink with such enthusiasm that I was certain they drank wine that was to be found flowing from the streams. In North Africa, because water is scarce close by the cities, you find foundations for water built at the tombs of some Muslims, and there is some sufi who is maintained by the foundation to keep the cisterns full of water, and to encourage passersby to pray for the soul of the departed and the living family. Such foundations for water on the roads are a common project of poor people. There are rich people more in Anatolia than any other part of Turkey, who, when they see travelers coming on the roads, they invite them to eat, drink and sleep in their homes, for the sake of their [own] souls, and take nothing for it from anyone; neither rich nor poor pays anything, and the next day one thanks them heartily, invoking God's blessing on them in recompense. And these kind of people are most respected among the Muslims because they send their charity to Paradise ahead of them.[4]

Postel is describing actions usually characterized as sadaqa or voluntary charity. In addition to paying zakat, Qur'anic verses and hadith continually encourage believers to give generously, reminding them how much God esteems beneficences. No penalty or sanction exists for those who do not give sadaqa, but giving is supposed to bring a donor closer to Paradise on the Day of Judgment, atone for sins, and contribute to the well-being of the entire community of Muslims. "Sadaqa" comes from a root which means "to be sincere" and charity is a reflection of the sincerity of the donor's belief. Sincerity of belief and intention are also necessary aspects of zakat, as we saw in the previous chapter.[5] While it has become common practice to distinguish between zakat and sadaqa, in fact zakat can also be understood as a form of sadaqa, and the Qur'an, as we saw above, sometimes uses the two words without making a clear distinction between them. The jurists who interpreted the Qur'an and hadith in the generations after Muhammad clarified the distinction, although at times they too continued to use the word sadaqa to refer to zakat.[6] Technically referred to in legal literature as *sadaqa al-tatawwu'*, voluntary charity in this book will be called simply sadaqa.

Voluntary charitable giving was integrated to the rhythms of annual and lifetime calendars, in predictable forms and spontaneous acts, in large formal endowments and small gestures. Postel's observations convey some sense of the variety and ubiquity of actions considered as sadaqa. The present chapter explores these actions to understand how they were woven into the quotidian

---

[4] Guillaume Postel, *De la République des Turcs, là ou l'occasion s'offrera, des meurs & ly de tous muhamedistes* (Poitiers: Enguilbert de Marnef, 1560), 56–63; my translation (AS). On Postel see Maxime Rodinson, *Europe and the Mystique of Islam*, translated by Roger Veinus (London: I. B. Tauris, 1987), 40–41 and George Saliba, "Whose Science is Arabic Science in Renaissance Europe?" (1999), Section 4, published at http://www.columbia.edu/%7Egas1/project/visions/case1. html (accessed December 12, 2006).

[5] Weir and Zysow, "ṣadaḳa," VIII:708–9; Rosenthal, "Ṣedaḳa, Charity."

[6] Al-Ghazālī, *Kitāb Asrār al-Zakāh*, 280; Faris, *Mysteries of Almsgiving*, 23.

and festival fabric of life, their importance and meaning as part of daily routines, normal and special rituals, and festive celebrations. In its second part, the chapter focuses specifically on the waqf endowments because of their particular importance in supporting a wide spectrum of activities and institutions. The cases presented offer only a minuscule sample of the extent, variety, and impact of voluntary giving, yet the visible breadth of activity stands in marked contrast to the practice of zakat discussed in the previous chapter.

Supplying the basics

The most basic necessities for existence, which quite naturally comprise the substance of much voluntary charity, are food, water, clothing, and shelter. While we have mostly talked about *paying* zakat it may well be the case that zakat distributions, especially when carried out in the absence of zakat collectors, were made in kind, similar to the way in which Abu Illya delivered sacks of flour to Lalla Fatiha's doorstep. However, Ebu's-Su'ud answered a query on this subject to clarify that if a person gave to the poor honey, oil, and raw meat from their domestic supplies, this could be zakat, but only if the goods themselves were donated such that they became possessions and not if they were served as a meal to be consumed.[7] Food provides basic nourishment without which people will starve. Repeated anecdotes in hadith, biographies of saints, and historical chronicles tell of benevolent people providing bread and soup, a basic meal for poor and rich alike. One story about Caliph 'Umar (d. 644) recounted how, when walking about one night in disguise, he met a destitute woman and her two children. The woman, not recognizing him, cursed the caliph's indifference to their hunger. Chastened, he left and returned carrying supplies which he himself used to build a fire, cook soup, and bake bread for the three hungry souls.[8] In recounting his time in Mecca, the fourteenth-century Moroccan traveler Ibn Battuta observed many poor Muslims in the city gathered at the communal ovens to wait for a handout of bread:

> When anyone has his bread baked and takes it away to his house, the destitute follow him up and he gives each one of them whatever he assigns to him, sending none away disappointed. Even if he has but a single loaf, he gives away a third or a half of it, conceding it cheerfully and without grudgingness.[9]

Thus, it is not surprising that in the annals of Islamic history, there were many places where needy people might find a free meal. These include sufi zawiyas,

---

[7] Düzdağ, *Ebussuûd Efendi Fetvaları*, 63–64, #216, #215, #218.
[8] Niẓām al-Mulk, *The Book of Government, or Rules for Kings. The Siyar al-Muluk or Siyasat-Nama of Nizam al-Mulk*, translated by Hubert Darke (London: Routledge and Kegan Paul, 1960), 143–44.
[9] Gibb, *Ibn Battuta*, vol. I, 215–16.

the homes of wealthy people (including imperial palaces), and buildings like mosques and tombs. Moreover, sharing food with those who had none was a standard recommendation in the exemplary lives of Muslim saints and sufis, and their biographies are replete with vignettes in which hungry people knock at the door to ask for food.

Distinctions in basic categories of subsistence were obvious markers of means and status. While the poor made do with coarse bread and a basic soup with whatever grains, pulses, or vegetables were cheap, perhaps with the addition of herbs, yogurt, cheese, fruit, or fish depending on location and season, the better-off ate finer bread, included meat more often, and had more varieties of food, served in handsome plates and bowls. These distinctions were preserved at public imperial banquets, for example those spread in 1539 for the circumcisions of Sultan Süleyman's sons, the princes Bayezid and Cihangir. On that occasion, the poor ate *dane* (mutton and rice stew) and *zerde* (sweet saffron rice), served to them in the great public kitchens of Istanbul; these same dishes were the ones cooked in these kitchens on Fridays and holiday evenings. All other guests at the banquet also received the same basic dishes, suggesting that they had a certain symbolic value. More privileged, the janissaries had chicken soup, kebabs, breads, and *muhallabi* (flavored sweet milk pudding) in addition, as did other ranking people like the 'ulama. Meanwhile, the pashas enjoyed all of the above together with additional stews and sweets, while the sultan and his particular guests tasted an even wider array of soups, grilled meats, stews, and desserts.[10]

Water is a basic requirement to sustain life and its supply cannot be taken for granted. It is a dietary staple and a necessary element of regular Muslim purification rituals, most commonly those performed before prayer. Charitable undertakings therefore regularly included the provision of a steady water supply, as Postel's description illustrated, whether in large public systems like those built through the desert on the hajj route and in Mecca, the cisterns and wells supported by waqfs in medieval Cairo, the aqueducts and fountains of Sultan Süleyman for Jerusalem, or more modest projects like a neighborhood well or a roadside fountain (Fig. 4)[11].

---

[10] Semih Tezcan, *Bir Ziyafet Defteri* (Istanbul: Simurg Yayıncılık, 1998), 8–15. For illustrations of feast tables from the eighteenth century, see the miniatures reproduced in Esin Atıl, *Levni and the Surname: The Story of an Eighteenth-Century Ottoman Festival* (Seattle: University of Washington Press, 2000).

[11] Sabra, *Poverty and Charity*, 115–16; O. Salama and Y. Zilberman, "Aspakat ha-mayim li-yerushalayim ba-meot ha-16 ve-ha-17 [Water Supply to Jerusalem in the Sixteenth and Seventeenth Centuries (Hebrew)]," *Cathedra* 41 (1986): 91–106; Cem Behar, *A Neighborhood in Ottoman Istanbul. Fruit Vendors and Civil Servants in the Kasap İlyas Mahalle* (Albany: State University of New York Press, 2003), 31.

Fig. 4. A modern fountain (*çeşme*) on the Aegean island of Cunda/Alibey, Turkey. The inscription reads: "Good Work (*hayrat*) of Uçarı Hasan Güzin Seviğ." Author's photo.

Clothing affords a degree of personal modesty while also providing some protection from extremes of weather. Unfortunately, physical evidence about the clothing of the poor is rare. No one has preserved their basic garments as interesting or valuable artifacts, and their clothing was probably used until it fell apart and was then reused for other purposes, and so largely disappeared from the historical record. However, some information is available through commercial records, inheritance lists, illustrations, and travelers' descriptions.[12] Robes were a regular component of dress, as well as of official recompense and honors from Abbasid times until recently. Al-Ghazali seemed to suggest that in his day a minimum amount of clothing would include separate garments for summer and winter when he said: "Since we reckon food on the basis of a day [for purposes of determining whether someone should pay zakat al-fitr] we should reckon home furniture and bodily clothing on the basis of a year. Consequently,

---

[12] Among the few scholars who have tried to fathom the material conditions of the pre-modern poor in Islamic societies, Adam Sabra studied the standards of living of the poor in medieval Cairo by following the evidence as far as possible for the class of artisans or working poor, and then inferring that there were many people who made do with even less. Sabra, *Poverty and Charity*, 109–12; Rafeq, "The Poor in Ottoman Damascus."

the summer clothes are not sold in winter time nor the winter clothes in the summer."[13] Madrasa students usually received new robes once or twice a year, depending on the endowment terms of the institution where they studied. At the higher end of the socio-political scale, commanders, ministers, officials, and notables of every rank could expect to receive robes made from rich fabrics, sometimes luxuriously decorated or fur-lined. The materials and the fineness of the workmanship of these robes reflected the status of their owners, as well as variations in climate, taste, and fashion. Under the Ottomans, even in some rural contexts, men recognized by the Ottoman government as village heads received a sum called a "robe price" as part of their compensation.[14]

The need for sturdy shelter may vary from one region or climate to the next but generally people create some form of dwelling for protection from natural and human threats, to define family and social units, as well as for storing belongings and establishing private space. Where climate allows it, such shelter may indeed be minimal.[15] Different kinds of institutions – zawiyas, mosques, caravansarays – offered a place to sleep and shelter to travelers (and their animals) for the night. Many of the working poor, especially doorkeepers and custodians, may have found a sheltered spot at their place of work. Not surprisingly, to the extent we have any information on it, we find that housing for the poor was more crowded than for others, ill-repaired, with less privacy, fewer furnishings, and in less desirable locations. Yet it was not necessarily the case that poor people regularly lived in quarters isolated from the rich. Some evidence shows that while there existed richer and poorer quarters in some places, neighborhoods often had an economic mix of residents.[16] Such mixing existed because people did not cluster according to economic class alone, but by family, origin, sect, religion, or profession. The organization of urban communities along these lines helps to explain the creation of endowments by better-off residents for the benefit of individual urban neighborhoods where the beneficiaries might be poor, but they were not strangers.

A calendar of charity

Over the normal course of a year, charitable distributions marked the holy days and seasons as regularly as they did the momentous events of a human lifetime.

---

[13]   Al-Ghazāli, *Kitāb Asrār al-Zakāh*, 292; Faris, *Mysteries of Almsgiving*, 56–57.
[14]   Sabra, *Poverty and Charity*, 109; Singer, *Palestinian Peasants*, 33–34; N. Stillman, "khil'a," in *EI²*, V:6–7; Y. K. Stillman, "libās: In the Central and Eastern Arab Lands; Muslim West; Iran," in *EI²*, V:737.
[15]   Sabra, *Poverty and Charity*, 108, cites Felix Fabri and other medieval European travelers to Cairo who described people sleeping outside as a common sight.
[16]   Compare Rafeq, "The Poor in Ottoman Damascus," 217; Behar, *A Neighborhood in Ottoman Istanbul*, 5; and Sabra, *Poverty and Charity*, 102–09.

Examining the rituals of celebration reveals how charity was part of each festivity, as integral to it as the prayers, new clothes, special foods, and family or other gatherings that marked the occasion. The origins of these charitable practices are not documented, yet more important is the fact that the practices were invented, adopted, or reinvented as Muslim, and justified with reference to Muslim texts. Not only does charity come to accompany most of the rituals and holidays of the year, but it also became a canonically acceptable substitute to replace a variety of ritual obligations. Someone who was unable to complete a fast or missed a Friday prayer could give sadaqa instead, as could pilgrims who failed to complete any part of the hajj rituals or had to make up for some flaw in the way they were performed.[17] The composite calendar of charity sketched here, blending time and space for the moment, illustrates the variety and ubiquity of charitable gestures in everyday life and as an inseparable aspect of annual and lifetime celebrations.[18]

Perhaps the most frequent formal occasion for giving was Friday, the weekly day of communal prayer. Among the advice offered to the medieval Persian ruler on proper Friday etiquette was that "he should give charity on this day, if only a bit of bread, for this brings a great reward."[19] With good reason beggars might especially gather at the entrances to mosques on Fridays, anticipating that those attending prayer would be generous and that some might be pleased to make a public demonstration of their charity. When the Fatimid general Jawhar conquered Egypt in 969, he made a point of going on Friday to the Mosque of 'Amr in Fustat, the busy economic and commercial center in the older part of Cairo, where the alms that he and his troops distributed would impress not only a large crowd of Muslims but also the local Jews and Christians.[20] In fifteenth-century Cairo, a European resident recorded that the lords who had their tombs constructed in the great cemetery of al-Qarafa "give alms to the poor every Friday. It is on this day that they have their holiday, say their prayers, and prepare large meals of meat. And it is on this day that all the poor of Cairo go there to eat and to receive the money which is given them."[21]

---

[17] Qur'an 2:184; 58:4. See the hadith on this in *Sunan Abu Dawud*, USC-MSA, Sunan, 3/1048–1049; and B. Lewis, "hadjdj," in *EI²*, III:36.

[18] Sabra, too, emphasizes the concentration of charitable giving at holiday celebrations. See Sabra, *Poverty and Charity*, 52–55.

[19] Julie Scott Meisami, *Persian Historiography to the End of the Twelfth Century* (Edinburgh: Edinburgh University Press, 1999), 170.

[20] Paula Sanders, *Ritual, Politics, and the City in Fatimid Cairo* (Albany: State University of New York Press, 1994), 44.

[21] "Alms" here refers to voluntary distributions, not to zakat. Observations of the long-time Cairo resident, Venetian merchant Emmanuel Piloti, as quoted in Christopher S. Taylor, *In the Vicinity of the Righteous: Ziyāra and the Veneration of Muslim Saints in Late Medieval Egypt* (Leiden: Brill, 1999), 60.

In describing the virtues of his patron, Sultan Abu 'Inan, Ibn Battuta portrayed Friday as a special occasion:

His justice is more renowned than can be recorded in a book. An instance is that he has sessions to hear complaints from his subjects; he devotes Fridays to the poor, dividing the day between men and women, giving women priority because of their weakness. Their petitions are read from after the [midday] Friday prayer until the afternoon prayer.[22]

Observers in eighteenth-century Aleppo described how beggars stationed themselves along the routes to the mosques in expectation of some beneficence from those attending prayers.[23]

Fridays were a day when many beneficent institutions like public kitchens and tombs had special distributions of food or better dishes than would be served the rest of the week. Instead of the usual soup, the public kitchen of Haseki Sultan in Jerusalem, like most other such Ottoman kitchens, served the meat stew with rice called dane together with the sweet saffron rice zerde. At the tomb of Qamar Banu Khanum, a wife of the seventeenth-century Uzbek ruler Subhan Quli, an evening meal of bread and soup was served on Friday and Monday, and if there was money enough, sweets and fruit after Friday and Monday prayers.[24] Friday distributions of charity along with the acceptance of petitions from the populace were also part of the Ottoman imperial processions from the palace to the great congregational mosques. Postel saw one of Sultan Süleyman's processions in Istanbul and noted that the sultan gave out alms to the needy after he had finished praying.[25] Under Sultan Abdülhamid II (1876–1909), the Friday distributions were organized to rotate throughout Istanbul, so that each week freshly sacrificed meat and coins were doled out to the students, sufis, and poor of a different quarter.[26] One can well understand that the extended absence of the sultan and the court from the capital city on military campaigns or while in residence at his Edirne palace would cause disappointment among the city's poor, as well as raising the documented ire of the merchants and artisans.

---

[22] Gibb, *Ibn Battuta*, Vol. IV, 927.

[23] Abraham Marcus, *The Middle East on the Eve of Modernity* (New York: Columbia University Press, 1989), 214.

[24] R. D. McChesney, *Waqf in Central Asia: Four Hundred Years in the History of a Muslim Shrine, 1480–1889* (Princeton: Princeton University Press, 1991), 131.

[25] Guillaume Postel, *Des Histoires Orientales et principalement des Turks ou Turchikes et Schitiques ou Tartaresques et aultres qui en sont descendus, oeuvre pour la troisième fois augmenté* (Paris: Imprimerie de Marnef, 1575), ed. with introduction and notes by Jacques Rollet (Istanbul: Isis, 1999), 115.

[26] Nadir Özbek, "Imperial Gifts and Sultanic Legislation in the Late Ottoman Empire, 1876–1909," in *Poverty and Charity*, ed. Michael Bonner et al., 203, 208–09; Nadir Özbek, *Osmanlı İmparatorluğu'nda Sosyal Devlet: Siyaset, İktidar ve Meşruiyet 1876–1914* (Istanbul: İletişim, 2002), 32, 34, 132; Mehmed İpşirli, "Cuma Selamlığı," in *Dünden Bugüne İstanbul Ansiklopedisi*, vol. II (Istanbul, 1993–95), 443–44.

During the course of a year, holy days punctuate the twelve months of the Muslim calendar, many marked by good deeds and generosity to the poor along-side devotional rituals. 'Ashura is a fast day on the tenth day of Muharram, the first month of the year. Shi'i communities celebrate 'Ashura with passion plays and mourning, recalling the martyrdom of Hasan and Husayn, grandsons of the Prophet and sons of 'Ali, the fourth caliph. A village boyhood memoir from twentieth-century Iran recalls that after one such play "people rushed to eat the special wheat stews (*ash-e gandom*) that were cooked in massive cauldrons. These communal meals were supplied either from perpetual endowments, vows made during the year, or as holiday donations by richer villagers."[27] Despite the different significance of 'Ashura for Sunnis and Shi'is – the Sunni Ayyubids under Saladin changed the day from one of mourning to one of celebration when they conquered Egypt from the Shi'i Fatimid dynasty (909–1171) – certain aspects of the celebrations, like beneficent distributions, were shared.[28]

In the early nineteenth century, the lexicographer and long-time resident of Cairo, Edward Lane, described his own experience of 'Ashura in Cairo:

It is common custom of the Muslims of Egypt to give what they can afford in alms during the month of Moharram, especially in the first ten days, and more especially on the tenth day; and many pretend though few of them really do so, to give at this season the "zekah," or alms required by their law . . . they give what, and to whom, they will.[29]

Lane's observation that zakat paying was conflated with the so-called "alms of 'ashura" suggests how different types of giving overlap in the Muslim calendar. Al-Ghazali, for example, recommended that the annual zakat be paid in one of four sacred months: Muharram, Ramadan, Dhu'l-Hijja, and Rajab.[30] Thus it is perhaps not surprising that both Lane and Abu Illya observed people paying zakat in these months, according to their own decisions and interpretations of the obligation. In the absence of centralized collection, people may have incorporated their annual zakat obligation into different kinds of distributions.

Lane's description of 'Ashura practices further illustrates how zakat became identified with other occasions for giving charity. Children came begging for

---

[27] Mehdi Abedi and Michael M. J. Fischer, "An Iranian Village Boyhood," in *Struggle and Survival in the Modern Middle East*, ed. Edmund Burke III (Berkeley: University of California Press, 1993), 328. Recipes for 'ashura puddings or stews may vary between Muslim communities. For one recipe of the 'ashura cooked in sufi convents in early twentieth-century Istanbul and the symbolic significance of the ingredients, see Grace Martin Smith, "'Ashure and, in Particular, the 'Ashure of Muharrem," *Journal of Turkish Studies* 8 (1984): 229–31.

[28] See M. Plessner, "al-Muḥarram," in *EI²*, VII:464; A. J. Wensinck and P. Marçais, "'Āshūrā'," in *EI²*, I:705–6; Sabra, *Poverty and Charity*, 52.

[29] Lane, *Manners and Customs*, 420.

[30] Al-Ghazālī, *Kitāb Asrār al-Zakāh*, I:282–83; Faris, *Mysteries of Almsgiving*, 29–30; Zysow, "zakāt," XI:417.

what they called "the alms of the ʿashr," which Lane learned could also be understood as "a corruption of "ʿoshr', a term improperly used for 'ruba el-ʿoshr' (the quarter of the tenth, or the fortieth part)." This is the same percentage to be taken in zakat when it is calculated on money or goods.[31] Even as a foreigner and non-Muslim, Lane was drawn into the distribution of alms expected on that day:

I had to provide myself with a number of five-faddah pieces [coins] before I went out this day, for the alms of the ʿashr already mentioned. In the streets of the town I saw many young children, from about three to six or seven years of age, chiefly girls, walking about alone, or two or three together, or carried by women, and begging these alms. In the course of the morning a small group of blind fakeers [sufis, or simply, poor people], one of whom bore a half-furled red flag, with the names of El Hoseyn and other worthies worked upon it in white, stopped in the street before my door and chanted a petition for an alms. One of them began, "O thou who hast alms to bestow on the blessed day of ʿAʾshoora!" the others then continued in chorus, "A couple of grains of wheat! A couple of grains of rice! O Hasan! O Hoseyn!" The same words were repeated by them several times. As soon as they had received a small piece of money they passed on, and then performed the same chant before other houses, but only where appearances led them to expect a reward. Numerous groups of fakeers go about the town in different quarters during this day soliciting alms in the same manner.[32]

Safar, the second month of the Muslim calendar, contains no major holidays, but in Herat, Afghanistan, this is the time when women traditionally cooked a dish of sweet milky rice they call *nazr* (vow), and distributed it to friends and neighbors "as a gesture of goodwill and an act of charity." During the year, women pledged plates of nazr to mark their supplications and vows to the holy women of the Prophet's family at key moments like the birth of a child, the illness of a family member, moving into a new house, or sending a son to the army. When the nazr was cooked, the female head of the house divided it into portions for the recipients, including for her husband's patrons. Nazr thus served as a token of family generosity and obligation, affirming horizontal and vertical ties, appealing for intercession from saints and secular powers alike. This practice of nazr also illustrates one way in which charitable distributions were gendered: here, the donors were women, seeking the intercession of holy women, while the beneficiaries include a wide economic and social cross-section of people, men and women alike.[33]

Mawlid al-nabi, the birthday of the Prophet, falls on the twelfth of Rabiʿ al-Awwal, the third month of the year. This festival became popular and widespread from about the thirteenth century and the first account of it is from the

---

[31] In North Africa, the day of ʿAshura was marked traditionally by almsgiving, and children went from house to house collecting for their teachers. See Ph. Marçais, "II-ʿAshūra," *EI²*, I:705.

[32] Lane, *Manners and Customs*, 420–23.

[33] Veronica Doubleday, *Three Women of Herat* (Austin: University of Texas Press, 1990), 46–53.

biography of one Muzaffar al-Din (d. 1283), brother-in-law of Saladin. We will meet Muzaffar al-Din again in chapter 3, but for now our interest is with his biographer's description of the mawlid celebrations he sponsored, which lasted for more than a month and culminated in a night of public feasts (*simat*), including a separate meal for the poor (*sa'alik*), recitations, and finally, distributions of money from Muzaffar al-Din to everyone in attendance. These celebrations established a kind of paradigm for the later development of *mawlid* observances elsewhere. Under the Mamluks (1250–1517), the sultans held banquets at which the poor and the privileged among the guests all received something while many people distributed alms.[34]

"Rajab is the month of God, Sha'ban is my month – and Ramadan is the month of my people," said the Prophet. The rewards for fasting and beneficent giving are said to increase when they take place during this trio of holy months. In pre-Islamic times, Rajab was a sacrifice month and this practice continued with the Prophet's recommendation that meat be distributed among the poor as it was at the sacrifice festival ('Id al-Adha) during the time of the hajj.[35] The Ottoman queen mother Kösem Sultan provided stipends to two hundred descendants of the Prophet during these three months. She also secretly arranged for the release of debtors and other lesser criminals from prisons, paying their debts and fines from her own purse.[36] Laylat al-bara'a, the night on which the leaves shaken from the tree of life reveal the identity of those who will die in the coming year, falls on the fourteenth of Sha'ban. Among Indo-Muslims, this night is marked by prayers and celebrations on behalf of the dead, including distributions of food to the poor.[37]

Fasting from dawn to dusk marks the month of Ramadan among Muslims around the world, but, as we have seen, it is also a month recommended for paying zakat and marked by the collection of zakat al-fitr for the poor. The twenty-seventh night of Ramadan, *laylat al-qadr*, is singled out as especially blessed because on that night the Qur'an was revealed and good works carried out then earn special merit.[38] During Ramadan, large-scale demonstrations of generosity, in addition to the minimal zakat al-fitr, are not uncommon. Wealthy people may set tables that accommodate whole neighborhoods and welcome

---

[34] Ibn Khallikān, *Ibn Khallikan's Biographical Dictionary*, vol. II, trans. Mac Guckin de Slane, (Paris: Printed for the Oriental Translation Fund of Great Britain and Ireland, 1842–71 repr. 1961), 539–40; H. Fuchs and F. DeJong, "mawlid," *EI²*, VI:895–96; and Sabra, *Poverty and Charity*, 52.

[35] M. J. Kister, "Radjab," in *EI²*, VIII:374.

[36] Mustafa Naima, *Tarih-i Naima* (Istanbul, 1285/1868–69), V:113, as quoted in Peirce, *The Imperial Harem*, 209.

[37] A. J. Wensinck, "Sha'bān," *EI²*, IX:154.

[38] M. Plessner, "Ramaḍān," in *EI²*, VIII:417. Different contemporary Ramadan traditions, including a variety of charitable practices, are discussed at www.ramadhanzone.com/ramadhan_world. asp (accessed December 11, 2006).

passersby for the iftar meal to break the fast. For rulers Ramadan was also an opportunity for large-scale generosity. Reports of food, such as meat and bread, prepared and distributed to thousands of people every night of the month were not uncommon. The Fatimid caliphs held large banquets during Ramadan and at 'Id al-Fitr from which the prominent guests were encouraged to take food away to redistribute to those outside, beneficence reiterating and reinforcing a chain of patronage ties.[39]

While traveling in Anatolia, Ibn Battuta described the generosity of the *akhi* brotherhoods at Ramadan and on 'Id al-Fitr:

> Every group of these artisans would come out with cattle, sheep, and loads of bread, and after slaughtering the animals in the cemetery give them away in alms, along with the bread . . .When we had prayed the festival prayer we went in with the sultan to his residence, and the food was brought. A separate table was set for the doctors of the law, the shaikhs, and the Young Brethren, and another separately for the poor and destitute; and no one, whether poor or rich, is turned back from the sultan's door on that day.[40]

Ibn Battuta's account illustrates clearly how charity is often designed to advance more than one agenda simultaneously. Here, the ruler sponsored festival celebrations that included the poor but preserved existing social and economic hierarchies by separating rich from poor at the tables. Ottoman public kitchens across the empire followed a similar practice when serving special meals during Ramadan that provided the more well-to-do guests as well as the poor with meals of meat stew, rich pilavs, and sweets for dessert.[41]

In Ottoman Istanbul, Turhan Sultan (d. 1683), daughter-in-law of the powerful Kösem Sultan and queen mother after her, regularly distributed basic commodities of rice, cooking oil, and firewood to the poor of the Asian quarter of Üsküdar at the beginning of Ramadan. The modern Iranian village memoir quoted above to describe 'Ashura also recounted: "In Ramadan one received double merit for good deeds. The rich paid their debts to God by cooking cauldrons of stew to distribute, sharing the meat of a slaughtered lamb, and sending gifts of dry provisions (e.g., rice) to their neighbors."[42] The custom in Morocco of the late twentieth century was to break the fast with a soup called *harira*. Everyone everywhere in the country ate the same thing with no distinction between rich and poor.[43] In Turkey today, local municipalities build

---

[39] Sanders, *Ritual, Politics, and the City in Fatimid Cairo*, 76–79; Sabra, *Poverty and Charity*, 53.

[40] H. A. R. Gibb, trans. and ed., *The Travels of Ibn Baṭṭūṭa AD 1325–1354*, vol. II (Cambridge, UK: Cambridge University Press, 1962), 427–28. The akhis seem to have been medieval young men's associations, perhaps linked to guilds. On them see Ziya Kazıcı, "Ahilik," in *TDVİA* (1988), I:540–42.

[41] Singer, *Constructing Ottoman Beneficence*, 58–60, 115.

[42] Abedi and Fischer, "An Iranian Village Boyhood," 328.

[43] Donna Lee Bowen and Evelyn A. Early, eds., *Everyday Life in the Muslim Middle East* (Bloomington: Indiana University Press, 1993), 207.

Fig. 5. *Iftar* tent for Ramadan. Istanbul, September 2007. The tent is sponsored by the Eminönü municipality, while the meals served there to break the fast have changing sponsors. Author's photo.

huge iftar tables in city squares, funded by public, private, or joint contributions, and sometimes sponsored by political parties (Fig. 5). While not a strict obligation, the sponsorship of meals to break the daily Ramadan fast appears to be a practice that in some places came to be expected (even today) from practicing Muslims of rank and wealth.

Dhu'l-Hijja, the month of the hajj, is the last month of the Muslim year. On the tenth day and to mark the end of the formal pilgrimage rituals, Muslims worldwide celebrate the ʿId al-Adha sacrifice festival, which is obligatory for free Muslims who can afford it. In the story of Abu Illya, ʿId al-Adha was the holiday on which his family discovered their neighbor's poverty, since she could only afford to buy a bit of meat from the butcher, not to slaughter a lamb or sheep.[44] The animal sacrificed signifies the ram that God gave Abraham to offer up instead of Isaac, and part of the meat is given away as charity. Postel left the following description of the sacrifice celebrations:

During these days and the seven preceding ones, the Turks give immeasurable charity; they especially slaughter many sheep because they prefer mutton. They invite all poor households to come collect their *bayram* [holiday] that is, meat, bread, coins, etc. They visit the sick and give aid to orphans. Others go to graves and bring food to the dead, for their souls. In short, the demonstrations of their charity make an impressive sight.[45]

---

[44] E. Mittwoch, "ʿīd al-aḍḥā," in *EI²*, III:1007.
[45] Postel, *De la République des Turcs*, 64–65; my translation (AS).

Accounts of great generosity at the time of the Sacrifice Festival are relatively easy to find. However, as evidence from medieval Cairo during the rule of the Mamluk Sultan Qaitbay suggests, it is important to examine each case in its separate historical context, in order to understand what signals were embedded in charitable distributions. Qaitbay distributed gifts of money to everyone from the caliph and the chief judges through the sufis and the weakest of the population, including the widows and orphans. Yet while gold and silver coins were distributed to those of greater status, more modest people – the lower-ranking jurists and the poor – received copper coins.[46] As at the iftar feasts attended by Ibn Battuta or the Ottoman imperial public banquets, here too an existing social hierarchy was preserved, even affirmed and emphasized. Likewise, Postel focused on the generosity of the Turks he observed, yet embedded in his description is a ritual – coming to the house of a wealthier person – that signals the dependent condition of the poor or the less well-off as emphatically as it does the capacity for largesse of their benefactors.

The Muslim calendar is thus marked weekly and throughout the months of the year with occasions for charitable giving. This calendar, however, rotates through the seasons, so that no one month remains fixed with respect to the natural seasons. These seasons, too, have their beneficence, most notably at harvest times. Local celebrations and distributions may be tied to these times of the year. Gleaning, collecting what remains fallen or uncut in the fields after any harvest, is recounted in the Bible (Lev. 23:22), and most notably in the story of Ruth (Book of Ruth 2:2–3) as the right of poor people. This tradition also persisted, for example, in eighteenth-century Salonica. A case there came before the *qadi* (judge) in which a woman had died in a field. Her brothers claimed she was murdered, while the owner of the field, the defendant, said that the woman had died from the heat as she and her daughter gathered wheat left after the harvesters were through with their work. (He claimed he had generously seen to her funeral.)[47] Gleaning was also observed in a contemporary setting in late twentieth-century Afghanistan, among other places. The *jats* in Herat were barber-musicians of low social standing who had a reputation as "notoriously grasping, loud and insistent in their begging." However, they also had "a customary right to collect alms in grain at harvest time. When they were given money or presents they shouted praise to generous patrons but insulted those who were mean."[48] These few examples of harvesting suggest there may have been other occasions for charitable giving that were tied to the seasons and to yields from other crops, and not only grains. In all instances the amount

[46] Sabra, *Poverty and Charity*, 53–54.
[47] Eyal Ginio, "Living on the Margins of Charity: Coping with Poverty in an Ottoman Provincial City," in *Poverty and Charity*, ed. Bonner *et al.*, 172.
[48] Doubleday, *Three Women of Herat*, 161.

obtained probably varied with the quality of local agriculture and the relative success or failure of individual agricultural cycles. However, since rural and agrarian history is almost always less well documented than urban events, it is more difficult to discover the details of social relations and local practices in the countryside.

A shared calendar of holidays and observances seems to provide Muslims in different locations with overlapping if not entirely identical occasions for ritual celebration and charitable giving. However, this calendar was not static over time. Individual holidays, like the Prophet's birthday discussed above or the Persian New Year (*Nawruz*), became more prominent or declined as important festivals and were not equally significant in every era or place, nor among Sunnis and Shiʿis, for example. Alongside the shared calendar, local celebrations and sacred sites might also be marked by charitable giving. Such distributions could be worked into various kinds of festivities, acts easily legible to large numbers of people in the lexicon of Muslim rituals, perhaps even markers of Islamization. However, each performance of these distributions had its own context and it is only by examining them individually that the full and particular historical significance of distributions can be appreciated.

A lifetime of giving

Charitable giving also accompanied key events in an individual human lifetime. Seven days after the birth of a child, Muslim law recommends a sacrifice called ʿ*aqiqa* in which an animal is slaughtered and some or all of its meat distributed to the poor. The baby's hair, also called ʿ*aqiqa*, should be shaved and weighed, and a sum worth not less than this weight in gold or silver distributed to the poor.[49] One contemporary local tradition expressing gratitude for the successful and safe delivery of a child is the Sunni custom in Afghanistan of cooking *halwa*, a sweet, at a saint's shrine and distributing some to the beggars there.[50]

Circumcision of boys is practiced in Muslim communities worldwide, as distant from each other as Morocco and Java.[51] The occasion of a boy's circumcision seems to have been a particular opportunity for Muslims to undertake charity of various kinds, linking two key ritual actions. Historically, when some well-to-do families circumcised their sons, they also included the sons of other members of the household or neighborhood who were less well-off. This

---

[49] Meisami, *The Sea of Precious Virtues*, 164; Th. W. Juynboll and J. Pedersen, "ʿakīka," in *EI²*, I:337; Denny, *An Introduction to Islam*, 270.

[50] Doubleday, *Three Women of Herat*, 46–48.

[51] In many Muslim societies, boys are traditionally circumcised at around the age of seven, but this varies from place to place with local traditions. See the article A. J. Wensinck, "khitān," in *EI²*, V:20–22.

practice did not go unnoticed by foreign visitors, among them the artist-traveler G. J. Grelot, who visited Istanbul in the late seventeenth century. He observed:

Now they never Circumcise any till they come to six or seven years of age: Elder than these are often Circumciz'd, but neer younger, sometimes at twelve, fifteen years or more, according to the pleasure of the Parents; Especially if they be poor people, for then not being able to defray the charges of a private, they must stay till the Rich make a publick Circumcision of their own . . . And often the liberality of Rich men at their Child's Circumcision amounts to large sums. For besides the almes which they give to a great number of poor Children which are Circumciz'd, frequently at their charges, at the same time they also distribute considerable Almes to the poor of the Neighbourhood, to the end they may obtain the blessing of God upon the new circumciz'd Lad, and all the rest of their Family.[52]

For the Ottoman sultans the circumcision of a son was an occasion for great public celebrations – the epitome of what Grelot described – and the event could include large numbers of boys, orphans as well as the sons of imperial notables and impoverished families alike. The magnificent illustrated albums of the *Surname-i Humayun* and the *Surname-i Vehbi* depict the circumcision celebrations of the sons of Murad III (1582) and Ahmed III (1720), respectively. As seen in the painting from the *Surname-i Vehbi* (Fig. 6), the boys sponsored by the sultan attended the special public entertainments under the watchful eye of their escort.[53] As noted above, the public feasts sponsored by the sultans on these occasions offered substantial fare to those who could get to the tables, though the poor had far fewer dishes (and smaller portions) than the craftsmen, janissaries, imperial guards, 'ulama, and other notables.[54] In feasts like these, the line between hospitality and beneficence faded as rich and poor alike enjoyed variants of the sultan's generosity. All imperial distributions were demonstrations of power and prestige which reminded each and every participant in the feast of their dependence on the sultan.

Education offers a popular and widespread opportunity for philanthropic endeavors in many societies into the present day. Before exploring the way in which charitable donations financed education, it is worth considering why education was a principal focus of beneficent giving. Learning and knowledge are central in Islam as they are in Judaism because of the importance of legal knowledge for the correct performance of religious ritual and because religious law orders most facets of life. In early Islamic societies, a curriculum of study

---

[52] Quoted from G. J. Grelot, *A Late Voyage to Constantinople (1680)* in Laurence Kelly, ed. and comp., *Istanbul: A Travellers' Companion* (New York: Atheneum, 1987), 337.

[53] For a description of the earlier festival of 1582, illustrated in the *Surname-i Humayun*, see Derin Terzioğlu, "The Imperial Circumcision Festival of 1582: An Interpretation," *Muqarnas* 12 (1995): 84–100. Other examples of such celebrations can be found in the Mamluk era, for which see Sabra, *Poverty and Charity*, 54.

[54] Tezcan, *Bir Ziyafet Defteri*.

Fig. 6. Painting from the *Surname-i Vehbi* of boys to be circumcised as part of the circumcision festivities in 1720 for the sons of Sultan Ahmed III (1703–30). The boys are escorted by surgeons and janissaries as they watch the *jereed* match played in front of the sultan (on foot instead of on horseback) as part of the entertainments staged during the two-week celebrations. A band, with male and female spectators behind, appears in the upper left-hand corner. *Surname-i Vehbi*, A.3593, f. 43a. With the permission of the Topkapi Palace Museum, Istanbul.

developed based on the need for instruction in the foundational texts of the Muslim faith, and Islamic law and jurisprudence. In essence, teaching the Qur'an to Muslim children was the basis for teaching Islam and of creating a shared cultural frame of reference for the community, whether people were rich or poor. Islam offered a spiritual order for the world, together with a legal and political framework. Thus studying the Qur'an was a means of socializing children, and it was in the interests of people with power and money to support the education of children so as to promote acceptance of the existing order of things. Advanced training in law and jurisprudence, largely but not exclusively the domain of men, created a corps of scholar-jurists who acted as spiritual and legal authorities.

Education first took place in mosques, and probably other venues as well. By the tenth century, hans were being founded next to mosques in order to house students and teachers, and from this pairing the institution of the *madrasa* (college) emerged in the eleventh and twelfth centuries, in particular in Iran, Iraq, Syria, and Egypt. These endowed educational institutions proliferated in Syria and Egypt roughly from the time of Saladin (d. 1193) through the Mamluk era (1250–1517). Primary schools (*maktab*), devoted mostly to teaching the Qur'an, were founded alongside the madrasas as well as independently. As purpose-built colleges, the madrasas contained spaces for prayer and study and living quarters, and were endowed by prominent individuals, often members of the ruling political elites. The endowments, with many variations in size and conditions, generally provided salaries for scholar-teachers, and students could expect a place to live, instruction, sometimes daily meals and a cash stipend, as well as a new set of clothes once or twice a year. The endowment deeds also stipulated support for managerial and custodial staff, building maintenance, and sometimes curricular details as well.[55]

Another kind of educational beneficence emphasizing the individual nature of patronage was recounted in the memoirs of the Ottoman-Turkish author and political activist Halide Edip Adıvar (1884–1964). She described a ceremony called *başlanmak* which marked the start of her studies as a little girl. Not only did her family distribute sweets and coins to her entire class, but as well-to-do people they included poorer children of the same quarter in the ceremony and then paid for their education as well. Halide Edip somewhat nostalgically

---

[55] Jonathan P. Berkey, *The Transmission of Knowledge in Medieval Cairo: A Social History of Islamic Education* (Princeton: Princeton University Press, 1992), 6–18, 67–69; Robert Hillenbrand, *Islamic Architecture: Form, Function, and Meaning* (New York: Columbia University Press, 1994), 173–251; on madrasas, see George Makdisi, *The Rise of Colleges* (Edinburgh: Edinburgh University Press, 1981) and Yaacov Lev, *Charity, Endowments, and Charitable Institutions in Medieval Islam* (Gainesville, FL: University Press of Florida, 2005), 85–112.

attributed this practice to Ottoman philanthropic traditions: "The old systematic philanthropy of the Ottomans, although fast disappearing, was not entirely dead yet."[56] Halide Edip's observation caught charitable practice and educational institutions at an important moment of change, for the nineteenth-century reforms and the twentieth-century creation of the Middle Eastern states included the gradual institution of widespread if not universal, state-sponsored education of the sort that was meant to make her parents' form of personalized charity and patronage unnecessary and obsolete.

Children's education also included learning about charity, whether from the many relevant passages in the Qur'an and hadith, or from the behavior of those around them. The insistence on affirming faith through prayer and charitable giving was something children memorized along with the other verses of the Qur'an. According to an early Hanafi scholar, Abu Mansur al-Maturidi (d. 944), Muslims should make sure their children learn to give: "The believer is obligated to instruct his child in generosity and charity just as he is obligated to instruct him in monotheistic doctrine and belief, for the love of this world is the source of all sin."[57] Quite likely, from an early age children witnessed and experienced alms either as donors or recipients, perhaps both, perhaps at their own or their siblings' ceremonies of circumcision. As Lane described in Cairo, children participated in holiday celebrations at which charitable distributions were an integral part of observance. Abu Illya's children, in a further example, tutored the children of the widow their father supported.

Marriage celebrations could also include charitable distributions. Under the Ottomans, wedding celebrations of imperial princesses were a counterpart to the circumcision ceremonies of their brothers, and included some of the same elements of public banqueting and beneficent distributions of coins. At the wedding of Fatma Sultan, daughter of Murad III (1574–96), "skirtfulls of shiny new coins were distributed . . . those who did not receive any sighed with longing." As has been suggested, such largesse may have been intended to ensure that suitably large crowds were present at these occasions, serving to witness and affirm the power and wealth on public display.[58] For the poor, distributions of food might offer real nourishment and a change from their routine menus, while a coin received on such occasions might be used to enjoy the holiday, discharge a debt, pay for necessary clothes or utensils, or be put away for more dire times. Marriage could also be the object of charitable

---

[56] Halide Edip, *The Memoirs of Halide Edip* (London: John Murray, 1926), 85–88, quote from p. 88.
[57] Abu Mansur al-Maturidi, as cited in Ibn Nujaym, *Al-Bahr al-Ra'iq* (Cairo 1334/1915), VII:284, according to Weir and Zysow, "ṣadaḳa," VIII:715.
[58] Peirce, *The Imperial Harem*, 123, quoting the Ottoman historian Selaniki (d. c.1600) on events in the year 1593–94.

donations; wealthy women sometimes directed their beneficence to assisting girls to marry by providing them with dowries.[59]

Charitable donations often celebrated success or joy, but they could be equally important in troubled times or following a tragedy. Setting off on a journey – often a dangerous proposition – could be marked by an act of beneficence or the promise of one upon a safe return. Ibn Battuta described how people departing on sea voyages to India and China would leave written commitments at the shrine of one Abu Ishaq (936–1035) in Kazuran (Iran), to be fulfilled upon their safe return. When and if these travelers did come home, employees at the tomb hospice would go to collect the pledges and distribute the promised monies to poor people.[60] At numerous times, characters in the stories of *A Thousand-and-One Nights* give alms in a stereotypical gesture of thanks for safe delivery from danger.[61] While these stories are not usually regarded as a historical source, literature may add insights into cultural practices.

Beneficent acts marked both sickness and health, with donations aiming to promote wellness through physical treatment as well as calling on or giving thanks for divine intervention. Hospitals were the largest and most impressive form of charity connected with treating sickness, though they were a rare donation because of their enormous cost and because the practice of medicine was not significantly situated in such institutions before the twentieth century. Created as endowments, the hospitals offered basic care comprising a clean, quiet, warm, and safe place to rest with adequate meals. Sometimes, regular and nourishing food given in a calm environment was an important and even sufficient part of medical treatment, although hospitals also provided surgical, pharmacological, and other therapies.[62] In the face of plague epidemics in Mamluk Egypt, sultans and simple people alike undertook beneficent gestures for the public welfare. In 1348 people prepared and buried the huge numbers of dead with no compensation, contributing their time and skills to wash the bodies and make coffins.[63] This instance of volunteerism provides a rare view of this form of charity, so organized and widespread in the modern world. Intuition suggests that such actions were a common, necessary, and unspectacular part of life in the pre-modern era. Burying dead bodies was as much a public health need as it was a charitable gesture toward the departed.

[59] Peirce, *The Imperial Harem*, 202; Ellison Banks Findly, "Women's Wealth and Styles of Giving: Perspectives from Buddhist, Jain, and Mughal Sites," in *Women, Patronage, and Self-Representation*, ed. Ruggles (Albany: State University of New York Press, 2000), 104.

[60] Gibb, *Ibn Battuta*, vol. II, 320–21.

[61] See several examples in the Sinbad stories, in *Arabian Nights' Entertainments*, ed. Robert L. Mack (Oxford: Oxford University Press, 1995), 151–67.

[62] See Yasser Tabbaa, "The Functional Aspects of Medieval Islamic Hospitals," in *Poverty and Charity*, ed. Bonner *et al.*, 95–120; Miri Shefer, *Living with Death: Medicine and Society in the Early Modern Middle East* (Albany: State University of New York Press, forthcoming).

[63] Sabra, *Poverty and Charity*, 55.

A common practice among the Mamluk sultans and *amirs* (commanders) was for a man to have "treated himself with alms" (*dawa bi'l-sadaqa*) by giving generously to the poor when ill.[64] Charity, large or small, also marked recovery from illness. The life of Melek Ahmed Pasha (d. 1662), uncle and patron of the Ottoman traveler and author Evliya Çelebi (d. 1684), has been documented extensively, including the following account of his recovery from a hideous infection.

> The Pasha improved daily until, God be praised, in two months he was returned to health. He distributed twenty purses among the poor and he waived the stewardship accounts of all his aghas [military officers], then dismissed them, and they went off hunting or partying in the gardens and the vineyards. He had several hundred orphan boys circumcized, gave each of them into the custody of one or another agha or master craftsman or teacher and bestowed on each one a splendid suit. He also found Muslim homes for quite a few orphan girls, outfitting them as well and giving them a start in life. In Silistre he constructed a stone pavement over the main road, from the head of the bazaar all the way to the Istanbul gate, a distance of 3,000 yards; and in several of the roads he dug out gutters, thus relieving the town from a sea of mud. He built a harness shop and a luxurious coffeehouse and several houses, and established this property as an endowment for the upkeep of the pavement on the main road . . .[65]

Melek Ahmed Pasha's beneficence touched a broad spectrum of people, from servants of his household to unknown orphans. Nor did he neglect the general public welfare, providing for infrastructure, industry, and popular leisure in his benefactions. Whether real or a literary construction, the list of beneficiaries presents the image of a generous donor, mindful to include as many people as possible in his philanthropy. More important for the purpose of understanding the place of charitable endeavor in the Ottoman Empire, the list of Melek Ahmed Pasha's public works illustrates how responsibility for the construction and maintenance of services like roads fell mostly on the shoulders of sultans, imperial officials, and notables, often in the form of endowments, although, according to Postel's account, road works on a minor scale were also undertaken by just about everyone in the empire.

Less happy than the recovery of Melek Ahmed Pasha, though the occasion for equal beneficence, was the story of his wife Kaya Sultan (d. 1659), daughter of Sultan Murad IV. Pregnant, she was unnerved by ominous interpretations of her dreams. As a result she "grew more pious day by day. She gave 20,000 goldpieces in trust for Mecca and Medina, and another 20,000 for the benefit of everyone in her household, great and small . . ." As with Melek Ahmed Pasha, Evliya has taken care to show that Kaya Sultan was generous both to her immediate household and on behalf of the public welfare; he also linked her increasing benefactions to increased piety, making a direct connection between

---

[64] Sabra, *Poverty and Charity*, 56.   [65] Evliya Çelebi, *Intimate Life*, 214.

religious belief and beneficent practice. However, none of Kaya Sultan's donations saved her, and Melek Ahmed Pasha, mourning her death, was prevented from making any in her memory. Their entire household had been sealed and confiscated because with her death Melek Ahmed Pasha fell from imperial favor, losing not only his wife but his imperial patroness.[66]

Charitable acts often accompanied death and funerals. Death was an important moment for the deceased, who now had to face the record of a lifetime and be judged for it. Before dying, people of means might endow a Qur'an reader's position for their tomb so that verses would be read on behalf of the donor's soul, or they might leave funds to distribute food to those who came to visit the grave and presumably add their prayers for the deceased. Freeing slaves as part of a last will and testament was a familiar act. The living could also contribute on behalf of the dead with distributions at the cemetery or by endowing Qur'an readings or prayers in addition to the beneficent acts arranged in advance by the deceased. That people might legitimately attend to the spiritual welfare of their beloved departed is recognized in hadiths such as that in which a man is reported to have said to the Prophet: " 'My mother died suddenly, and I think that if she could speak, she would have given in charity. May I give in charity on her behalf?' He said, 'Yes! Give in charity on her behalf.' "[67] However, reading Qur'an verses and offering prayers were not forms of intercession sponsored only by the living on behalf of the departed; at the same time those praying hoped that the dead would intercede on behalf of the living.

Intercession (shafaʿa) is explicitly labeled as "sadaqa of the tongue" in one hadith, which recommends it should be practiced among the living on behalf of the living. In fact, the capacity for this kind of intercession, which relies on individual status, is also labeled as the zakat due on that status. The intercessor, therefore, is a donor, who is then part of a donor–beneficiary relationship between the one receiving mercy or justice as a result of the intercession and the one who granted it. Shaun Marmon's discussion of intercession with reference to Mamluk society suggests that there is a complex relationship to be explored between the ideas of shafaʿa and sadaqa in Islamic thought, one which may help to explain further how networks of loyalty and obligation are formed and utilized.[68]

Descriptions from Mamluk Cairo recount how meals there were organized in cemeteries as part of funerals, so that food distributions could also be incorporated in mourning rituals. In some cases, however, the meals attracted large and

---

[66] Evliya Çelebi, Intimate Life, 226.
[67] Al-Bukhārī, Ṣaḥīḥ al-Bukhārī, 55 (wasaya), bab 19; USC-MSA, Bukhari, 51/22.
[68] On intercession, see: Shaun E. Marmon, "The Quality of Mercy: Intercession in Mamluk Society," Studia Islamica 87 (1998): 125–39, and especially pp. 132–33.

unruly crowds of people, all anxious to have a share.[69] The great Cairene cemetery of al-Qarafa developed from the seventh to the fifteenth century into a veritable "city of the dead" whose large tombs and many *khanqahs* (sufi hospices) were endowed to enable regular distributions of alms and charity, thereby attracting living inhabitants to the same space.[70] When Şehzade Mehmed, son of the Ottoman Sultan Süleyman (mentioned in the Introduction of this book), died in 1543, his father publicly mourned the death of this beloved son. The imperial public kitchens served food free for three days and the sultan personally gave alms to the poor during the forty days of mourning prayers at Mehmed's tomb. The foundations for an imperial mosque complex were laid in the following year, and alms and meat from sacrifices were handed out to the poor of every Muslim quarter of Istanbul. There were more than 250 such quarters at the time![71] (Figs. 7 & 8.)

Lane described how the funeral procession of a wealthy man in nineteenth-century Cairo included some poor people as professional mourners, adding volume to the public obsequies in expectation of a handout. The procession "is sometimes preceded by three or four or more camels, bearing bread and water to give to the poor at the tomb . . . A buffalo, to be sacrificed at the tomb, where its flesh is to be distributed to the poor, sometimes closes the procession." Lane explained that: "This custom is called 'el-kaffárah' (or the expiation), being supposed to expiate some of the minor sins of the deceased, but not great sins." On the Friday following the funeral, the women of the family returned to the tomb, carrying, among other things, cakes or bread to distribute to the poor. The same ritual took place on the following two Fridays, and on Thursday and Friday following the forty-day mourning period.[72] Generous distributions at tombs lasted far beyond the moment of burial or formal mourning period, and were an important factor in establishing the cemetery at al-Qarafa as a place where the living poor might hope to find subsistence.

The calendar of annual holidays together with the cradle-to-grave celebrations of birth, death, and important milestones in between depict beneficent distributions as a constant feature of life in Islamic societies, an aspect of every kind of notable occasion. Weaving them together into hypothetical annual and lifetime calendars is intended to demonstrate how regularly charity might punctuate people's lives. Moments at which donations could occur were mostly predictable for donors and recipients alike, for they followed standard patterns in where and what to distribute. Yet even where predictable, each donation still depended on the capacity of an individual and was vulnerable to

---

[69] Sabra, *Poverty and Charity*, 96.   [70] Taylor, *In the Vicinity of the Righteous*, 20.

[71] Necipoğlu, *The Age of Sinan*, 192. For an example from the funeral of an Ottoman queen mother, see Peirce, *The Imperial Harem*, 198, 210.

[72] Lane, *Manners and Customs*, 508, 510, 518.

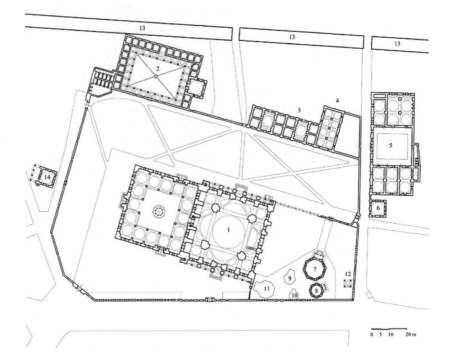

Fig. 7. Plan of the Şehzade Mehmed complex which comprises: (1) mosque, (2) madrasa, (3) guest rooms, (4) caravansaray with stables, (5) imaret, (6) maktab, (7) tomb of Şehzade Mehmed, (8–12) additional tombs, (13) fountains of the Valens aqueduct, and (14) earlier minaret. Plan by Arben N. Arapi, in Gülru Necipoğlu, *The Age of Sinan* (Princeton: Princeton University Press, 2005), Illustration #154, p. 192. With the permission of the author.

personal idiosyncrasies and therefore not an entirely dependable source of assistance.

Waqf

The Prophet said: "When a person dies, his achievement expires, except with regard to three things – ongoing charity (*sadaqa jariya*) or knowledge from which people benefit or a son who prays for him."[73]

---

[73] Muslim b. al-Ḥajjāj al-Nisābūrī, *Al-Jāmiʿ al-Ṣaḥīḥ*, 5:73; Muslim b. al-Ḥajjāj, "Kitāb al-Waṣiyya," in *Ṣaḥīḥ Muslim*, vol. IV (Cairo: Dar al-Ghad al-ʿArabi, 1987–90), 4; USC-MSA, Muslim, 13/1005.

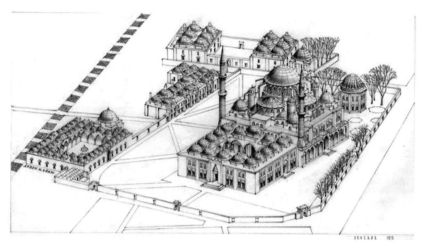

Fig. 8. Axonometric projection of the Şehzade Mehmed complex. See Fig. 7 for indentification of the buildings. Projection by Arben N. Arapi, in Necipoğlu, *The Age of Sinan*, Illustration #155, p.193. With the permission of the author.

One major exception to the relative invisibility of many charitable gestures is the large foundations (waqfs) that began to appear in greater numbers in the Islamic world from roughly the ninth century. Scholars agree on the central role of waqfs in Islamic societies: their influence on religious practice, social inter-action, cultural transmission, aesthetic production, political legitimation, eco-nomic organization, and the physical structure of towns and villages alike. With roots in Roman, Byzantine, and Sassanian laws and practices, waqfs developed within the context of Muslim legal and cultural demands, together with local political, social, and economic realities. The historian Marshall Hodgson main-tained that from about the tenth century, private waqfs replaced zakat as "the vehicle for financing Islam as a society" and that they offered "the material foundation for most specifically Islamic concerns," supporting religious, social, cultural, and economic activities, while equally serving political functions. Hodgson continued: "Through the waqfs the various civic essentials and even amenities were provided for on a private yet dependable basis without need or fear of the intervention of political power."[74]

Many eye-catching buildings, like mosques, schools, and tombs, were con-structed and supported by waqfs, and this has often made endowments the most public form of charity in Islamic societies. Waqfs are also the most visible

[74] Marshall G. S. Hodgson, *The Venture of Islam*, 3 vols. (Chicago: University of Chicago Press, 1974), II:124; McChesney, *Charity and Philanthropy*.

evidence of charity for historians, since they established and sustained large buildings as well as leaving a broad paper trail of evidence about their founding and operation. In comparison with the waqfs, informal acts of charity often went unrecorded, and can be retrieved only sporadically from the historical record through anecdote and accidental accounts. The cumulative mass of these informal gestures probably far outnumbered the waqfs and is ultimately no less significant for understanding how charity created ties that bound individuals and sustained communities. Unfortunately, such gestures are mostly lost from historical view.

Waqfs have been researched extensively, probably as much because of the prominence of particular foundations as because of the relatively large amount of evidence available about them. Foreign visitors and colonial rulers alike carefully scrutinized waqfs, especially in the nineteenth and twentieth centuries, because the entire institution seemed to interfere with the establishment of modern private property regimes and the reform of landholding for purposes of agricultural modernization and development. None of these reforms had much to do with charity, and when people did stop to comment on the ostensibly charitable nature of the foundations, it was usually to criticize an apparently cynical or self-interested attitude toward charity on the part of the founders or the parasitic attitude of the beneficiaries.[75] This section discusses what waqfs are: their component parts and some of the considerations that went into waqf making.

Basic parameters

Waqfs, known also as *habs* or *hubus*, were probably the most widespread form of "ongoing charity" historically in Islamic societies and they aimed to establish and sustain beneficent endeavors over time. Founding a waqf constituted a

---

[75] The first to point out that the study of waqfs should be focused on their character as social institutions was M. Fuad Köprülü, in a 1942 article, but he did not go so far as to suggest that this included the study of charity. See M. Fuad Köprülü, "Vakıf Müessesesinin Hukuki Mahiyeti ve Tarihi Tekâmülü," *Vakıflar Dergisi* 2 (1942): 5–6. Research on waqfs abounds in scholarly literature and continues to be a prominent and fruitful field of research. For some examples, see the recent collections: Faruk Bilici, ed., *Le waqf dans le monde musulman contemporain (XIXe–XXe siècles): fonctions sociales, économiques et politiques* (Istanbul: Institut Français d'Études Anatoliennes, 1994); the special issue of the *Journal of the Economic and Social History of the Orient*, "Waqfs and Other Institutions of Religious/Philanthropic Endowment in Comparative Perspective," 38, no.3 (1995); Randi Deguilhem, ed., *Le waqf dans l'espace islamique: outil de pouvoir socio-politique*, preface by André Raymond (Damas: Institut Français de Damas, 1995); the special issue of *Islamic Law and Society*, 4, no.3 (1997); Miriam Hoexter, "*Waqf* Studies in the Twentieth Century: The State of the Art," *Journal of the Economic and Social History of the Orient* 41, no. 4 (1998): 474–95; and Randi Deguilhem and Abdelhamid Hénia, eds., *Les fondations pieuses (waqf) en Méditerranée: enjeux de société, enjeux de pouvoir* (Safat, Kuwait: Kuwait Awqaf Public Foundation, 2004).

charitable act, defined by the intentions of the founder. Making a waqf is also a legal act, one defined and circumscribed by specific sections of Muslim law books, and subject to numerous variants in the different schools of law. The discussions here rely on the rules of waqf making according to the Hanafi school, which was organized in the eighth to ninth centuries, later spreading east to Central Asia, Afghanistan, and South Asia, as well as westward into parts of the Central Muslim lands, eventually including the Ottoman Empire (1300–1923).[76] (How the variant stipulations of the schools affected the practices of waqf making and the social history of waqfs is worth considering in greater depth.) Waqf making continues today in large parts of the Muslim world, although it is subject to modifications according to separate contemporary legal developments in different countries.

In its most basic outline, a waqf consisted of specific endowed properties, the revenues of which were designated in perpetuity to sustain defined beneficiaries; the properties or capital of the endowment were managed by a specified succession of managers. The founder, male or female, had to be of sound mind, adult, and free, and could endow only those properties owned fully, free, and clear of any lien. Beneficiaries had to constitute a valid pious purpose, which could be the support of Muslim ritual, social and cultural institutions (their buildings, staffs, and activities), public works, poor and needy persons, or even family members. Once constituted, an endowment was irrevocable and unalterable, except according to conditions laid down in the original deed or otherwise approved by a judge. The manager (*mutawalli*) was supposed to serve the beneficiaries capably and honestly, and a local judge could intervene if the required succession of designated managers lapsed or if the manager failed in his or her duties. The founders could appoint themselves as salaried managers and members of their families after them, or designate other capable people to the task. Local judges, imams, or other prominent people often served as managers, whether by initial arrangement or as the default choice when the stipulated line of managers expired.[77]

It became the practice to register an endowment deed (*waqfiyya*) before a judge, listing the revenue-yielding properties together with the succession of beneficiaries and managers. Endowment deeds exist as exquisite certificates and plain utilitarian copies. Many are preserved from the Mamluk and Ottoman periods, yet there are significant examples from earlier periods and other regions as well. The earliest inscription mentioning a waqf, and also referring

---

[76] Peter Charles Hennigan, *The Birth of a Legal Institution: The Formation of the Waqf in the Third Century AH Ḥanafī Legal Discourse* (Leiden: Brill, 2004).

[77] On the earliest waqf inscription, see M. Sharon, "A Waqf Inscription from Ramlah," *Arabica* 13 (1966): 77–84. For further detail on the legal stipulations concerning the founding of waqfs, see Rudolph Peters et al., "*wakf*," in *EI*², XI:59–99.

to a more extensive written deed, describes an inn (*funduq*) founded in 913 in the early Muslim Palestinian town of Ramle. Endowment deeds and accounts registers, the latter particularly numerous for the Ottoman period, supply extensive details about subjects as varied as urban development, agricultural production and revenues, currency values, building materials, soup recipes, school curricula, food and labor prices, and medical practices and supplies. Depending on its size, management history, and economic resources, as well as local political and environmental factors, an endowment might also generate extensive daily ledgers and management reports, and leave its tracks in local judges' registers and official correspondence. Because they were institutions governed by law and deeply embedded in the local (often urban) fabric, the activities, properties, personnel, and beneficiaries of endowments naturally caught the attention of imperial officials, local chroniclers, and travelers alike.[78] All this evidence stands in marked contrast – in volume, texture, and depth – to the sources about zakat or other forms of charity. A simple comparison of entries in the *Encyclopaedia of Islam*, the most authoritative general reference in English, shows that the entry "*wakf*" is almost three times as long as that on "*zakat*," and was written by multiple authors because a review of the sources on this topic along with a discussion of the state of scholarly research is too extensive for any single person to cover.[79]

Scholars of Islamic societies have always noticed waqfs, yet earlier research focused mostly on the laws that governed waqf making, waqf management, and the documents generated by the founding of waqfs, in some cases as much for their aesthetic value as for the contents of their texts. It was only from the 1970s

---

[78] Historical endowment deeds (*waqfiyya, vakfiye, vaqfnama*) can be found in libraries, archives, and private collections around the world, notably the Dār al-Wathā'iq and Wizārat al-Awqāf in Cairo and the Vakıflar Umum Müdürlüğü in Ankara. Many published examples are in specialized journals such as *Vakiflar Dergisi, Belleten, Annales Islamologiques, Bulletin d'Etudes Orientales*, and others. Published deeds or guides to collections are also in, for example, Daniel Crecelius, "The Organization of *Waqf* Documents in Cairo," *International Journal of Middle East Studies* 2 (1971): 266–77; Muḥammad M. Amin, *Al-Awqāf wa'l-ḥayāt al-ijtimā'iyya wa'l-iqtiṣādiyya fī Miṣr: 648–923 (1250–1517)* (Cairo: Dār al-Nahḍa al-'Arabiyya, 1980); Muḥammad M. Amin, *Catalogue des documents d'archives du Caire de 239/853 à 922/1516* (Cairo: Institut Français d'Archéologie Orientale, 1981); Donald P. Little, *A Catalogue of the Islamic Documents from al-Ḥaram Aš-Šarīf in Jerusalem* (Beirut and Wiesbaden: Franz Steiner Verlag, 1984); Daniel Crecelius, *Fihris waqfiyyat al-'asr al-'Uthmani al-mahfuzah bi-Wizarat al-Awqaf wa-Dar al-Watha'iq al-Tarikhiyyah al-Qawmiyyah bi-al-Qahirah* (Cairo: Dar al-Nahdah al-'Arabiyyah, 1992); Birgitt Hoffmann, *Waqf im Mongolischen Iran: Rashiduddins Sorge um Nachruhm und Seelenheil* (Stuttgart: Steiner, 2000). For the Ottoman period, waqf accounts registers can be found among the holdings of the Topkapi Palace Archives and the Prime Minister's Archives (Başbakanlık Osmanlı Arşivi) in Istanbul, as well as in other collections of Ottoman materials. Color reproductions of the opening pages of numerous Ottoman waqfiyyas can be found in Tülay Duran, ed., *Tarihimizde Vakıf Kuran Kadınlar. Hanım Sultan Vakfiyyeleri* (Istanbul: Tarihi Araştırmalar ve Dokümentasyon Merkezleri Kurma ve Geliştirme Vakfı, 1990).

[79] Zysow, "zakāt," XI:823–28; Peters et al., "*wakf*," XI:59–99, supplement 823–28.

that waqf research systematically began to address topics other than the legal, structural, and organizational aspects of the foundations, and scholars turned to writing the social history of waqfs, as well as to using waqf documents to write social history more generally. Research focusing on waqfs has predominated in the investigation of charity in Islamic societies, probably because endowment deeds and related records are readily available together with the normative legal literature. For the study of charity, all of these sources make it possible to explore the evolution of norms and their relationship to practice. The subjects to which waqf study provides entry are numerous; for obvious reasons, the list offered here includes only those related to charity. These topics include the roles of different social, economic, and political classes as founders; the place of women in the business of beneficence; the integration or exclusion of minority communities, as both founders and beneficiaries; the physical distribution of large endowments as an indication of the type and availability of social services in the cities and countryside, center and periphery; and the relative standing of beneficiaries, be they buildings or people, scholars or paupers. Gabriel Baer and his students pioneered the study of waqfs as a key to understanding the social history of the Middle East and Islamic societies.

Waqfs are not actually mentioned in the Qur'an but numerous hadiths discuss aspects of waqf making, including the notable anecdote repeated in several authoritative collections, which named the second caliph, ʿUmar b. al-Khattab (634–644), as the person who began the practice. Having acquired some land at the battle of Khaybar (635), ʿUmar asked the Prophet what he should do with it:

ʿUmar said, "O Allah's apostle! I have some property which I prize highly and I want to give it in charity." The Prophet said, "Give it in charity with its land and trees on the condition that the land and trees will neither be sold nor given as a present, nor bequeathed, but the fruits are to be spent in charity." So ʿUmar gave it in charity, and it was for Allah's cause, the emancipation of slaves, the poor, guests, travelers, and kinsmen. The person acting as its administrator could eat from it reasonably and fairly, and could let a friend of his eat from it provided he had no intention of becoming wealthy by its means.[80]

The basic principles articulated in this hadith lie at the heart of the ramified system of waqf. Notably, this text not only legitimates the practice of perpetual endowment and the beneficent use of revenues, but also describes the appropriate beneficiaries and allows the administrator of the waqf and some others close to the administrator to be supported from these revenues.

One example of a waqf is the public kitchen of Hurrem Sultan in Jerusalem. Established to feed four hundred of "the poor and pious, the weak and needy," this kitchen relied on the revenues from more than twenty villages in the

---

[80] Al-Bukhārī, *Ṣaḥīḥ al-Bukhārī*, 55 (wasaya), bab 28; USC-MSA, Bukhari, 51/26.

surrounding countryside as well as income from a double bath house (*hamam*) built especially to support the kitchen. Income from all these properties was intended to cover the cost of food supplies, staff salaries, and repairs to maintain the buildings in good working order. Because this waqf was founded by a member of the ruling dynasty, a paid manager was appointed from the imperial administrative corps (and not from the founder's family) to manage the waqf locally, submitting regular and detailed financial statements to a supervisor in the imperial palace in Istanbul. From the late sixteenth century, the supervisor of such waqfs was the chief black eunuch of the imperial Topkapı Palace. Hurrem Sultan's waqf demonstrates several basic features of waqfs as well as suggesting how complex a task it could be to establish and manage a large endowment. While quite specific in its aims and organization, including a list of functionaries, their salaries, the basic recipes for the meals to be cooked, and a list of revenue-producing properties, the endowment deed does not describe how a manager should cope with day-to-day challenges of food supply, revenue collection, problematic personnel, or people clamoring for a meal, except to demand that he or she behave in an honest and just manner.[81]

Each individual waqf, therefore, constitutes a discrete story of individual intentions and local circumstances, and each was integrated to its local political, economic, and social context through its functions, personnel, and properties. Depending on the size of a foundation, its own history formed a smaller or larger part of local events. The specific case of the Jerusalem kitchen draws attention to the way in which the Ottoman central authorities established and maintained relationships with provincial authorities, how the endowed properties were managed, the functions the waqf served that were not defined in its charter, and how these things changed over time from the mid-sixteenth century until the end of the empire. Specifically with respect to the original charter of this waqf, it is possible to see the fluctuations of income and expenditure, the changing cast of beneficiaries, and eventually the switch from ladling out cooked food to distributing raw foodstuffs such as flour and oil. Periodic reports speak of large numbers of poor people seeking access to the facility and offer some clues as to how that access was regulated. With hundreds of years of court records (*sijill*, Tur. *sicil*) for historians to comb, a far more detailed account can be written of this and many other similarly well-documented endowments.[82]

---

[81] For an account of the founding and early operation of this endowment, see Singer, *Constructing Ottoman Beneficence*.

[82] For more on this endowment, see Oded Peri, "The Waqf as an Instrument to Increase and Consolidate Political Power: The Case of the Khassekî Sultân Waqf in Late 18th Century Jerusalem," *Asian and African Studies* 17 (1983): 47–62; Oded Peri, "The Muslim *Waqf* and the Collection of *Jizya* in Late Eighteenth-Century Jerusalem," in *Ottoman Palestine 1800–1914: Studies in Economic and Social History*, ed. Gad G. Gilbar (Leiden: E. J. Brill, 1990), 287–97; Oded Peri, "Waqf and Ottoman Welfare Policy," *Journal of the Economic*

Because a waqf was irreversible, its conditions had to be defined in perpetuity. Buildings could collapse and families die out, but poor people always exist, and so the line of beneficiaries defined in most endowment deeds ended by naming the poor, sometimes those of the city where the endowment was located, sometimes the poor of the holy cities of Mecca and Medina. For example, Muhammad Bey Abu al-Dhahab, briefly the governor of Ottoman Egypt (1772–75), endowed an enormous waqf in 1774, with a long list of properties to support his mosque, college, fountain, and a zawiya in Cairo. After a lengthy description of the beneficiaries and the properties, the deed stipulated that any revenues remaining after distributions to the beneficiaries belonged to the founder, and after his death to his freed slaves, and after their deaths the money would support the blind residents of al-Azhar mosque and its neighboring zawiya in Cairo. "But if this is not possible," the document continued, "it should then be spent for the poor and the needy among the Muslims wherever they are found."[83]

The endowments of Hurrem Sultan and Muhammad Abu Dhahab are only two from among the thousands of waqfs established throughout Islamic history. Among the beneficiaries of waqfs were buildings like mosques, colleges, schools, hospitals, and sufi convents, and all their personnel, students, patients, and devotees; public works like water supply systems, bridges, and roads; emergency funds like community trusts for paying taxes; individual people like the founder's kin; and the poor. Other items found in endowments included books for schools and libraries, carpets for mosques, and swords and horses for holy war. The Jerusalem kitchen was a much smaller operation than the huge multi-purpose mosque complexes built in the Ottoman capitals of Istanbul, Bursa, and Edirne, or the Rabʿ-i Rashidi foundation of the Ilkhanid minister and physician Rashid al-Din (1247–1318).[84] Yet the people who made endowments were men and women from a wide range of social and economic classes

and Social History of the Orient 35 (1992): 167–86; Yusuf Natsheh, "Al-ʿImara al-ʿAmira: The Charitable Foundation of Khassaki Sultan (959/1552)," in *Ottoman Jerusalem: The Living City, 1517–1917*, ed. S. Auld and R. Hillenbrand (London: Altajir World of Islam Trust, 2000), 749–90; Singer, *Constructing Ottoman Beneficence*; and Singer, "The Privileged Poor of Ottoman Jerusalem," in *Pauvreté et richesse dans le monde musulman méditerranéen/Poverty and Wealth in the Muslim Mediterranean World*, ed. Jean-Paul Pascual (Paris: Maisonneuve et Larose, 2003), 257–69.

[83] Daniel Crecelius, "The *Waqfīyah* of Muḥammad Bey Abū al-Dhahab, I," *Journal of the American Research Center in Egypt* 15 (1978): 105.

[84] On the Ottoman capitals see the relevant articles in *EI²*, *İA*, and *TDVİA*. For a sense of the huge variety of waqfs in Istanbul and Edirne, see O. L. Barkan and Ekrem Hakki Ayverdi, eds., *Istanbul Vakıflar Tahrîr Defteri, 953 (1546) Tarîhlî* (Istanbul: Fetih Cemiyeti, 1970) and M. Tayyib Gökbilgin, *XV–XVI. Asırlarda Edirne ve Paşa Livâsı: Vakıflar, Mülkler, Mukataalar* (Istanbul: Üçler Basımevi, 1952). On the Rabʿ-i Rashidi, see Hoffmann, *Waqf im Mongolischen Iran* and Fariba Zarinebaf, "Feeding the Poor: The Rabʿ-i Rashidi ʿImaret in Il-Khanid Tabriz," in *Feeding People, Feeding Power: Imarets in the Ottoman Empire*, ed. Nina Ergin, Christoph K. Neumann, and Amy Singer (Istanbul: Eren, 2007), 59–67.

who met the basic legal qualifications defined above. The Jerusalem waqf was mammoth compared with the roadside fountains described by Postel at the beginning of this chapter, or the small neighborhood endowments that provided oil for mosque lamps or the maintenance of a local well.[85] In February 1358, Shaykh ʿUthman made an endowment of his house in Hebron to benefit his children, after them their descendants, and finally the poor.[86] Two men and two women were joint owners of a house in the sixteenth-century provincial town of Aintab (today, Gaziantep); each of the four made an endowment of his or her share to support the mosque of their neighborhood.[87]

Not everyone chose to set up something new. Some people contributed properties to benefit existing institutions, like prominent, even distant, Muslim establishments: the central mosques in Mecca, Medina, Jerusalem, and Hebron, as well as other important monuments like the Mazar-i Sharif shrine of ʿAli b. Abi Talib in Balkh, Afghanistan and his traditional burial site in the town of Najaf in Iraq.[88] For example, a centralized endowment fund for Mecca and Medina (al-Haramayn al-Sharifayn) existed in the city of Algiers from at least the seventeenth century. Eighteenth-century records show how the annual revenues of the endowment were collected in Algiers, forwarded in a heavily guarded caravan to the holy cities, and distributed there according to a detailed register of individual recipients that accompanied the sacks of money.[89] Funds that supported such places distributed charity for hundreds of years, while employing dozens, perhaps hundreds, of people to look after the sites and manage the properties. In general, however, research like that on the Haramayn waqf of Algiers is rare, and many questions remain unanswered about the aggregate value or management of endowments, as well as about how belonging to an important if remote charitable institution affected local revenue-generating properties.

The properties endowed to produce revenues were as varied as the founders and the beneficiaries of waqfs. Agricultural fields and gardens yielding grains, fruits, and vegetables; urban residential and commercial buildings earning rents; baths and mills charging fees; an entire orchard or a single tree, a multi-story house or a single room could all be valid properties of an endowment, as long as the endowing owner held title free and clear. Cash waqfs relied on yields generated from investments in order to create revenues for their beneficiaries, mostly in the form of interest on loans. These waqfs were not regarded as legal by many scholars because of the prohibition on taking interest in Islamic law but

---

[85] Behar, *A Neighborhood in Ottoman Istanbul*, 35.   [86] Little, *Catalogue*, 319.
[87] Leslie P. Peirce, *Morality Tales: Law and Gender in the Ottoman Court of Aintab* (Berkeley: University of California Press, 2003), 225.
[88] McChesney, *Waqf in Central Asia*; E. Honigmann and C. E. Bosworth, "al-Nadjaf," in *EI²*, VII:859–61.
[89] Miriam Hoexter, *Endowments, Rulers and Community: Waqf al-Ḥaramayn in Ottoman Algiers* (Leiden: E. J. Brill, 1998).

they were accepted by the Ottomans despite acrimonious debates. Ebu's-Su'ud Efendi, an eminently practical man, enabled the practice in two ways: (1) by allowing a legal device redefining the transaction to be a form of sale; and (2) by affirming that interest of up to 15 percent was allowable. Cash waqfs were limited mostly to Anatolia and the Balkans, and were rarely if ever found in the Arabic-speaking parts of the empire, where a long tradition of Islamic rule and legal practice pre-dated the Ottoman conquest of 1516–17. However, the cash waqfs, together with surplus revenues from other endowments, constituted significant sources of affordable credit before the establishment of banks in the Ottoman Empire during the nineteenth century.[90] As such, they served a crucial function in the Ottoman economic, political, and social world.

Jews and Christians living in Muslim lands also founded waqfs. Because the purpose of the waqf had to be legal under Muslim law, synagogues and churches were not legitimate beneficiaries, but many other personal and communal goals were permitted. Thus, a Moroccan Jewish woman, Bannita bint Barakat, who lived in Jerusalem in 1458, endowed her house and named her son as the beneficiary and his children and theirs after him. If the line of descendants ended, the poor of the Jewish community would become the beneficiaries, a purpose accepted in Muslim law. If, for some reason, the revenues could not be spent on the poor, then the money should be used for the Dome of the Rock in Jerusalem.[91] Thus in her waqf, Bannita articulated the seemingly remote possibility that there might one day be either no poor people among the Jews in Jerusalem or no Jews left in the city.

Even though non-Muslim religious institutions were not legally valid as waqf beneficiaries, churches and monasteries in some parts of the Ottoman Empire, notably in Lebanon and in the Balkans, were able to create endowments for their own benefit. This was accomplished through various legal stratagems, the most obvious of which was naming "the poor of the church" as beneficiaries in lieu of the church itself, or else "the poor and travelers."[92] These examples demonstrate how flexible waqf was as an institution in terms of its purposes and how inclusive it could be of populations within any state or even across political boundaries. That some Jews and Christians saw fit to make endowments according to Muslim law, recorded before Muslim legal authorities, suggests

---

[90] Imber, *Ebus's-Su'ud*, 145; J. Mandaville, "Usurious Piety: The Cash Waqf Controversy in the Ottoman Empire," *International Journal of Middle East Studies* 10 (1979): 289–308; Murat Çizakça, "Cash Waqfs in Bursa, 1555–1823," *Journal of the Economic and Social History of the Orient* 38 (1995): 313–54.

[91] Amnon Cohen, *Jewish Life under Islam* (Cambridge, MA: Harvard University Press, 1984), 211.

[92] Imber, *Ebus's-Su'ud*, 159–61; Eugenia Kermeli, "Ebū Su'ūd's Definitions of Church *Vakfs*: Theory and Practice in Ottoman Law," in *Islamic Law: Theory and Practice*, ed. Robert Gleave and Eugenia Kermeli (London: I. B. Tauris, 1997), 141–56; Richard van Leeuwen, "The Maronite Waqf of Dayr Sayyidat Bkirkī in Mount Lebanon during the 18th Century," in *Le waqf dans l'espace islamique*, ed. Deguilhem, 259–75.

that they acknowledged the strength of Muslim legal institutions in safeguard-
ing their own interests.[93]

Waqfs obviously were far more than engines of beneficence. They were
integral actors in the realms of property, finance, and labor, and their economic,
social, and cultural influence could be extensive. In the course of their lives, few
people in Muslim societies remained unaffected by endowments. Many people
enjoyed direct personal benefits from them, like students or poor people who
were immediate recipients of stipends or assistance. Others enjoyed impersonal
if direct benefits, such as the people who prayed in a local mosque or drank from
a fountain. Numerous merchants rented their shops from waqfs, since bazaars
were often endowed for the benefit of a local institution, and the same could be
true for the tenants of rented dwellings. Thus the physical infrastructure of a city
could result from its endowments. Waqfs also employed people up and down
the economic scale: to manage, collect revenues, teach, make repairs, cook,
clean, and perform a long list of tasks related to function and maintenance. Yet
waqfs could also exclude individuals or groups intentionally, as a signal of their
weaker or inferior status or undesirable presence. During their rule over
Baghdad, the Ottomans made numerous waqfs to support the Sunni ʿulama of
the town, but pointedly ignored the Shiʿi scholars.[94] Madrasas offered an
education only to select stipendiaries; public kitchens only admitted people
who could prove their claim to a meal.

Why found a waqf?

Why would a donor choose to make a waqf, alienating property so that the
revenues served a charitable purpose? If we read endowment deeds for answers,
they seem to articulate only two principal aims: spiritual benefit in the next life
for the donor and the well-being of the Muslim community (maslaha) in this
world, including the provision of ritual, social, and cultural services.[95] Postel's
observations quoted above seem to admit only piety and goodwill as motives for
beneficence, suggesting that his own perceptions were at least partly shaped by
the normative Muslim texts that he read, and probably his own notions of

---

[93] Jews also made endowments (heqdesh) under Jewish law to support synagogues and the poor.
For more on the heqdesh in Muslim societies, see Moshe Gil, Documents of the Jewish Pious
Foundations from the Cairo Geniza (Leiden: E. J. Brill, 1976) and Cohen, Poverty and Charity.

[94] Meir Litvak, Shiʿi Scholars of Nineteenth-Century Iraq: The 'Ulama' of Najaf and Karbala'
(Cambridge, UK: Cambridge University Press, 1993), 35–38. Among the Shiʿi tribes of Iraq,
there was no custom of founding waqfs and in some places no significant concentration of wealth
to make endowments possible. Beneficent support for Shiʿi scholars, students, and shrines came
in donations from Shiʿis outside Iraq.

[95] Khadduri, "maslaha." See the list of motives discussed in Bahaeddin Yediyıldız, Institution du
vaqf au XVIIIe siècle en Turquie – étude socio-historique (Ankara: Imprimerie de la Société
d'Histoire Turque, 1985), 11–12.

charity. Hurrem Sultan's deed for the public kitchen, issued in 1552, clearly states these goals:

in compliance with the noble content of the holy verse: "Do good, as Allah has done good unto you," [she] unlocked the cupboards of favours and gifts and opened the doors of unlimited kindness to mankind at large, pouring bounteous gifts and favours in abundance; thus people of distinction and mankind at large were nurtured by her favours. Her aim thereby was that people should benefit by her kindnesses, which – in order to procure her eternal bliss – were granted freely and were intended to be perpetual as days wear into months and years into ages, and that no disorder should befall them, so that her prosperity and luck should continue unchanged to the end of time.[96]

The sentiments expressed in this passage are familiar from the discussion of zakat in the previous chapter: the blessings of this life and the next come from God; material wealth enables people to act beneficently toward others; charitable giving improves the donor's chances of ultimately attaining Paradise.

One means of promoting community well-being was to set up institutions that created and maintained spaces for ritual observance, education, social welfare services, commercial activity, and residence. A huge mosque complex like the Süleymaniye in Istanbul (only a few hundred meters from the Şehzade) comprised a congregational mosque meant to hold several thousand people at Friday midday prayer; four colleges; a primary school; a hospital and a medical school; a public kitchen; an inn for travelers; a vast courtyard shaded by trees and open to the breezes with a spectacular view north to the Golden Horn and the Bosphorus; the tombs of the founder and his wife in the garden; a covered market; a bath; and public toilets.[97] Access to the schools, the public kitchen, and the inn was limited, but the courtyard was an ample park for anyone to enjoy. Any Muslim could pray in the mosque and some stopped there by the great tombs of Süleyman and Hurrem, since people appealed for intercession to powerful as well as holy people, whose aura of authority remained even in death. The nearby markets built to sustain the complex from their rents housed both manufacturing and sales venues for craftsmen and merchants; the baths were a place for ritual purification, general hygiene, relaxation, and gossip. Markets and baths alike served a wide range of customers. As part of the waqf's endowment, urban residences provided rental living for the city's laboring classes, and the revenue-producing villages endowed to the waqf enjoyed certain tax exemptions.[98] By founding the complex, therefore, Süleyman affected thousands of people, contributing to their welfare, and enhancing his capital city while attending to his own salvation.

---

[96] St. H. Stephan, "An Endowment Deed of Khâsseki Sultân, Dated 24th May 1552," *Quarterly of the Department of Antiquities in Palestine* 10 (1944): 178, 180.
[97] Necipoğlu, *The Age of Sinan*, 207–22.
[98] See the terms set down in the endowment deed for the Süleymaniye complex in Istanbul, in Kemal Edib Kürkçüoğlu, *Süleymaniye Vakfiyesi* (Ankara: Resimli Posta Matbaası, 1962).

Fig. 9. The complex of Bayezid II (1481–1512) in Amasya. The complex, built in 1481–86, includes (right to left): a madrasa, mosque, şadirvan (ablutions fountain) in front of the mosque, an imaret perpendicular to the mosque with a caravansaray linked to it at a right angle. The mosque precincts are planted with trees to form a park alongside the river. Author's photo.

The size of the Süleymaniye makes it an extraordinary achievement by any standard, and today its many buildings still serve multiple purposes. The mosque, tombs, park, markets, and toilets continue in their original functions, while one of the colleges is now a research library. The public kitchen, after serving as a depot and then a museum, holds a touristic Ottoman restaurant and a large tea garden frequented by university students. Moreover, the Süleymaniye is not the only large complex in Istanbul and there were others founded in cities around the empire, like the complex of Bayezid II (1481–1512) in Amasya (Fig. 9). Nor were the Ottomans the only ones to found multi-functional complexes of buildings, though they seem to have undertaken far more of this and made it a kind of architectural icon of their rule. As one non-Ottoman example, the so-called madrasa built by the Qarakhanid ruler Ibrahim b. Nasr in Samarkand in the mid-eleventh century included a college, tomb, mosque, rooms, garden, library, and cells for contemplative retreat. The poor received meat here on the Sacrifice Festival of ʿId al-Adha, and food and clothing on ʿAshura.[99]

---

[99] Lev, *Charity*, 98–99.

The size of complexes and the choice of component buildings depended on the means and goals of the individual founders, as well as on the needs of the places themselves. A complex along a busy trade route might boast a huge caravansaray while one in a town of scholars included a large madrasa. Sometimes, endowments existed to achieve a beneficent goal of local concern or of special importance to the founder. In an Ottoman city quarter, wealthy inhabitants made waqfs to help pay the share of poor residents when the government imposed extraordinary taxes (*avariz*). In the late eighteenth century, the Kasap Ilyas quarter of Istanbul had such a waqf that included a house, a charcoal and timber shop, and a mill. At times when no avariz taxes were levied, the manager could use the funds to help the poor or improve local public services. Waqfs in Tabriz and in the Anatolian city of Sivas paid to feed birds there during the cold winter months, while one was established to nurse sick storks in nineteenth-century Fez. The fourteenth-century traveler Ibn Battuta enthusiastically described the waqfs he found in Damascus, including those that sponsored people to go on the hajj in place of those who could not go themselves, to keep the streets paved and sidewalks in order, and to pay the cost of replacing dishes broken by servants.[100]

Waqfs, however, served a wide range of additional purposes beyond their obvious and stated goals. This was recognized by scholars and observers over many centuries. Chronicles, legal treatises, advice literature, and travelogues contain many references to the establishment and functioning of waqfs, as well as critiques of the ways in which waqfs were managed or their purposes undermined. A historian will find it difficult to judge the sincere good intentions of any beneficent person in the absence of substantial autobiographical records – diaries, letters, memoirs – that might illuminate individual personality. No such evidence exists in most pre-modern Islamic societies. The discovery of unstated motives is a precarious historiographic endeavor, yet between the lines and against the background of what we know of specific historical situations, it is possible to infer reasons for making waqfs beyond providing for the salvation of the donor and promoting the social welfare of the Muslim community. Endowment deeds can be read together with other evidence such as inheritance records, judicial proceedings, or historical chronicles. The inscriptions and Qur'an verses found on mosque walls and at the entrances to endowed buildings also provide insights into the aims of the

---

[100] Behar, *A Neighborhood in Ottoman Istanbul*, 67–68; Kishwar Rizvi, "Gendered Patronage: Women and Benevolence during the Early Safavid Empire," in *Women, Patronage, and Self-Representation*, ed. Ruggles, 128; A. K. S. Lambton, "Awqaf in Persia: 6th–8th/12th–14th Centuries," *Islamic Law and Society* 4 (1997): 316–17; M. Fuad Köprülü, *The Origins of the Ottoman Empire*, trans. and ed. Gary Leiser (Albany: State University of New York Press, 1992), 64; Edward Westermarck, *Ritual and Belief in Morocco*, vol. II (London: Macmillan, 1926), 330; Gibb, *Ibn Battuta*, vol. I, 148–49.

founders. Though they may seem formulaic, all these texts are nonetheless composed from a huge repertoire of possibilities.[101] In some cases, it is difficult to judge whether unstated aims produced results that were intentional or accidental on the part of the founder. Motives that might be deduced from the effects of waqf making include: urban and rural development; imperial legitimation; the desire for personal prominence; avoiding restrictions on the division of inheritance; the protection of wealth from imperial confiscation; the promotion of community or sectarian interests; and the preservation of social hierarchies and cultural norms. These diverse possibilities probably contributed to the enduring popularity of waqfs. Moreover, it bears remembering that although specific waqfs might attract objections from disinherited family members, government officials, or educated observers, the institution was integral to the well-being of state and society in Muslim communities for hundreds of years, another reason perhaps for its persistence.

Waqfs have long been a vehicle for urban and rural development. In addition to creating spiritual, economic, residential, and commercial spaces, these foundations were important agents of settlement in newly conquered regions. Rural development, Islamization, and security could be promoted by the establishment of zawiyas, which included ritual spaces, living quarters, kitchens, guest facilities, and sometimes cultivated land. In areas of sparse settlement, the zawiyas attracted not only temporary visitors but also permanent neighbors, who benefited from the spiritual services of the sufis and the proximity of a protected institution promoting a viable economic undertaking, as in the Moroccan example described in chapter 1.[102] Looking again at the illustrations of the Şehzade and Amasya complexes (see Figs. 7, 8, and 9), it is easy to understand how a neighborhood of the city grew up around them, taking advantage of the public and commercial spaces, and the social services they offered, as well as opportunities for employment. Seen from this perspective, the Süleymaniye and other complexes were high-profile urban development projects and answered the obvious needs of a growing metropolis.[103] Economic and political development was also fostered by endowments such as the mosque-caravansaray-bazaar complex founded alongside a fortress in Payas on the

---

[101] For examples that discuss the circumstances surrounding the founding of individual waqfs, see Singer, *Constructing Ottoman Beneficence* and Peirce, *Morality Tales*, 236–38. On texts and their importance, see Lucienne Thys-Şenocak, "The Yeni Valide Mosque Complex at Eminönü," *Muqarnas* 15 (1998) and Pınar Kayaalp-Aktan, "The Atik Valide Mosque Complex: A Testament of Nurbanu's Prestige, Power, and Piety," Ph.D. dissertation, Harvard University, 2005.

[102] On the importance of Ottoman zawiyas to the Ottoman colonization of the Balkans, see O. L. Barkan, "Osmanlı İmparatorluğunda bir İskân ve Kolonizasyon Metodu olarak Vakıflar ve Temlikler: I. İstila Devirlerinin Kolonizatör Türk Dervişleri ve Zaviyeler," *Vakıflar Dergisi* 2 (1942): 279–386.

[103] Halil Inalcik, "Istanbul: An Islamic City," *Journal of Islamic Studies* 1 (1990): 1–23.

much-traveled but not always secure southern coastal road from Anatolia into Syria.[104]

Ottoman officials, many drafted into service at a young age from Christian families in the Balkans (*devşirme*), sometimes invested in their home towns or in the places where they served. One example is the grand vizier Sokollu Mehmed Pasha (*c.*1505–79), founder of the complex in Payas. Recruited to Ottoman service from the Bosnian village of Sokolovici, Mehmed rose through the ranks of military-administrative service to serve as grand vizier for fourteen years. His very numerous endowments are found scattered from the Balkans to the Hijaz, a testament to his wealth and beneficence, as well as to his competitive instinct to outdo the philanthropy of his predecessor, the grand vizier Rüstem Pasha.[105] Rüstem's and Sokollu Mehmed Pasha's endowments promoted public welfare while writing their reputation in stone for all to see.

Waqfs came in all sizes. There is no doubt that the imposing buildings of the large imperial waqfs attracted attention, whether the premier mosques in the great Muslim cities like Baghdad and Damascus or Mamluk madrasas in Cairo and Jerusalem or Seljuq caravansarays in Anatolia. They were intended to do so, advertising power while at the same time bolstering and legitimizing it. A maxim from the twelfth-century "Mirror for Princes" volume articulated the expectation that rulers would look after the basic needs of their populations, and that such actions were to be reckoned as charity: "Know that those deeds by which kings gain fame and achieve greatness are threefold." The first kind of deeds had to do with prayer, the Qur'an, and ritual; the second, with waging holy war; and the third was "building cities and roads, border forts, mosques, bridges, and the like. Each day that you perform acts of charity and benevolence, know that that day is blessed; and each day that you do not bring charity and ease to Muslims, and have not discharged the people's needs, that is an evil day."[106] Obviously rulers had to provide physical security from attack. Yet they were also supposed to ensure basic subsistence and the possibility of fulfilling ritual obligations. This did not necessarily mean feeding whole populations on a daily basis or creating jobs for everyone. Rather, it meant worrying about regular food supply to urban areas and storing up grain against the event of famine, as well as making it possible for people to be good Muslims by providing spaces to pray and water for ritual purification, and by helping to provide for the poor, especially on holy days and festivals.

The Ottomans, as a long-lived dynasty ruling a vast and resource-laden empire, could afford to build and did so virtually everywhere they ruled as

---

[104] Necipoğlu, *The Age of Sinan*, 355–62.
[105] See Gilles Veinstein, "Soḳollu Meḥmed Pasha," in *EI²*, IX:706–11 and Necipoğlu, *The Age of Sinan*, 345–68, 579 (the map of Sokollu Mehmed Pasha's foundations).
[106] Meisami, *The Sea of Precious Virtues*, 223.

part of the work of consolidating their conquests. While their buildings were stamped with elements of Ottoman style and design, they varied throughout the empire under the influence of local building skills and materials, changing technologies and fashions, and sometimes as a result of the reuse of existing structures. More importantly, the buildings varied because the message of imperial beneficence in each place was somewhat different, shaped by the importance of a location to Ottoman needs and policies, the status and means of the founder, and local needs and resources. The absence of monumental structures could be just as telling as their presence, as can be seen in the example of Ottoman Cairo. As the imperial capital of the Mamluks, Cairo enjoyed the investment of major endowments as a succession of sultans built in the city. Ottoman Cairo enjoyed the benefits of Ottoman power and protection, thrived and expanded commercially, but it was no longer the site of the largest and most impressive new buildings.[107] These were saved for the capital cities of Bursa, Edirne, and Istanbul, for the holy cities of Mecca and Medina, and even for a city like Damascus, which although Mamluk for centuries, was not the former capital of an enemy empire. Rather, it was the first imperial Muslim capital under the Umayyads (661–750) and a key hub on the hajj route. Thus, the endowment of large mosques there by Selim I and Süleyman I linked them to early Muslim dynasties. Deputies, ministers, and people of power at every rank followed the lead of sultans in making waqfs. Many chose to communicate and reinforce their positions through endowments, and like the sultans, used them not only to claim status but to preserve it. Certainly Sokollu Mehmed Pasha's waqfs helped achieve this for him, as had the famous colleges of the Seljuq vizier Nizam al-Mulk (1018–90) in Baghdad, Nishapur, Balkh, Mosul, Herat, and Marv.[108]

Other, more material considerations also played a role in some decisions to found waqfs and how to configure them. Property endowed no longer belonged to the founder and therefore could not be distributed as part of an estate after death. According to Islamic law, the division of inheritances should proceed along carefully prescribed guidelines; as a result, large property holdings might be parcellized within a few generations. One way to prevent this subdivision without disinheriting people entirely was to constitute the property as a waqf while assigning paid positions or benefits in the waqf to family members.[109] In addition to keeping together family holdings, the process of making a waqf and assigning beneficiaries could also be used to disinherit family members entirely,

---

[107] A. Raymond, "The Ottoman Conquest and the Development of the Great Arab Towns," *International Journal of Turkish Studies* 1, no. 1 (1979–80): 84–101.

[108] H. Bowen and C. E. Bosworth, "Nizām al-Mulk," in *EI²*, VIII:71–72; J. Pedersen, G. Makdisi *et al.*, "madrasa," in *EI²*, V:1125–28.

[109] On the *dīwān al-mawārith*, see Rabie, *Financial System of Egypt*, 128–29, 132.

change the amount of property available for distribution, or even benefit people who ordinarily would not have inherited anything. Thus a son or daughter might be excluded from a share, while the portion of women – who normally inherited only half as much as men in the same relation to the deceased – could be further reduced or, alternatively, expanded. A household slave could be designated as the beneficiary of a waqf while she or he would have no portion at all in the inheritance from a master. For example, some eunuch freedmen of Mamluk sultans and notables were appointed as tomb guardians with handsome salaries paid from the endowments.[110]

Endowments have sometimes been characterized as "family" (*ahli*) and as "public" or "charitable" (*khayri*), according to their beneficiaries. This division can be misleading, since there is no legal distinction between the two categories. Many waqfs were founded to support a mix or succession of family and public beneficiaries, and all waqfs ultimately were destined to become public according to the provisions made for the final beneficiaries. The demarcation of the two categories may have evolved as a result of critical discussions of waqf, when authors wanted to praise the founding of "public" endowments while disparaging "family" endowments as self-serving and a distortion of the true purpose of waqfs.[111] It has been suggested, too, that the critique of waqfs as serving to disinherit legitimate heirs was itself part of the French colonial attempt to discredit local Muslim institutions that were inimicable to the goals of the regime. French attempts to undermine the overall legitimacy of waqfs aimed to make more property available for colonial settlement. In fact, the impact of waqf making on inheritance seems to have been interpreted in comparison with the normative legal rules of inheritance and waqf making, and less according to investigations of the actual effect of waqfs on inheritance in any specific time and place. The same is true regarding claims that endowed agricultural lands and buildings suffered more from lack of repairs and investment than non-endowed properties.[112]

---

[110] See Beshara Doumani "Endowing Family: Waqf, Property Devolution, and Gender in Greater Syria, 1800–1860," *Comparative Studies in Society and History* 40 (1998): 3–41, which presents an extensive comparative analysis of the strikingly different waqf-making strategies in nineteenth-century Tripoli (Syria) and Nablus. On the eunuchs, see Shaun Marmon, *Eunuchs and Sacred Boundaries in Islamic Society* (New York: Oxford University Press, 1995), 22–26.

[111] See Peters *et al.*, "*wakf*," XI:60. This distinction between family and charitable waqfs deserves an entirely separate investigation and discussion.

[112] See D. S. Powers, "Orientalism, Colonialism and Legal History: The Attack on Muslim Family Endowments in Algeria and India," *Comparative Studies in Society and History* 31 (1989): 535–71 on whether the importance of inheritance laws is a later Orientalist "invention." Powers criticizes the extensive emphasis placed on this aspect of waqf by nineteenth-century French Orientalists. For purposes of colonial rule, including land acquisition, scholars advising the colonial regime highlighted the displacement of heirs, perhaps to an exaggerated degree.

Another material consideration was the fact that property endowed in waqfs was theoretically protected from confiscation. The principal endowed property no longer belonged to the founder, but rather to God, from whom, in theory, one might hesitate to reclaim it. Ottoman imperial officials were liable to have their property confiscated when they fell out of favor, not an uncommon event in the sometimes turbulent political climate. As described above, Melek Ahmed Pasha lost his fortune along with his wife when she died and he lost her protective shield against the political rancor of his rivals. In such a situation, endowments could provide a steady source of income to the official who had fallen out of favor. If the founder of a waqf was executed, income would continue to flow to the designated beneficiaries, who might be his children. Just as important, through public endowments important people could preserve their public persona long after they had lost the immediate source of their power and wealth or passed away entirely. Thus, the Ottoman grand vizier Kara Mustafa Pasha was executed in December 1683, blamed for the failed second siege of Vienna. Yet the mosque complex he endowed in his native town of Merzifon in north-central Anatolia lived on, as did his fountains in Istanbul and his caravansarays at İncesu and Vezirhan.[113] In a similar fashion, the Mihrimah mosque near the Edirne gate of the Istanbul city walls and another with the same name across the Bosphorus in Üsküdar continue to bear the name of Süleyman's daughter, reminding everyone of her existence.

Lest we idealize the waqf system of organizing property to sustain charitable endeavors, it is important to point out that there were disadvantages and risks in making endowments, some of which were common to property holders in general. For one thing, the founder lost the ability to liquidate property for ready cash. Moreover, though waqfs were inviolable in principle, in practice mismanagement, wars, economic collapse, natural disasters, and normal wear and tear could all wreak havoc on property, undermining its value to the point of worthlessness. Political disruptions, too, could step in to cripple an endowment. The plans of Muhammad Bey Abu al-Dhahab for his magnificent madrasa-takiyya in Cairo, described above, were barely complete when he died in 1775. In the chaotic period of factional rivalries that followed his reign, virtually all the properties intended to support his waqf were seized and redistributed, and the madrasa closed owing to lack of funds.[114] The fate of Abu al-Dhahab's waqf demonstrates the imperfect reality that accompanied pious intentions.

---

[113] Godfrey Goodwin, *A History of Ottoman Architecture* (Baltimore: The Johns Hopkins University Press, 1971), 361–62.
[114] Crecelius, "The *Waqfīyah* of Muḥammad Bey Abū al-Dhahab, I," 84; Daniel N. Crecelius, "The Waqf of Muḥammad Bey Abū al-Dhahab in Historical Perspective," *International Journal of Middle East Studies* 23 (1991): 71–72.

While some misfortune might undo all the aims of a founder and leave the beneficiaries stranded, this fate did not impinge on the spiritual benefit to the founder, whose intentions were untainted by what happened later.

Although rarely, rulers did confiscate waqf properties altogether, especially strong rulers who could risk the predictable discontent of the beneficiaries, including the elites who often benefited most from the largest waqfs. Sultan Mehmed II ("the Conqueror," 1451–81) and Muhammad 'Ali Pasha of Egypt (1805–48) both seized vast properties for the state fisc from endowments made or controlled by notables, thereby increasing state revenues and weakening powerful subjects. They justified these confiscations with the claim that the property had been improperly alienated from the state to the founders in the first place. Competing claims to property between rulers and individuals (waqf managers or beneficiaries) sharpened in the nineteenth century as new state institutions began to take over some of the functions of waqfs along with their properties, while the state apparatus in general captured waqf revenues through administrative reforms, directing them to public purposes other than those originally defined. (This will be discussed further in chapter 5.) Ultimately one should perhaps be impressed at the longevity of those waqfs, like the Süleymaniye, that endured for hundreds of years. In part, this is due to the provisions for maintenance in their original endowment deeds, although it also has much to do with local historical conditions.[115]

Like many philanthropic endeavors, the founding of waqfs was a means to preserve social hierarchies and cultural norms. For the most part, endowments funded activities that reinforced the dominant values of a society: the place of religion and ritual; the accepted curriculum of study and the goal of education; the physical shape of cities; the conventional practice of medicine; the preservation of family wealth; and the status of the poor as poor and dependent. Much of the poor relief distributed through waqfs was aimed at supplying subsistence or relief rather than what is today called development aid. Much good work was accomplished, but it did not have radical aims such as the redistribution of wealth, the promotion of general literacy, or the eradication of need.

The waqfs were flexible enough to accommodate a wide variety of particularistic aims while enjoying legal sanctity and protection. They could accommodate and serve both religious and secular motives, even stretching the limits of the law, as in the case of Christian or cash endowments, or serving to circumvent them, as with regard to inheritance. The establishment of charitable endowments served religious beliefs, altruistic and more selfish human instincts, perhaps all equally well, which may help to explain the popularity

---

[115] Nina Ergin, "Taking Care of Imarets: Repairs and Renovations to the Atik Valide İmareti, Istanbul, circa 1600–1700," in *Feeding People, Feeding Power*, ed. Ergin *et al.*, 151–67.

of endowments as a form of charitable giving.[116] Many contemporary states in the Muslim world preserve the legacies of past philanthropy effected through waqf. These physical remains are only the most obvious traces of earlier waqf making. Equally important are other kinds of legacies. An intellectual legacy remains in the form of long traditions of scholarship and rich library collections. In economic terms, where prevalent, waqfs created and reinforced systems of property relations and urban commercial organization. As they modernized, Islamic societies have almost all been mindful of existing endowments and have allowed for the establishment of new ones, either in their traditional form or within the context of foundation or trust laws.[117]

Waqfs were only one aspect of voluntary giving, which stretches to a vast range of activity. The waqfs are conveniently conspicuous, perhaps so much so that they distract attention from other important institutions. As discussed in the first part of this chapter, even without a legal framework like waqf to structure it, much voluntary giving can be considered formal and institutionalized because it comes at predictable times and places, perhaps even in predictable quality or quantity. Yet much charity remained spontaneous and unpredictable, even if ubiquitous: handouts to beggars in the street, help to sick neighbors, contributions in supplication for a speedy return to health or to mark that recovery, and donations of thanks for good fortune.

People who lacked the property or funds to make endowments were still able to give. No one was excluded from this possibility, even those at the very bottom of the economic scale. Postel recounted that in his travels he learned that the proper reply to the hospitality offered by people along one's way was to ask for "God's blessings on them in recompense."[118] To ensure that even people of few means found a place in a community created not only by belief and shared ritual, but also through ties of voluntary giving, numerous hadiths reminded everyone that people who possessed little or nothing could invoke God's blessings on others. In fact, Muslim tradition allowed for the possibility that a large number of common daily actions might be considered as sadaqa, feasible for any Muslim.[119]

Informal voluntary giving has few legal restrictions or requirements and so is far easier than paying zakat or making a waqf. Any amount can be given, of

---

[116] For additional discussions of motives for waqf making, see, for example, Lambton, "Awqaf in Persia" and Lev, "Charity and Social Practice,"475–86.

[117] Amy Singer, "Charity's Legacies: A Reconsideration of Ottoman Imperial Endowment Making," in *Poverty and Charity*, ed. Bonner *et al.*, 304–10; Peters *et al.*, "*wakf*," 78–81, 97–99, and *passim*.

[118] Postel, *De la République des Turcs*, 59.

[119] See the hadith quoted at the opening of this chapter, and also the list of acts considered sadaqa, as described in Muslim b. al-Ḥajjāj al-Nisābūrī, *Al-Jāmiʿ al-Ṣaḥīḥ*, 3:482; Muslim, *Ṣaḥīḥ Muslim*, 482–83; USC-MSA, Muslim 5 (zakat), 2198.

almost anything, at any time, in any place, to any appropriate person, including members of the family as well as neighbors and strangers. From the simplest blessing to the most magnificent building, anyone can participate and contribute to strengthening the Muslim community by contributing to its welfare in some way. Sadaqa is a far more flexible and adaptable instrument than zakat. A donor may choose a precise purpose, and structure giving according to personal preferences or goals. Zakat, despite being obligatory, does not offer nearly as many additional and tangible benefits to the donor.

Zakat al-fitr presents an interesting contrast to zakat, since it seems to have endured more publicly than zakat over time, practiced everywhere. Why would this be so? Is it because the minimum amount is smaller than regular zakat and because it falls due in the holy month of Ramadan? Did willingness to pay have to do with the communal nature of some Ramadan break fasts and the 'Id al-Fitr holiday celebrations? Have communities historically taken a larger role in enforcing the collection of zakat al-fitr? Calculating zakat al-fitr is also less complicated than assessing zakat, with a fixed rate for everyone. Nor are there any competing obligations to zakat al-fitr, like the state taxes that existed alongside zakat. Perhaps, however, in emphasizing a legal distinction between zakat and sadaqa we have lost sight of the fact that the functional and social distinctions may not always be so clear.

A final question to consider with respect to voluntary charity is whether donors really were free to make independent decisions regarding the philanthropic use of their wealth. The waqfs discussed in this chapter seem most often to be conventional within the context of their times. Donors, at least at the upper end of the economic scale, varied the size and scope of their projects without straying far from the philanthropy of their peers, acting within relatively fixed and expected parameters. Philanthropy, to be most effective for donor and recipient, needs to occur in a known idiom, one easily comprehensible and so appreciated by both those it aims to serve and those it is intended to impress. Shifts in the nature of philanthropic giving and institutions, therefore, may be read as signs of other changes in society and culture.[120] Although we usually ascribe donation decisions to individual conscience and preference, in fact such decisions are equally if not more likely to be the product of individual volition as shaped by structural norms, cultural practices, and immediate circumstances, including family decisions, urgent need, and fashion. Mauss' analysis of gift-giving suggested that in the repeated cycle of giving and receiving, givers and recipients are obliged to play their parts or endure the repercussions, which may include forfeit of power and status, on the one hand, or of protection and favors on the other. Zahavi's view of the altruistic impulse also implied that giving is a

---

[120] For the specific question of motivation, see Cavallo, "The Motivations of Benefactors," 46–62, especially 54–60.

necessary aspect of power relations, and not really optional for whoever is engaged in them. In his animal world, opting out of the altruistic giver–recipient relationship is probably suicidal, either immediately or genetically. For humans, ostracism may not be fatal, but its impact can have varied and sometimes negative implications. The Qur'an and hadith together send a clear message to Muslims that the choice to do sadaqa is one they can ill afford to ignore. Given the human tendency to err, whether through unintentional blunders or purposeful omissions, sadaqa becomes a crucial means for redressing one's personal balance sheet before God. Sadaqa, however, is not only a powerful corrective; it is also an external sign of a good Muslim, one who looks out for the well-being of family, neighbors, and Muslims in general, and so contributes to establishing reputation and status in a community.

The imperial response to the threat of famine in Mamluk Cairo illustrates this idea clearly. The local food economy there was based on two major dynamics. First, peasants in this tributary economy paid taxes in kind and cash to the central government; the sultan redistributed foodstuffs as patronage to his officials. Second, foodstuffs were sold to most of the city's population in the Cairo markets as part of the larger urban economy. When they occurred, Cairo's food shortages and famines resulted from low annual flood levels of the Nile and the resulting low crop yields, or else from the hoarding that took place in anticipation of shortages. In the event of real or anticipated shortages, the sultan responded by opening the state granaries and forcing grain or bread distributions at low prices or for free to the poor of Cairo. Stockpiling grain against low flood years was a habit of Cairo's rulers, stretching back to Pharaonic times, and it emphasized their dependence on the fluctuating annual Nile flood levels. Yet, even in good times, Cairo's rulers were obliged to distribute food to some number of the urban poor, preserving their own status and reputation. Together with the distributions to officials and amirs, they were thus running a food distribution operation parallel to that of the market, one that fueled an economy of patronage and beneficence. In emergencies, the sultans obliged those who had earlier enjoyed their patronage to redirect some of what they had received to others further down the food chain. The sultan might assign several hundred poor people to each of his officials and amirs, who were then responsible for feeding them for the duration of the crisis.[121]

As in some other examples cited previously, here again the distinction between hospitality or patronage and charity was fuzzy, seemingly defined by the class of the recipient, not necessarily the essence of the act. All these distributions enabled their recipients to maintain themselves in a style commensurate with their habits and expectations, a legitimate goal of charity as

---

[121] Boaz Shoshan, *Popular Culture in Medieval Cairo* (Cambridge, UK: Cambridge University Press, 1993); Sabra, *Poverty and Charity*, 138–66.

inferred from descriptions of who could be counted as poor.[122] For the one the goal was subsistence, for the other comfortable luxury. Those who fell into the latter category, however, were expected to open their storehouses and convert their wealth into charitable distributions if circumstances required. Such actions were not without their rewards, however, for they could in turn be counted as acts of sadaqa, worthy of God's recognition.

The situation in Cairo has been characterized as reflecting the "moral economy" of the medieval city, recalling the thesis articulated by historian E. P. Thompson. Thompson proposed that culturally shaped moral norms could influence economic decision-making at the expense of profit. In the Mamluk case, Cairo's populace had certain expectations about how the grain markets should operate, and about the role of rulers in intervening to correct abuses or responding to shortages. Failure to react according to expectations could provoke popular unrest and violent reactions.[123] Historical chronicles make clear that the Mamluk sultan took an active role in persuading his amirs to make distributions when necessary. This suggests a line of investigation that might be opened in the Ottoman context. Ottoman pashas and viziers, those who profited most from their regular wages, a share in the booty of Ottoman conquests, and imperial gifts, were active patrons in the empire. To what extent were their donations and waqfs made according to independent decisions, and to what extent did sultans play some role in "apportioning beneficence" among Ottoman subjects? Mapping the establishment of waqfs with this question in mind may reveal additional dynamics in the changing relationships between rulers, members of the elites, and the broader population. More difficult still to understand are the individual reactions or emotions of the recipients to their benefactors and to the distributions themselves. To what extent did notions of obligation and entitlement not derived from the Islamic ritual being celebrated shape the expectations and behavior of donors and recipients alike? These questions will be addressed further in chapters 3 and 4.

---

[122] See the discussion in al-Ghazālī, *Kitāb Asrār al-Zakāh*, 291–93; Faris, *Mysteries of Almsgiving*, 53–60; and the more extensive discussion of poverty and the poor in chapter 4.

[123] Shoshan, *Popular Culture*, 52–66; E. P. Thompson, "The Moral Economy of the English Crowd in the Eighteenth Century," *Past and Present* 50 (1971): 76–136; Adam Sabra, " 'Prices are in God's Hands': The Theory and Practice of Price Control in the Medieval Islamic World," in *Poverty and Charity*, ed. Bonner *et al.*, 73–91. The *Oxford English Dictionary* defines moral economy as "the regulation of moral or ethical behaviour; an economic system in which moral issues, such as social justice, influence fiscal policy or money matters." Michael Bonner raises the notion of a moral economy in his discussion of the meaning of poverty and almsgiving in the earliest Islamic period, emphasizing the idea of redistributing surplus, on which see Michael Bonner, "Definitions of Poverty and the Rise of the Muslim Urban Poor," *Journal of the Royal Asiatic Society* 6, 3rd series (1996): 335–44.

3   The upper hand

The upper hand is better than the lower one, the upper being the one that gives and the lower the one that begs.[1]

In the Prophet's time an unbeliever was brought to be executed. They struck him with a sword several times but it was of no avail. The Prophet was astonished.

Gabriel appeared, saying, "God commands (you thus): 'He gives alms to the poor; he is a generous man; leave him alone.' " So the Prophet left him alone.[2]

Be known for wealth, not for poverty.[3]

Weighing in

The present chapter examines individual donors to explore how charitable acts were integrated to biographical accounts as part of the portrait of ideal lives. The painting on the cover of this book, *Emperor Jahangir Weighing his Son Khurram in Gold*, depicts the weighing ceremony that the Muslim Mughal emperors adapted from local Hindu culture. As practiced by the Mughals, it was the custom to weigh the sultans and princes on their birthdays, loading them on to one side of a huge balance while on the other were placed, each in succession, gold, silver, silk, perfume, copper, iron, butter, starch, salt, grains, rice, or other commodities. The amounts balanced in the scales were then distributed to the poor. In the painting, small red sacks of coins are being added to balance the weight of Prince Khurram (the future Shah Jahan). Trays of gifts to the prince are displayed on the ground in front of the scales.

One seventeenth-century Mughal author set down an explanation of the weighing practice during the reign of Shah Jahan (1628–58) and its origins in the reign of Jahan's grandfather, Akbar (1556–1605), in the following words:

---

[1] Al-Bukhārī, *Ṣaḥīḥ al-Bukhārī*, 24 (zakat), bab 18; 55 (wasaya), bab 2; USC-MSA, Bukhari, 24/508–509; 51/5.
[2] Meisami, *The Sea of Precious Virtues*, 78.
[3] Popular saying in eighteenth-century Aleppo, quoted in Marcus, *The Middle East on the Eve of Modernity*, 50.

Since it is His Majesty's custom and habit to have beggars sought out, and his generous nature is always looking for a pretext to relieve those who are in need, therefore twice a year he sits, like the orient sun in majesty, in the pan of the scale of auspiciousness in the solar and lunar weighing ceremonies. Twice a year by solar and lunar calculation a magnificent celebration and a large-scale banquet is arranged by order of His Majesty. An amount equal to his weight in gold and silver is distributed among the destitute and the poor according to their deservedness and merits. Although this type of alms is not mentioned in the [Muslim] religious law, nonetheless since scholars of this country are all in agreement that such alms are the most perfect type of alms for repelling corporeal and spiritual catastrophes and calamities, therefore this pleasing method was chosen and established by His Majesty Arsh-Ashyani [Akbar], whose personality was, like the world-illuminating sun, based upon pure effulgence. By this means the poor attained their wishes, and in truth the custom of *aqiqa* – which is an established custom in the law of the Prophet and his Companions, and in which on the seventh day after birth the equivalent weight of an infant's shaven hair in silver is given in alms, and a sacrificial animal is divided and distributed among the poor – has opened the way to making this custom permissible ... In short, from that time forward this praiseworthy act has become usual and customary in this mighty empire. The princes are also weighed once a solar year.[4]

Weighing people to set the size of their contributions pre-dated Muslim rule in the Indian subcontinent and has continued down to this day in a practice called *tulabhara* or *tulabharam* among Hindu men and women.[5] Muslim jurists in Mughal India allowed the imperial weighing to continue by associating it to the 'aqiqa ceremony (mentioned in chapter 2) as an immediate precedent for adopting the Hindu practice. The original aim of the ceremonies – to prevent spiritual and material disasters – was interpreted by Muslim scholars at the Mughal court to accord with their understanding of charitable good works. Using a person's weight to define the size of their charitable donation was not unknown in Islamic societies of the Middle East. For example, the Mamluk sultan Al-Ashraf Barsbay (d. 1438) donated his son's weight in silver to the poor in hopes that he would recover from a serious illness.[6]

The Mughal painting clearly shows the prince dressed in gorgeous clothes and jewels as he sits in the scales.[7] This impressive aspect of his appearance was

---

[4] From the seventeenth-century author Muhammad Salih Kanbo, *'Amal-i Salih or Shahjahannama*, ed. Wahid Quraishi, 2nd edn., 3 vols. (Lahore, 1967–72), as quoted in M. C. Beach and E. Koch, *King of the World: The Padshahnama* (London: Thames and Hudson, 1997), 39.

[5] T. B. Birchall, "Notes and Queries: The Weight in Gold of the Maharjah given to the Poor," *The Folk-Lore Journal* 3 (1885), 280–81; Edgar Thurston, *The Madras Presidency with Mysore, Coorg, and the Associated States* (Cambridge, UK: Cambridge University Press, 1913), 4. The newspaper announcement of a ceremony held in December 2004 (www.hinduonnet.com/2004/12/03/stories/2004120303250300.htm, accessed January 30, 2007) is only one of hundreds of such notices easily found on the World Wide Web by searching "tulabhara" or "tulabharam."

[6] Sabra, *Poverty and Charity*, 58.

[7] One of these paintings is reproduced on the cover of this book. The other, *The Weighing of Shah-Jahan on his Forty-Second Lunar Birthday*, painted c.1635, in the manuscript of the *Padshahnama*, belonging to The Royal Library (Windsor Castle), can be found in Beach and Koch, *King of the World*, plates 12–13.

also emphasized by the Portuguese priest Sebastian Manrique, who described the weighing of the former prince, now Sultan Shah Jahan, in 1641:

> The Imperial Majesty came forth to attend this solemn function dressed in a white satin robe covered with most precious stones of many colours ... He also wore round his neck very rich collars of most valuable jewels; so that when I mentally summed up everything estimated I could only think that all this adornment must serve rather as a troublesome burden than an elegant ornament.[8]

The description emphasizes the immediate tactile and corporeal aspect of the weighing ceremony, which uses a royal body to define the scale of royal magnanimity. While the imperial personage was always arrayed to be impressive in public appearances, attired so as to reflect wealth and power, here the body was also dressed up to add further to its natural weight before being converted into measurable commodities. The things weighed were then distributed to recipients designated as worthy and needy, although their worthiness may not always have been purely a function of indigence. A later painting of Shah Jahan suggests that some of the recipients were religious scholars and courtiers, already known to be regular and valid recipients of charitable distributions in other Muslim societies.

For the Mughal sultans, there were obvious advantages to adopting an existing practice like the weighing ceremony. Since their subject population in the Indian subcontinent was not entirely Muslim, preserving the practice of weighing rulers incorporated a familiar action into Mughal ceremonial, perhaps demonstrating that the Islamization of India was not only foreign but also familiar. Moreover, the weighing ceremonies were good theatre, easily described and broadcast to a population already accustomed to their shape and meaning. Adopting ceremonial charitable practices that were easily "readable" by a target audience was good politics for a regime seeking legitimacy.[9] The ceremony also allowed a single act of charity to be divided into two distinct actions of giving and receiving. While the former could be emphatically public, the latter could be conducted with as much or as little discretion as desired.

It is not clear how far weighing was practiced by the ranks of Mughal officials and notables, Muslim or otherwise. Ibn Battuta told a story that suggested there were various ways of conducting weighing ceremonies for charitable purposes. The king of India during Ibn Battuta's stay there, renowned for his expansive generosity, once came to see a visitor who was unwell. He asked the ailing man

---

[8] Sebastian Manrique, *Travels of Fray Sebastian Manrique 1629–1643*, 2 vols. (Oxford, 1927), as quoted in Beach and Koch, *King of the World*, 42.

[9] For more on the idea of readability, see the discussion of aesthetics in Gülru Necipoğlu, "A *Kânûn* for the State, a Canon for the Arts: Conceptualizing the Classical Synthesis of Ottoman Arts and Architecture," in *Soliman le Magnifique et son temps*, ed. Gilles Veinstein (Paris: La Documentation Française, 1992), 195–216.

to sit on the balance he brought with him, encouraging him to put on as many garments as he wished. The king then balanced the man's weight with gold, and gave it to him saying: "Take this and give it in alms for your recovery."[10] The weighing ceremony, then, fixed a measure for charitable giving, while the things given served a variety of charitable purposes, familiar from other contexts. What Ibn Battuta described is noteworthy because it also explicitly articulated what we have only inferred elsewhere, such as with respect to Mamluk Cairo, namely, that some beneficent giving was intended to have a trickle-down effect, with the original recipients passing on the largesse they received to others. In this way, the sultan (or some other initial donor) enabled the first recipients to act beneficently and so obtain the benefits of giving charity – both spiritual and temporal – for themselves. Emulating their patrons, the recipient-donors gave to their own clients or selected needy persons to receive their beneficence. At the same time, this practice of apportioning the power of donation could take advantage of the individual knowledge of less wealthy donors so as to reach more and worthy recipients. The story illustrates another point, to which we will return later; that is, that many people (perhaps most) were by turns donors and recipients, sitting neither at the top nor at the bottom of a vertical hierarchy.

Ceremonies similar to those of the Mughals were held in the first half of the twentieth century by the late Sir Sultan Mahomed Shah Aga Khan (1877–1957), leader of the Isma'ilis. While a comprehensive history of weighing in its general Islamic and specifically Isma'ili contexts remains to be written, one might speculate that the Isma'ilis were inspired to adopt the ceremony after the Nizari Isma'ili community fled from Iran to India in 1843. The Aga Khan was weighed in the successive jubilee years of his reign against gold, diamonds, and platinum contributed by members of the Isma'ili community from around the world. The fortune collected each time was donated to support an array of social and cultural services organized within the community itself and for needy people around the world. Photos of the diamond jubilee capture the full figure of this man as he sits in an armchair on a huge scale watching the cases of diamonds placed on the opposite balance. These weighing ceremonies have not continued under Prince Karim al-Husayni, the present Aga Khan. Today, the philanthropic traditions of the Isma'ili community are embodied in the Aga Khan Development Network, a private fund supporting health, culture, rural, and economic development around the world through a broad variety of programs.[11]

---

[10] Gibb, *Ibn Battuta*, vol. II, 312.

[11] On the history of the Isma'ilis, see Daftary, *The Ismā'īlīs*. For photographs of the Aga Khan diamond jubilee, see "Weighing the Aga Khan in Diamonds," *National Geographic Magazine* (March 1947), 317–24. On the Aga Khan Development Network and its component funds, see www.akdn.org (accessed February 15, 2007).

The images described above are very far from the recommendations for anonymous and discreet charity found in the Qur'an and hadith, and the scholarly commentaries on Muslim law and practice discussed in earlier chapters of this book. However, they may be closer to a popular imagining of imperial wealth and beneficence. Indeed, just as sultans and other leaders often demonstrated their strength with parades of soldiers, they and their consorts also displayed their wealth in imperial processions and sometimes performed charity with equal pomp and publicity.

The history of charity often takes prominent donors as a point of departure. The lives of the wealthy are more thoroughly documented than those of more modest people because the sum total of their lifetime activities produced more documents – legal, commercial, financial, aesthetic – and also because they were more likely to be the subject of writings by their contemporaries, some of whom were sponsored by wealthy donors themselves. Records of beneficent giving can be found in written and graphic histories, as well as in built monuments and crafted items, because the gifts themselves often survived as physical testimony to the beneficence of their patrons. The Bimaristan al-Nuri (1154), the hospital built by Nur al-Din b. al-Zangi in Damascus, the Ibn Tulun mosque, or the hospital complex of the Mamluk sultan Al-Mansur Qalawun (1284–85) in Cairo are just as evocative of their patrons as are Carnegie Hall in New York City and Balliol College in Oxford.[12] At the same time, as discussed earlier, every Muslim is supposed to give something, even if he or she can afford only to wish a neighbor well or simply to act according to the fundamental prescription of the Qur'an to command the right and forbid the wrong.[13] Modest donors (and recipients), far more numerous than sultans or the super-wealthy, have been less prominent and less frequently recorded as individuals in historical memory, even if they were readily visible to their immediate community of contemporaries.

In theory, Allah is the source of all wealth and therefore the true benefactor of any charitable act; at the same time, belief in Allah and adherence to the teachings of the Qur'an are the true motivation for all beneficence. This spiritual calculus, discussed in chapter 1, holds giver and recipient as equally valued in any act of charitable giving. However, the hadith from which the title of this chapter is taken tells a different story. In it, the ideal vision of equal and reciprocal roles for giver and receiver is replaced by a clear preference for the giver. Moreover, despite the stories about pious people who gave away all their

---

[12] An excellent resource for images of these buildings is www.archnet.org, which includes an extensive on-line database of information and images of the built environment of Muslim cultures.

[13] On this fundamental concept, see Michael Cook, *Commanding Right and Forbidding Wrong in Islamic Thought* (Cambridge, UK: Cambridge University Press, 2001).

wealth, different Muslim texts admonish people not to beggar themselves or their families through their beneficent giving. The obligation to support one's family is fundamental – the family is a legitimate target of sadaqa (though not of zakat) – and family members should not suffer a decline in their status or standard of living as a result of donations made to others.[14] At the same time, however, the lives of ascetic saints and sufis were also written as models of beneficence, and some authors applauded them for giving away all their material possessions in the quest for spiritual wealth, believing that material poverty and even the humiliation of begging were a necessary experience on the road to achieving a closer understanding of God. Altogether, the different attitudes to the proper and permissible extent of charitable actions reflect the wide spectrum of Islamic thought that emerged over several centuries, influenced by internal dissent over theology and practice, as well as by external models like that of the Christian ascetics.

Because charity is a very different experience for giver and recipient, the present chapter focuses on givers while the next looks at recipients. The two parties play distinct, yet related, roles in charitable giving. However, givers do not always require a specific recipient in order to make a donation. Previous chapters examined charitable giving as part of a belief system and explored the motivations and results of obligatory and voluntary giving. Now, the lives of specific individuals depict the central role of philanthropy in shaping identity and status. The charity of sultans, imperial women, high-ranking office-holders, and powerful local figures will be considered in light of the responsibilities and expectations of office or status, where rank often presupposed beneficent action. The identification of an individual with his or her status created ambiguities between the individual and the office or station he or she held, particularly when considering the motivations and means for undertaking charitable acts. It is individuals who most capture our attention, because only in the later nineteenth and twentieth centuries, did the relative importance of individuals decline with the formation of government agencies and non-governmental associations (to be discussed in chapter 5).

Written biographies emerged relatively early in Islamic literary tradition owing to the prominence of hadiths as an authoritative reference for Muslim practice and the need to verify the transmitters of individual traditions in order to ascertain the soundness of these accounts of the life and deeds of the Prophet. Over time, biography became one of the central literary genres of Islamic societies. The first collections from the mid-ninth century focused almost exclusively on religious scholars, but from the later tenth century a more diverse array of people, including rulers, scholars, artists, and even bureaucrats, were

---

[14] Al-Bukhārī, *Ṣaḥīḥ al-Bukhārī*, 55 (al-wasaya), bab 2; USC-MSA, Bukhari, 51/5.

included in specialized biographical dictionaries. These biographies became "the crucial building blocks of Islamic moral traditions" and the lives of exemplary pious individuals were studied because they embodied models of behavior and values.[15] Magnanimity became the mark of some individuals, who served as paradigms to be emulated (but perhaps never equalled) in later eras.

The individual lives in this chapter portray charitable giving as a social good in Muslim communities. The paintings of Khurram/Shah Jahan capture the grandeur of the prince and emperor, as well as illustrating how his wealth was assessed in order to be given away to those in need. However, the Prophet Muhammad is the obvious place to begin this discussion, since his life in all its details became the paradigm of proper comportment for all Muslims. The Prophet's biography leaves no doubt as to the central role that charitable giving between members of the young community must have played in sustaining it in its earliest days in Mecca and after the hijra to Medina. Muhammad's first followers faced many difficulties, challenging the prevailing religious ethos as well as becoming a threat to the dominant social and, ultimately, political hierarchy. There were those among the group who probably cut themselves off from family resources and social networks by joining with Muhammad, and although the Prophet attracted additional adherents after the hijra and his increasing military successes, the original Muslim community seems to have relied on voluntary contributions as well as on tribute or taxes of various kinds. Social realities may thus have contributed to the Qur'anic emphasis on almsgiving as a companion to prayer to serve as a visible demonstration of adherence to the new faith. Muhammad's personal history as an orphan seems to have contributed further to the stress laid on beneficence to orphans and widows. In the broader cultural perspective, the pre-Islamic Arabian emphasis on generosity and hospitality was incorporated into the Qur'an and recast in terms of the new faith.[16]

The life of the Prophet Muhammad as sketched in the Qur'an and elaborated in the hadiths and in his biography (*sira*) has become a fundamental point of reference for all Muslim belief and practice. As we saw in previous chapters, these texts furnish the guidelines for obligatory almsgiving as well as the rules and recommendations for additional charitable undertakings. Muhammad's personal generosity, as well as that of his family and companions, stands as a paradigm for charitable giving. Many examples from hadith highlight the constant, sometimes urgent character of the Prophet's giving. For example, it is said that Muhammad never missed an occasion to give nor did he delay

---

[15] Humphreys, *Islamic History*, 187–208; Nimrod Hurvitz, "Biographies and Mild Asceticism: A Study of Islamic Moral Imagination," *Studia Islamica* 85 (1997): 64–65.

[16] W. Montgomery Watt, *Muhammad at Medina* (Oxford: Oxford University Press, 1956), *passim*; Bonner, "Poverty and Charity in the Rise of Islam."

giving. 'Uqba b. al-Harith reported: "Once the Prophet offered the 'Asr (late afternoon) prayer and then hurriedly went to his house and returned immediately. I . . . spoke to him and he said, 'I left a piece of gold at home which was from the charity and I did not like to let it remain a night in my house, so I had it distributed.' "[17] After seeing to his own families and dependants, the Prophet devoted his resources to charity: "The Prophet said, 'My heirs will not inherit a dinar, for whatever I leave, after the sustenance of my wives and the wages of my employees, is given in charity.' "[18] Together with the emphasis on beneficence, the Prophet is also portrayed as someone who did not run from or despise poverty. He accepted no alms for himself of any kind, either zakat or sadaqa, and his family was barred from accepting zakat.

Charity seems to have been, at various times, a necessary component in the biography of a successful ruler, perhaps of any notable, and so we examine two sovereigns – Muzaffar al-Din (d. 1233), ruler of Irbil, and Abu 'Inan (d. 1358), Marinid ruler of Morocco. The royal patronesses Zubayda (d. 831) and Hurrem Sultan (d. 1558), although controversial figures, were both remembered for their charitable undertakings as well. Members of elite groups who were not part of the ruling dynasty in their societies usually controlled more limited and fluctuating resources than sovereigns. Melek Ahmed Pasha has already provided one example of this. The Moroccan traveler Ibn Battuta (d. c.1368) and Mehmed Ağa (d. c.1623), architect of the famous Blue Mosque in Istanbul, were men whose status afforded them significant means; their stories depict the beneficence of men of learning and skill. Finally, the lives of saints and sufis as they appear in biographies and hagiographies describe the charity of the pious poor.

Muzaffar al-Din

One of the most renowned biographical collections, and the first to cover a general list of distinguished men other than scholars, was written by Ahmad b. Muhammad b. Khallikan (1211–82).[19] He was born in Irbil, southeast of Mosul, moved to Aleppo and Damascus to continue his studies, and worked in Cairo and Damascus, where he ultimately died. In his *Wafayat al-a'yan wa anba abna al-zaman* (Deaths of Notables and Information on Contemporaries) Ibn Khallikan included only famous people whose date of death he could determine. Because he thought adequate information was available on all of them elsewhere, he excluded the companions of the Prophet, the caliphs, and the second generation of hadith transmitters.[20]

---

[17] Al-Bukhārī, *Ṣaḥīḥ al-Bukhārī* 24 (al-zakat), bab 20; USC-MSA, Bukhari, 24/510.
[18] Al-Bukhārī, *Ṣaḥīḥ al-Bukhārī* 55 (al-wasaya), bab 32; USC-MSA, Bukhari, 51/37.
[19] Humphreys, *Islamic History*, 188.   [20] J. W. Fück, "Ibn Khallikān," in *EI*², III:832–33.

Among the biographies written by Ibn Khallikan is that of one Muzaffar al-Din, known as Gökburi or Kukuburi (d. 1233). Muzaffar al-Din was born in Mosul and succeeded his father as ruler of the city of Irbil at age fourteen; he was subsequently imprisoned, and then left the city when his younger brother managed to oust him from power. He next entered the service of Saladin (d. 1193), who was sufficiently impressed to make him governor of the cities of Urfa and Harran (in southeastern Turkey) in recompense for his services, as well as to marry Muzaffar al-Din to his own sister, Rabi'a Khatun. In particular, Muzaffar al-Din earned his reputation for an extraordinary performance at the decisive defeat of the Crusaders at the battle of Hittin (1187). Following this victory and the death of his brother, Muzaffar al-Din asked to be reinstated at Irbil, a request which Saladin granted. Returning there in 1191, Muzaffar al-Din made that city his home until his death more than forty years later.

Ibn Khallikan did not write at great length about Muzaffar al-Din's military exploits, and did not mention any further military activity during the period of his rule over Irbil. In fact, the bulk of Ibn Khallikan's biography is given over to a long and detailed description of the charitable works of Muzaffar al-Din, who is introduced thus: "as to the proceedings which mark his character, we may say that, in works of charity (khayrat), he performed what no single man was ever known to have done before."[21] Muzaffar al-Din's days were regularly punctuated by acts of charity, beginning with distributions made before and after the first morning prayers, including giving out bread to needy persons around the city. His week was similarly organized: on Mondays and Thursdays he personally visited the facilities he had built for the blind and chronically ill, greeting each resident. He also regularly toured the hospice for widows, the orphanage, and the foundling home, as well as his other foundations, often making additional donations directly to residents during these visits.[22] The list goes on. Muzaffar al-Din founded a guesthouse for visiting jurists, dervishes, and others, where each received two meals a day and an allowance when resuming his journey. Shafi'i and Hanafi scholars taught at the madrasa he founded and he would sometimes join them for dinner and stay to hear religious music afterwards. Two sufi convents established by him were provided with generous endowments to ensure their continuous functioning, furnishing, and provisions for residents and guests. These, too, he visited regularly.

In addition to buildings in Irbil, Muzaffar al-Din also funded the redemption of Muslim captives and granted assistance to any of them who arrived at his court. He annually sent money to sustain the needy pilgrims on the hajj and the poor of Mecca and Medina. In and around Mecca, Muzaffar al-Din established

---

[21] Ibn Khāllikān, *Biographical Dictionary*, vol. II, 537.
[22] Before the end of the nineteenth century, there is no other evidence for the existence of orphanages as a separate type of institution. R. Shaham, "yatim," in *EI²*, XI:300.

buildings, fountains, and a tomb structure for himself. (Ironically, after his death, his own body never reached Mecca because the caravan bearing it turned back for lack of water.) Finally, as noted in the previous chapter, Muzaffar al-Din sponsored annual celebrations of the Prophet's birthday, described by Ibn Khallikan as beginning from the month of Muharram and continuing in a crescendo of activity until the actual festival evening two months later on the twelfth day of Rabi' al-Awwal. Muzaffar al-Din erected facilities to house all the visiting celebrants and entertainers, and provided an enormous public feast for the poor.[23]

Ibn Khallikan asserted the veracity of all he recounted, claiming to have witnessed everything, presumably during his own youth in Irbil. Muzaffar al-Din died when Ibn Khallikan was twenty-two, by which time the latter had left Irbil to study in Aleppo. We might be a bit skeptical of Ibn Khallikan's assertion that he "has avoided even the slightest exaggeration," because Muzaffar al-Din was the patron of both Ibn Khallikan and Ibn Khallikan's father, a fact which Ibn Khallikan stated clearly.[24] What is less obvious is that Muzaffar al-Din's biography was unusual in the extent to which Ibn Khallikan dwelt on his patron's good works, far more than in his biographies of more illustrious individuals like Saladin and the other Ayyubid princes. Ibn Khallikan also did not specify the source of Muzaffar al-Din's resources for all of his undertakings. Some part of his wealth must have derived from the booty he earned during his earlier military career, but there is no mention of local taxes and fees that may also have fed his treasury.

We are, however, less concerned with the absolute truth of what Ibn Khallikan had to say about Muzaffar al-Din's life than with how he chose to memorialize it. The portrait drawn was that of an exemplary Muslim, just, generous, and a successful warrior for the faith against the infidels. This biography was a tribute from a loyal subject and a personal client. Those who benefited regularly from Muzaffar al-Din's good works can be categorized as the poor and needy, students and scholars (like Ibn Khallikan himself), debtors, sufis, travelers, and captives, notably representing six of the eight categories specified in the Qur'an as zakat recipients (excluding the zakat collectors and "those whose hearts should be reconciled"). The descriptions of Muzaffar al-Din's philanthropic actions were intended to impress readers (or listeners), and his life was narrated as a model for other rulers. Ibn Khallikan's text articulated expectations, commenting implicitly on the nature of sovereignty and setting standards of imperial behavior. He constructed buildings to serve the public welfare and provided food, clothing, and shelter. Since the Qur'anic injunctions regarding charity give few if any details of how exactly assistance should be

---

[23] Ibn Khāllikān, *Biographical Dictionary*, II:537–40.
[24] Ibn Khāllikān, *Biographical Dictionary*, II:541.

given, biographies such as this one became important because they illustrate how the commands were interpreted, at least by one particular donor (and his biographer).

No less important than the charitable works he accomplished were the things Muzaffar al-Din did not do. He apparently built no mosques or baths. Although he did found one madrasa, he seems to have invested more resources in facilities for sufis and for the weak and needy than for scholars and students. These choices may reveal something of the social composition of the town of Irbil, the nature of its competing political factions, and the character of local religiosity and religious practice. Was Muzaffar al-Din more comfortable in the company of sufi dervishes than that of learned legal scholars? The establishment of dervish lodges by local amirs in the thirteenth-century Anatolian towns of Tokat and Sivas replaced the imperial Seljuq patronage of mosques and madrasas; these shifting forms of patronage signaled the reliance of the up-and-coming amirs on the dervishes and the shift of power away from the Seljuq rulers based in Konya.[25] The many madrasas established by Mamluk sultans, on the other hand, were important in garnering and sustaining necessary support for their rule from the ʿulama.[26] Muzaffar al-Din's emphasis on facilities for sufis and celebrations of a more popular kind all suggest that either the learned mosque-based ʿulama were not a central component of local spiritual authority and Muslim practice in Irbil or for some reason they had failed to attract the patronage of the town's ruler.[27] However, Ibn Khallikan's biography alone does not explain fully the nature of Muzaffar al-Din's charity in Irbil. Nor does it tell us anything about the charitable practices of local notables, merchants, and craftsmen, or the population of women, children, and unskilled laborers. Charity as practiced below the top tier of society remains a complete enigma in this text, as in most. Moreover, even though the town was an active Christian center, Ibn Khallikan gave no evidence of Christian charitable works or the inclusion of Christian beneficiaries in Muzaffar al-Din's own philanthropy.

Ibn Battuta and Abu ʿInan

Among medieval Muslim travelers of renown was Ibn Battuta (d. c.1368), who left Tangiers in June 1325 and returned to Sijilmasa in 1353 after having journeyed across North Africa through the Middle East and Central Asia, including to India and the East Indies, as far as the cosmopolitan port of Zaytun (Quanzhou) in China. Upon his return, at the request of the Marinid

---

[25] Ethel Sara Wolper, "The Politics of Patronage: Political Change and the Construction of Dervish Lodges in Sivas," *Muqarnas* 12 (1995): 39–47.

[26] See the discussions in Berkey, *The Transmission of Knowledge.*

[27] D. Sourdel, "Irbil," *EI*², IV:76.

ruler of Morocco, Abu 'Inan (d. 1358), Ibn Battuta dictated an account of his travels to the scholar Ibn Juzayy (d. *c*.1355–7).[28] Ibn Battuta's account contributed three important perspectives to the discussion of individuals and philanthropy in Islamic contexts: his descriptions of his own charitable acts, the extensive beneficence he enjoyed as a traveler, and, finally, the generosity of his patron, Abu 'Inan. Travelers, as explained in chapter 1, constitute one category of legitimate recipients of sadaqa because they are considered to be vulnerable strangers, lacking the ready home support network of friends and family. (Recall that Muzaffar al-Din built a guesthouse for scholars, dervishes, and others.) Ibn Battuta will reappear in chapter 4, since most of his accounts of great charity find him on the receiving end. Yet his account is another reminder that most people did not live at the extremes of wealth or poverty, nor could they be characterized either as very generous or stingy. In the course of a lifetime many were donors and recipients by turns or even at the same time.

Only during the period when he found employment as a high official in the court of the sultan of Delhi did Ibn Battuta have the capital to undertake the kinds of large donations he had hitherto praised in others. In Delhi, he built a mosque opposite his own house. He was also charged to oversee the building of the mausoleum of Sultan Qutb al-Din (1316–20) and its endowment, which supported daily food allocations to the salaried employees of the tomb and its visitors, as well as distributions of famine relief to the broader population and food for the poor and dignitaries on holidays.[29] Ibn Battuta also recounted the responsibilities assigned to officials during a drought-induced famine. The sultan ordered:

> that the inhabitants of Dihlī [Delhi] should be given an allowance of food at the rate of a pound and a half per person per day. The vizier assembled them and distributed the indigent inhabitants amongst the amirs and qāḍīs so that these latter should be responsible for supplying them with food. My share of them [the indigents] was five hundred souls; I built for them galleries in two houses and lodged them there, and I used to give them provisions for five days every five days.[30]

This practice of the ruler of Delhi recalls the organization of famine relief in Mamluk Egypt in the same period. Here again, food distributions may not always have been considered sadaqa by the ruler who ordered them, by the notables who carried them out, or even by the recipients. However, just as we have noted intersections between charity and hospitality, these distributions illustrate the indistinct boundaries between different forms of giving. Ibn

---

[28] On Ibn Battuta and his travels, including a discussion of whether he actually went to China, see Ross E. Dunn, *The Adventures of Ibn Battuta: A Muslim Traveler of the 14th Century* (Berkeley: University of California Press, 1986).

[29] P. Hardy, "Dihlī Sultanate," *EI²*, II: 267–69. Gibb, *Ibn Battuta*, vol. III, 760–61.

[30] Gibb, *Ibn Battuta*, vol. IV, 789.

Battuta did not say much of smaller acts of generosity which he may have undertaken, even when he was not very well-off, but perhaps to speak of these would have been an unacceptable form of boasting.

More than recounting his own endeavors, Ibn Battuta focused on those of people who helped him. His description of his patron, Abu 'Inan, recalls Ibn Khallikan's biography of Muzaffar al-Din. Having expounded at length on the philanthropic deeds of rulers and ordinary people alike whom he met during his twenty-five years on the road, Ibn Battuta had to draw a portrait of his patron's beneficence that was not inferior to these.

> As for the stream of alms he [Abu 'Inan] dispenses and the hospices he has ordered to be built throughout his domains to provide food for all who come and go, that is something which no other king has done except the Sultan Atabak Ahmad, and our master, God strengthen him, is his superior in giving food to the poor every day and in giving grain to those hermits who hide themselves away.[31]

Not surprisingly, in each comparison with his eastern experiences, Ibn Battuta invariably found a reason to prefer Abu 'Inan's benefactions and endowments as superior. In fact, after reading the lengthy description of Abu 'Inan's good works, one wonders how there were any poor people left in his realm or whether those called poor did not enjoy a reasonably secure and comfortable life.

> Our master, God strengthen him, has devised practices in benevolence and almsgiving of which no one had thought and which the Sultans had not attained. Among them are the constant distribution of alms to the poor in every place in his realms; the designation of abundant alms for prisoners in all his realms; the stipulation that those alms should be in the form of baked bread that is easy to use; clothing for the poor, the sick, old women, old men, and those serving in the mosques throughout his realms; the allocation of sacrificial animals for these classes of people for the Feast of Sacrifice; the giving in alms of the tolls exacted at the gates in his realms on the twenty-seventh day of Ramadan in honour of that noble day and in support of its sanctity; feeding the people of the whole country on the night of the noble birth [mawlid al-nabi] and assembling them for its ceremonies; the circumcision, feeding and clothing of orphan boys on the day of 'Ashura; his help to the chronically sick and infirm in providing them with partners to work their land and so ease their burdens; his giving to the poor in his capital soft rugs and wraps of good quality for them to spread out and sleep on, an unparalleled kindness; building hospitals in every town of his realms providing ample endowments for feeding the sick, and appointing doctors to cure them and take charge of their treatment, as well as other kinds of beneficence and varieties of memorable acts which he has been the first to do. May God repay the favours he has bestowed and recompense his benefactions.[32]

---

[31] Gibb, *Ibn Battuta*, vol. IV, 930–33. For a description of Atabak Ahmad's charity, see Gibb, *Ibn Battuta*, vol. II, 288–90. He belonged to the dynasty of Kurdish Atabegs of Great Lur (1155–1423) in western Persia; see C. E. Bosworth, "Īdhadj", *EI²*, III:1016.

[32] Gibb, *Ibn Battuta*, vol. IV, 930–33.

Like Ibn Khallikan's description of Muzaffar al-Din, this passage describes Abu 'Inan as paying meticulous attention so that his charitable distributions reached all the categories of recipients listed in the Qur'an, not missing any of the year's holy days or festivals. Such descriptions, as noted earlier, seem typical of the praises sung by the learned class to their patrons and they appear to constitute one topos in biographical literature.[33] One wonders, however, whether praise for beneficent acts was especially reserved for descriptions of patrons, as a superlative form of panegyric. Perhaps the biography was akin to the prayers said for the dead, emphasizing beneficence as a quality of the deceased in order to enhance his or her reputation before God. Ibn Battuta's accounts of the charity of rulers were also infused with a competitive tone. He set Atabak Ahmad over everyone else and then placed Abu 'Inan even above him. Ibn Khallikan, too, proclaimed Muzaffar al-Din to have carried out charitable works unequalled by his predecessors. While the words come from their biographers, one should ask to what extent the donors themselves consciously vied with their predecessors and their contemporaries in the performance of charitable acts. How important were these competitions in shaping the philanthropic choices of any individual? Certainly comparisons with a competitive echo can be found in the beneficence of the Ottoman Hurrem Sultan, whose philanthropy is discussed below.

Haseki Hurrem Sultan

Voluntary giving was equally important for men and women, but served women (particularly elite women) as a rare vehicle to participate in public displays of power and patronage, as well as to support other women in ways complementary to the sponsoring of madrasas and circumcisions that mostly benefited boys and men. In Muslim law, women's rights over their property and wealth are similar to those of men. This situation stood in significant contrast to the rights of women in many European countries and the United States until well into the nineteenth century, where adult women either lost control over their own property when they married or had circumscribed property rights in general.[34]

---

[33] This was also pointed out in Gibb, *Ibn Battuta*, vol. IV, 930–33.

[34] Shulamith Shahar, *The Fourth Estate: A History of Women in the Middle Ages*, rev. edn. (London: Routledge, 2003), 91ff., 176ff.; Lee Holcombe, *Wives and Property: Reform of the Married Women's Property Law in Nineteenth-Century England* (Oxford: Martin Robertson, 1983); Norma Basch, *In the Eyes of the Law: Women, Marriage, and Property in Nineteenth-Century New York* (Ithaca: Cornell University Press, 1982); Ginzberg, *Women and the Work of Benevolence*, 50. Compare the situation of Russian women, who gained property rights almost a century earlier, in Michele Lamarche Marrese, *A Woman's Kingdom: Noblewomen and the Control of Property in Russia, 1700–1861* (Ithaca: Cornell University Press, 2002) and Adele Lindenmeyr, *Poverty is not a Vice: Charity, Society, and the State in Imperial Russia* (Princeton: Princeton University Press, 1996).

Historically where there existed discrepancies between the financial capacities of men and women in Islamic societies, they derived from their disparate access to sources of wealth and not from their right to possess or utilize it independently.[35] In Muslim law, women in the same relationship to a deceased person inherited only half as much as men. Women were largely excluded from the military and so did not enjoy shares in booty or other rewards of conquest. They were rarely in positions of political authority or administration that might bring them fortunes in the shape of salaries, taxes, gifts, or other revenues, although Ottoman imperial women received allowances, including set incomes based on tax revenues and regular gifts, and one is tempted to assume that this was perhaps a norm among members of other dynasties.[36] Even though women engaged regularly in economic activities – agriculture, manufacturing, money-lending, peddling, and as landlords – they generally did not control the largest shares of these enterprises in any particular time or place.

Women could and did make endowments or donations as they saw fit, although they may not have initiated every endowment on which their names appeared. Sultans might furnish women of the imperial household (their mothers, sisters, wives, or daughters) with the resources needed for specific philanthropic projects, even where regular stipends and other periodic gifts already amounted to significant sums. A man might also make an endowment in the name of a particular woman. The practice was widespread and persistent enough to suggest that the participation of women in charitable giving was not only effected for the personal spiritual welfare of the women as donors, but also as part of the larger beneficent calculus of the dynasty or family. Endowment decisions or donations ascribed to women may have been decided in a family context, where the power of individual women varied tremendously. However, the same could be said for all individuals in the complex network of family, household, or dynastic politics. Ottoman princes, for example, did not endow at all until they became sultans, which is a clear indication that decisions about public philanthropy were at least partly controlled or managed by the head of the family.[37]

Certain Muslim women became paradigms of philanthropy, cited as examples by and for other women. Muhammad's wives were portrayed as models of generosity, of whom 'A'isha (d. 678) is probably most frequently invoked. One hadith quotes her as saying: "A lady along with her two daughters came to me asking (for some alms), but she found nothing with me except one date which

---

[35] See the discussion in Randi Deguilhem, "Gender Blindness and Societal Influence in Late Ottoman Damascus: Women as the Creators and Managers of Endowments," *Hawwa* 1 (2003): 329–50, especially 335ff.
[36] See Peirce, *The Imperial Harem*, on the financial resources of women in the Ottoman harem.
[37] Peirce, *The Imperial Harem*, 199.

I gave to her and she divided it between her two daughters, and did not eat anything herself, and then she got up and went away."[38] According to another hadith some of the wives of the Prophet asked him:

"Which of us will be the first to die after you?" He replied, "Whichever of you has the longest hand." So they began measuring their hands with a stick and discovered that Sawda had the longest hand. Later they came to know that giving charity was called "the longest hand." She was the first to follow the Prophet and she loved giving charity.[39]

Hurrem Sultan was one of the most powerful and prolific Muslim patronesses. The extent and location of her patronage was unique in the context of Ottoman women before and during her lifetime, "formally modest yet functionally magnanimous." It was part of a concerted public relations campaign to counteract the criticisms of those who disliked her unprecedented status and influence as Süleyman's wife and mother of several of his sons. Her foundations included a mosque complex and large double bath in Istanbul, public kitchens in Jerusalem, Mecca, and Medina, numerous smaller mosques and tekkes in Istanbul and additional cities, a bridge, waterworks, and additional donations for pilgrims and janissaries.[40] However, she was only one of a large number of Ottoman imperial patronesses who left their philanthropic stamp on Ottoman space and society. Despite the Christian origins of most of these women, either Christian princesses married to Ottomans as part of diplomatic alliances or concubines acquired as war booty through sale or gift, and in spite of whatever affinities they may have retained for their original faith, all of their endowments were framed in the context of Muslim charity and as heirs to a tradition of Muslim female beneficence. Hurrem Sultan, apparently a Ukrainian princess, known as Roxelana in western sources, was called the "'A'isha of her times" and further compared to the saintly ascetic Rabi'a al-'Adawiya (d. 801) and to Zubayda (d. 831), wife of the Abbasid caliph Harun al-Rashid (d. 809).[41]

Zubayda was renowned for her looks and her intelligence, and both she and her husband were famous for their extravagance and patronage to artists of all types as well as their support of large-scale charitable endeavors. The family fame as benefactors also included Harun's mother, Khayzuran.[42] Perhaps the

[38] Al-Bukhārī, Ṣaḥīḥ al-Bukhārī 24 (al-zakat), bab 10; USC-MSA, Bukhari 24/499.
[39] Al-Bukhārī, Ṣaḥīḥ al-Bukhārī 24 (al-zakat), bab 11; USC-MSA, Bukhari, 24/501; Calder et al., Classical Islam, 40.
[40] Necipoğlu, The Age of Sinan, 269 (quote), 268–80.
[41] Stephan, "An Endowment Deed," 178; additional waqfiyya, made by Süleyman after Hurrem's death, dated Awākhir Shawwāl 967 (July 1560) in Kāmil Jamīl Al-'Asalī, Wathā'iq Maqdisiyya Ta'rīkhiyya (Amman: Matba'a al-Tawfīq, 1983), 148; Margaret Smith, "Rābi'a al-Adawiyya al-Ḳaysiyya," EI², VIII:354–56. On the patronage of Ottoman imperial women, see Peirce, The Imperial Harem, 198–212.
[42] See Nabia Abbott, Two Queens of Baghdad: Mother and Wife of Hārūn al-Rashīd (Chicago: University of Chicago Press, 1946; repr. London: Al Saqi Books, 1986), 236–64 and Renate Jacobi, "Zubayda," in EI², 11:547–48.

Fig. 10. Birqat al-Aqiqa, Saudi Arabia, one of the pools on the Darb Zubayda.
Photo by Patricia Barbor.

most enduring and best-known contribution of Zubayda's philanthropy was the
water supply system she had built along the route from Baghdad to Mecca and
the local aqueduct at Mecca to ensure water for Muslim pilgrims on the hajj to
the desert city.[43] Zubayda personally made the pilgrimage several times, a trip
that itself provided an important opportunity for philanthropic acts and one of
the rare opportunities for a woman to travel on her own.[44] She thus knew first-
hand of the chronic need for water and the problems in obtaining it. At
enormous, even legendary cost, she funded the "Darb Zubayda" (Zubayda's
route) lined with wells, reservoirs, underground pipes, and then, finally, 'Ayn
Zubayda (the spring of Zubayda) as part of the water supply system in Mecca
(Fig. 10). Construction work on this project went on for years and Zubayda
reportedly continued to pay huge sums in order to see it through to completion.
The inscription on the gate of the reservoir from 809–10 (194 AH) in Mecca is
telling. It reads:

---

[43] Zubayda probably repaired an older aqueduct. See R. B. Winder, "Makka: The Modern City," in
EI^2, VI:179.

[44] Marina Tolmacheva, "Female Piety and Patronage in the Medieval 'Hajj'", in *Women in the
Medieval Islamic World: Power, Patronage and Piety*, ed. Gavin R. G. Hambly (New York: St.
Martin's Press, 1998), 162–63.

In the name of Allah, the Merciful, the Compassionate. There is no God but Allah alone without any partners. The blessings of Allah be on Mohammed his servant and messenger. The grace of Allah (be with us all)! Umm Ja'far [Zubayda] the daughter of Abū al-Faḍl Ja'far the son of the Commander of the Believers Manṣūr – Allah be pleased with the Commander of the Believers – ordered the construction of these springs in order to provide water for the pilgrims of the House of Allah and to the people of his Sanctuary, praying thereby for Allah's reward and seeking to draw nigh unto him.[45]

Zubayda pretended no anonymity in funding this project but rather took full and public credit for it, and today the 'Ayn Zubayda spring and water system are still important sources of water in Mecca.[46] In fact, Zubayda was even said to be displeased with the governor of Mecca when she discovered he had written to the caliph and not directly to her for support in repairing the water system. It was, after all, her project, and she may have been loath to let anyone else diminish the recognition due to her.[47] Competition could be just as fierce in charitable endeavors as in any other route to power and glory because beneficence contributed so directly to enhancing reputation, status, and legitimacy. In particular, expensive projects in the holiest cities of Islam brought their sponsors both spiritual benefit and invaluable public recognition. This may be one reason why the Ottoman sultan Abdulhamid II banned charitable giving in Mecca by non-Ottoman Muslims. In this way, the title "Protector of the Holy Places" remained uniquely Ottoman, even while it imposed a larger financial burden on them to maintain the holy city.[48]

Zubayda's reputation as an exemplary philanthropist was consolidated in her own day and contemporary and later historians further secured it. From her public works to an ongoing concern for the welfare of the poor, chroniclers celebrated Zubayda's deeds and she became a conscious point of reference for female imperial patrons. A story, perhaps apocryphal, recounts how Hurrem Sultan explicitly requested that Süleyman allow her to carry out the repairs needed on the Meccan waterworks in the sixteenth century, thus setting herself up as Zubayda's heir and equal. The implicit comparison of Süleyman and Hurrem to the legendary Harun al-Rashid and his wife was intended to flatter and to enhance the image of the Ottoman imperial couple, whether it was made by their contemporaries or later chroniclers. Ultimately the Ottomans gained a keen appreciation of the magnitude of Zubayda's original patronage when the necessary repairs in Mecca continued for almost a decade and at great cost, completed eventually under the patronage of Mihrimah Sultan, daughter of Süleyman and Hurrem.[49]

---

[45] As cited in Abbott, *Two Queens of Baghdad*, 244.   [46] Winder, "Makka," VI:179.

[47] Abbott, *Two Queens of Baghdad*, 246–47.

[48] Selim Deringil, *The Well-Protected Domains: Ideology and the Legitimation of Power in the Ottoman Empire 1876–1909* (London: I. B. Tauris, 1997), 57.

[49] Abbott, *Two Queens of Baghdad*, 255; Peirce, *The Imperial Harem*, 204, 330n.79; Necipoğlu, *The Age of Sinan*, 190, 269–70, 300–301.

Elite Muslim women like Hurrem Sultan circumvented the social restrictions on appearing in public when their names or titles were given to public buildings. Hurrem's many endowments were called "Haseki" (the favorite), recalling Hurrem's status with respect to Süleyman but not her own name. The same was true for the Atik Valide (Old Queen Mother) and Yeni Valide (New Queen Mother) mosque complexes endowed in Üsküdar by Nurbanu (d. 1583) and Emetullah Rabia Gülnuş (d. 1715), the mothers of, respectively, Sultan Murat III (1574–95) and Sultan Ahmet III (1703–30). Another well-known example is the Taj Mahal (Crown of the Palace) in Agra, the tomb complex built and endowed by the Mughal Shah Jahan (d. 1658) for his beloved wife, Arjumand Banu Begum (d. 1631), known in court formally as Mumtaz Mahal ("Chosen One of the Palace"). In each case, the buildings were the site of regular (daily or annual) charitable distributions or public services. The Valide Sultan complexes added mosques, fountains, public kitchens, and other buildings to the Asian quarter of Istanbul. The endowment of the Taj Mahal provided for money to be distributed to poor men and women on the anniversary of Mumtaz Mahal's death, and for the maintenance of the Qur'an readers who prayed for her soul day and night.[50]

The patronage of women in Safavid Iran (1501–1722) provides a contrast to that of the Ottomans and serves as a useful caution against assuming parallels too broadly across the breadth of Islamic societies, even among the ruling dynasties or particularly among women. For the Shi'i Safavid rulers, the shrines of holy men and women, to whom people appealed for intercession with God, were a more popular focus of building patronage by both men and women than were the mosques so preferred by the Ottoman elites. In addition, the paradigmatic female figure for the Safavids was the Prophet's daughter Fatima, wife of 'Ali, the fourth caliph, and mother of the martyrs Hasan and Husayn. References and comparisons were more likely to be drawn to her than to other women.[51] In Mughal India, too, the patronage of Muslim women was distinctively shaped by the influence of local Hindu and Jain practices, as the ritual of imperial weighing has already suggested might be the case.[52]

In general, the charitable endeavors of women in Islamic societies elucidate how women used their wealth and resources. Personal concerns and local needs shaped their choices, as did their identity as women and as Muslims. One source tells that Hurrem Sultan sold her gold, jewelry, and pearls to make donations to the novices laboring on the building site of the Şehzade complex after she saw how miserable and unkempt they looked.[53] Women used waqf making as a way

---

[50] On the Ottoman women, see Peirce, *The Imperial Harem*, 198–210. On the Taj Mahal, see Ebba Koch, *The Complete Taj Mahal and the Riverfront Gardens of Agra* (London: Thames and Hudson, 2006), 97–101.

[51] Rizvi, "Gendered Patronage," 125–29.   [52] Findly, "Women's Wealth."

[53] Necipoğlu, *The Age of Sinan*, 194–95.

to protect their own property and income from encroachment by other interested parties like husbands, guardians, or in-laws, and as a form of insurance against future uncertainties. They set up endowments to benefit themselves and named themselves as managers, sometimes to be succeeded by other women, their daughters or freed slaves for whom control of these resources was equally important as a basis for independence and influence.[54] Women without the resources to build large buildings could still be patrons on a smaller scale, as could men. The large numbers of extant waqf deeds and documents afford valuable insights into women's identities – middle class as well as elite women – the nature of their property holdings, and their ability to affect their own societies. The particular accessibility of waqf making in Islamic societies makes it possible to explore gender relations through charitable giving, both within Islamic societies, and in comparison with women and men in other societies.[55]

There are many more donors from Muslim dynasties who could be discussed and the charity and patronage of rulers deserves extensive further attention, partly because the distinctive differences between dynasties in their philanthropic choices – the kinds of endeavors, their size, location, timing, funding, and the extent to which they engaged the other members of their households in these endeavors – all further highlight the specificities of each dynasty and state. However, examining the charity of less powerful and prominent people is equally significant for understanding specific charity dynamics as well as the larger society: popular forms, changing fashions, limitations imposed by social or economic status, and the impact of family dynamics or broader political forces.

Mehmed Ağa

Mehmed Ağa (d. c.1623), originally a Christian recruited into Ottoman service, rose from janissary to become the chief imperial architect to Sultan Ahmed I (1603–17). Mehmed Ağa's architectural works included repairs and restorations to the holy sanctuaries and other buildings in Mecca and Medina,

---

[54] Mary Ann Fay, "Women and Waqf: Toward a Reconsideration of Women's Place in the Mamluk Household," *International Journal of Middle East Studies* 29 (1997): 36–37; G. Baer, "Women and Waqf: An Analysis of the Istanbul Tahrîr of 1546," *Asian and African Studies* 17 (1983): 27.

[55] See Singer, *Constructing Ottoman Beneficence*, chapter 3; Baer, "Women and Waqf"; Leslie Peirce, "The Family as Faction: Dynastic Politics in the Reign of Süleyman," in *Soliman le Magnifique et son temps*, ed. Gilles Veinstein (Paris: La Documentation Française, 1992), 105–16; R. Stephen Humphreys, "Women as Patrons of Religious Architecture in Ayyubid Damascus," *Muqarnas* 11 (1994): 35–54; Margaret L. Meriwether, "Women and *Waqf* Revisited: The Case of Aleppo, 1770–1840," in *Women in the Ottoman Empire: Middle Eastern Women in the Early Modern Era*, ed. Madeline C. Zilfi (Leiden: Brill, 1997), 128–52; Gregory C. Kozlowski, "Private Lives and Public Piety: Women and the Practice of Islam in Mughal India," in *Women in the Medieval Islamic World*, ed. Hambly, 469–88.

and the imposing Sultan Ahmed or Blue Mosque complex in the historic center of Istanbul on the site of the Byzantine Hippodrome. The biography of Mehmed Ağa contains several chapters that constitute a treatise on sciences and terminology related to architecture. His biographer was one Ca'fer Efendi, who enjoyed Mehmed Ağa's patronage for more than twenty years, but of whom little is known outside what the author himself tells us. Ca'fer, in a manner reminiscent of Ibn Khallikan and Ibn Battuta, devoted one of four biographical chapters in his work entirely to the philanthropy of his patron, beginning thus: "[The chapter] describes the kindness (*lutf*) and generosity (*karam*) and benevolence (*ihsan*) and charity (*ni'am*) of the aforementioned Ağa. There was no need to write this chapter because the Ağa's kindness and generosity are, like the day, manifest and evident to all the world."[56]

Despite this statement and though he also noted that Mehmed Ağa quite intentionally did not advertise his charity, Ca'fer then launched into a catalogue of his many acts. First, Ca'fer said, Mehmed Ağa was a model of generosity such as existed in the previous century under sultans like Selim II and Murad III but not after them. Second, Mehmed Ağa continued to give even when he himself had financial troubles. Third, Ca'fer's own father, an exceedingly pious man whose every act was canonically correct, was nonetheless stingy when it came to his own son. Fourth, Mehmed was extremely modest about his good works and constantly felt he needed to improve on them, even though Ca'fer saw them as exemplary. Finally, Ca'fer believed that Mehmed's generosity was better told briefly, in his own summary narrative, rather than having each person who had benefited from it come forward to give a separate account. As it was, Ca'fer said, when people heard he was writing the Ağa's biography, they hurried to him in great numbers, each eager to describe a personal experience of Mehmed's generosity.

Ca'fer depicted Mehmed to readers as a prosperous, pious, and generous man, well worthy of imitation, but the beneficence that Ca'fer praised in Mehmed Ağa was recounted very differently from that of Muzaffar al-Din or Abu 'Inan. Mehmed appeared extremely modest in his acts, most of which Ca'fer was unable even to specify; in fact, his descriptions were almost all very general, mentioning only that Mehmed's beneficiaries were numerous and his donations generous. Mehmed did not, apparently, endow grand buildings or sponsor great public feasts, probably because this scale of philanthropy was beyond his means. What was admirable in a ruler whose charity was conducted as part of his public persona would perhaps be inappropriate, not to mention impossible, for a man of Mehmed Ağa's status. As a successful professional and a state office-holder, he conducted his philanthropy at a level commensurate

---

[56] Ca'fer Efendi, *Risāle*, 42.

with his own standing. Although in his work as an architect for various patrons, he built mosques, madrasas, bridges, and fountains, Mehmed Ağa's own benefcent constructions focused on fountains, apparently more than forty in one town.[57] The charitable works of Mehmed's predecessor, the renowned architect Sinan, also stood in marked contrast to those of his patrons. While for them he built enormous mosques and magnificent bridges, Sinan himself sponsored a primary school, some fountains, smaller neighborhood mosques, and Istanbul's sidewalks.[58]

Curiously, Caʿfer does not mention any constructions at all in the chapter on Mehmed's charity; these appear in an earlier chapter. Rather, he talks about other kinds of giving. Mehmed Ağa was scrupulous in calculating what he owed in zakat from his earnings. His house, even when he himself was pinched financially, operated like a public kitchen (imaret) "for travelers free and slave, and equally for the great and the humble and for all neighbors and strangers," distributing food as well as gifts. Mehmed was generous to Caʿfer Efendi, supporting him and always favoring him with a good meal. Finally, he gave generously to many deserving people in the community, including shaykhs, just people, and poor religious students. In refusing to list Mehmed's individual acts of generosity, despite being encouraged to recount them, Caʿfer excused himself, saying: "would His Excellency that illustrious Ağa be pleased that gifts given secretly and covertly become well known and legendary in public?"[59] Mehmed Ağa seemed to be guided by the sentiment of hadiths such as: "Seven people will be shaded by Allah under His shade on the day when there will be no shade except His. They are . . . [among others] a person who practices charity so secretly that his left hand does not know what his right hand has given."[60] Caʿfer's own sensitivity may have derived, too, from the fact that he himself threatened this secrecy by composing his text.

Yet he did this with a declared purpose, using his biography of Mehmed Ağa to reproach others for their weak performance. (European travelers, too, sometimes made unfavorable comparisons between their own countries and the Ottoman Empire in order to sharpen their critiques.) Caʿfer took the opportunity to castigate his father for being ungenerous to his own son while readily giving to others. Since family members are among the preferred recipients of sadaqa, Caʿfer perceived his father to have been hypocritically stingy. In addition, Caʿfer reproached the Ottoman officials of his own day, who "do not give a thing or support anyone," and who compared unfavorably with men of the previous generation.

Being content with little, all of them were renowned for generosity. This was their noble custom, that if someone wanted to give something to them, they would not take it. In fact,

---

[57] Caʿfer Efendi, *Risāle*, 14.   [58] Necipoğlu, *The Age of Sinan*, 147–52.
[59] Caʿfer Efendi, *Risāle*, 44.
[60] Al-Bukhārī, *Ṣaḥīḥ al-Bukhārī*, 24 (al-zakat), bab 16; USC-MSA, Bukhari, 24/504.

even those high state officials who had little wealth would expend their own resources in order to give alms to the poor, and would search continuously for men worthy of benevolence and for a reason for mercy. Finding a poor and deserving person, they, of course, spared no effort in giving him help and assistance. Now none of the men of that age or generous ones of those times remain.[61]

The publication of donations was a useful way to criticize what Ca'fer perceived as a declining sense of public responsibility among people who should have been active philanthropists on behalf of the public welfare. Nostalgia like this may be a set piece in Ottoman history writing, but it also articulated the expectations of members of the Ottoman elites that were current among members of the professional classes like Ca'fer.

Even when it existed not all charity earned the praise and admiration of contemporary chroniclers. The late sixteenth-century Ottoman author Mustafa 'Ali (d. 1600), often critical of his era, was not at all dazzled by the public works of sultans, some of whom, he claimed, had no right to be undertaking grand acts of philanthropy.

As long as the glorious sultans, the Alexander-like kings, have not enriched themselves with the spoils of the Holy War and have not become owners of lands through the gains of campaigns of the Faith, it is not appropriate that they undertake to build soup kitchens for the poor and hospitals or to repair libraries and higher *medreses* or, in general, to construct establishments of charity, and it is seriously not right to spend and waste the means of the public treasury on unnecessary projects. For, the Divine Laws do not permit the building of charitable establishments with the means of the public treasury, neither do they allow the foundation of mosques and *medreses* that are not needed. Unless a sultan, after conducting a victorious campaign, decides to spend the booty he has made on pious deeds rather than on his personal pleasures, and engages to prove this by the erection of [public] buildings.[62]

Donors, according to Mustafa 'Ali, had to earn the right to give. Mustafa 'Ali was addressing some of the successors of Sultan Süleyman who had no significant conquests from which to build in the way they did. Essentially, they were taking funds from the public treasury (to which they had not added) to finance their personal philanthropy instead of contributing from their own monies. His critique is a reminder that, fundamentally, the purpose of giving was not to score points with the populace but rather to bring the founder closer to God by giving away his or her own property. Only charity carried out with pious intent would be considered genuine by God. Perhaps this was also the unstated message behind the hadith that told of a man who gave charity three times and each time was dismayed to discover that the recipient – a thief, an adulteress, and a rich man – was apparently unworthy. Yet someone reassured him that his donations had not

---

[61] Ca'fer Efendi, *Risāle*, 42.
[62] Andreas Tietze, ed., trans., and notes, *Muṣṭafā 'Ālī's Counsel for Sultans of 1581*, 2 vols. (Vienna: Verlag der Österreichischen Akademie der Wissenschaften, 1979 and 1982), I:54.

missed the mark: because of them the thief might give up stealing, the adulteress mend her ways, and the rich man be persuaded to give his own charity.[63]

Like the man in this hadith, most givers assumed that their donations reached needy and deserving people as defined in the Qur'an and that the recipients would benefit from the distribution, if not from any long-term remedy to their impoverished condition. We can imagine the dismay of the man who believed that his charity failed both to reach deserving people and to earn credit for him from God for good deeds, and his subsequent relief at being reassured that such was not the case. One might argue, too, that if the man's intention (niyya) in giving was honest, then his reward was in any case assured. However, this hadith seems to remove the donor's burden of identifying worthy recipients, since it implies that charity given may find an unseen mark and so do good. Moreover, by focusing on such questionable recipients, the hadith emphasizes the possibility that charity might act as a social corrective and restrain individuals within the bounds of normative behavior so as to strengthen society and serve the public good. In either case, the recipients are portrayed as utterly passive and the hadith speaks only about the giver.

Charitable giving was constrained by belief, ethics, and manners, all of which had to be sincere and correct for an individual charitable act to be valid before God. However, as we have noted, charity had several layers of meaning and motivation for givers, some of them quite worldly and important to the day-to-day functioning of communities. This perspective is articulated in the text of a tenth-century Buyid judge:

Al-Munajjim [a tax collector in Iraq] . . . used to be praised for establishing pious endowments in his district, for repairing the local irrigation system, and for giving alms to the appropriate people. Privately, al-Munajjim said that he did these things for God; but, he added, if he had done them for appearances, that would be good too, and why shouldn't the local people keep up appearances by a matching hypocritical pretense that they believed in the high-minded motives of the benefactor? Nowadays, he complained, if a man is munificent they say he is "making commerce with his munificence" and consider him a miser.[64]

Al-Munajjim described a no-win situation in which beneficence was criticized as self-interest. Such a charge is difficult to prove, and the Qur'an often reminds its readers that only God knows the truth and that the truth is never hidden from God. In the living world of humans, al-Munajjim suggested, many motivations may be at work behind the scenes, yet the immediate material impact of beneficent giving – improved community welfare and assistance to needy individuals – should remain valid and praiseworthy. Since the spiritual aspect of beneficent

---

[63] Al-Bukhārī, *Ṣaḥīḥ al-Bukhārī* 24 (al-zakat), bab 14; USC-MSA, Bukhari, 24/502.
[64] Mottahedeh, *Loyalty and Leadership*, 82, quoting from al-Tanukhi, *Nishwar al-Muhadara*, vol. II (Beirut, 1971–72), 21. On the Buyids, see C. Cahen, "Buwayhids or Būyids," *EI*², I:350–57.

giving depends on the relationship between the believer and Allah, it is not the place of other human beings to question its sincerity. Although this claim sounds reasonable in the context of what we understand about God in Muslim belief, Ibn Battuta and Ca'fer Efendi both offered accounts wherein they took charitable giving to be a direct indication of individual piety and belief. In general, too, biographies have offered philanthropy as transparent evidence of generosity and correct behavior. Ca'fer's critiques of the officials of his era (and of his father) also recall that in societies that valued beneficence highly, not giving was judged a serious failing.

Through examining individual donors, the impact of a moral economy on habits of charitable giving can again be detected. Expectations about the proper uses of wealth were an inseparable aspect of beneficence. Non-market considerations were not only part of the population's expectations of its ruler, as discussed above with respect to Mamluk Cairo. They could be equally salient in the actions of a single subject. Moreover, they could shape the demands people made on themselves. The generosity of one retired Ottoman pasha illustrates the moral economic expectations rooted in late Ottoman culture.

Toward the end of the reign of Abdulhamid II (1876–1909), a certain Enis Pasha was forcibly retired from imperial service on a meager pension. According to an account by the niece who grew up in his household, Enis Pasha nonetheless maintained the kitchen of his own home in Istanbul as he had on his previously more substantial income. Daily, the two dozen people who formed his household ate at his table, and never fewer than ten other guests. In addition to these, there were many "poor of the mansion" (*konağın fukarası*) who had grown accustomed to receive food and whom the pasha expected he would feed. He further maintained a bath attached to his house, open for use by people in the neighboring quarters. Even when the pasha's household itself had no water, its depot still fed the faucets used by the neighborhood residents. As the retired pasha gradually slipped into penury, he continued to maintain his open table and the neighborhood bath as long as possible. Over the years, explained his niece, the pasha had come to perceive these services as his obligation and an entitlement of the people dependent on him. As she said:

All these were the customary practices of a well-known, notable family, based on habits of hundreds of years. Entrenched customs cannot be broken. How is it possible to serve a meal to the people of a great house with no soup, no vegetables, no meat, no rice, no sweets, no savory pastries, no puddings, no stewed fruit? How can one reduce the amount of oil, flour, salt, and pepper in these foods, and their quantity? How could the plates of the indigents who come [to the house] be turned away empty? How could permission be denied for them to bathe in the warm bath?[65]

---

[65] Cahit Uçuk, *Bir İmparatorluk Çökerken* (Istanbul: Yapı Kredi Yayınları, 1995), 58–59. This memoir about the last years of the Ottoman Empire was written by one of Turkey's prominent female writers, famous from the 1930s.

Fulfilling these minimum commitments was a sign of the pasha's status; after so many years, providing for the local poor and the neighbors was no longer an option but an obligation. Stripped of office, his petitions to the sultan ignored, and his funds dwindling, Enis Pasha tried to sustain the actions which had defined him as a member of the Ottoman elite and the wealthy man of the neighborhood. According to his niece, he was ultimately undermined both by his fall from imperial favor and by his inability to fulfill long-standing commitments to his own community of dependants. When he could no longer manage even these, he died.[66]

The pasha's actions, which look so much like voluntary good works, had become, in his eyes, an intrinsic aspect of his identity and status. To put it another way, Enis Pasha was part of a moral economy that restricted his ability to make self-interested decisions. Whether other pashas, beys, and sultans had a similar appreciation of the obligations of office is a matter for further investigation. Based on the circumstantial evidence of the good works (*hayrat*) of the Ottoman elite, one might posit that there was indeed a moral economy of high office that persisted over the course of Ottoman history, although the specific extent and shape of the expectations differed over time, and across the vast space of the empire. (Enis Pasha's idea of a minimal meal from a pasha's kitchen was obviously different from that of the people who decided that soup and bread were sufficient for the clients of a public kitchen.) A map of the specific beneficent acts of members of the Ottoman elite would further explain the dynamics of the Ottoman household (*kapı*), one of the key institutions of the Ottoman Empire, and also uncover the networks that reached beyond and between such households.[67] In the immediate context of Enis Pasha's biography, this story helps to rewrite his life history as one of successful and selfless service to his community (perhaps more so than most?), even if his career as an Ottoman pasha was cut short and ended ingloriously. For Ca'fer Efendi, the inclusion of a chapter on Mehmed Ağa's philanthropy was the opportunity to demonstrate the piety and humanity of a man whose biography was otherwise a story of technical achievements.

Sufis and saints

The story is told of a merchant and jurist named Abu al-Hasan 'Ali b. Muhammad b. 'Abd al-Ghani who for forty years gave away all his profits as alms, believing

---

[66] Uçuk, *Bir İmparatorluk Çökerken*, 51.

[67] Some of the key works on the structure, function, and culture of Ottoman households include I. Metin Kunt, *The Sultan's Servants: The Transformation of Ottoman Provincial Government, 1550–1650* (New York: Columbia University Press, 1983); Peirce, *The Imperial Harem*; Jane Hathaway, *The Politics of Households in Ottoman Egypt: The Rise of the Qazdağlıs* (Cambridge, UK: Cambridge University Press, 1997); Ehud Toledano, "The Emergence of Ottoman-Local Elites (1700–1800): A Framework for Research," in *Middle Eastern Politics and Ideas: A History from Within*, ed. I. Pappe and M. Ma'oz (London: I. B. Tauris, 1997), 145–62.

that God would always provide for him. When he married, he was reduced to tears at the realization that his wife's well-being would take priority over his almsgiving. Upon learning the cause of his distress, she decided to share his trust in God and urged him to continue as before. Shortly thereafter a man appeared on their doorstep with one thousand dinars for Abu al-Hasan, a deposit left with him by Abu al-Hasan's father years before. Abu al-Hasan refused to take the money and sent the man away. However, a dream sent the man back to Abu al-Hasan, to insist that he take the money, since it came from God as a reward for his unswerving faith.[68]

In this story, found in texts from the fourteenth and fifteenth centuries, Abu al-Hasan and his wife exemplify the charitable giving and generosity characteristically attributed to Muslim saints, also known as "friends of God" (*wali*), and sufis. Saints and sufis were the focus of veneration and appeals for divine intercession, and their lives were written into hagiographies and biographies to illustrate what was expected of people and perhaps to inspire generous acts of charity even if people could not fully emulate them. In another story, a wealthy merchant named 'Affan b. Sulayman al-Misri was famous for giving away money and food to large numbers of people, both on a daily basis and at special moments. He made it a habit to supply food to the hajj caravan when it reached the port of Aqaba on the return trip from Mecca. As seen in many previous examples, feeding large numbers of people was one typical action of wealthy pious people. Biographical dictionaries and the hagiographies are replete with acts of beneficence in which men and women like Abu al-Hasan, his wife, and 'Affan continually gave away money to provide for others. Like wealthy benefactors, the saints and sufis also had a reputation for defraying the costs of circumcisions, dowries, and burials.[69]

Sufism comprised many different practices and the organization of sufis has changed dynamically during the course of Islamic history, from a largely itinerant and ascetic phenomenon to one that became centered in tariqas around spiritual masters, sometimes in endowed convent buildings (zawiya, tekke), sometimes with branches throughout large parts of the Islamic world. Sufism was not necessarily a phenomenon isolated from the mainstream of Islamic societies although there were always sufis who practiced extreme forms of asceticism, which set them apart from society. In certain periods and places, sufis drew the reproaches (at times violent) of mosque-based religious leaders, like the seventeenth-century Kadizadelis in Istanbul. Yet the orders also attracted adherents from among the majority communities of Muslims, who

---

[68] The story is found in the fourteenth–fifteenth-century author Ibn al-Zayyāt's, *Al-Kawākib*, and also in the fifteenth-century author al-Sakhāwī's, *Tuʿfat*, as quoted in Taylor, *In the Vicinity of the Righteous*, 102.

[69] Taylor, *In the Vicinity of the Righteous*, 99.

continued to follow orthodox Sunni or Shiʻi practices even while participating in sufi rituals.[70]

Charity played a central role in the lives of Muslim saints and sufis because it was a means to approach God, which was their chief goal, even in Paradise. One of the obligations of the sufis is to give alms and charity, and God is said to be present in every such act. Wealth is seen as a test for the sufi *murid*, the one who seeks God, and the sufi is supposed to resist the lure of wealth and the temptations it brings. Poverty has long been associated with the sufis, such that the Arabic word *faqir* refers both to sufis and to indigent people, sometimes indistinguishably. Beneficent giving was the immediate cause of sufi poverty in many cases, since people who became sufis often gave away their possessions and chose material poverty in pursuit of spiritual wealth. However, not all sufi adherents adopted a life of poverty. The biography of Molla Shams al-Din al-Fanari, the first Ottoman shaykh al-Islam, described him as a sincere participant in sufi rituals even while he was a prosperous man and a respected scholar and judge.[71]

Over the course of Islamic history there have been vociferous debates about how poor sufis should be and the role of poverty in pursuit of piety. Representative of the debate at a certain point were the opinions of al-Ghazali, who supported adopting poverty as a means to attain greater piety and focus on God. His views were attacked by Ibn al-Jawzi (d. 1200) who argued against the withdrawal of sufis from the material and temporal world.[72] While they could not agree on the particular degree of poverty or modest living appropriate for sufis, it seems that all those who wrote about sufism did continue to support giving sadaqa as an expression of true piety and one means for sufis to further their search for God. The debate represented by al-Ghazali and Ibn al-Jawzi also appears to assume some underlying consensus about what has been called "mild asceticism" with regard to an earlier period. Studying the biographies of pious individuals, and in particular the noted jurist Ahmad b. Hanbal (d. 878), one contemporary scholar has come to the conclusion that they express a shared ethical and moral adherence to ideas and practices that describe, among other things, a modest life. While not necessarily impoverished – some, like

---

[70] On sufism see J. S. Trimingham, *The Sufi Orders in Islam* (Oxford: Clarendon Press, 1971); the articles "*ṭarīḳa*," "*taṣawwuf*," and "*walī*" in *EI²*; and Fritz Meier, "The Mystic Path," in *The World of Islam*, ed. Bernard Lewis (London: Thames and Hudson, 1976), 117–40. I am grateful to Ateret Aharon for permission to cite her MA thesis, "Poverty and Charity in Sufism" [Hebrew] (School of History, Tel Aviv University, 2006), which focuses on the eleventh to the fourteenth centuries. On the Kadizadelis, see Madeline C. Zilfi, "The Kadizadelis: Discordant Revivalism in Seventeenth-Century Istanbul," *Journal of Near Eastern Studies* 45 (1986): 251–69.

[71] Ibn Tashköprüzade, "The Biography of an Ottoman Jurist," from *Al-Shaqa'iq al-Nuʻmāniyya*, in *Islam*, vol. II, ed. and trans. Bernard Lewis (New York: Harper Torchbooks, 1974), 45–49.

[72] Sabra, *Poverty and Charity*, 17–31.

Abu al-Hasan, earned handsomely in order to be able to give – these exemplary pious individuals minimized their personal material needs, eating, drinking, and living simply. On the other hand, they rejected extremes like extended fasting, wearing rags, abandoning their families, and withdrawing from the world.[73]

It is difficult to know whether the many stories and anecdotes that illustrate sufi generosity are based in fact but they are clearly meant to be inspirational. The anecdotes reiterate the purpose of giving, which is to shed the desires of this world in an attempt to approach God. Many stories talk about food, a basic human need and so a focus of desire. One story tells of al-Rabi' b. Khaytham who longed to eat chicken, but for forty days denied himself the pleasure. Finally, he gave in and asked his wife to prepare one. She gladly cooked a dish for him, making a sauce and baking bread to accompany it. As he sat down to eat, a beggar knocked at the door and asked for charity, saying, "Give me charity and God will bless you." Al-Rabi' stopped eating and asked his wife to wrap up the chicken to give to the beggar. She protested and instead offered to give the beggar money equal to the cost of the food. Al-Rabi' agreed that they should give the sum she mentioned, but then insisted on giving the food as well. In this way, he was charitable to the beggar while also giving up his own desire in favor of a pious act.[74] Other stories make clear the cost of not being generous at appropriate moments. One Abu Ja'far b. Tarkan told of how he sat one day among the poor and received one dinar as charity. He wanted, he said, to give it to the poor, and then decided to keep it in case he should need it. Suddenly, he felt a sharp pain in his tooth and to relieve it pulled the tooth out. The next tooth began to hurt and that too was pulled. Then Abu Ja'far heard a voice telling him: "If you don't give the dinar to the poor, you won't have any teeth left in your mouth."[75]

The sufis, however, were both givers and recipients, and so serve as perhaps the most obvious reminder that the division of people into givers and recipients is not meant to be permanent. In the hadith that gives the title to this chapter, the upper hand is assumed to be the one that gives. However, in another interpretation, sufis are said to give with the bottom hand, that is, the lower hand open and facing up, such that the hand of the recipient takes from above.[76] For the sufi, the upper hand would be the hand of God, taking back what originally came from God. Yet another interpretation is that of the Iranian mystic Hujwiri (d. 1072) who said that the upper hand of the sufi was better than the lower hand, but specified the lower hand as the one that gives, while the upper is the one that takes. In taking

[73] Hurvitz, "Biographies."

[74] Aharon, "Poverty and Charity," 65, citing Jamal al-Din Abu al-Faraj Ibn al-Jawzi, *Sifat al-Safwa*, vol. II, (Beirut: Dar al-Fikr, 1412/1991), 31.

[75] Aharon, "Poverty and Charity," 68, citing 'Ali b. al-Hasan Ibn 'Asakir, *Tarikh Madinat Dimashq*, vol. 21, (Beirut: Dar al-Fikr, 1995), 35–36.

[76] Aharon, "Poverty and Charity," 63, citing al-Makki, *Qūt al-Qulūb* (Misr: Mustafa al-Babi al-Halabi, 1961), 218.

the sufi helps the believer to fulfill his or her obligations to pay zakat or give sadaqa.[77] The multiple versions and interpretations of the hadith offer one example of how no one position or clear agreement exists among Muslim scholars about some textual traditions and interpretations. The variant interpretations in this case also demonstrate specifically that, while there is agreement about the necessity to give charity, scholars have taken different positions regarding the relative merits of donors and beneficiaries in the gesture. The saints and sufis, meanwhile, have established themselves in written sources and popular imagination alike as models of both charitable generosity and poverty.

Charitable giving can play an important role in constituting the identity of the powerful and wealthy. The portraits examined here, whether literary or visual, projected an image of generosity and pious attendance to the responsibilities for community welfare that inhered in sovereignty, wealth, and exemplary piety. As expressed equally in the medieval "mirrors for princes" literature and in the proclamations of Ottoman sultans, the ruler was expected to secure the welfare of his subjects and promote justice. The idea of justice contained a strong component of social justice, that is, that subject peoples had a just claim to basic subsistence and freedom from abuse. People from the ruling and wealthy classes had a responsibility to ensure this, as was demonstrated by the apportioning of famine relief among high officials or by the impoverishment of Enis Pasha, who maintained his household even as his wealth disappeared. Any stronger person had some responsibility for weaker or dependent people, like the head of a family for relatives and retainers, or a neighbor like Abu Illya for those next door. Writ large or small, the power gradient entailed social responsibility, and social justice was seen as an aspect of the public good. Al-Ghazali emphasized this specifically, attributing his words to al-Hasan al-Basri, the famous preacher of the first Muslim century:

"If God had so desired He could have made you all rich, not a single poor or pauper among you. But He had willed that some of you be responsible for the support of the others."[78]

The central role of charitable giving in the biographies of some Muslims is not so surprising given the insistence on charity in the texts that are meant to guide them. Their biographies thus became part of the corpus of texts describing ideals and can be used to teach these ideals as well as measure the behavior of others. However, there are also many biographies that relate few if any charitable undertakings. Notably, Ibn Khallikan's entire collection of biographies contains only a handful of extensive charitable portraits. Among all of them, that of Muzaffar al-Din was by far the most detailed. We might assume that it

---

[77] Sabra, *Poverty and Charity*, 36.
[78] Al-Ghazālī, *Kitāb Asrār al-Zakāh*, 298; Faris, *Mysteries of Almsgiving*, 76.

was the personal connection between him and Ibn Khallikan which inspired the unique portrait; Ibn Battuta's descriptions of Abu 'Inan, Ca'fer Efendi's biography of Mehmed Ağa, and Evliya Çelebi's portrayal of Melek Ahmed Pasha all suggest that the authors' positions as clients may have prompted them to praise the beneficence of their patrons. However, the portraits of the benefactors did not focus on their support of the people who wrote about them, but rather on a standard if not entirely formulaic list of good works.

Whether or not the biography presents a true or an idealized portrait of the giver, it is nonetheless a valuable source about the culture of charity in the society in which the biography was created. The portraits served as models of both good and bad behavior for people who read them, although the readership and audience for these texts need to be further studied. If we compare the benefactions of rulers and other high-ranking members of society, male and female (like Mehmed Ağa or Hurrem Sultan), clear hierarchies of giving emerge to which people had to adhere, configuring their charity to their status. Religious belief was doubtless a significant factor in encouraging people of all ranks to undertake beneficent acts. At the same time, the ambition of people to establish and maintain a position of relative power, anywhere on the social scale, seems to have demanded that they undertake charitable acts on behalf of their constituents and so for the Muslim community at large.

While the discussion thus far might be read to imply that everyone with the means to do so gave, this was probably not the case. The variations in biography were not all a result only of choices by the authors; some must have reflected real situations. In the contemporary world, examples abound of people with enormous or only moderate wealth who do not make donations, for a variety of reasons. Research into charity can also ask about them, about the way their wealth was used, and about the extent to which anyone noticed or criticized their choice not to give. It is generally asserted that some segments of the Ottoman elite were less active in large-scale, highly visible charity – notably waqf making – despite the fact that they appeared to have had extensive resources. Among these were the scholars and the commercial elites. Some of these men earned healthy profits from trade and manufacturing or substantial salaries from their teaching or judicial posts, but for the most part they did not have access to booty won in conquests nor did they benefit from the profits of tax farming. Perhaps they were more conscious of various admonitions to give secretly, such that their philanthropy left fewer obvious traces or, not needing the kind of political legitimation derived from the large public donations that motivated rulers and governors, they chose not to give, openly or at all. Perhaps, too, ruling elites reserved to themselves certain forms of giving, excluding intellectual or commercial elites. Again, further study is needed. Systematic study can establish a more complex picture of the role of charitable giving in individuals' lives and in the construction of their reputations, as well as describing more precisely the distribution of giving in any particular society. In general, the wealth of biographical literature among Muslim historical texts offers a ready field for research of this kind. The perspective of biographies will probably always yield far more on the givers than on the recipients, but the study of charity is not concerned only with them. The next chapter turns to the beneficiaries, specifically, the most stereotypically needy and deserving: the poor (Fig. 11).

Fig. 11. Design on velvet showing a repeating pattern of a young man and a beggar. Persian 1610–40. Karlsruhe Turkish Booty. Inv. D 200. With the permission of the Badisches Landesmuseum, Karlsruhe.

4   The poor and the needy

The alms are for the poor and needy, those who work to collect them, those whose hearts are brought together, the ransoming of slaves, debtors, in God's way, and the traveller.

Qur'an 9:60

It is not piety, that you turn your faces to the East and to the West. True piety is this: to believe in God, and the Last Day, the angels, the Book, and the Prophets, to give of one's substance, however cherished, to kinsmen, and orphans, the needy, the traveller, beggars, and to ransom the slave, to perform the prayer, to pay the alms (zakat).

Qur'an 2:177

The reward of him who gives alms from his abundance is not superior to that of him who receives alms because of need.[1]

Charitable giving has rarely been examined historically from the perspective of the recipients, in part because the means to do so are not always readily available, in part because of the assumption that recipients were mostly indigents. As such, their lives may seem to offer little that demands description or explanation, their individual stories to be of little historical consequence. One way to broaden our understanding of the role of charity and its impact on people of different status and on whole societies, is consciously to seek out evidence that in some way reflects the experience of the recipients, first-hand accounts to the extent possible. Sources by and about recipients are more plentiful than perhaps imagined, particularly if we include non-poor recipients like Ca'fer Efendi or Evliya Çelebi, or the foreigners who encountered charity in the large caravansarays and through their local acquaintances or interlocutors. Muslim travelers like Ibn Battuta and Evliya Çelebi described their use of endowed caravansarays and fountains as did Europeans like Guillaume Postel during his travels in Muslim lands. Authors such as Ibn Khallikan enjoyed their patrons' beneficence and in articulating their gratitude, they provided at least a literary rendition of their attitudes to these patrons. Of Muzaffar al-Din, Ibn Khallikan said:

---

[1] Hadith quoted in Al-Ghazālī, *Kitāb Asrār al-Zakāh*, 297; Faris, *Mysteries of Almsgiving*, 72.

Were I to enumerate all his virtues and noble deeds, I should be obliged to give a great extension to this work, but they are so well known that it is needless to enter into any details . . . our family were under such obligations to Muzaffar al-Din, that, to repay even a part of them, our utmost efforts would be in vain; gratitude to a benefactor is, however, a binding precept. May God reward him for us with the best of retributions! inasmuch as the benefits and favours conferred by him on us, and by his forefathers on ours, were boundless and men's affections are gained by acts of kindness.[2]

The preceding chapters focused on the ideals and practices of charitable giving and historical examples of benefactors. The present chapter focuses on the recipients of charity, particularly on the poor and the needy, including a brief discussion of poverty. To the extent that they have been visible, the recipients of charity appeared mostly as passive actors in the drama of philanthropy. Like Lalla Fatiha and her children, they were the beneficiaries of decisions made by others about what and how much they should receive, when, and in what manner. No matter what their status, recipients are assumed to have had little say in such decisions, which ultimately stressed their relative weakness and dependence on the donors, even if a particular moment brought them the benefits of great generosity. This weakness may be overemphasized, especially with respect to the non-poor. Nor should we assume that poverty, while in some cases the result of disability and itself debilitating, necessarily stripped people of intelligence or agency. Instead, our working assumption about poor people should be that even they could make choices about how to cope with poverty and make selections from among the options of available assistance. This was certainly the assumption of al-Ghazali, who, after focusing most of his attentions on the givers in his *Kitāb Asrār al-Zakāh*, also recommended to recipients that they adhere to a code of behavior. For their part, they should be sure that they qualified to receive zakat or sadaqa before taking it and thank the donor and praise the donation. Moreover, recipients were responsible, in theory, for verifying the source of what they received so as to avoid taking anything acquired by questionable or unlawful means.[3] In al-Ghazali's eyes, the recipients, even the poor, were theoretically not devoid of agency or responsibility. The challenge for the historian is to explore sources for clues to the struggles and strategies of the poor.

The Qur'an lists the legitimate recipients of zakat and sadaqa in the two verses quoted at the opening of this chapter, while other verses, hadiths, and legal texts further interpret who may or may not properly receive zakat or sadaqa. The Qur'anic categories are broad, allowing room for subjective interpretations of the legitimate recipients. This elasticity made possible an inclusive culture of charity and allowed room for local initiatives and individual

---

[2] Ibn Khāllikān, *Biographical Dictionary*, vol. II, 541.
[3] Al-Ghazālī, *Kitāb Asrār al-Zakāh*, 293–95; Faris, *Mysteries of Almsgiving*, 60–66.

idiosyncrasies. At the same time, the definition of categories also led to selection and exclusion, imposing hierarchies of need and deservedness that helped to define who was entitled to assistance. The privilege of receiving beneficent distributions was circumscribed and contingent, sometimes a prerogative of office, birth, or profession, sometimes a predictable event, at times haphazard and dependent on passing good will and a generous spirit. The fact that categories existed at all meant there were those who were intentionally excluded, despite the fact that they may have been neither wealthy nor strong. These were the unlucky and unprivileged poor. Moreover, although the annual rhythm traced in chapter 2 identified regular occasions for giving, these did not necessarily include fixed groups of recipients. Endowments, although promising stipends to some, could not always ensure their own prosperity and the continuous distribution of the assigned benefits.

Most Muslims (and some non-Muslims) have been the beneficiaries of Muslim philanthropy. Mosques and fountains served diverse populations, whether in cities, neighborhoods, or villages. Everyone from the neighborhood beggar to the most senior scholar might enjoy the benefits of a sultan's multifunctional mosque complex, just as everyone from the poorest to the richest pilgrim benefited from Zubayda's waterworks in Mecca or bridges built and maintained as endowments. The markets and baths built to sustain these endowments also made a contribution to the general welfare by creating commercial spaces and providing for ritual and general hygiene. By their nature, many of these institutions benefited people who suffered no immediate economic hardship and many others who were even quite wealthy, and such was apparently the intent of their founders. Large beneficent institutions and facilities often had no way to select or discriminate between their beneficiaries. (The same is true of contemporary philanthropy when it sponsors disaster relief, hospitals, museums, sports centers, and libraries.)

Lists of clients served by Ottoman public kitchens are one example of a source that provides valuable insight into the range of beneficiaries of a specific charitable endeavor. According to their foundation deeds, the kitchens were intended to serve scholars, students, sufis, functionaries of the mosque complexes, and travelers of all ranks, although some indigents also ate in them. By the mid-sixteenth century, after operating for one hundred years, the imaret in the complex of Sultan Mehmed II in Istanbul fed approximately 1,500 people twice a day. Among the diverse group of regular diners were visiting dignitaries, travelers, scholars and students from the prestigious colleges attached to the mosque, the doorkeepers and guards of these colleges, the students of three other nearby colleges, the residents of four dervish lodges, 600 student candidates and their 8 proctors, 56 members of the imaret staff, 47 hospital staff members, and 51 other functionaries, including those working at the Fatih mosque and the tombs in the complex. After all these people finished eating, what was left over was distributed to the indigent poor. The Süleymaniye complex in the same city stipulated a similar roster of clients. Indigence, often assumed to be the principal motivation for charity, was only one basis for determining need or eligibility at these large kitchens. In contrast, the deed of Hurrem Sultan's complex in Jerusalem, endowed in the same years as the Süleymaniye, provided food for 50 staff, the guests in its 55 rooms, and for 400 "poor and pious" people twice daily.[4] The contrast between its clientele and that of the imarets of Fatih and Süleyman is emphasized by a contemporary report sent back to Istanbul, which related: "the poor of this region are many . . . I was amazed at the crowds and the cry for help from the sort of people who said 'we are still hungry,' not receiving [food] because the food and bread did not reach [them]."[5] Yet whether in endowment deeds or historical chronicles, the indigent beneficiaries of charity usually appear in undifferentiated groups. For the kitchen in Jerusalem, no details were given about who the 400 "poor and pious, weak and needy" were meant to be, nor how they should be selected.

Only occasionally is it possible to learn something about a needy individual. On October 6, 1598, a letter of patent was issued by the Ottoman sultan Mehmed III (1595–1603) to Kamer, daughter of Abdullah, a poor woman (*fakire*). It confirmed her original entitlement, granted three years earlier, to receive one full serving of food per meal at the public kitchen founded in Istanbul by Sultan Selim I (1512–20). Additional signatures on the back of the same document reconfirmed the patent in 1601 and 1614. Finally, years later, Kamer voluntarily transferred her food right to a woman named Nafise.[6] In another example, a certain Ahmed obtained an imperial Ottoman decree in mid-August 1601 to reconfirm his right to receive a full serving of food at the public kitchen of the Süleymaniye complex in Istanbul. Ahmed had requested that his right be renewed for the third time, explaining that since he had lost both legs in the battle of Eğri (1595) during the Hungarian campaign of Mehmed III, he and his family had become poor (*fakirülhal*) and he could not undertake any kind of regular work.[7]

The cases of Kamer and Ahmed constitute brief encounters with individuals defined as poor, each granted a daily meal as a right or privilege at one of Istanbul's public kitchens. Through them, we catch a rare glimpse of the particular historical circumstances of individual poor people. On what grounds Kamer secured an imperial patent for the right to eat at the imaret of Selim I is a mystery. Neither the origins of her poverty nor the means by which she drew

---

[4] A. Süheyl Ünver, *Fâtih Aşhânesi Tevzî'nâmesi* (Ankara: İstanbul Fethi Derneği Yayınları, 1953); Kürkçüoğlu, *Süleymaniye Vakfiyesi*; Singer, *Constructing Ottoman Beneficence.*
[5] Topkapi Palace Archives, Evrak 7301/2, translated in full in Singer, *Constructing Ottoman Beneficence,* 100.
[6] Topkapi Palace Archives, E.5411/3.
[7] Topkapi Palace Archives E.5411/7. Eğri = Erlau (Hungary).

attention to her plight are described. Perhaps she was formerly a member of an important household, and the privilege was part of her pension. Ahmed's story provided more concrete details about his situation. A severely disabled veteran of an imperial campaign, he petitioned for and received a daily serving of food. He had a family whom he could not support, but they were not included in the patent that granted him the right to a daily meal. The privilege he received was personal, earned for himself alone, presumably in recognition of his military service and injury. Yet as indicated in Kamer's letter of patent, these privileges could also be passed on, either to people nominated by their holders or as part of an inheritance. So perhaps Ahmed's heirs could look forward to some small measure of social insurance at his death.

Kamer and Ahmed might be compared with the group of anonymous boys depicted in the painting of the circumcision celebrations held in 1720 for the sons of Ahmed III (see Fig. 6).[8] The boys stood as spectators watching one of the many performances put on during the two-week celebration, while at the same time, they were also part of the spectacle. Their circumcisions were taking place at the sultan's expense, one aspect of the imperial beneficence on display for whomever attended the performances or might be privileged to see the painting. Each boy was dressed in new clothes awarded him for the occasion and each received a sum of money along with access to the festivities and a meal.[9] All of these poor recipients appear to have only "walk-on" roles in the larger theater of historical action. Historians, however, must bear them in mind and work to write them into the web of human relationships that impelled the actions of more visible and presumably more consequential actors. The poor, the needy, and others deemed deserving of charity laid claims to and consumed the resources and energies of wealthy and more powerful individuals, while the charity they received affected their own perceptions of identity and entitlement.

Thinking about poverty

What does it mean to call someone poor? Individuals and societies confront this question regularly and the answer affects virtually everyone in a society because the condition of poor or not-poor entails rights, responsibilities, authority, status, or stigma. The label "poor" can routinely qualify people to receive benefits or assistance as well as exempting them from paying taxes. In the past, the lack of property was one way to define poverty that served to deny people rights in a polity or community.

Michel Mollat, an early scholar of the history of poverty in the European Middle Ages, offered the following definition:

[8] *Surname-i Vehbi* (1720), Topkapi Palace Museum A.3593, f. 43a.
[9] Peirce, *The Imperial Harem*, 192. See also Terzioğlu, "The Imperial Circumcision Festival."

A pauper was a person who permanently or temporarily found himself in a situation of weakness, dependence, or humiliation, characterized by privation of the means to power and social esteem (which means varied with period and place): these included money, relations, influence, power, knowledge, skill, nobility of birth, physical strength, intellectual capacity, and personal freedom and dignity. Living from hand to mouth, he had no chance of rising without assistance. Such a definition is broad enough to encompass the frustrated, the misfit, the antisocial, and the marginal. It is not limited to any one era, region, or social setting. Nor does it exclude those who in obedience to ascetic or mystical ideals chose voluntarily to live apart from the world or those who out of a spirit of self-sacrifice chose to live as paupers among the poor.[10]

Mollat's definition is a useful one, encompassing many possible meanings and implications of poverty in a language applicable to different societies. He included the social, political, and economic effects of poverty, recognizing that strength, independence, and honor derive from both material and social capital, and acknowledging that lack of one of the latter may affect the ability to acquire or maintain any or all of the former. In investigating particular historical situations and cultures, some of Mollat's "means to power and social esteem" will be more prominent, others perhaps irrelevant. To his list, drawn up some thirty years ago, one might also add a number of prejudicial factors widely recognized today as inhibiting access to these means, including gender, age, religion, race, ethnicity, or ecology.[11]

General discussions of poverty in history employ some further categories for thinking about what poverty means and its implications for those called poor. Two main analytic divisions are used to understand the causes of, and, by implication perhaps, to decide the proper responses to, poverty. Conjunctural or accidental poverty is brought on by sudden events like illness, injury, natural disasters, or war. Such events can make even normally self-sufficient people poor, and are largely unpredictable and unavoidable. However, the ensuing poverty can often be met with aid distributions and pre-crisis standards of living restored within a period measurable by normal harvest seasons or business cycles, with the return of rain, the absence of disease, or the end of war, for example. Conjunctural events may affect a few individuals but can also be responsible for widespread famine and starvation, subsequent epidemics or

---

[10] Michel Mollat, *The Poor in the Middle Ages: An Essay in Social History* (New Haven: Yale University Press, 1986 (originally published in French, 1978)), 5.

[11] The experience of poverty, as distinct from charity, has been researched more in European history than in the history of Islamic societies. On this, see C. Lis and H. Soly, *Poverty and Capitalism in Pre-Industrial Europe* (London: Humanities Press, 1973); the series of volumes (three, to date) edited by Thomas Riis, *Aspects of Poverty in Early Modern Europe* (Stuttgart and Odense, 1981–90); Bronisław Geremek, *Poverty: A History* (Cambridge, MA: Blackwell, 1994); and Robert Jütte, *Poverty and Deviance in Early Modern Europe* (Cambridge, UK: Cambridge University Press, 1994). For Africa, there is the comprehensive work of John Iliffe, *The African Poor: A History* (Cambridge, UK: Cambridge University Press, 1987).

migration, depending on the availability or lack of emergency assistance and the access to or exclusion from it. Conjunctural poverty is usually recognized as a sufficient qualification for relief.[12]

Structural poverty is a long-term phenomenon, more complex than conjunctural poverty but not always unrelated. It is deprivation created or maintained by shifting demographic or economic cycles, lack of land or work, life-cycle stages such as youth, childbearing, or old age, lack of marketable skills, or social prejudices against gender, age, or race. All of these can contribute to forming barriers that prevent people from overcoming poverty. Many of the more universal categories of poor people – such as widows, orphans, the elderly, prisoners, and the disabled – are victims of structural poverty, made permanently dependent on others for their basic needs and unable to escape this condition. Historically these categories have included large numbers of women and children as the more vulnerable people in most societies.[13] Structural impoverishment demands more complex and longer-term responses than the immediate assistance that is often most crucial to alleviating conjunctural poverty. Obviously, people of means may be less vulnerable to structural and conjunctural events alike, particularly if their assets and revenues are diversified so as to mitigate risk. However, long-term changes in sources of wealth and status, together with diminishing natural resources, shifting patterns of trade, developments in manufacturing or transportation, or political shifts that favor certain social groups can all impoverish established families or whole societies. The texts referred to in this chapter acknowledge these variations in the causes of poverty either directly or through references to charity and how it should be distributed.

Any study that examines pre-modern societies must also point out the precariousness of wealth or well-being in general. Conjunctural events may ultimately produce structural changes, creating poverty that lasts for more than a generation. Thus, while the causes of poverty may be classified separately, their discrete results are not always distinguishable. Famine, disease, war (including the enslavement of prisoners), natural disasters, political upheavals, and economic crises could leave even the wealthiest person materially destitute and dependent on the generosity of others. A severe crisis such as plague or extended famine could turn thousands of people in the artisan and laboring classes into indigents by forcing up the price of food or destroying family networks that provided regular mutual assistance.[14] Hence, it is perhaps useful to think about a potential for poverty that affected everyone alongside the continually poor.

---

[12] Iliffe, *The African Poor*, 4–6.   [13] Jütte, *Poverty and Deviance*, 21–44.

[14] Abraham Marcus, "Poverty and Poor Relief in Eighteenth Century Aleppo," *Revue du Monde Musulman et de la Mediterranée* 55–56 (1990): 171–80.

Poverty was not an absolute or uniform condition. Its origins in specific circumstances as well as the response of the poor influenced how other people reacted to such individuals and their plight as much as did the prevailing ideologies and individual inclinations of the beneficent. Thus, in addition to characterizing the causes of poverty as structural or conjunctural, ideological and historical discussions of poverty describe the poor as "deserving" and "undeserving," either explicitly or by implication. Religious precepts, social norms, economic or political conditions, and personal experience shape attitudes toward the poor and divide them in most societies into these two broad categories. Deservedness may be defined according to the circumstances of poverty, as well as by origin, confession, profession, residence, gender, or age, in order to include or exclude people from assistance. Dividing the poor into deserving and undeserving is a powerful means of marking the boundaries of a community or neighborhood, strengthening identities and loyalties, and promoting ideologies, be they religious, ethnic, or otherwise. Likewise, the initiation of specific poor relief efforts implies a distinction between deserving and undeserving within the immediate context of distributing particular resources.[15] Miriam Hoexter has pointed out, for example, that over time Muslim endowments for specific solidarity groups proliferated, whether these were defined by association with a particular school of law, a sufi order, a neighborhood, or geographic origins. In eighteenth-century Salonica, the "outsider poor" who were not part of any social network in the city included rural migrants, fugitive slaves, unskilled workers, beggars, dismissed domestic servants, and solitary women. Their need was not perceived as legitimate by most individual donors and institutions.[16]

Poverty as a subject extends far beyond its intersection with the topic of charity. Although it is no less compelling a subject of study the space here allows for only a brief discussion. As with charity, the Qur'an provides one shared textual frame of reference for Muslims which, together with other texts, has inspired a broad range of attitudes toward poverty, further shaped by historically specific conditions. The causes of poverty in any Islamic society – other than the conscious choice by some sufis to adopt a pauper's life – belong more to universal contexts than to those specifically shaped by Muslim beliefs or experiences. Ahmed, disabled in battle, belongs to a universal category of people who fall into poverty through unfortunate accident, in particular the category of war veterans. Lalla Fatiha, impoverished by widowhood and the costs of raising children, belonged to another such category, and resembled

---

[15] For a comparative discussion of the distinction between "deserving" and "undeserving" in Europe, see Jütte, *Poverty and Deviance*, 145.
[16] Miriam Hoexter, "Charity, the Poor, and Distributions of Alms in Ottoman Algiers," in *Poverty and Charity*, ed. Bonner *et al.*, 149. On Salonica, see Ginio, "Living on the Margins," 169–70.

women and children worldwide who become poor when the male head of their family disappears or is no longer able to work. It is the experience of poverty as it relates to charity that may have some specifically Islamic aspects because of the ethos described in earlier chapters, but this too remains to be investigated further.

One group of traditionally deserving poor in Islamic societies were the poor of Mecca and Medina, and to a lesser extent perhaps those of Jerusalem and Hebron, Kerbala and Najaf, and some other sacred cities and sites. These people included men and women who lived in the holy cities, some as religious functionaries and some simply as devout believers who sought to spend their days in close proximity to the holy places. As discussed in chapter 2, endowment deeds often named "the poor of the two holy cities" (the Haramayn al-Sharifayn) or "the poor of this town" as the last in the succession of recipients. In Ottoman Algiers, money sent annually from the waqf of the Haramayn al-Sharifayn to the holy cities was distributed to office-holders of all ranks in the various institutions of Mecca and Medina, and individual men and women who were shaykhs, freed slaves, former mosque servants, people originally from Algiers, and others. Some were probably on the list ex-officio, while others had sent petitions to the managers of the Algerian waqf asking for support.[17]

Historically, ideas about poverty and attitudes to the poor have been far from static and have ranged from glorification to acceptance to censure. The pious poor of different faiths have often secured support and admiration, though not consistently. Holy cities like Mecca, Medina, and Jerusalem have long attracted pilgrims of every station, while their residents have exhibited a greater (if not boundless) tolerance for the presence of impoverished co-religionists.[18] Yet scholars of Western Europe, for example, have found that after the Middle Ages attitudes toward the poor there shifted and became more judgmental of those who were now described as able-bodied or "sturdy," capable of working but too lazy to find jobs and hence undeserving of help or special consideration. Such changes reflected at least in part the association, justified or not, of poverty with criminality, vagrancy, heresy, or with marginalized groups such as gypsies, prostitutes, thieves, or strangers.[19] Similar studies for Islamic societies that explore changes over time in both intellectual and practical attitudes to the poor do not yet exist.

In Muslim texts, neither wealth nor poverty is consistently portrayed as inherently good or bad, perhaps because both were attributed to God. No intrinsic shame adheres to poverty, no stain to wealth, especially if people are

[17] Hoexter, "Alms in Ottoman Algiers," 151–57.
[18] See, for example, the various cases that have to do with poor Jews in Jerusalem, in Amnon Cohen, *Jewish Life under Islam*.
[19] Geremek, *Poverty*, 7; Mollat, *The Poor in the Middle Ages*, 7.

assiduous in paying zakat.[20] The practical effects of this attitude are reflected in widespread reports of beggars and sufis who were tolerated and sustained. The scholars who interpreted Islamic theology and law came to constitute a class supported by donations. Seeking to establish a religious ethic which was in some ways the antithesis of the socio-economic definition articulated by Mollat, the Qur'an insists that material wealth is ultimately without value when compared with sincere belief and a life of good works (of any size) performed with true intention. It cautions donors to avoid shaming or insulting recipients and continually emphasizes belief and almsgiving as the key to Paradise, and not riches or power (2:262–64). In this way the Qur'anic verses seek to counterbalance the resultant loss or absence of worldly power and status suffered by the poor, whether by insisting that in the spiritual world material wealth has no value or by claiming that charity aims to restore people to their rightful status. Nonetheless, most texts express a preference for wealth over poverty.

As in some Jewish and Christian texts, Muslim authors recognized the particular poverty of those who were forced into reduced circumstances from a position of some status. In European history, such people were known as the "shamefaced poor" because of the loss of social status that accompanied their economic misfortune. They deserved some deference while being provided with assistance. Not only did poverty bring them shame, but in some places they could not work because of their noble status, and so were dependent on charity to survive or recover. In Italy of the fourteenth and fifteenth centuries, the shamefaced poor were a popular target of charitable distributions made in a spirit of class solidarity to people who were perceived as having exceptional qualities and deserving assistance.[21]

Familiar from the Qur'an and al-Ghazali are more general discussions of the care and attention demanded of donors for the regard and self-respect of recipients of charity, lest they be further humiliated in receiving assistance. Al-Ghazali essentially recognized a category of shamefaced poor when he said that a person whose only means to earn a living is one for which he lacks appropriate tools, or that one "unworthy of his honor" should be considered a pauper, that is, eligible for charity.[22] In describing how distributions were carried out after the Mughal weighing ceremony, the Portuguese priest Manrique explained that the fourth weighing of "eatables, such as wheaten cakes, flour, sugar, *ghi* [ghee = clarified butter], and common kinds of cotton cloth" was "distributed amongst the poor Bramenes and Baneanes [brahmins

---

[20] Eric Chaumont, "Pauvreté et richesse dans le Coran et dans les sciences religieuses musulmanes," in *Pauvreté et richesse*, ed. Pascual, 24.

[21] Geremek, *Poverty*, 24.

[22] Al-Ghazālī, *Kitāb Asrār al-Zakāh*, 291; Faris, *Mysteries of Almsgiving*, 54.

(priests) and *bania*s (merchants)], but with much secrecy that, save those who actually gave the gifts or those who received them, no one saw them."[23]

The definitions of need and of appropriate levels of assistance are also crucial indicators of the way in which a society understands the just distribution of resources. In the early Shafi'i legal discussions, for example, poverty was determined by the relative status of individuals and the proper response to it was to restore lost status.[24] In this context, obligatory zakat and voluntary sadaqa alike aimed to provide more than basic subsistence; they were intended to preserve the existing socio-economic order and so posed little threat to those in established positions of power.[25]

In Islamic historiography, few scholars have taken up any aspect of the history of poverty before the end of the twentieth century. The article *"fakīr"* (poor) in the second edition of the *Encyclopaedia of Islam* is scarcely more than a long dictionary entry. Adam Sabra, author of the first book to examine poverty in a historical context in any period of Islamic history, recalled that people believed he would find little material when he began his work. His broad chapter titles reflect the status of research: Poverty; Begging and Almsgiving; Waqf; Standards of Living; Food Shortages and Famines. Any one of these topics has already provided material for several monographs in American and European history, not to mention contemporary works of political science, economics, anthropology, and sociology for many regions of the globe. Mine Ener also studied poverty and the poor in Egypt, focusing her research on the nineteenth and twentieth centuries. Like Sabra's, her research on poverty and the poor drew skeptical comments from some people she worked with, but she ultimately demonstrated that the resources are more than sufficient to explore the experience of poverty as well as attitudes and actions directed toward the poor. Together, Sabra's and Ener's works established that the poor and their poverty can be a viable subject for research in Islamic history without discovering new sources.[26]

---

[23] Manrique, *Travels of Fray Sebastian Manrique 1629–1643*, as quoted in Beach and Koch, *King of the World*, 43.

[24] This discussion is based on Mattson, "Status-Based Definitions of Need."

[25] For a more extensive discussion of definitions of need and poverty in the earliest Muslim society, see Bonner, "Definitions of Poverty."

[26] Sabra, *Poverty and Charity*, 1–7; Mine Ener, *Managing Egypt's Poor and the Politics of Benevolence, 1800–1952* (Princeton: Princeton University Press, 2003). Some works that include material on poverty and the poor, although these topics are not their main focus, are Eliyahu Ashtor, *A Social and Economic History of the Near East in the Middle Ages* (Berkeley: University of California Press, 1976); Ira M. Lapidus, *Muslim Cities in the Later Middle Ages*, rev. edn. (Cambridge, UK: Cambridge University Press, 1984); Sanders, *Ritual, Politics, and the City*; Shoshan, *Popular Culture*. In his work on eighteenth-century Aleppo based on local court records, Abraham Marcus was one of the earliest to discuss poverty directly. See Marcus, *The Middle East on the Eve of Modernity*.

Research by Marcus, Hoexter, and Ginio has also directly addressed the condition of the poor in historical terms, although this is not the main focus of their scholarship. Not only did they write in some detail about who people were and what happened to them, disaggregating "the poor" into individuals, but they have also analyzed individual strategies for dealing with need and the experience of poverty. The central Ottoman archives and the judicial protocols that remain from towns around the empire introduce people like Kamer and Ahmed, whose lives can now be incorporated into a historical analysis. Yet, it bears remembering that even where such individuals appear in Ottoman documents, they almost always speak to us through the medium of a record created by an institution or authority of the imperial administration, at least one step removed (if not more) from an autobiographical text or first-hand account.

The poor and the indigent (*al-fuqara wa'l-masakin*)

These are the first two groups in the list of people eligible to receive zakat. Both faqir and miskin can be translated as "poor," although this translation explains very little about the actual significance of the words. Faqir (pl. fuqara), the most common word for "poor" in Arabic, has a variety of meanings. Anyone may refer to him- or herself as "one in need of God's mercy" (*al-faqir ila rahmat Allah*). The expression emphasizes the essential distinction between God, who is "al-Ghani" (rich, self-sufficient, and independent) and people who are essentially needy. In the Qur'an, faqir is used as the opposite of ghani. Literally, a faqir is someone whose back is broken, a condition that produces absolute disability and dependence. The quality of dependence is central to understanding the meaning of poverty, the aims of beneficence, and relationships between donors and recipients in Muslim contexts. However, the word is used most frequently to mean "indigent" or "destitute." Sufis were often called "faqir" to emphasize their utter spiritual dependence on God's mercy and perhaps because many renounced their worldly possessions as a basic aspect of their spiritual practice. Because poverty was widely associated with the sufis, in some contexts faqir means specifically "sufi" and not just any group of poor people. *Fakir* or *fakeer* entered English usage as early as 1609 to refer to a pious Muslim beggar and in British-ruled India also included Hindu ascetics. Finally, the word faqir was used by Muslim authors to refer to themselves, the equivalent in English of "your humble servant."[27] In chronicles, the literary juxtaposition of this phrase with the familiar refrain "and God knows best" emphasized the

---

[27] Quran 47:38, 35:15; K. A. Nizami, "fakīr," in *EI²*, II:757–58; E. W. Lane, *An Arabic–English Lexicon* (London: Williams and Norgate, 1863–93), s.v.; *Oxford English Dictionary* (online edition, August 9, 2005), s.v.; Rafeq, "The Poor in Ottoman Damascus," 217; Chaumont, "Pauvreté et richesse," 19–20.

author's humility and tenuous claim on knowledge or expertise when compared with divine wisdom. In addition, the author's modesty may be directed at patrons, at whose request many literary texts were produced or whose sponsorship an author hoped to win. Here again, the power gradient is a central and ongoing aspect of relations between all benefactors and their clients, one which creates ties of responsibility and dependence as well as exploitation and suffering.

The Qur'an, hadith, and subsequent legal writings call the poor both "faqir" and "miskin." The labels denote different degrees of poverty. Faqir designated a pauper, one who has nothing and does not (or cannot) work. Without help, he or she is unable to scrape together even a day's subsistence. In comparison, a miskin is a needy person who barely has the means to cover the most basic needs. Miskin includes the working poor, who, despite their labors, cannot make ends meet, as well as those who have been well off and are now unable to maintain themselves at their accustomed level, as dictated by their status.[28] Distinctions like this exist outside of normative Muslim texts; in one way or another most societies recognize the difference between paupers who cannot maintain even a basic existence without assistance and the working poor whose labors do not enable them permanently to cross whatever poverty line a society establishes.

In his study of eighteenth-century Aleppo based on contemporary chronicles and court records, Marcus compiled a vivid description of the indigent and working poor and their general conditions:

They inhabited small and crowded courtyard houses often shared with other households or rented mean rooms ... or found shelter in public buildings. Their clothes were often old and shabby ... They subsisted on a diet limited in both its quality and quantity ... Those of them who worked pursued lowly and poorly paid occupations, making their living as unskilled laborers, peddlars, servants, prostitutes, petty thieves, and beggars. Wives and children usually worked ... [They owned] few personal possessions. Altogether they dwelt on the threshold of hunger, cold, and disease ...[29]

While this description refers to a specific time and place, it imparts a sense of the meager dress, living conditions, food, and employment possibilities of the poor in general and the more concrete meanings of economic inequality. Aleppo in the eighteenth century was an urban society with a small wealthy group at the top who enjoyed significant power and luxury, a somewhat larger middle class employed in trade and manufacture and perhaps administrative and military

---

[28] Michael Bonner, "Poverty and Economics in the Quran," *The Journal of Interdisciplinary History* 35, no. 3 (2005): 399. The jurists of different schools sometimes reversed the labels, although the substance of the distinction between them remained the same; on which see Zysow, "zakāt," XI:415.

[29] Marcus, "Poverty and Poor Relief," 173.

tasks, and the largest group, which comprised people who were more and less poor, their poverty fluctuating according to individual and local economic, social and political conditions. Theirs was:

the increasingly precarious material world inhabited by most of the townspeople. Here were the multitudes of residents who lived at bare subsistence levels, surviving from hand to mouth in wretched conditions: families crowded into congested dwellings often shared with other households; parents reduced by poverty to putting their children in the custody of others; debtors who languished in prison for months for the inability to pay back petty sums; the victims of hunger and starvation in periods of high bread prices; and the host of those dependent on charity.[30]

Al-Ghazali's discussion of the distinctions between the faqir and the miskin offers one example of how a legal scholar described the two groups as well as providing useful definitions of what can also be called absolute and relative poverty, both equally legitimate to qualify someone to receive zakat. He stressed the relative condition of the miskin, explaining that "a person may possess a thousand dirhams and yet be poor while another may own nothing more than an ax and a rope and yet be rich." Even with a house, furniture, and clothing, a person could still be considered poor if lacking the things required by a specific position and status. Al-Ghazali reminded his readers, too, that the reason for defining who is poor is to determine who must pay zakat and the smaller sum of zakat al-fitr, or only zakat al-fitr, or who cannot pay either and so may accept them.[31]

The two main factors by which someone was judged to be poor were the existence of need (haja) and absence of surplus (fadl). A needy person did not possess sufficient resources (kifaya) for sustenance and could legitimately seek charity. However, need and sufficiency were not defined by all Muslim authorities and jurists as absolute conditions, but rather, most definitions depended on a combination of absolute and relative factors. For example, the early Iraqi scholar Abu 'Ubayd (d. 838) cited a hadith that prohibited people seeking assistance if they had enough food to sustain themselves and their dependants for a day and a night. He also quoted another hadith that said a person could beg until acquiring what would support him. Finally, Abu 'Ubayd himself recommended that a person should not ask for charity (that is, be considered legitimately needy) if they still possessed the value of 40 dirhams (silver coins) after fulfilling all their obligations to provide food, clothing, and shelter for themselves and their dependants, including their slaves.[32] Another kind of poverty line was fixed by some jurists according to the nisab, the minimum quantity of

---

[30] Marcus, *The Middle East on the Eve of Modernity*, 48.
[31] Al-Ghazālī, *Kitāb Asrār al-Zakāh*, 291; Faris, *Mysteries of Almsgiving*, 53–55.
[32] Mattson, "Status-Based Definitions," 34–35. See also, for example, the text of Qudama b. Ja'far, a tenth-century jurist, who included a chapter on the distribution of sadaqa in his *Kitāb al-Kharāj*, a treatise on taxation. Ben Shemesh, *Qudāma b. Ja'far's Kitāb al-Kharāj*, 65–68.

revenues or goods on which zakat was due for the period of one year. Possessing the nisab effectively meant that someone had a surplus, "a specific amount of wealth in excess of what is needed to support and protect life" and so could pay zakat and therefore not be considered poor.[33]

Such discussions aimed not only to establish who was needy but also to determine how much zakat might legitimately be given to someone. If need was defined in an absolute sense, then the amount to be given was also fixed. Yet if need was a subjective condition, one based on the accustomed circumstances of the recipient, then the proper amount to be given could vary tremendously and people of many different economic conditions became the legitimate recipients of zakat. This way of thinking about need appears to be tied to the considerations employed for determining questions of maintenance (nafaqa) in Islamic law, not usually discussed in the context of zakat or sadaqa. Maintenance was conceived as a male obligation to support immediate family members including parents and children together with wives, other women and children under a man's formal guardianship (wilaya), and his slaves. Being protected by maintenance obligations, a man's dependants were not eligible to receive his own zakat. However, the man himself might be eligible to receive zakat if by selling the house and using its proceeds he would be unable to meet his obligations, including buying a more modest house for his family. Maintenance laws were frequently invoked in matters of divorce, and payments to a wife were fixed according to her status at the time of her marriage, taking into consideration the means of her husband. Thus, one person's luxury might be another's need.[34]

In real terms, maintenance obligations did appear as an important measure of economic capability. For example, in a judicial decision from eighteenth-century Aleppo, a man was released by the court from the obligation to support his siblings when it was confirmed that his monthly income was inadequate. The same court also heard cases where widows, orphans, the elderly, and the disabled demanded assistance, whether charity or maintenance, from their relatives and communities. Among these cases were lawsuits by individuals who had grown accustomed to regular, if minimal, donations from benefactors who subsequently ceased giving for one reason or another. The disappointed beneficiaries – a son who expected that his father's benefactors would continue to give him the same half piastre per week; poor Jews getting help from wealthier Jews to pay their poll-tax; a recent convert to Islam who no longer received the occasional few piastres from his former Christian co-religionist – turned to the court to try to regain those small sums that were so crucial to navigating poverty.[35] The margins of survival were slim and had to be defended.

---

[33] Mattson, "Status-Based Definitions," 33; Zysow, "zakāt," XI:411.
[34] See the discussions that link nafaqa and sadaqa in Mattson, "Status-Based Definitions."
[35] Marcus, The Middle East on the Eve of Modernity, 49, 215.

For orphans or impoverished children in eighteenth-century Salonica, support was sometimes available through the practice of taking poor children into domestic service, with the expectation that the children would form part of the household, often becoming domestic servants. This was a chance to grow up in a more secure material environment, housed, clothed, and sheltered, perhaps even dowered or educated. Orphanages did not, as a rule, exist in pre-modern Islamic societies, although there were schools for orphans, endowments specifically to assist them, and as was evident in previous chapters, they were a popular target of beneficence. Children were usually adopted by a family member owing to a ubiquitous expectation that extended families would care for children wherever possible, a practice that stemmed at least in part from concerns about property remaining within the family. In more desperate situations, children might be placed with non-relative families. In all cases, their fate varied and while some experienced life as members of the family or as protected household servants, others suffered near-enslavement. Such situations provided an opportunity for exploitation and abuse of all kinds. Where they worked as servants, children not only were a cheaper source of labor than domestic slaves, but were also more dependent and beholden to their benefactors. Some of them, dismissed from service or moved to protest their own mistreatment, brought their cases before the qadi for arbitration.[36]

Beneficence, then, was yet another aspect of life that might be contested and claimed (at least in the Ottoman period) through the medium of Muslim legal authorities. The records of these claims – articulation, justification, adjudication – describe the parameters of justified and unjustified appeals for family and community support, the functional (as opposed to theoretical) definitions of need, and the realistic responses to it. As scholars working with court records have cautioned, the actual, spoken claims made before a qadi were not necessarily identical to the recorded protocol of the registers.[37] Yet the appearance of poor people before a judge to claim assistance demonstrated that they did engage the legal system to negotiate their survival.

Representations of individual poor people in the medieval Muslim world have also come down to us in the petitions for assistance from Jews to other Jews. These were found among the documents of the Cairo Geniza, the unique trove of religious and secular papers discovered in an old Cairo synagogue in the late

---

[36] Ginio, "Living on the Margins," 165–84. On orphans, see E. Chaumont and R. Shaham, "yatim," *EI²*, XI:298–300 and Amira al-Azhary Sonbol, "Adoption in Islamic Society: A Historical Survey," in *Children in the Muslim Middle East*, ed. Elizabeth Warnock Fernea (Austin: University of Texas Press, 1995), 45–67.

[37] For a salient discussion of the judicial registers (*sijillat al-qadi, kadı sicilleri*) as sources, see Dror Ze'evi, "The Use of Ottoman Sharī'a Court Records as a Source for Middle Eastern Social History: A Reappraisal," *Islamic Law and Society* 5, no. 1 (1998): 35–56. On cases brought by poor people before a qadi, see Ginio, "Living on the Margins," 166–67.

nineteenth century. In particular, S. D. Goitein has studied the personal, communal, and commercial practices of the Jews who lived as a minority among Muslims in Egypt, and his work demonstrates the extent to which one may read the letters as a source for the history of the medieval Mediterranean world. The petitions addressed Jewish community authorities in Cairo and not the ruling sultan. Albeit couched in rather formulaic language, designed to elicit generous responses from their recipients, they offer a rare look into the straitened circumstances of individuals who lived in the tenth to the thirteenth centuries. The petitions identified and situated the poor – their origins, family circumstances, the reasons for their poverty, and their professions – while articulating the expectations of such petitioners and, in some cases, the responses of their potential benefactors.[38] The poor Jews of medieval Cairo included the working poor, pushed to seek help as a result of the overwhelming burdens of taxation, providing for a family and fulfilling ritual obligations, or brought to crisis by illness or injury.

The medieval Geniza letters provide an interesting comparison to the later Ottoman patent letters of Kamer and Ahmed. The letters of these poor Jews in Cairo, written by them or on their behalf in order to persuade a donor of their worthiness and misery, are more detailed than the patent letters of Kamer and Ahmed, issued by an imperial office to confirm a privilege. The poor Jews included captives, refugees, proselytes, debtors, widows, divorcees, orphans, and the foreign poor who passed through the city. Some people fit more than one category, as is evident in the following petition. The author of the letter quoted below introduced the case of its bearer. One of the working poor, the man was reduced to poverty by the combined weight of illness, debt, and taxation. His request was for help to "maintain his standard of living" and the author stressed the poor man's humiliation at his condition and at his inability to hide the poverty of himself and his family:

I am writing this letter to the illustrious elders, may God preserve them, to inform them that the bearer of this (letter) is a man who was healthy, working strenuously in order to "conceal" . . . himself and his family, when Fate betrayed him and he became weak . . . such that anyone looking at him needs no explanation about his condition. In addition, debt . . . and the poll tax (*jizya*) caught up with him. Whoever assists him with something with which he can maintain his standard of living shall be deemed to have made an offering (to God). He is ashamed . . . for this has never been his habit. Whoever does him a good turn shall be deemed to have done so for the sake of God, and the Creator will magnify his reward. *And peace.*[39]

---

[38] On the documents of the Cairo Geniza and the story of their discovery, see S. D. Goitein, *A Mediterranean Society, vol. I: Economic Foundations* (Berkeley: University of California Press, 1967), 1–28. This topic and the rich materials of the Cairo Geniza have been analyzed with great insight in recent works, for which see Cohen, *Poverty and Charity*, and the companion book of texts, Mark R. Cohen, *The Voice of the Poor in the Middle Ages: An Anthology of Documents from the Cairo Geniza* (Princeton: Princeton University Press, 2005).
[39] See Cohen, *Poverty and Charity*, 33.

This private appeal for assistance was typical of other Geniza letters, whereby a person who usually managed to live "concealed," that is, able to maintain a proper level of personal and family privacy and avoid "uncovering his face" to the shame of public charity, had to expose his or her misfortune in the hopes of obtaining the necessary help. The concealment–uncovering ideas are ones that appear to have made their way from the Muslim culture of medieval Cairo into the vocabulary of the local Jewish community.[40]

For Jews and Christians living in Muslim lands, the poll-tax was a familiar burden, but it was nonetheless one which could upset the financial situation of any household; any tax, unexpected expense, or drop in income could undermine the economy of most medieval households, minority or Muslim. Wealthy members of the community were called upon to help the weaker. In sixteenth-century Jerusalem, Jewish community leaders negotiated continually with Ottoman authorities to make sure that the jizya rolls were corrected to reflect population loss in order to mitigate the collective burden on the community.[41] In Ottoman times, unemployed poor Jews and Christians were exempt from the jizya as were people with handicaps or limitations. For this reason, a Christian man named Isa from Bayt Jala, a village south of Jerusalem, appeared before the qadi in that city in the mid-sixteenth century to complain that the people in his largely Christian village had increased the jizya they took from his blind son. Isa then produced a fatwa stating that no jizya at all was due from a blind man, and the judge ordered the villagers to leave the son alone.[42]

The preceding example reminds us that evidence about the poor comes mostly from the urban context. We know less of the rural poor in the pre-modern era, and the information where available more often describes the poverty of a community or a region and not necessarily the indigence of an individual. Nonetheless, imperial decrees and sijill documents recorded examples of peasants who could not pay their taxes in certain years, together with the reasons they gave in the petitions they submitted or if called to account before a qadi. Other than the abuses of tax collectors, the causes of their impoverishment

---

[40] See Mark R. Cohen, "Maimonides and Charity in the Light of the Geniza Documents," in *The Trias of Maimonides: Jewish, Arabic and Ancient Culture of Knowledge*, ed. Georges Tamer (Berlin: Walter de Gruyter, 2005), 72–74.

[41] A. Cohen, *Jewish Life under Islam*, 20–35; C. Cahen, H. Inalcik, and P. Hardy, "*djizya*," in *EI²*, II:563.

[42] Jerusalem Court Registers (*Sijill*), vol. 44, #64/p. 11, and Singer, *Palestinian Peasants*, 81–82. Conditions varied from place to place; for example, the Shafi'i scholars in the Ayyubid period in medieval Syria and Egypt seem to have interpreted the law far less generously, with no exemptions, on which see Eli Alshech, "Islamic Law, Practice, and Legal Doctrine: Exempting the Poor from the Jizya under the Ayyubids (1171–1250)," *Islamic Law and Society* 10 (2003): 348–76. A useful discussion (one of many) of the status of Jews and Christians under Ottoman rule is Bruce Masters, *Christians and Jews in the Ottoman Arab World: The Shifting Boundaries of Political Communities 1516–1918* (Cambridge, UK: Cambridge University Press, 2001).

included natural disasters and personal tragedies alike. While the countryside often lacked the kinds of charitable institutions more characteristic of towns, peasants had networks for mutual assistance as well as access to a wider range of agrarian resources, like animal fodder, seed grain, and wild plants, which, while not ideal, could nonetheless help to bridge subsistence gaps in hard times. Ottoman evidence also shows some mechanisms for tax relief in bad years, like loans for seed from waqfs or the rescheduling or even complete forgiveness of tax payments by Ottoman officials.[43] Yet hardship brought on by natural disasters or the heavy exactions from landholders or tax collectors could also lead to migration, temporary or permanent, since this was one effective means of finding relief for the rural poor. Migration ultimately meant a loss of labor, a drop in production (and so in tax revenues), and likely the influx of poor and unskilled laborers to nearby urban centers or the creation of mobile bands of unemployed and impoverished poor people. Thus it was in the interests of land- or revenue-holders not to remain utterly indifferent to rural hardship.

Among the different categories of fuqara, sufis were the epitome of the poor and worthy object of charity, devoting their lives to the pursuit of a spiritual goal. Their devotion was expressed not only in rituals and modest if not ascetic lifestyles, but also in good works. Like many other people, sufis probably negotiated an existence that teetered between sufficiency and want. Although they continually received donations, these were often small, and some stories about sufis recount how they habitually gave away what they had in order to help others. Ibn Battuta described the local sufis in one place he visited:

It is part of their regular practice to assemble in the hospice after the afternoon prayer every day, and then make a circuit of the houses in the city; at each house they are given one or two loaves, and from these they provide food for wayfarers. The householders are used to this practice, and include [the extra loaves] in their [daily] provision in readiness for the faqirs, as a contribution to their distribution of food.[44]

Many tariqas enjoyed the beneficent patronage of rulers and wealthy people alike such that their lodges – part hostel, part ritual space – prospered. Zawiyas appeared in urban and rural sites across the Muslim world.

Different attitudes prevailed among the sufis toward accepting alms and sadaqa. On the one hand, it was important to take zakat as offered, since this act enabled another Muslim to fulfill the obligation to pay zakat.[45] Accepting sadaqa in the form of endowed lodges and subsistence support also allowed patrons the benefits of giving sadaqa while enabling the sufis to devote

[43] Singer, *Palestinian Peasants*, 115–16, and *passim* on abuses of revenue holders.
[44] Gibb, *Ibn Battuta*, vol. II, 405–06.
[45] Vincent Cornell, "Fruit of the Tree of Knowledge: The Relationship between Faith and Practice in Islam," in *The Oxford History of Islam*, ed. John L. Esposito (Oxford: Oxford University Press, 1999), 63–107.

themselves to spiritual goals. Some of their lodges were impressive structures with endowments to sustain the buildings. Yet the existence of a building did not necessarily ensure subsistence. In a petition to the Ottoman sultan Selim II (1566–74), the qadi of Konya claimed that the sufis living at the zawiya attached to the tomb of Mevlana Jalal al-Din Rumi had trouble obtaining food, despite the fact that Selim's father had invested generously in repairs to the complex of Mevlevi buildings. On these grounds, the qadi requested that the twenty-five dervishes living there be added to the list of people receiving daily meals at the endowed public kitchen belonging to Selim's mosque next door, since they suffered from the smell of food cooking as it wafted in their direction.[46]

To work or to beg?

People in need who did not enjoy some ongoing form of support could either seek work to support themselves or beg for assistance in public places like markets, mosques, or going from door to door. One theme that weaves in and out of normative discussions of charity is the obligation of a poor person to try to work as opposed to seeking charity or relying on it. Various sources make it clear that earning a living (*kasb*) is not only a priority but a religious obligation. One hadith quotes the Prophet as saying: "It is better for one of you to take a rope and cut wood and sell it than to beg from someone who might or might not give."[47] The hadith suggests that any menial labor is better than begging. Labor provides food as well as the means to give sadaqa. In a similar vein, the eighth-century jurist al-Shaybani (d. 805) characterized earning a living as a religious obligation comparable to that of seeking knowledge. Moreover, once a person obtained enough to fulfill basic needs, the surplus could be given away as sadaqa in an effort to ensure the giver's fate after death.[48]

Al-Ghazali elaborated further on the related topics of poverty and work with the aim of clarifying under what circumstances someone could receive charity as well as determining the type of assistance that might be appropriate:

But if the person is able to earn a living he will no longer be a pauper. If he were able to earn his living by means of an instrument which he does not possess, then he would be a pauper and it would be permissible to purchase the instrument for him. If he were able to earn a living [only] through means unworthy of his honour and not befitting his station, then he would be a pauper. If he were a student of jurisprudence or law and work in order to earn his living would prevent him from continuing his studies then he would be regarded as a pauper and his ability to secure a living will not be taken into consideration.

---

[46] İbrahim Hakki Konyalı, *Âbideleri ve Kitabeleri ile Konya Tarihi* (Konya: Yeni Kitap Basımevi, 1964), 977.

[47] Al-Bukhārī, *Ṣaḥīḥ al-Bukhārī* 24 (al-zakat), bab 50, bab 53; USC-MSA, Bukhari, 24/549–50.

[48] Michael Bonner, "The *Kitāb al-Kasb* Attributed to al-Shaybānī: Poverty, Surplus, and the Circulation of Wealth," *Journal of the American Oriental Society* 121 (2001): 419.

If he were a devotee [*muta'abbid*, a pious person] and work to secure a living would prevent him from fulfilling the act of worship and observing the set hours of prayer, let him work for his livelihood as much as possible because his work to earn a living is the more important.[49]

Al-Ghazali's point of departure was that people should work and they should be helped to do so; beneficent support was preferable only in specific situations. He recognized the shamefaced poor and the limitations on their ability to work, making them an exception to the recommendation of the hadith quoted above. Al-Ghazali's discussion implied that the amount of zakat paid to one person might be quite large if it restored him to his former status or supplied him with the equipment to practice his profession and become self-sustaining: "Others have gone to the extreme in generosity and said that a person may take as much as would buy him a whole village which will make him independent for the rest of his life, or as much as would establish him in a business that will make him secure for the rest of his days . . ."[50] At the same time, menial work was thus better than none and it was those who were needy and incapacitated whom people were obliged to help. Providing orphan boys with jobs or skills and giving dowries to orphan girls were charitable contributions to ensure them a place in the social order and provide basic economic security. Ibn Battuta described how the Meccans found work for orphan boys, equipping them with baskets in the bazaar so they could earn a living as porters carrying home groceries, that is, working honestly.[51] Large waqfs created many jobs for unskilled laborers (for example, cleaners, porters, and doorkeepers) or for those who had managed only a basic education in the Qur'an but could serve as reciters at tombs.

Not surprisingly, al-Ghazali distinguished between the professional scholar and the devout believer: the former deserved zakat to support him while the latter should find a time to pray that did not interfere with earning a living. The devout poor were an obvious object of charity for some, but al-Ghazali did not find that piety was a sufficient reason for seeking out or receiving charity. Scholars and students, on the other hand, deserved to be maintained in their rightful occupations of study and teaching the religious sciences, acting as judges, and giving learned opinions on questions of law. Their job was to provide spiritual and temporal guidance to rulers and subjects alike, working to ensure the overall welfare of the Muslim community.[52]

Another passage from al-Ghazali dwelt on the professional needs of scholars or literate people like himself and offered an interesting example of how poverty

[49] Al-Ghazālī, *Kitāb Asrār al-Zakāh*, 291; Faris, *Mysteries of Almsgiving*, 54.
[50] Al-Ghazālī, *Kitāb Asrār al-Zakāh*, 295; Faris, *Mysteries of Almsgiving*, 67.
[51] Gibb, *Ibn Battuta*, vol. I, 215–16.
[52] Al-Ghazālī, *Kitāb Asrār al-Zakāh*, 291; Faris, *Mysteries of Almsgiving*, 53–55.

was subjectively defined. He said that books used for instruction or for personal benefit (Qur'an, hadith, works of jurisprudence, etc.) could be considered as basic needs and not counted as surplus wealth. If the books were necessary for a man's livelihood and they were all he owned, he was even exempt from zakat al-fitr. Books for recreation and pleasure (like poetry and history), on the other hand, were a form of surplus wealth and should be sold for sustenance and to allow their owner to pay zakat. Al-Ghazali cautioned people that if they had two copies of a book, they should, for example, keep only the most correct copy and give up the more beautiful if it was less accurate.[53] That books continued to be considered a basic necessity for students and scholars was brought home in an appeal from one unfortunate Mehmed, who was accosted and robbed on the road in Anatolia one day in the mid-nineteenth century. As a poor student, Mehmed petitioned the Ottoman sultan Abdülmecid (1839–61), invoking his beneficence to replace the stolen books without which Mehmed could not complete his studies. Mehmed obviously regarded the sultan as personally responsible for the protection of his subjects (as, in fact, the sultan claimed to be) and as a source of individual succor in times of need.[54] Mehmed's case is important for the present discussion because it offers another rare first-person testimony about one kind of poverty and a strategy for managing it. Unlike Kamer or Ahmed, however, Mehmed's was a one-time request intended to restore his ability to earn his living.

A similar emphasis to that of al-Ghazali on charity that restores people's capacity to work and support themselves was put forward in the "ladder of charity" of the Cairo-based Jewish physician and theologian Maimonides (d. 1204) in his hierarchy of giving as recorded in *Matnot 'Aniyim*. Maimonides, author of several documents from the Geniza, was apparently the first to codify the dispersed Jewish laws of charity. He ranked eight degrees of benevolence, starting from giving alms grudgingly and culminating in granting a gift, loan, business partnership, or job which was intended to make the recipient self-sustaining.[55] However, despite the recommendations of these two prominent theologians, most concrete examples of medieval charity discovered thus far have consisted of distributions of aid while lacking any aspect identifiable with late twentieth-century ideas of development, that is, providing training or tools to people so that they might become less dependent on charitable distributions. No example in the pre-modern era has yet come to light of an endowment or other charitable endeavor which sought to train people in a craft or trade which could

[53] Al-Ghazālī, *Kitāb Asrār al-Zakāh*, 291–92; Faris, *Mysteries of Almsgiving*, 55–57.
[54] Başbakanlık Osmanlı Arşivi, Sadaret, A.DVN 99/86 (1270/1853–54), reproduced and discussed in Orlin Sabev (Orhan Salih), "Tales of Ottoman Book Theft (19th Century)," *Journal of Ottoman Studies/Osmanlı Araştırmaları* 29 (2007): 173–201.
[55] Abraham Cronbach, "The Gradations of Benevolence," *Hebrew Union College Annual* 16 (1941): 164–65; Mark R. Cohen, "Maimonides and Charity."

bring them into the ranks of skilled laborers and craftsmen. Perhaps we know too little of professional guilds to rule out this possibility, but the limited evidence to hand suggests that the relative economic security provided by having a trade and being part of a guild was passed on within families and rather jealously guarded. The integration of surplus labor into various professions also depended at least partly on local economic trends and so should be studied at that level.

The education of religious scholars who functioned as judges, teachers, and legal experts might be interpreted as an exceptional example of the use of beneficence to train people for professions. From the medieval period, Muslim education took place almost entirely in maktabs and madrasas endowed by rulers and other wealthy individuals. Having graduated, those who qualified as scholars could work as teachers, remaining in the schools, or else find employment in mosques. Others might use the literacy they initially obtained in religious studies as the basis for further training in the bureaucracy or go on to find work as judges or muftis. Many of the students were probably not born into poverty; rather, they earned the right to subsidized study through their intellectual talents, as a result of their family heritage, with the support of a patron, or a combination of these.

Historically, the ability of graduating scholars to find work was not consistent. Aside from the question of individual capability, the number of positions available fluctuated depending on political and economic factors. In an expansionist era such as that from the origins of the Ottoman Empire *circa* 1300 until the later sixteenth century, the learned class absorbed increasing numbers of educated religious experts from all classes into endowed schools because the state needed more people qualified to fill crucial posts in the educational and judicial systems. During that period, this legal-academic system had room for both the "sons of" as well as intelligent poor boys. As expansion slowed and posts became more jealously guarded, entry to the learned professions and even to the madrasas became increasingly difficult for anyone who did not belong to the established scholarly families, eventually further restricted to the learned families of Istanbul.[56] Yet it was the philanthropic apparatus sustaining the educational system that funded the privileged and exclusionary policies of these families.

Begging, the alternative to work or crime for poor people, was a topic of ongoing concern in discussions of charitable giving. With all the praise for the poor expressed in the texts discussed, it is interesting to note rather ambivalent or even negative attitudes to begging found in the Qur'an and hadith. The Qur'an pays specific attention to begging as a response to need and includes beggars as a category worthy of charity (2:177), but it praises the poor who do not beg importunately (2:273). The Prophet recommended that people should not beg, but rather trust God to provide, a companion idea to other statements

---

[56] Madeline C. Zilfi, *The Politics of Piety: The Ottoman Ulema of the Postclassical Age (1600–1800)* (Minneapolis: Bibliotheca Islamica, 1989).

condemning the fear of poverty and advocating work. People were encouraged to undertake even the most menial tasks rather than humiliate themselves by begging, and those who begged when they had alternatives were compared to the stingy and miserly. Begging carried an additional burden associated with poverty: shame. The European notion of the "shamefaced" poor echoed in Muslim contexts in the phrase "uncovering one's face" used by both Muslims and Jews to characterize the situation created by poverty.

Different Muslim authors allowed begging in specific circumstances, although they were not in agreement as to what these might be. According to one hadith, begging was allowed if a person incurred a debt, if someone's property was destroyed by a disaster, or if a person was struck by poverty and this was confirmed by people who knew him or her. In each case, begging was permissible only until the person received sufficient sustenance, which again raises the question of how to define sufficiency.[57] For al-Ghazali begging might be permissible, though not necessarily laudable, if one was truly a pauper. His discussion, and those of other scholars, criticized begging for two types of reasons. First, begging suggested that one's belief in God was flawed, either through lack of confidence that God would provide or by the intimation that a person might somehow share in God's attributes, either as a provider or as a source of shame for the one who begs. Second, begging risked testing another believer in an inappropriate manner by demanding charity and so perhaps compelling a person to give to or refuse someone for the wrong reasons, as implied by the words "from someone who might or might not give" in the hadith quoted above.[58] The Prophet was quoted as saying: "A man keeps on asking others for something till he comes on the Day of Resurrection without any piece of flesh on his face."[59] Shame and humiliation were the cost of begging. In theory, therefore, anyone risking these was truly indigent. How much more preferable it was to hope for the private delivery of aid from relatives or neighbors.

Sufis were imagined to be beggars par excellence. Among them, some saw begging as a necessary humiliation, an obligatory aspect of their spiritual practice in which they abased themselves utterly in order to approach God. Many paintings depicted sufis in rags or in mendicant postures that represented their poverty and dependence on the generosity of others. One symbol of sufi poverty was the *kashkul* (Fig. 12). This bowl, in the form of a boat, was large enough to hold food or drink. It was actually identified with the wine-boat in sufi poetry, shaped like the crescent moon and holding the wine that leads to divine love. Not uncommonly, sea coconut shells that washed up on the shores of the Arabian Sea served as natural bowls for some mendicants; some elaborately carved bowls and even

---

[57] Muslim, *Ṣaḥīḥ Muslim*, vol. II, :498; USC-MSA, 5/2271.
[58] Sabra, *Poverty and Charity*, 41–50.
[59] Al-Bukhārī, *Ṣaḥīḥ al-Bukhārī*, 24 (zakat), bab 52; USC-MSA, Bukhari, 24/553.

Fig. 12. Undecorated kashkul (begging bowl) made from a sea coconut. Author's collection. Photo by Dana Katz.

elegant kashkuls made from metals may also be found in art collections around the world. One example is engraved, appropriately enough, with the Qur'anic verses: "And they give food for the love of Him, to the needy, the orphan, the captive [saying]: 'We feed you only for the sake of God; we desire no recompense from you, no thankfulness.' "(76:8–9)[60] This same verse reminding recipients that the donor was aiming to please God, to whom they should first give thanks, is inscribed above the entry to the public kitchen at the shrine of Eyüp (Abu Ayyub al-Ansari) in Istanbul (Fig. 13). The kitchen was endowed by Mihrişah Sultan (d. 1805), mother of the Ottoman sultan Selim III (1789–1808).

Based on relatively little evidence about actual beggars, it seems that beggars were for the most part tolerated in Islamic societies before the nineteenth and twentieth centuries, for a combination of reasons: the merits associated with charitable giving in general; the legitimacy of begging by sufis; and because they did not often constitute a serious threat to the established social order. This order was usually the responsibility of the *muhtasib*, the urban authority who oversaw public behavior and moral comportment within the bounds of commanding the right and forbidding the wrong. He supervised the business and social conduct of merchants and shoppers alike, maintained security, and, among other things, ensured that beggars did not annoy people too much, particularly in places like the mosque precincts in which the needy could traditionally seek shelter. Worth noting, however, are complaints like those of the writer Mark Twain from his travels in the Middle East in 1867, recounting how his group was aggressively accosted by beggars at Christian and other holy sites in Jerusalem. However, although begging was frowned upon but tolerated

---

[60] On the bowls, see A. S. Melikian-Chirvani, "From the Royal Boat to the Beggar's Bowl," *Islamic Art* 4 (1991): 21–22, 31–34 and the illustration in Sheila Blair and Jonathan Bloom, *Images of Paradise in Islamic Art* (Hanover, NH: Hood Museum of Art, Dartmouth College, 1991), 72. The plant from which they were frequently made is called Maldive coconut, *Lodoicea maldivica*, and is today found commonly in the Seychelles.

Fig. 13. Inscription from the imaret of Mihrişah Sultan at Eyüp, Istanbul. "We feed you only for the sake of God; we desire no recompense from you, no thankfulness" (*Innama nata'amkum li-wajh Allah la nurid minkum jaza'an wa-la shukuran*) (Qur'an 76:9). Author's photo.

in both normative literature and apparently in practice, there are other writings which portray beggars as calculating and mean. They appear as unattractive physically, either naturally or intentionally disfigured, plaguing people in cities with their obnoxious requests for money. In these sources, professional beggars were disparaged for the various tricks and deceptions they used to create illusions of greater poverty and suffering in order to evoke sympathy and material support. They were also portrayed by some as organized in professional groups and thereby constituting a certain social or even political force in cities.[61]

---

[61] Mark Twain, *The Innocents Abroad* (Sciute, MA: DSI Digital Reproduction, 2001), chapter 53. For some examples from Islamic literature, see Abū 'Uthmān ibn Baḥr al-Jāḥiẓ, *Book of Misers (al-Bukhalā')*, trans. R. B. Serjeant (Reading: Garnet Publishing, 1997) and C. E. Bosworth, *The Mediaeval Islamic Underworld: The Banū Sāsān in Arabic Society and Literature. Part One: The Banū Sāsān in Arabic Life and Lore* (Leiden: E. J. Bill, 1976), 1–47.

Many questions remain for historians regarding the recipients or consumers of charity. It is relatively easy to make lists of the beneficiaries from the Qur'an or from thousands of endowment deeds that have survived from the past. The categories were not established solely on the basis of economic need, but rather reflected the communal concerns, norms, and cultural practices of the early Muslims and the communities that emerged from them. Poverty was only one reason that qualified someone to receive charity, and even poverty could be broken down into different categories to distinguish between those considered more and less worthy.

Definitions of need and eligibility constitute key aspects in the study of charity. Such definitions necessarily include and exclude people according to specific yet varying criteria, which are key indicators of who is valued in any society and how much. The Qur'anic definition of zakat recipients left the categories broad, to be interpreted depending on available resources, on who was doing the interpreting, and on the immediate constellation of social and political power. Changing interpretations, traceable in legal literature as well as literary and documentary evidence, constitute valuable indicators for historians of broader social and cultural shifts in attitudes and approaches to charitable giving and to different members of society.

The line drawn between the poor and the not-poor indicates how a society defines minimal necessities. Theoretical discussions based on the Qur'an and hadith ultimately do not seem very strict in their qualifications of poverty. Yet in practice, to the extent we have evidence, local communities or institutions seem to have been fairly discerning in their attitudes toward poor people. Beggars could belong to neighborhoods just like anyone else, orphans were formally attached to relatives, but marginal, dubious, or criminal elements could be excluded altogether.

Less easy is the task of discovering what actually happened to the poor, how they experienced charitable giving, and how it affected them. To what extent, ultimately, were the recipients of charity consumers, active and even discerning in their selection of opportunities and venues? What induced them to approach a particular individual or institution? Who did in fact have access to the benefits of charitable institutions and beneficent distributions in any particular time and place, and what specific factors affected inclusion and exclusion? How did people who had different options for assistance make their choices and implement them? How did they negotiate with those who determined distributions? As discussed above, the sufis in Konya successfully appealed and won the right to a regular meal. Would a beggar in the same neighborhood have had equal success in trying to claim a fixed place at the local imaret table?

The various examples in this and preceding chapters suggest that the savvy beggar or attentive person of little means could seek out distributions of food or coins at known places in a city and at predictable times throughout the year. For the needy, a map of regular charity events might guide their search for food and shelter between mosques and zawiyas, from imarets to private homes. Yet in most such instances people probably never received more than enough to sustain them in the short term and achieved no significant change in their status. They remained vulnerable to economic hardship and had few if any resources for surviving long-term economic crises, no matter what the cause of these. Moreover, because the poor were chronically undernourished, ill-clothed, and poorly housed, they remained more vulnerable to hardship and disease than the non-poor, while their economic weakness kept most of them socially and politically marginalized.

What also bears further consideration is how the size and frequency of donations might vary according to financial or political circumstances, as well as personal tendencies to be more or less open-handed. Thus the expectation of the poor that they would receive something on holidays was tempered by the uncertainty of how much it would be or how long it might be made to last. Moreover, access to general beneficent distributions was probably not uniform among the population. As is clear from various accounts, there were those deemed deserving who were probably not poor, and those who received their handouts with a certain amount of pomp or dignity in controlled and protected circumstances like in a palace or other enclosed and orderly space. Not all charity was haphazard. In Mamluk Cairo, money distributed on 'Id al-Adha was paid when someone, rich or poor, presented a voucher that affirmed their entitlement.[62] During the circumcision celebrations for the sons of Murat III, more than ten thousand robes with money in the pockets were apparently distributed to orphans and poor people in the Hippodrome of Istanbul (Fig. 14).[63] In public kitchens of the Ottoman Empire, all those with the right to eat were admitted by doorkeepers to receive their food in an orderly fashion.[64] Only further research, however, will explain how people other than employees or students acquired the right to a bowl of soup. Less fortunate indigents might have to scramble for coins tossed by parading sultans or to elbow their way up to a public banquet table in order to grab a share. Descriptions of events such as the one below from the Ottoman circumcision feasts suggest that they were not for the infirm or faint of heart:

Next the common people were given their usual meal and as was always done hundreds of loaves were set out on the ground. The sultan, from his own window, and his son, from another immediately adjacent to it, would then strew not just thousands of akçes but also many silver groschen as well for half an hour. Besides this, gold-plated pans were tossed

---

[62] Sabra, *Poverty and Charity*, 53–54.
[63] Nurhan Atasoy, *1582 Surname-i Hümayun: An Imperial Celebration* (Istanbul: Koçbank, 1997), 127.
[64] Singer, *Constructing Ottoman Beneficence*, 63–64.

Fig. 14. Painting from the *Surname-i Hümâyûn* showing the robes, their pockets filled with coins, to be distributed to needy people and orphans. *Surname-i Hümâyûn* H.1344, f. 411b. With the permission of the Topkapi Palace Museum, Istanbul.

out to the commonfolk below. This caused such a scramble and struggle that, on every occasion, one or two people would be crushed to death.[65]

Even in less competitive or aggressive situations, there was still the question of proximity, that is, getting close enough to the place where coins were strewn or food set out.

Despite some indications that access to institutional assistance from endowments was regulated, one important characteristic of the charitable distributions discussed in this chapter is the agglomeration of highly personal or individually institutionalized episodes. Even where distributions were formally authorized, defined, and recorded to allow repeated distributions on a daily or annual basis, all the distributions observed were of what is called in European or US contexts "outdoor relief," that is, without requiring that recipients be incarcerated or live in a closed and controlled situation like the English poorhouses or workhouses. Except for emergency interventions like the expulsion of non-residents or the distribution of relief, the control and management of the poor in Islamic societies remained largely informal and in private hands until the nineteenth century, which is usually characterized as a period of modernization and reform. The final chapter of this book will explore some of the shifts of the past two hundred years in order to understand how they affected private charity, how state welfare services developed, where competition existed between state and private initiatives, and how the emergence of charitable associations introduced additional agents to the practice of charity in Islamic societies.

---

[65] Johannes Löwenklaw, *Neuwe Cronica Türkischer Nation* (Frankfurt am Main, 1595), p. 489, cited in Atasoy, *1582 Surname*, 44–45.

5   A mixed economy of charity

Isn't the state required to care for us? ... I am going to the Directorate of Health. I want to reprimand the director and say, "Your patients are here." If I saw the governor, believe me I would explain our situation. Because we don't have parents, isn't the state supposed to act as our parent?

Interview with a boy caring for his dying tubercular sister *Cumhuriyet*, 1934[1]

Zakat Foundation of America is an international charity which aims to foster charitable giving and help generous and caring people reach out to those in need with direct aid. We strive to bridge the gap between our financially privileged donors and our beneficiaries in financial need, as we believe that the first group has responsibilities toward the second. ZF is dedicated to alleviating the immediate needs of the poorest communities by providing food, shelter, health care and by delivering relief in emergencies. ZF also provides education and training in order to equip people with the skills to help themselves. ZF pursues this mission with compassion and strict standards of efficiency and accountability.

From the mission statement of the Zakat Foundation of America[2]

Once upon a time the history of charity was written to recount a linear transition from family-centered care and individual beneficence to the creation of the modern welfare state. This same transition was accompanied by the development of modern secular philanthropy and the non-governmental voluntary associations whose members came together for the collective support and execution of an extraordinary diversity of good works. Many studies of charity and the changes in beneficent practices have organized their analyses along a chronological continuum and according to the dichotomies of public/private, formal/informal, local/centralized, and individual/collective. Globally, however, there is no neat chronological passage of welfare responsibilities from the hands of individuals to the state or to non-governmental associations over time. Individual charitable efforts have never ceased, nor did they necessarily decline as the modern welfare state emerged. Rather, with the development of

---

[1] Kathryn Libal, "'The Child Question.' The Politics of Child Welfare in Early Republican Turkey," in *Poverty and Charity*, ed. Bonner et al., 267.
[2] Http://www.thezakat.org/Mission-Statement.aspx (accessed September 10, 2007).

government agencies and new non-governmental forms of association, an increasingly "mixed economy of charity" emerged in which multiple agents supplied social welfare, public works, and cultural services. Upon closer historical examination, public and individual social and welfare services have always been provided by a range of benefactors. Organizations like churches or guilds (whether identified with the state or independent) seem to have been involved from their inception in collecting and distributing beneficence or community support, while some states, such as England, created state poor relief systems well before the nineteenth century. Over time, new actors have joined and left the mix of individuals, families, geographic communities, rulers, dynastic households, religious orders, professional guilds, governments, purpose-defined associations, and other institutions, while the proportionate contribution of each expanded or contracted, so that the mix has never been static.[3]

In the preceding chapters, the discussion focused largely on charitable individuals. The most visible among them, then, as now, were wealthy and powerful people, especially rulers and dynastic families, and the highest-ranking members of the government and society. Beneficence was the business of individual believers as part of their ongoing practice of piety and good works, which aimed at contributing to the public good. In the nineteenth century, newly created government agencies and non-governmental associations began to participate in the work of beneficence, taking over or sharing in the creation and support of social services, public works, and cultural projects, joining individuals as agents in the distribution of what we have discussed until now under the heading of charity and philanthropy. This innovation was part of the deliberately modernizing reform movements introduced and shaped by domestic and foreign critics of government and society. It was sustained by a growing middle class with the education and engagement to seek ways of influencing societies in which political power was still largely monopolized by a small elite. A power struggle emerged between the new agencies and individuals whose long-standing influence was rooted in personal status and the loyalty of family, local, or professional followers. In addition, non-governmental confessional and secular associations emerged, based on the cooperative efforts of groups of like-minded individuals. State agencies, individuals, and non-governmental organizations all worked – sometimes in cooperation, sometimes in competition – to supply welfare, social, and public services.

---

[3] "Introduction," in Katz and Sachsse, *The Mixed Economy of Social Welfare*; Peregrine Horden and Richard Smith, "Introduction," in *The Locus of Care: Families, Communities, Institutions, and the Provision of Welfare since Antiquity*, ed. Peregrine Horden and Richard Smith (New York: Routledge, 1998), 1–18; Nadir Özbek, "The Politics of Welfare: Philanthropy, Voluntarism and Legitimacy in the Ottoman Empire, 1876–1914," Ph.D. thesis, Binghamton University, State University of New York, 2001, 4.

Fig. 15. Supermarket advertisement for discount Ramadan package, including basic foodstuffs like flour, rice, tea, coffee, sugar, oil, spaghetti, tomato paste, sweets, etc. Istanbul, September 2007. Author's photo.

Many traditional aspects of charitable giving in Islamic societies remained compelling throughout these shifts, as religious belief continued to provide one fundamental impetus for beneficent giving. Holidays and especially the month of Ramadan have remained occasions marked by charity (Fig. 15). Zakat, sadaqa, and waqf have persisted as the rubrics under which people give, and giving continues to range from large public projects to small individual acts. What was new were the governmental and corporate non-governmental bodies (local, national, and transnational) that participated in collecting and distributing charitable donations, often with a greater emphasis than in the past on economic need as a criterion for deserving assistance. New, too, were modern financial instruments, technologies for publicizing and carrying out charitable projects, and the potential reach of assistance extended by modern communications and transportation.

This chapter follows the changing mix in the economy of charity drawing largely on examples from the Ottoman Empire and the Middle East. While not necessarily paradigmatic of the shifts and changes in beneficent practices in all Muslim societies, the Ottoman Empire was the largest Muslim state of its day and the state from which most of the modern Middle Eastern and Balkan nation states emerged. Thus, the experiences of the Ottoman Empire and its successor states may offer insights into the kinds of shifts that affected beneficent practice and thinking in a larger group of Islamic societies, as well as some of the issues that faced practitioners and scholars as a result of the transitions.

State giving in the modern era of elected, bureaucratic, impersonal rule is not called charity. Yet contemporary governments also make contributions which might once have been recognized under a broad definition of charity, in the form of social welfare assistance, public services, relief payments, international aid grants to countries facing subsistence or medical crises, as well as funds and advisors for economic and social development. State giving today comes under the aegis of ministries like those for health, education, welfare, and public works and is also effected through disbursements, sometimes referred to as "entitlements," that include, for example, unemployment, disability, maternity, or retirement benefits. These payments have become the (sometimes-contested) obligation of modern states toward their citizens. We may find it odd to think of "welfare" as somehow connected to "charity," particularly since (in principle) there is nothing voluntary about paying the taxes which sustain government budgets for disbursing welfare payments.[4] However, the connection becomes apparent when we try to trace historically who was responsible for supporting weak and dependent members of the population, and inquire into the ways governments use their wealth as compared with individuals.

There are few countries today where the role of government institutions as providers of minimal subsistence and other welfare services is not being debated: what should "basic needs" include, for whom, how much, and for how long? In addition, the list of "basic needs" has expanded in many places

---

[4] For a discussion of the relationship between government and philanthropy, particularly for large donors' perspectives on the roles of government spending and private giving, see Francie Ostrower, *Why the Wealthy Give: The Culture of Elite Philanthropy* (Princeton: Princeton University Press, 1996), 113–31.

from a simple list of food, water, clothing, and shelter, to include health care, literacy, vocational training, and some form of old-age and disability assistance. Countless publications around the world – academic, policy, and popular – contain articles about failing welfare systems or arguments about the justice of increasing or reducing state-funded assistance to the indigent, single parents, the unemployed, elderly, children, immigrants, disabled, or any other category defined as having special needs or being of questionable status.

State motivations for distributing assistance are somewhat different from those of individuals. Most obviously, spiritual considerations of individual religious belief may have relatively less influence on state agencies. Moreover, the personal political calculus of how to sustain a household of allies, which characterized Ottoman society in the seventeenth and eighteenth centuries, for example, declined although it did not disappear. Yet motivations do not diverge entirely, as political considerations of aid distribution do come into play for govern-ments that view welfare distributions as a form of political patronage and party platform. Moreover, the work of individuals and governments as donors overlaps because they share concerns about actual need, definitions of deserv-edness, decisions about the allocation of limited resources, and strategies for effective distribution. At the same time, aid distribution can become a field of conflict and competition between individual donors, governments, and NGOs as each seeks to benefit from the prestige and influence that accrues to prom-inent benefactors. This same prestige has today also become a crucial factor in the ability of beneficent organizations to continue to raise money to fund their operations.

In order to explore the mixed economy of charity described above, this chapter focuses on a few key topics: the characterization of the Ottoman Empire as a welfare state; government reforms to the organization and management of waqf endowments; the reinvention of imperial beneficence and zakat; changing atti-tudes to the poor; and the role of associations and NGOs. The changes of the nineteenth and twentieth centuries are far more visible historically because they are usually more densely documented and have already been the subject of some scholarly investigation. However, this focus on change is not intended to suggest that the practices and ideologies of charity were static in previous centuries. Doubtless, as research continues, the changes and fluctuations of earlier periods will become more evident and will then need to be incorporated into a larger analysis of how charity was both an agent and an object of historical change.

The Ottoman Empire: a "welfare state"?

Quite close to the beginning of *An Economic and Social History of the Ottoman Empire*, the definitive synthesis of the subject published in 1994, Halil Inalcik included an essay entitled "The Economic Mind" in which he characterized the

Ottoman Empire as a welfare state. His argument rests on the idea, discussed in various contexts above, that the fundamental aim of an Islamic ruler was to promote public welfare and it was this consideration that served as a basic organizing principle for the economy. The Ottoman government strove to sustain an economy of plenty, ensuring the provision of necessities at relatively low prices, especially to urban markets. Maslaha was also supported and strengthened through the extensive distribution of charity by individual Muslims, with the sultan taking the lead role in beneficent giving. The result, however, was that a disproportionate amount of private wealth was directed toward charity rather than toward commercial or mercantile investment and capitalist profit-making. The redistribution of wealth in society was partly carried out through the waqfs, which controlled large amounts of capital and revenues, as well as the distribution of gifts on holidays and special occasions, both in the form of reciprocal gifts at all levels of society, starting with the sultan, and in the form of beneficent distributions of money and objects. To supply imperial beneficence, whole workshops existed to manufacture the goods distributed on such occasions, everything from robes made of precious fabrics and furs to simple woolen cloaks, the cloth given to the janissaries for their uniforms, and small precious or semi-precious objects of wood, ceramic, metal, glass, or paper. The basic form of economic activity that sustained all of this was agriculture on state-owned lands, which supported the peasants and the military. Additional revenues came chiefly from non-agricultural taxation, and from commerce, manufacture, conquest, and tribute.[5]

It is worth considering the term "welfare state" for a moment as it is of relatively recent origin. Widespread use of the word "welfare" in connection with relief activity seems to have begun in the later nineteenth century, and included public and private, outdoor and enclosed relief and rehabilitation efforts.[6] "Welfare state" emerged as a specific term after the Second World War. The ideological shift that occurred to bring it into being has been described as one

from the ideas of a social service state, improvising and extending welfare networks for people in misfortune, to that of a "welfare state" providing a basic minimum for everybody. The "welfare state," to use a different metaphor, was seeking to provide a fence to ensure that people do not fall over a cliff, whereas the older social-service state provided an ambulance at the bottom of the cliff to carry away for treatment all those who fell.[7]

This goal required the kind of bureaucratic institutions associated with modernity, in order to systematize and regularize the gathering of information about

---

[5] Inalcik and Quataert, *An Economic and Social History*, 45–52.
[6] Michael B. Katz, *In the Shadow of the Poorhouse: A Social History of Welfare in America* (New York: Basic Books, 1986), 293.
[7] Asa Briggs, "Welfare State," in *Dictionary of the History of Ideas*, vol. IV, ed. Philip P. Wiener (New York, 1973), 513.

individuals, to classify their means and needs, to define, assign, and distribute assistance, and (neither last nor least) to ensure the collection of adequate funds, matériel, and expertise for distribution.

The modern welfare state, therefore, is predicated on the presence of state-sponsored institutions and tied to formal government initiatives and activities aimed at providing or fostering the ability to attain an objective norm, some basic minimum level of subsistence, health, living conditions, etc. for all its subjects. Most studies of the welfare state place its development in the nineteenth and twentieth centuries, whether they tie its rise generally to modernization and the increasing strength of the state or specifically to the growing political capacities of workers' movements and their leadership.[8] However, it is also important to recognize that the welfare state has almost never sustained social services solely on its own as a government-run and -sponsored operation. Rather, alongside the growing reach and ambition of government agencies, an amalgam of private and public non-governmental organizations and partnerships between various groups have contributed significantly to ensuring individual welfare.

Inalcik, it seems, used the term "welfare state" somewhat differently, in order to emphasize how central public welfare was to the entire logic and functioning of the Ottoman Empire. Rather than claiming that the Ottoman Empire measured up to an anachronistic and contested ideal, Inalcik's portrayal suggests a fundamental characteristic of Ottoman state and society. His comments focused on the impact of Islamic ideals about charity that shaped the ethical norms underlying the moral economy, an enduring ethos that he identified in both state *and* society, rather than a single form of state structure or institution.[9] Based on citations from modern Muslim scholars and examples of the redistributive mechanisms found in Ottoman society, Inalcik's analysis pointed to the existence of a moral economy in the Ottoman Empire that prompted the establishment of service and relief initiatives by state-sponsored and private undertakings alike. The idea of a moral economy, discussed in chapter 2, posits that ethical values have a significant influence on economic behavior such as to override market or fiscal concerns. Scholars writing the history of Islamic states and societies have invoked the idea of a moral economy to explain, for example, the behavior of Fatimid and Mamluk sultans during food shortages in medieval Egypt as well as the attitudes of Malay peasants to the state imposition of zakat.[10]

---

[8] Koven and Michel briefly summarize the historiography of welfare states, including extensive references, for which see Seth Koven and Sonya Michel, "Womanly Duties: Maternalist Politics and the Origins of Welfare States in Germany, Great Britain, France and the United States, 1880–1920," *American Historical Review* 95 (1990): 1080–84.

[9] Inalcik and Quataert, *An Economic and Social History*, 45–46.

[10] Shoshan, *Popular Culture*, 52–66; James C. Scott, "Resistance without Protest and without Organization: Peasant Opposition to the Islamic *Zakat* and the Christian Tithe," *Contemporary Studies in Society and History* 29 (1987): 417–52.

The Ottoman Empire, and perhaps some of the other states referred to in this book, might usefully be characterized not as welfare states but as welfare *societies*, made up of welfare networks. People belonged to and tried to tap into overlapping networks formed by families, neighborhoods, villages, professional groups, sufi tariqas, households, and people of similar geographic origin or confession. As discussed in different parts of this book, within each network assistance was more or less formalized, routinized, or institutionalized, ranging from passing handouts in the street to familiar holiday celebrations to endowments that offered food or tax assistance. The welfare ethos and the responsibility for providing relief were rooted in the society at large and it was the entire society, including the sultan, which participated in providing social services and not the state, alone or even primarily.

It is perhaps the large imperial waqfs that come closest to being state welfare agencies during much of the Ottoman period. One might point to these constructions as a reflection of a larger state policy implemented through the agency of the Ottoman elite, but the distance between this ultimately decentralized agglomeration of independent relief nodes and a single state-sponsored agency is too great to justify calling the Ottoman Empire a welfare state. For most of the Ottoman period, the expectation that people of wealth would be generous toward the rest of society focused on certain individuals, primarily the sultan, because of their wealth and rank and it was not an expectation of something called "the state." While the Ottoman government developed an impressive bureaucracy, even from quite an early era, the distribution of social services was not bureaucratized. Donations overall were not impersonal, nor uniformly systematized and coordinated, at least not as we understand them today.

Nor were recipients chosen according to uniform criteria based on an assessment of economic need as in today's welfare states. Rather, need was defined according to criteria that were economic for some and social for others. Some of the services provided by Ottoman philanthropy, like fountains and bridges, were available to the population at large, and might today be classified as public utilities rather than social services. Yet many of the facilities supported by Ottoman philanthropy were not available to everyone, nor were they intended to be. For example, people outside of the cities were largely excluded because of where they lived; girls mostly did not attend schools (maktab and madrasa); libraries belonged to the literate; Christians and Jews obviously did not benefit from the mosques (one wonders whether they would even avail themselves of the shady urban parks created by mosque courtyards); and hospitals were too few in number and had too few beds to offer care to any but a small number of people.[11]

---

[11] On hospitals, see Shefer, *Living with Death.*

Another difference between the Ottoman Empire and welfare states is that the latter also seek to provide what we today call development aid, and not only relief services. Modern welfare states aspire to develop people's ability to sustain themselves, building "fences" so that people do not "fall over cliffs" or teaching them to use a rod instead of just giving them fish. Welfare states not only bridge the gaps to provide food, clothing, and shelter when these are lacking, but try to provide education and vocational training so that people who are able can work and become self-supporting. Governmental attempts to achieve these goals may not always succeed, nor have they always been carried out with sensitivity and skill, but their aim is generally broader than temporary respite. As discussed in the previous chapter, this idea did exist in medieval writings, but there is little evidence to demonstrate how it may have been implemented systematically in earlier eras.

Finally, the capacity for distributing assistance in welfare states is predicated on the steady inflow of revenues, largely from taxes. Unless these revenues fluctuate in wild ways or political decisions are taken to change the nature of welfare distributions, the state maintains a fixed level of benefits and social services. As Inalcik has pointed out, the provision of social services in the Ottoman Empire was largely through waqfs endowed with individual wealth obtained through war booty, military salaries, and agrarian tax revenues, and was not a regular expenditure from the state coffers before the second half of the nineteenth century, when one can perhaps talk about the emergence of an Ottoman welfare state in a more familiar form. Various Ottoman state mechanisms contributed to urban provisioning, including requisitioning and price fixing (*narh*) in city markets. Controlling food delivery to towns and cities, including bans on sales of grain to outsiders, were additional facets of the Ottoman welfare society. They often constituted state-coerced subsidies or contributions from private individuals to ensure basic food supplies.[12] Water supply and distribution within towns was funded in a similar way to food distributions, partly through imperial beneficence, partly through endowments made by members of the elite.[13]

Ottoman public kitchens further illustrated why the Ottoman Empire might usefully be called a welfare society and not a welfare state. More than two hundred imarets were built in the Ottoman Empire over a period of approximately 550 years. Standard features reappear in almost all of them: soup and bread were served twice a day, with special, richer dishes cooked on holidays. All these public kitchens seem to have been alert to class distinctions among their clients, serving more or better foods to people of some standing than they

[12] See M. S. Kütükoğlu, "narkh," EI^2, VIII:964–965.
[13] On water supply in general, and specifically in the Ottoman Empire, see T. Fold *et al.*, "mā'," EI^2, V:859–889 (878–883).

did to the indigents who obtained permission to eat a meal.[14] Yet imarets were only one component of food distributions in the Ottoman Empire. Although various institutions – imarets, zawiyas, palaces, private houses – may have acted like a comprehensive project to ensure basic and affordable minimal provisioning and subsistence to urban populations, they were not. There is no evidence that their activities were coordinated by a central authority nor even among themselves.

By examining the imarets closely it also becomes clear that the distribution of assistance in the Ottoman Empire was not systematic, or impersonal. Although aid may have reached large numbers of people, the recipients were not evaluated according to some set criteria of economic need. Rather, it was their social classification as scholars, students, mosque employees, travelers, sufis, Ottoman officials, or loyal retainers that earned most of them the right to a meal. One problem with the term "welfare state" is that it conjures up the notion of a state supporting the poor and the weak in the same way that "charity" suggests beneficence aimed at the poor, whereas the distributions of the Ottoman sultans and waqfs also supported large numbers of people who were not poor. Economic need was only one criterion and not always a sufficient or the most important one.[15] Moreover, there is nothing in the organization of food distributions that suggests that the Ottomans aimed to enable the recipients to provide for themselves in the future. In fact, the opposite may be true: the mechanisms of food supply were designed to perpetuate the food distributions as part of what defined and located power within Ottoman society. Changes in the structure of government that took place from the late eighteenth century deeply influenced the nature of power in the empire, as well as the networks of relief agents and the organization of social and welfare services. This process itself reflected how diffuse the organization of social services had been previously. New attitudes and assumptions about the expanding role of government fundamentally affected the waqfs with far-reaching consequences for people dependent on them across the Ottoman Empire.[16]

---

[14] On imarets in general see Amy Singer, "Imarets," in *The Turks*, vol. III, ed. Hasan Celâl Güzel, C. Cem Oğuz, and Osman Karatay (Ankara: Yeni Türkiye Publications, 2002), 657–64. Recent studies of imarets may be found in *Feeding People, Feeding Power*, ed. Ergin *et al*.

[15] Amy Singer, "What's so Charitable about Ottoman Charity? [Hebrew]," *Jama'a* 15 (2006): 9–30.

[16] For a general discussion of the large-scale changes in waqf law and administration, see John Robert Barnes, *An Introduction to Religious Foundations in the Ottoman Empire* (Leiden: E. J. Brill, 1987), chapters 5, 7, and 8; Seyit Ali Kahraman, *Evkâf-ı Hümâyûn Nezâreti* (Istanbul: Kitabevi, 2006), who provides a synopsis of Ottoman waqf administration, including lists of the responsible authorities for the entire period; Nazif Öztürk, *Türk Yenileşme Tarihi Çerçevesinde Vakıf Müessesesi* (Ankara: Türkiye Diyanet Vakfı Yayınları, 1995).

Waqf reforms

Historically, as discussed in chapter 2, waqfs were the main vehicle for "financing Islam as a society," central to the establishment and maintenance of social and cultural institutions of all types.[17] They were the most prominent form of voluntary charity. Nineteenth-century reforms had a far-reaching impact on waqfs, whether in the Ottoman Empire, Egypt, French-occupied Algeria, or British-ruled India. For this reason it is important to understand the changes that attacked and weakened the institution in this period.

By the nineteenth century, large amounts of property all over the Muslim world belonged to endowments, including an estimated 75 percent of arable lands in the area of today's Turkey, one-fifth in Egypt, one-seventh in Iran, one-half in Algeria, one-third in Tunisia, and one-third in Greece. At the end of the eighteenth century, an estimated 20,000 waqfs in the Ottoman Empire had a total annual income equal to one-third of annual government revenues, and perhaps including as much as one-half to two-thirds of arable land. The amount of urban property in waqf was also considerable.[18] Many of these properties also escaped taxation entirely and the sums they remitted to Istanbul as surplus revenues landed in the pockets of the handful of officials who served as overseers of different groups of endowments. The perception became widespread that the expansive waqf system, particularly the so-called family endowments, was directly detrimental to the fiscal capacity of the empire at a time when the government especially needed resources to fund military and bureaucratic reforms. The deleterious effects of waqfs were also pointed out regularly by colonial regimes in Islamic countries. Foreign observers and scholars alike pointed to waqfs as a major stumbling block in the path of agricultural modernization because they hindered land transactions and development, and prevented access to capital through the usual instruments of sale and mortgage.[19]

At the same time, the legitimacy of waqfs as beneficent endeavors was being called into question, again with special focus on the so-called family waqfs, which supported public purposes only after the disappearance of the original line of family beneficiaries. This is not the place to undertake an extensive examination of the historical criticism of waqfs. However, it is important to point out that jurists, memorialists, and chroniclers alike had long criticized and debated specific aspects of waqf law and practice – conflicts with property laws, the harm caused to the founders' heirs, corrupt management, etc. – and waqfs were periodically

---

[17] Hodgson, *The Venture of Islam*, vol. II, 124.

[18] Figures collected in Powers, "Orientalism, Colonialism," 537; Timur Kuran, "The Provision of Public Goods under Islamic Law: Origins, Impact, and Limitations of the Waqf System," *Law and Society Review* 35 (2001): 849.

[19] See Powers, "Orientalism, Colonialism," 538, as well as a pessimistic assessment of waqf's legacy in Kuran, "Provision of Public Goods."

confiscated or subjected to more stringent legal controls. Yet the institution as such had not been called into question until the nineteenth and twentieth centuries.[20]

One of the largest problems for the Ottoman Empire with regard to waqfs sprang from the decentralization of waqf management. Day-to-day management of waqfs was dispersed in the hands of local individuals, often members of city or provincial notable families. Each imperial waqf had a local manager who came under the general oversight of a higher Ottoman official in Istanbul. One of the most powerful among these overseers was the chief black eunuch (*darüsseadet ağası*) of the imperial Topkapı Palace. From the late sixteenth century he supervised almost all imperial waqfs: these endowments, often quite large, were by then already numerous and their numbers increased continually. The responsibilities of the darüsseadet ağası also included the ever-growing agglomeration of endowments for the two holy cities of Mecca and Medina (al-Haramayn al-Sharifayn).[21] The rights to collect surplus revenues from these waqfs and to appoint or confirm appointments to posts in them lay in his hands, a situation which enhanced his influence greatly and gave him (and his successors) a keen interest in preserving the entire system of waqf management. Other central figures such as the grand vizier, the commander of the janissaries, and the shaykh al-Islam each gradually accumulated responsibility for large numbers of waqfs as well, often as the managers of waqfs founded by people from their branch of the government who had died. Ultimately, the totality of waqf revenues was a substantial sum that was not available to the central government for its own budgetary needs, while the system of waqf management was not easily challenged because the overseers represented entrenched interests in the capital, capable of undermining imperial power by supporting competing factional interests around the sultan.

Attempts to reform the management of Ottoman waqfs so as to redirect revenues toward the central treasury began in the late eighteenth century and continued well beyond the collapse of the Ottoman Empire into its successor states in the Middle East and the Balkans. Long-term trends in waqf reform sought, in general, to relocate the management of waqfs into the hands of bureaucrats and to redirect the flow of waqf revenues into the central treasury, and from there back to the original beneficiaries as well as to the new ministries to be used for public expenditures. Waqfs that benefited family members were gradually circumscribed, and transformed under the influence of European trust laws. Since it was the public waqfs which funded social services, we will turn our attention to the reforms as they affected these waqfs, to understand how the Ottoman state gradually recovered control over revenues. This reorganization of what were essentially or originally charity funds is an important aspect of

---

[20] Powers, "Orientalism, Colonialism," 563–65; Singer, *Constructing Ottoman Beneficence*, 30–32.
[21] Barnes, *Introduction*, 65–66; Bahaeddin Yediyıldız, "Vakıf," in *İA*, XIII: 160.

understanding how the relationship developed between state welfare services and private charity in the late Ottoman Empire.

The nineteenth-century tug-of-war over waqf revenues was not a new contest. Since the days of Sultan Mehmed II in the fifteenth century, if not earlier, Muslim rulers had tried periodically to confiscate waqfs or create a government agency to oversee their management in order to recapture revenues lost through the alienation of lands, mostly to high-ranking officials who then created endowments. Waqf reform also periodically tried to address the abuses of imperial waqf managers who kept surplus revenues instead of using them to maintain or improve the institutions they managed. It was in an attempt to correct this that oversight of the imperial waqfs was originally transferred to the chief black eunuch at the end of the sixteenth century.

An early Ottoman institutional innovation in waqf management was the establishment of the ministry of Imperial Waqfs (*Evkaf-ı Hümayun Nezareti*) by Sultan Abdülhamid I (1774–89). In its first incarnation, the ministry was to oversee the sultan's own new endowments and begin to create a counterweight to the control of the chief black eunuch. Under the sultans who followed Abdülhamid I, this effort faltered when the chief eunuch was named as waqf minister. Yet during the nineteenth century, and especially after the reforms of Sultan Mahmud II (1808–39) that inaugurated the Tanzimat reform era (1839–76), the sultan's own power gradually strengthened and dispersed authority was recentralized to Istanbul and to the sultan himself. The destruction of the janissary corps in 1826 made possible the incorporation of all janissary waqf holdings under the ministry, as well as the further expansion of the ministry's authority over imperial waqfs to include those under the control of the chief eunuch, the grand vizier, the shaykh al-Islam, and the Istanbul qadis. This trend continued, notably with the incorporation of the Haramayn waqf administration into the ministry in 1838, so that gradually the holdings that had constituted the economic basis for the independent power of these high-ranking officials, as well as the financial basis of much of the Muslim learned class throughout the empire, were brought under the direct control of the ministry.[22]

In practice, the reorganized system forwarded waqf revenues directly to the ministry, which then allocated an annual sum to each waqf as the budget for its expenses. At the beginning of the nineteenth century, most mosques, schools, tekkes, imarets, and other public services and social welfare institutions were funded by waqf money. With the reforms, individual local waqf managers in the provinces were relieved of their financial authority, which consequently

---

[22] Barnes, *Introduction*, 69, 80; Nazif Öztürk, "Osmanlılar'da Vakıfların Merkezi Otoriteye Bağlanması ve Sonuçları," in *Le waqf dans le monde musulman contemporain*, ed. Bilici, 21–22; S. Yerasimos, "Les waqfs dans l'aménagement urbain d'Istanbul au XIXe siècle," in *Le waqf dans le monde musulman contemporain*, ed. Bilici, 46.

undermined their administrative power. The ability of the waqfs to fulfill their original purposes also diminished with their shrinking budgets. All appointments were handled through the ministry and if additional funds were needed, an application had to be submitted. Even worse for the waqfs, their annual budgets were determined not by the yields of their own individual properties, but by considerations of the central administration, which appropriated waqf revenues to cover other expenses of the empire such as military and bureaucratic reform. Thus, the creation of the ministry added a layer of central bureaucracy over the local salaried functionaries of the individual waqfs without contributing to the available budget. When the Ministry of Imperial Waqfs at times found itself short of funds, it appealed to the Ministry of Finance, from which it could receive donations (*iane*). More often, however, the shortfall was felt by local staffs and beneficiaries of the waqfs themselves.[23]

The sufi orders throughout Anatolia seem to have been particularly affected by the nineteenth-century reforms in waqf administration. Together with the elimination of the janissaries, the sultan ordered the abolition of the Bektashi order which had long been closely identified with the corps. The Ottoman government took over all Bektashi property and in 1840 issued a decree to take over the endowed properties of the other sufi tariqas. This left the tekkes deprived of their immediate sources of revenue, and the petitions to the sultan that followed revealed how the tekkes had been supporting not only the dervishes but also local poor people throughout the empire.

For example, a petition of 1846 asked that the government reinstate support for the local tekke of Seyyid Ahmed Zemci in Kütahya. Since 1839, shortages of daily provisions of bread, oil, rice, and cheese, from which it customarily fed travelers, dervishes, the poor, and the custodian of the place, had reduced the dervishes and the custodian to desperate straits. An imperial order restored the former level of provisions. Thus, although not yet establishing new institutions, the government was taking into its own hands the immediate responsibility for distributing welfare assistance both through existing institutions that could no longer function independently, being deprived of their usual budgets, and directly to individuals in response to specific appeals. As it undermined the traditional welfare institutions, the government gradually accepted the responsibility and also acquired more widespread authority to decide who would continue to receive support and how much. All stipends had to be approved from the center and were assigned from vacant salary posts, sometimes with a decrease in payments. For example, the widow of a Naqshabandi shaykh appealed for help for herself and six children after her husband's income was seized upon his death. As with similar petitions, the government responded by appointing the family a reduced

---

[23] Barnes, *Introduction*, 102–17; Yerasimos, "Les waqfs," 46–49.

monthly stipend, only slightly more than half their former income.[24] In effect, the Ottoman government was reorganizing what had been an agglomeration of micro-economies of individual charity into the beginnings of a state welfare system. Seemingly, it did this without directly intending to do so; rather the larger purpose was to retrieve previously dispersed revenues.

In addition to controlling and reducing the revenues of the dervish orders, the government also initiated a policy of recording the names of all the dervishes in Istanbul. The purpose of this was to limit the number of people who would be eligible to receive stipends at all, thereby curtailing the total funds necessary to support the dervishes in the city. Recording names and distinguishing between deserving dervishes and unworthy vagabonds associated with the tekkes reflected changing attitudes toward this group of poor people who had, in the past, been among the most worthy, the natural recipients of charitable donations, and the beneficiaries at the many endowed tekkes. As a group they were much diminished, and as individuals their level of living sank, mirroring the cutback in funds.[25]

These changes were visible, marked by Ottoman and foreign observers alike. Even allowing for exaggeration and a dramatic flourish, the deterioration is evident in the description by the English writer Charles MacFarlane (1799–1858), who toured Istanbul and the Ottoman provinces for sixteen months in 1828 and then returned at the end of the 1840s. After his later visit he wrote:

Still, I believe, in the great majority of cases, where the property was *vakouf* [waqf], some portion of the proceeds was from time to time devoted to the repairs of the bridges, fountains, khans, etc., and none of these things were left to go utterly to ruin. I can speak confidently to the fact that a considerable number of these works which are destroyed and useless now, were in a tolerable good state of repair no farther back than the year 1828. But the reformers, who are uprooting religion, and a respect for it in every direction, have utterly destroyed the security which the mosque, and the mosque alone, could give to any landed property; they have destroyed the independence of the Turkish Church – if I may so call it; they have laid their greedy hands on nearly all the *vakoufs* of the empire, and are undertaking to provide out of the common state treasury, for the subsistence of the Ulema, Mollas and college or medresseh students, to keep up the mosques and the medressehs, to repair the bridges, khans, etc., and to do, governmentally, that which the administrators of the vakouf had done or ought to have done. Hence, with very few exceptions, we see the heads of the mosques and the medressehs in abject poverty, the rabble of (religious) students in rags, the most beautiful of the temples and the minarets shamefully neglected and hurrying into decay, the bridges, fountains, and khans in the state I describe. It is notorious that since the vakoufs have been administered by the government nothing has been done to maintain the works of public utility.

MacFarlane was not alone among foreigners in making such remarks, and they seem to concur with the evidence of the Ottoman archives, at least insofar as the

---

[24] Barnes, *Introduction*, 93–94.   [25] Barnes, *Introduction*, 100–01.

status of impoverished religious functionaries can be gauged.[26] MacFarlane's observations also capture precisely the period when the support of both public works and individual welfare payments was in transition from being funded discretely and disparately by separate waqfs to being taken under the government's care. It was a moment, too, when the government, through its reforms, was undercutting the status of the large class of religious scholars and students.

Accompanying the obvious decline in immediate external appearances of buildings and other structures was the decline in the quality of education and relief services to the poor. While the original deeds of waqfs had proclaimed the intentions of their founders and outlined the initial instructions to their managers, the evidence cited above testifies to a diminished ability to fulfill these goals. Corruption among officials at the Ministry of Imperial Waqfs – embezzlement of funds and tampering with the transfer of properties – further undermined the institutions. Based on evidence from Ottoman chronicles and archives, it seems that by the 1860s, the ministry existed mostly to serve itself and its officials, but contributed little to the waqfs themselves. In an attempt to safeguard waqf properties from further mishandling, the authority for their registration, taxation, and supervision was transferred at that time to the Ministry of Land Registry (*Defter-i Hakani Nezareti*).[27] In 1863, a new regulation for waqf management further refined and specified the ongoing reforms, and this regulation served as the basis for waqf administration in the Ottoman Empire and then in Turkey until the 1936 law on foundations.[28] The Ministry of Waqfs in Turkey was replaced by a General Directorate of Waqfs in 1924, which managed the Ottoman waqfs in the Turkish Republic. All waqfs whose administration was in the hands of an official authority at the time of the founding of the Republic were nationalized. In 1954, the Turkish Vakıflar Bankası was established using the capital from the nationalized waqfs. Although it functions like any other bank, the Vakıflar Bankası also regularly devotes a portion of its profits to the maintenance of monuments originally founded as waqfs as well as for student stipends and dormitories. Few new waqfs were founded until 1967 when a new waqf law drawing on American foundation law as well as on traditions of Muslim law provided the impetus for a renewed interest in establishing foundations.[29]

---

[26] Quote from Charles MacFarlane, *Turkey and its Destiny: The Result of Journeys Made in 1847 and 1848 to Examine into the State of that Country* (London: John Murray, 1850), 396–97. Writing in 1840, Bishop Southgate made similar observations about Baghdad and blamed them on the government seizure of the endowments. In *A Tour through Armenia, Persia and Mesopotamia* for which see MacFarlane, *Turkey and its Destiny*, 396–97, note.

[27] Barnes, *Introduction*, 150.   [28] Öztürk, "Osmanlılar'da Vakıfların Merkezi," 23.

[29] Faruk Bilici, "Introduction," in *Le waqf dans le monde musulman contemporain*, ed. Bilici, 12, 57–58.

Waqf reforms were not unique to the Ottoman Empire but took place in Egypt under Muhammad Ali (1805–48) as well as in French-occupied North Africa and British-occupied India. Ultimately, waqf laws were reformed in all the colonized and newly independent Muslim states, either replacing shariʻa law completely with western foundation law or, as in most places, creating new laws based on aspects of both shariʻa and western laws. Waqfs that supported public works projects were usually treated somewhat differently from those with family beneficiaries.[30]

The decline in the use of waqf had many causes. In some places, revolutions did away with waqf as such, as for example in Soviet Central Asia, Syria, and Egypt. British rule in South Asia, the introduction there of English charity laws and the English interpretation of Muslim law were not especially favorable to continued waqf making. The impetus for changing waqf laws and the overall decline in importance of waqf varied from place to place, but contributing factors usually included: the secularization of law codes; changes in inheritance laws that obviated the need for waqf as an instrument of redivision; greater protection of property rights overall that also made waqfs less relevant; the establishment of state welfare agencies; and reforms to waqf law that decreased their attraction, sometimes in favor of other forms of trusts.[31]

"Liberating" property from waqfs was commonly held up as vital to modernization projects. However, very little research has been done on the actual effects on immovable property of belonging to a waqf, beyond the fact that transactions of such properties were more cumbersome (but not impossible) to negotiate. Research into this question would be particularly important since many reforms were conceived and implemented based on the assumption that waqfs constituted a major obstacle to the modernization of agriculture and property ownership. It would be helpful to substantiate the claims regarding agricultural development as distinct from the political, commercial, and financial objections that were raised against the existence of waqfs, or the doubts that were cast upon the sincere charitable intentions of their founders.

The fate of the waqfs and of the Ottoman Ministry of Waqfs was tied not only to attitudes toward the endowments but also to changing notions of the role of the state in the effective distribution of assistance. The diminished financial capacity of most waqfs left them less able to help the poor and pay stipends to students and teachers, to feed anyone who came to the public kitchens, to maintain buildings and other structures, in brief, to supply the range of social, cultural, and welfare services that people had grown accustomed to having the endowments support. The key question is then: what agents filled the gap left by

---

[30] See Peters et al., "wakf," 11:78–81 and the articles in Bilici, ed., Le waqf dans le monde musulman contemporain.

[31] Peters et al., "wakf," XI:78–81, 94–99.

the diminished capacities of waqfs throughout the empire? Did wealthy individuals find new ways to fulfill old obligations or were their responsibilities taken over successfully by new state institutions? As we have seen, waqf was an institution rooted in Islamic law and religious practice, though it had quite a healthy secular existence as an economic agent. In examining what replaced it, one must also ask to what extent new forms were deliberately Islamic or secular in their inception, justification, or operation.

Reinventing imperial charity

Sovereigns persisted as important individual donors, although they increasingly ruled through the apparatus of a modernizing bureaucratic state, which was itself increasingly active in the provision of social and welfare services to the population. Two cases highlight the continuing imperial role alongside innovations in state charitable distributions and welfare services in the nineteenth century: reforms in the Egypt of Muhammad Ali Pasha (1805–48) and his successors, and developments in the imperial capital of Istanbul, especially during the reign of Abdülhamid II (1876–1909) and the Young Turk era (1908–18). These rulers combined old and new forms of distributing social welfare in order to legitimize and enhance their own power and position in the new state context and with the emergence of an educated and professional middle class.[32]

Changes in Egypt beginning from Muhammad Ali's rule were part of an aggressive program of modernization in which the state intervened more and more to control the movement and location of its subjects. Military campaigns and large-scale agricultural and industrial innovations alike demanded increased manpower for which peasants were drafted from around Egypt. In the large cities of Cairo and Alexandria, the modernization drive aimed to impose greater order on people through more insistent policing of markets and public spaces, including expelling migrant non-residents and trying to remove beggars from the streets. As part of this effort, new state institutions opened their doors to enclose the local poor and unfortunate. In Cairo, these included the *maristan*, the medieval hospital of Sultan Qalawun (built in 1284) which became known as *Mahall al-Fuqara* (Residence of the Poor), and then the mosque of Ibn Tulun, now called Takiyyat Tulun (closed by 1880 to be restored as a monument). They served as both poorhouses and insane asylums. Two additional institutions were founded in Alexandria: Qishla al-Sadaqa and Takiyyat Qabbari, a new orphanage and a foundling home providing food and

---

[32] Ener, *Managing Egypt's Poor*, xxiv; Nadir Özbek, "The Politics of Poor Relief in the Late Ottoman Empire 1876–1914," *New Perspectives on Turkey* 21 (Fall 1999): 1–33; Nadir Özbek, "Osmanli İmparatorluğu'nda 'Sosyal Yardim' Uygulamaları: 1839–1918," *Toplum ve Bilim*, no. 83 (Winter 1999/2000): 111–32; Özbek, "Imperial Gifts."

shelter but with no plans to put people to work.[33] While hospitals and hospices of various kinds were nothing new in the urban landscape of Cairo, the activist involvement of the state in placing people in them was. In the past, insane people who had no one to care for them or who represented a threat to public order were confined to hospitals, but the poor were cared for mostly by families, neighbors, public kitchens, and sufi zawiyas. Takiyyat Tulun served simultaneously as a shelter and prison, since people were granted space there either at the recommendation of the police or at their own request with police approval, if they made a successful case for why they should be given public support. For release, a resident had to produce a guarantor who ensured that s/he would not become a beggar or public nuisance in any other way.[34]

Familiar locations for distributing relief like mosques and public kitchens persisted alongside new kinds of relief institutions. While for centuries there had been endowed schools and funds to help orphan boys and girls study, acquire skills, and marry, formal institutions to care for and accept responsibility for orphans were founded only later in the nineteenth century. These were not open only or primarily to homeless indigent orphans, but rather seem to have taken in at least some children having only one parent or parents incapable of working. Thus one Ahmad al-Bahiri, having lost a leg while working for the Egyptian railroad, sent a petition to the Khedive Abbas Hilmi asking that his sons be accepted into the industrial training school and orphanage established in Alexandria by the Muslim Benevolent Society (founded 1879) so that they could eventually support him and themselves. This Ahmad, like the wounded Ottoman veteran Ahmed three hundred years earlier, appealed personally to his sovereign for the specific permission needed to access poor relief. Unlike his predecessor, however, the Egyptian Ahmad sought not a guaranteed handout for himself from an imperially endowed public kitchen, but vocational training for his sons from an institution founded by a beneficent organization.[35]

In comparison with Egypt, significant changes other than the waqf reforms are visible in a slightly later period in the Ottoman Empire. Abdülhamid II increased substantially the traditional alms distributions and gifts from the imperial purse and added to them new kinds of poor relief in an effort to highlight his own role as the chief source of beneficence. Imperial Friday distributions continued, both as part of the ceremonial surrounding the sultan's procession to and from any particular imperial mosque and at other imperial mosques in different quarters of the city. These events took advantage of new

---

[33] Ener, *Managing Egypt's Poor*, 20–21.

[34] The most serious study of the treatment of the insane within the context of medical charity in an Islamic society is Michael Dols, *Majnūn: The Madman in Medieval Islamic Society* (Oxford: Clarendon Press, 1992).

[35] Ener, *Managing Egypt's Poor*, 102–3. On Ahmed, the Ottoman soldier, see chapter 4.

Fig. 16. Photo of boys whose circumcision at the *Hamidiye Etfal Hastahane-i 'Alisi* (Imperial Hamidiye Hospital for Children) in Istanbul was sponsored by Sultan Abdülhamid II (r. 1876–1909), in August 1906. The photo appears in a statistical yearbook published by imperial order on the thirtieth anniversary of the sultan's accession. Courtesy of Nadir Özbek.

technologies and tapped into new discourses that made Abdülhamid II's projects modern on the one hand while serving to shore up the power of the sultan in what seemed to many a reactionary attitude.

Among these projects were the poorhouse called *Darülaceze*, completed in 1896, and the Imperial Hospital for Children (*Hamidiye Etfal Hastahane-i 'Âlisi*) opened in 1899. Both were built with substantial and highly publicized contributions from the sultan and their ongoing achievements were continually advertised in a national press funded and controlled principally from the imperial palace. Few people could have missed these advertisements of the sultan's beneficence. The impact of ceremonies connected with the new institutions, like the annual circumcision of thousands of poor boys in modern, sanitary conditions at the Children's Hospital, was widespread. A 1906 photograph documented one group among the thousands of boys who were circumcised that year on the anniversary of Abdülhamid's accession to the throne (Fig. 16). The photo echoes the eighteenth-century painting commemorating a similar event (see Fig. 6) sponsored by Abdülhamid II's ancestor Ahmed III (1703–30). Yet while the eighteenth-century painting was created for an album presented to the sultan and kept in the library of the palace, the photo of Abdülhamid's charity was published in a yearbook of the hospital as well as in the newspapers of the day, where extensive stories covered this and similar occasions. The long-familiar sultanic act of charity was now staged in a thoroughly modern medical setting and recorded in print and photographs in the popular media. Imperial charity immediately and concretely demonstrated its scope to enormous numbers of people far beyond the circle of the boys themselves, their families, and friends. Naturally most patients in the hospital were from Istanbul or nearby provinces, but they also came from the farther parts of Anatolia.[36] The words of a news report describing such a ceremony evoked the imperial household, not a modern public institution, and emphasized the creation of a single family around the sultan: "At the courtyard [of the sultan's hospital] the sons of both poor and rich fathers gather like members of a single family, as if they were the sons of one father, and as if they were the beloved brothers of one another."[37]

The traditional rhetoric together with the use of imperial ceremonial and symbols maintained an important tie to long-standing Ottoman traditions. In Muhammad Ali's Egypt, new and more specialized government institutions were established to care for the poor, but they were still perceived as deriving from the personal charity of the Egyptian ruler, the *khedive*. Petitions were addressed directly to him asking for help, some of them sent from outside the cities and some coming even from Mecca. The positive responses to these petitions also noted specifically that help was provided "*ihsanan min al-Khidiwi*," through the beneficence of the ruler. It was not only the identity of an individual imperial donor which persisted but also the ideological frame of Islamic charity as reflected in the use of language, timing, and venues. Ottoman sultans and Egyptian khedives alike consciously portrayed their individual welfare and relief projects as modern in their technique while using the familiar Qur'anic vocabulary of *ihsan* (beneficence), sadaqa, and *khayrat* (good deeds) to talk about them. Just as there were multiple sources of support to which the poor might turn, there were several layers of ideology which motivated and shaped the behavior of givers as imperial, bureaucratic, secularizing forces interacted with confessional, communal, and professional identities. Both in Egypt and in the Ottoman imperial center at Istanbul, the role of the state as an institutional and corporate agent of social welfare and poor relief gradually increased throughout the nineteenth century.

Managing poor relief

One aspect of the changes was a shifting attitude toward the poor and poverty. While institutional changes like the waqf reforms reflected new ideas about the

---

[36] Özbek, "Imperial Gifts," 213–15.
[37] Özbek, "Imperial Gifts," 203, quoting from the Ottoman newpaper *Sabah* (no. 3429, June 7, 1899).

nature and locus of responsibility for care, new attitudes with regard to the objects of care, increasingly the poor, were linked to shifting definitions of need and entitlement. As we saw above, the status of religious scholars and function-aries was being circumscribed, though perhaps not questioned outright, with the creation of government ministries of justice and education that promoted secular legal codes and schooling in subjects outside of the traditional madrasa curriculum in order to prepare people, mostly men, to fill new kinds of bureau-cratic and official positions. The formation of ministries of education, health, and public works integrated functions previously filled by waqfs into the growing state bureaucracy. Care and support for the poor also changed with the creation of new government offices and associations, and the redefinition of old institutions. These have been little studied before the nineteenth century. In the past, indigents had been tolerated to a greater or lesser extent in any location based on its immediate economic conditions, and the extent to which poor people were identified with threats like disease and social unrest, especially in cities.

In comparison, legislation regulating the behavior of paupers became more widespread throughout Europe in the early modern and modern periods. In these centuries, as discussed in chapter 4, concern broadened from defining who the poor were and who deserved help, to include finding the means to control them by holding them physically in workhouses, poorhouses, and prisons, forcing them to work in crafts or trades, excluding them from certain urban areas or from some cities altogether, as well as reshaping their lives by prohib-iting begging as a means to deter would-be criminals. Poverty, in fact, had become more closely identified with criminality as part of a stricter distinction between the able-bodied and undeserving, and those whose poverty was in some way legitimate and therefore deserving.[38] A companion shift ensued toward defining the obligations of the state toward poor people, including the level, range, and duration of state-funded assistance. Necessary bureaucracies and systems were implemented to select recipients and determine the levels of support provided to them. From the later nineteenth century, the subject was also debated in the United States and Europe within the context of arguing the optimal extent of government involvement in managing people's lives: how much responsibility should be assumed by the state and the public treasury and how much left to the beneficent impulses of individuals and the initiatives of associations? The discussion of how to deal with the poor

---

[38] Increasing control over the poor achieved by enclosing them can be seen as part of a larger movement to shut up and cure people whose lives deviated from a perceived norm, including criminals and those emotionally or mentally disturbed. On these latter, see Foucault, *Madness and Civilization* and Foucault, *Discipline and Punish*.

gradually expanded to encompass the broader and more depersonalized ques-tion of what to do about poverty.[39]

In Istanbul, the closure of the dervish tekkes and the declining funding of these and other endowed institutions throughout the empire in the nineteenth century reduced one major locus of care. One apparently new practice that emerged to replace the tekkes was the distribution of government-funded "poor stipends" (*muhtacin maaşı*) on a regular and long-term basis to people who were recognized as needy and added to an official list, reminiscent of the distributions to the poor of Mecca and Medina from the Algerian Haramyan waqf.[40] Here too, more stringent criteria were increasingly drawn up for receiving relief based on distinctions between the deserving and undeserving poor. One example from mid-nineteenth-century Egypt illustrates this distinc-tion and its connection to new forms of poor relief. Three people of one family applied for admission to the Takiyyat Tulun poorhouse in Cairo: a blind man, his half-blind mother, and his sister. The doctors responsible to the police for recommending admissions approved the man and his mother, but rejected the sister's request on the grounds that she was healthy and, presumably, could find work to support herself. Blind people, traditionally and still considered deserv-ing of support, were readily admitted to the new state institution. However, a younger woman with no apparent physical limitations was assumed to be employable and in no need of assistance.[41]

Takiyyat Tulun was run by the police in conjunction with medical authorities. Its procedures illustrated how the police increasingly assumed functions from earlier authorities (like the muhtasib) in controlling access to government-sponsored relief, and also in distinguishing between the deserving and unde-serving poor, all as part of their responsibilities for managing and maintaining public order. The Egyptian Dabtiyya of Muhammad Ali Pasha was established in 1835, while the Ottoman police administration was founded in 1846, becoming a ministry in 1870.[42] With regard to the poor, the police took on an increasingly aggressive role toward vagrants – defined in the Ottoman Empire by the late nineteenth century as people without work – who came to be regarded not

---

[39] As discussed more fully in the previous chapter, there is an extensive literature on the European and North American history of the poor. See, as examples of the large and growing body of literature, Jütte, *Poverty and Deviance*; Geremek, *Poverty*; Paul Slack, *The English Poor Law, 1531–1782* (Cambridge, UK: Cambridge University Press, 1995); Gertrude Himmelfarb, *The Idea of Poverty: England in the Early Industrial Age* (New York: Alfred A. Knopf, 1984); Gertrude Himmelfarb, *Poverty and Compassion: The Moral Imagination of the Late Victorians* (New York: Alfred A. Knopf, 1991); and Koven and Michel, "Womanly Duties."

[40] Özbek, "'Sosyal Yardim' Uygulamaları," 115–16; Hoexter, "Alms in Ottoman Algiers."

[41] Ener, *Managing Egypt's Poor*, 53.

[42] Khaled Fahmy, "The Police and the People in Nineteenth-Century Egypt," *Die Welt des Islams* 39 (1999): 340–77; Ferdan Ergut, "Policing the Poor in the Late Ottoman Empire," *Middle Eastern Studies* 38 (2002): 150; Ener, *Managing Egypt's Poor*, Preface, 10–11.

only as undesirable and unsightly but also as criminal. Earlier Ottoman vagrancy regulations had aimed at keeping the agrarian population in the villages to ensure steady revenues and prevent population pressure in the cities. The changing role of the police vis-à-vis the population in general and toward the poor in particular can be seen in the police records used today by scholars as historical sources. These records contain significant information about poor people, whether through the records of admission and release from institutions like Takiyyat Tulun, petitions for assistance, or in the reports of abandoned children, beggars, and other poor people. By 1890, Ottoman law regarded those with no specific residence or job as "vagrants," while the 1909 "Law on Vagrants and Suspected Persons" criminalized vagrancy and left those convicted forever suspect and subject to police surveillance.[43]

Changing attitudes toward the poor and the new institutions and authorities for dealing with them were the result of both local factors and external influences, which also shifted during the nineteenth and twentieth centuries. Modernization projects aimed not only at introducing new technology and knowledge, but also at changing the appearance of public urban spaces. This meant removing beggars and the vagrant poor from view to the extent possible, and while on the one hand travelers continued to observe beggars as part of the Egyptian (and Middle Eastern) landscape, the policies of Muhammad Ali's government and those of his successors worked to clear them out of sight.[44] Caring for and controlling the public visibility of the poor continued to be linked to the creation of a modern state in the minds of the Europeans who came to the Middle East, and became increasingly so in the policies of local Middle Eastern governments. Gradually, the inability to manage the poor came to be seen as an indication to Europeans that local governments were unable to handle their affairs more generally. On the other hand, by the twentieth century care for the poor, and especially for poor children, was held up by citizens around the world as fundamental to the building of healthy new national populations, including in the emerging states of the Middle East.[45]

Underlying many of these changes was the idea not only of responsible individuals, but of a responsible state, as articulated in the writings of the preeminent nineteenth-century Egyptian intellectual, Rifaʿa Rafiʿ al-Tahtawi (1801–73). Tahtawi pointed to the tradition of caliphs and later sultans making beneficent donations as a direct precedent for the contemporary welfare responsibilities of the

---

[43] See, for example, Fahmy, "The Police and the People"; Ener, *Managing Egypt's Poor*; Liat Kozma, "Women on the Margins and Legal Reform in Late Nineteenth-Century Egypt, 1850–1882," Ph.D. dissertation, New York University, 2006; Ergut, "Policing the Poor," 151–60.

[44] Ener, *Managing Egypt's Poor*, 26–48.

[45] This development is traced explicitly in Ener, *Managing Egypt's Poor*. On the place of care for poor children in the context of building a healthy nation, see also Libal, "The Child Question."

state and of private philanthropy to ensure the welfare of the poor. Tahtawi also made a distinction between the able-bodied poor who were simply lazy and the disabled poor who deserved ongoing state assistance. Influenced by various Islamic and European thinkers, Tahtawi placed great value on work, including manual labor, as a factor contributing to public welfare and he did not think the 'ulama deserved public support, although he included students among the deserving poor. In this he echoed those Muslim thinkers, discussed in chapter 4, who stressed the obligation of able-bodied people to work for their livelihood. Whether directly influenced by Tahtawi or not, Egyptian reforms of waqf management effectively reduced subsidies to all the 'ulama. Tahtawi also gave considered thought to the nature of a third class of poor, the working poor, chiefly peasants but also urban craftsmen, who were largely if unfairly at the mercy of the landowning and propertied urban elites of Egypt.[46]

While attitudes to the indigent poor were changing, Tahtawi also excluded the non-poor as beneficiaries where they had previously figured prominently among those receiving support from waqfs. By the later nineteenth century, many of these people had become state employees paid regular salaries by the relevant departments of government. The imarets, on the other hand, seem to have become more exclusively centers of food distribution to the poor. Indirect evidence for this comes from the Young Turks' closure of all but two public kitchens in Istanbul in 1911. The measure was meant, in part, to distract public attention from imperial charitable works, which were to be replaced by new government institutions. However, the government was soon forced to reopen the imarets owing to the pressing needs of an increasingly poor population whose ranks were swelled by Muslim refugees flowing into the Ottoman Empire in the wake of the Balkan Wars as well as by the hardships brought on at home by those wars and by the ensuing World War.[47] It is not surprising that the Young Turk revolution that revived the constitutional monarchy and ultimately ended Abdülhamid II's reign also tried to eliminate as many practices associated with the sultan as possible, most especially those that cast him in a favorable light. In their place, the Young Turks encouraged associations like the Ottoman Red Crescent Society and continued the bureaucratization of poor relief, stripped of imperial symbols.

Reinventing zakat

While the nineteenth-century reforms saw increasingly bureaucratized and secular Ottoman and Egyptian government organizations providing welfare

---

[46] Juan R. I. Cole, "Al-Tahtawi on Poverty and Welfare," in *Poverty and Charity*, ed. Bonner *et al.*, 223–38.
[47] Singer, "Imarets."

services, a long-familiar language of Islamic charity persisted, as did the personal beneficence of rulers and individuals alike. A moral economy also endured, continuing to view responsibility for public welfare and poor relief as dispersed throughout society in the hands of private individuals, the new independent associations, governors, and state institutions alike. Zakat collection as an officially organized project became increasingly visible through the twentieth century in the Islamic states that emerged as colonial and then independent nations in the Middle East, Asia, and Africa. It is difficult to characterize this as a "zakat revival," however, since the payment of zakat on an individual basis was always possible and assumed to be widespread, even if it left few documentary traces for the historian to follow. Since zakat payment is one of the obligations of Muslims, one should assume that people mostly found a way to fulfill it even where the state did not intervene.

As discussed previously, zakat collection by official zakat collectors seems to have had an erratic history. Yet the principle of state collection was embedded in shari'a and official collection was at times revived. The periodic *re*imposition of zakat by Muslim governments throughout history is one indication that state collection lapsed repeatedly in the many states of the Islamic world. Thinkers or rulers with a reformist program chose to reintroduce zakat at the state level as part of an official economic system. Examples of this are scattered across time and space: the Almoravids and Almohads in eleventh- to thirteenth-century North Africa and Spain; Saladin in twelfth-century Syria and Egypt; Imam Nasir al-Din of the Znaga Berbers in the Senegal valley in the mid-seventeenth century; the Sokoto Caliphate (1817–1903) in Nigeria; the Wahhabis who ruled in the Arabian peninsula from the eighteenth century; and the Mahdists in the Sudan from the late nineteenth century. Many of the Muslim states in pre-colonial sub-Saharan Africa also imposed zakat collection in one form or another. Zakat was centrally organized by the state in Morocco and Kuwait from some time in the past until the turn of the nineteenth century and in Yemen until the revolution of 1962. The contexts for reintroducing official zakat collection were not identical. For some, like the Almohads or Wahhabis, the intent was to assert a fundamentalist program. Saladin, on the other hand, seems to have imposed zakat collection as one way to emphasize the reassertion of Sunni control over areas formerly ruled by the Shi'i Fatimids as well as the Christian Crusaders. As might be expected, official zakat, where implemented, was not always or even principally directed toward helping the poor but rather supported a broad range of clients, including military personnel, court figures, and scholars.

In the twentieth century, zakat was accorded renewed importance by Islamist thinkers as a fiscal mechanism for increasing social justice and public welfare in the context of states with a strong official Muslim identity. Numerous Muslim states officially imposed zakat as a tax to be collected and disbursed by the government, including Saudi Arabia (1951), Malaysia (1955), Libya (1971), Yemen (1975), Pakistan (1980), and Sudan (1984). In Jordan, Bahrain, Kuwait, and Egypt there are government-sponsored or overseen agencies that collect zakat.[48] For example, the Jordanian *Sunduq al-Zakat* is managed in the Ministry of Awqaf and has committees throughout Jordan which both collect and distribute zakat, as well as running clinics, giving scholarships, and organizing vocational training.[49] The reintroduction of government-organized zakat has taken different forms and affected the citizens of these countries in different ways, while assessments vary about how successful the measures have been. The redistribution of wealth effected by regular and full zakat payments was expected to be an important basis for social welfare projects as well as a means to defuse class tensions. In its ideal incarnation, Muslim intellectuals like Sayyid Mawdudi (1903–79) in Pakistan proposed that the adoption of zakat by Muslim governments would be a key step on the road to the establishment of Islamic states grounded firmly in shari'a and freed of the inequalities of capitalism and the rigorous restrictions of socialism. "Islamic economics," a term Mawdudi coined, has emerged not only as a field of intellectual inquiry but also as a practice guiding Muslim businessmen and banks like Al Baraka, run according to Muslim principles, where profit and rent replace interest as the means to earn money.[50] The application of zakat to modern financial forms and instruments has produced an extensive body of technical literature addressing these topics. One example, cited in chapter 1, is the government and private websites that offer answers to specific queries about zakat and calculation aids to figure out the correct zakat on various kinds of investments and revenues.

Sayyid Qutb (1906–66), the Egyptian intellectual and ideologist of modern Sunni fundamentalism, promoted zakat as a powerful corrective to economic inequality and an agent of increased social justice. It is worth taking a careful look at his writings on zakat since he has been the leading philosopher of the

---

[48] Zysow, "zakāt," XI:410, 420; Holger Weiss, "*Zakât* in Pre-Colonial Sub-Saharan Africa. A Tentative Survey. Part One" (Helsinki, 2000), 26–29, http://www.valt.helsinki.fi/kmi/Julkais/WPt/2000/WP100HW.HTM (accessed July 5, 2007); Holger Weiss, "*Zakât* in Pre-Colonial Sub-Saharan Africa. A Tentative Survey. Part Two" (Helsinki, 2000), http://www.valt.helsinki.fi/kmi/Julkais/WPt/2000/WP2004.HTM (accessed July 5, 2007); Holger Weiss, "Attempts to Establish an Islamic Economy: A Survey on Zakāt in Some Nineteenth-Century Muslim States of the Bilād as-Sūdān" (Helsinki, 2000), 2, www.valt.helsinki.fi/kmi/Tutkimus/Sal/Weiss%20accrapaper.htm (accessed December 27, 2006); Jonathan Benthall and Jérôme Bellion-Jourdan, *The Charitable Crescent: Politics of Aid in the Muslim World* (London: I. B. Tauris, 2003), 72.

[49] Janine A. Clark, *Islam, Charity, and Activism: Middle-Class Networks and Social Welfare in Egypt, Jordan, and Yemen* (Bloomington: Indiana University Press, 2003), 109.

[50] Timur Kuran, "On the Notion of Economic Justice in Contemporary Islamic Thought," *International Journal of Middle East Studies* 21 (1989): 171–91; Timur Kuran, "Islamic Redistribution through Zakat: Medieval Roots of Contemporary Problems," in *Poverty and Charity*, ed. Bonner et al., 275–94.

Muslim Brotherhood in Egypt and one of the most widely read Islamic thinkers of the twentieth century throughout the Islamic world. In his well-known work *Social Justice in Islam*, Qutb described zakat as integral to achieving social justice in a society of practicing Muslims:

As for the proceeds of the *zakat*, this is the law: It is to be received as a right, not given as charity. [As it says in the Qur'an:] "And of their wealth there was a settled share for the beggar and the deprived." (51:19) This share is taken by the state and is spent on the welfare of Muslims to support their bodily needs, to preserve their dignity, and to protect their power of conscience.[51]

Qutb explained zakat as fundamental to a moral economic outlook which rejected a purely capitalistic basis for organizing society. He claimed that there is a natural balance in Islamic economic thought:

Islam, then, does not demand a literal equality of wealth, because the distribution of wealth depends on men's endowments, which are not uniform . . . It prescribes the claims of the poor upon the wealth of the rich, according to their needs, and according to the best interests of society, so that social life may be balanced, just, and productive.[52]

The idea of a just claim (*haqq*) of the poor to the wealth of the rich is fundamental in Islamic thought, and as we have seen, constitutes one basis for the obligation to pay zakat and the encouragement generally to be charitable. In this way it constitutes a central aspect of the moral economy of Islam. Qutb also reiterated that society has a collective responsibility toward the poor, saying: "If any individual pass the night hungry, the blame attaches to the community because it did not bestir itself to feed him."[53]

An important factor in the contemporary application of zakat has been the extent to which the classic regulations have been adapted or reinterpreted to take into account forms of income and investment that did not exist in the early Islamic centuries when zakat law was refined and codified. At the same time, the categories of zakat recipients have also been reinterpreted to expand the possibilities of distributing zakat monies. This flexibility is not new; rather, it has been evident throughout this book in examples such as the fatwas of Ebu's-Su'ud and the story of Abu Illya. Qutb addressed the question of how to impose zakat in his own day, by which time the early Muslim discussions of how to calculate zakat were only partly relevant, focusing as they did on pastoral and agrarian sources of income. His approach, like that of Ebu's-Su'ud in his day, was pragmatic.

---

[51] Sayyid Qutb, *Social Justice in Islam*, trans. John D. Hardie, rev. trans. and intro. Hamid Algar (Oneonta, NY: Islamic Publications International, 2000), 67.
[52] Sayyid Qutb, *Social Justice*, 48–49.   [53] Sayyid Qutb, *Social Justice*, 89.

Again we must consider the sources of the zakat as including all types of property, some of which are not at present included because they were not familiar in the early days of Islam . . . The fact that the *zakat* was prescribed as a duty only upon such types of property as were familiar in the time of the Prophet does not prevent its being prescribed today as a duty on all that is known as property or wealth and on all that produces an income. It makes no difference that such things may not be of the kind on which the tax was originally imposed.

In addition, Qutb had innovative ideas about how to distribute zakat:

Similarly, we can modify the outlets for the tax money, just as 'Umar modified them when he stopped payments designed to support recent converts. It need not be given in cash or kind to those who are eligible for it. Factories and workshops might be established on their behalf, or they might be given shares in various enterprises to serve as a source of income. This would distance the *zakat* from any kind of temporary or haphazard charity; for these things are not in accord with the needs of modern life.[54]

Sayyid Qutb clearly envisaged the state as the agent of taxation and disbursement and argued for a modern interpretation of aid that emphasized investment in development programs rather than emergency relief.

Malaysia provides one example of the official national zakat systems that have been created, although it is not necessarily representative since each country has organized its collection and distribution apparatus individually. A state zakat authority was set up by law in 1955, by which the central government took over enforcing zakat collections which had formerly been local and often voluntary, and also became more involved in making decisions about zakat recipients. Research conducted in the mid-1970s found that the peasants, on whom the bulk of the zakat assessment fell, resented state intervention in what they perceived as a local process of donation and redistribution. They found ways to avoid the government collections and complained of corruption. In addition, they were unhappy with what they saw as the small return to their villages from the zakat they paid whereas in the past zakat had been used to address the immediate needs of local people. Despite government claims that the funds supported schools, clinics, poor people, and the hajj, the villagers continued to subvert the official zakat process, continuing to give voluntary charity even as they tried to minimize their payments to the state zakat fund.[55] The case of Malaysia describes active opposition to an official zakat system and the reasons for it. Whether an official zakat system is inherently more vulnerable to corruption than a welfare ministry is not obvious. What is more evident, however, is the tension that exists as an impersonal state system steps in to take

---

[54] Sayyid Qutb, *Social Justice*, 304.

[55] Scott, "Resistance without Protest." For a contemporary assessment of the distribution of zakat in Malaysia, see n.a., "The Efficiency of Zakat Distributions" (2001), posted in the publications section of http://www.iiu.edu.my/iaw (accessed on September 12, 2007).

over what had previously operated as an individual and local mechanism of social support and imposes a centrally established agenda for using the funds collected.

In Pakistan, an official zakat system has been in place for more than twenty-five years, established with the Zakat and Ushr Ordinance of 1980 by General Zia ul-Haq. It oversees the collection of zakat from financial wealth and 'ushr from the harvest, both contributions that had previously been voluntary. A highly ramified distribution bureaucracy is organized in the Ministry of Finance: the Central Zakat Fund controls the Provincial Zakat Funds, and below them the local zakat committees, whose members are partly elected though also often illiterate. As a separate but companion effort, there exists a National Zakat Foundation funded entirely with government appropriations, which makes grants to groups, not to individuals, the traditional recipients of zakat. Interpretations of the effectiveness of Pakistan's zakat system range from enthusiastic to critical; all seem to confirm that it has been relatively effective at identifying and targeting real need, with varying assessments of the impact of these distributions in alleviating or even removing poverty.[56]

Problems with the system in Pakistan include the popular perception that it was corrupt, while at the same time, there are those who see a difference between making tax payments to the state and voluntarily fulfilling religious obligations. Nor have the zakat committees been able to remain non-partisan, and through the various political changes in Pakistan, the funds have been steered toward uses that support the causes favored by those in power.[57] However, in the case of Pakistan, it is worth noting the results of surveys of individual and corporate giving carried out in 1998. They show that the worth of non-zakat giving exceeds that of zakat contributions, and when widespread volunteerism is factored in as well, those forms of charity which we have characterized as voluntary in this book outweigh the obligatory. An over-whelming majority of businesses also engage in philanthropic giving. This suggests that voluntary charity today still inspires a much greater response than does zakat, as the evidence has seemed to show for earlier eras in the history of Islamic societies and over the long term.[58] The familiar claims of corruption against state zakat officials are also a persistent theme where official

---

[56] Grace Clark, "Pakistan's Zakat and 'Ushr as a Welfare System," in *Islamic Reassertion in Pakistan: The Application of Islamic Laws in a Modern State*, ed. Anita M. Weiss (Syracuse: Syracuse University Press, 1986), 79–95.

[57] Clark, "Pakistan's Zakat"; Kemal A. Faruki, "Pakistan: Islamic Government and Society," in *Islam in Asia: Religion, Politics, Society*, ed. John L. Esposito (Oxford: Oxford University Press, 1987), 53–78; D. Novossyolov, "The Islamization of Welfare in Pakistan," in *Russia's Muslim Frontiers*, ed. D. F. Eickelman (Bloomington: Indiana University Press, 1993), 160–74.

[58] Http://www.asianphilanthropy.org/countries/pakistan/overview.html (accessed September 12, 2007). One should, nonetheless, also allow for certain distortions that arise from the fact that data are based on survey respondents' self-reporting.

zakat systems have existed. This complaint needs to be investigated further, perhaps to pose the question of whether official systems are typically perceived as corrupt when they step in to replace a highly personal form of transaction with an impersonal method.

Associations and NGOs

In addition to reinventing or reviving more long-standing forms of charitable giving with the help of new bureaucracies and technologies, innovations in philanthropy included the introduction of associations, volunteerism, and NGOs. Individual donors, initially mostly members of the elites, formed associations to cooperate in furthering particular goals. The Egyptian thinker Tahtawi described the role of associations as philanthropic agents based on what he had seen in France. Like de Tocqueville on his visit to the United States in 1831, and like other Egyptians who had participated in study missions to Europe, Tahtawi was impressed by the role he thought associations played in strengthening society and culture. He stated: "The hand of God is with the group, and the establishment of these philanthropies for the public good requires that an association of the wealthy endow them, and make charitable donations which are inalienable and subject to exploitation in perpetuity."[59] In Tahtawi's mind, the association had replaced the individual as the preferred agent of large charitable endeavors.

Examples of such associations appeared in Egypt in the latter part of the nineteenth century. The Muslim Benevolent Societies (founded 1879 and 1892) and the Coptic Benevolent Society (founded 1881) aimed to improve the quality of health, education, and welfare services available to the poor. While founded along confessional lines, the societies offered assistance to poor people from different faiths in Egypt. In addition to helping the poor, associations founded in the early twentieth century and particularly following the Egyptian revolution of 1919 framed their beneficent efforts in the language of strengthening the nation. Organizations established by elite women often focused on education, training, and support, especially for poor women and girls. These societies included, for example, the Muhammad Ali Charity (*Mabarrat Muhammad 'Ali*) and the New Woman's Society (*Jam'iyyat al-Mar'a al-Jadida*).[60]

The Society of Egyptian Ladies' Awakening (*Jam'iyyat Nahdat al-Sayyidat al-Misriyyat*) was founded by a woman named Labiba Ahmad (1870s–1951)

---

[59] Cole, "Al-Tahtawi," 228–29; Ener, *Managing Egypt's Poor*, 101; de Tocqueville, *Democracy in America*, 595.

[60] Ener, *Managing Egypt's Poor*, 97–111, 126–31; Beth Baron, "Islam, Philanthropy, and Political Culture in Interwar Egypt: The Activism of Labiba Ahmad," in *Poverty and Charity*, ed. Bonner et al., 241.

shortly after 1919 with the express aim of educating girls, particularly orphaned
or abandoned girls, and training them in practical skills, all within the framework of an emphatic instruction in nationalist ideals and Islamic values. It was
this latter aspect that distinguished her endeavor from many of the other elite
women's projects of the same era. Ahmad established a school and a workshop
for the girls and started a monthly journal, *al-Nahda al-Nisa'iyya* (Women's
Awakening) to disseminate her ideas in Egypt and in the Arabic-speaking
world. She made herself into a public figure, advocating her vision of assistance
to women and girls in the pages of the journal and on a weekly radio show.
Ahmad successfully raised money among Muslim leaders inside Egypt and
abroad, earning more support from them than some of the secular women's
organizations. Her charitable endeavors brought together a reformist Islamic
ideology, an Egyptian nationalist project, and modern techniques of communication and fund-raising to create a development project aimed at Egyptian
women. The society was very much her personal vision, but she was only one
of a number of educated elite Egyptian women in the early twentieth century
who created philanthropic associations that specifically targeted women and
girls.[61]

The Like women around the world until the late twentieth century, the bulk of the
wealth used by women in their philanthropic endeavors was theirs through gift
and inheritance from men, primarily their fathers and husbands. One characteristic of associations was not only the joining together of personal fortunes for a
common goal, but also the solicitation of funds from other sources, including
small donations from middle-class people. In the past, people of more modest
means had made individual contributions that left few traces, established small
endowments, or else made their endowments to contribute to larger existing
foundations like the waqfs for the Haramayn al-Sharifayn. Through the formation of associations, men and women of varying means were able to contribute money, time, and expertise to philanthropic projects. What distinguished
the endeavors of early twentieth-century Egyptian women and their associations
from the great waqfs of earlier sultanas and princesses was their personal
commitment of volunteered time and personal public activism. Where women
in the past had been a known but often invisible presence in philanthropic
endeavors, now they could be visible benefactors. Moreover, their increasing
presence in the public arena was ultimately linked to other fields such as politics
and professions.[62]

The comparison between the actions of women and men in their charity is a
particularly valuable one for historians, since both had long been active as

---

[61] Baron, "Islam, Philanthropy."
[62] Beth Baron, *The Women's Awakening in Egypt: Culture, Society, and the Press* (New Haven:
Yale University Press, 1994), 175; Ener, *Managing Egypt's Poor*, 111.

benefactors at various levels of society and there is largely comparable evidence to trace their actions, even from early periods, with respect to endowment making. Thus it is possible to consider their ideology, rhetoric, and practices in a common domain of endeavor as a way of studying the depiction of men and women as philanthropists and their choices of donations and acts.

The Ottoman Empire offers a useful comparison to Egypt in the development of philanthropic associations from the end of the nineteenth century. Unlike Egypt, occupied by the British from 1882, the Ottoman Empire remained independent although constrained by a foreign Public Debt Administration from 1881. In addition, beginning from the Russo-Turkish War of 1878, the empire had to cope with an increasing flood of refugees from former Ottoman lands who streamed into (or at least through) the capital of Istanbul. The sultan, Abdülhamid II, was an enthusiastic modernizer although he ruled as a paranoid autocrat, having suspended the constitution and prorogued the nascent parliament in 1878. In his philanthropic endeavors, Abdülhamid II intended his projects to overshadow those of any other individual or state office and to employ beneficence in the service of imperial legitimation. His founding of the Darülaceze and the Imperial Hospital for Children were both framed and advertised as the personal endeavors of the sultan despite the substantial contributions to them from members of the elite and middle classes. The history of the Ottoman Red Crescent Society (ORCS) up to the Young Turk revolution of 1908 demonstrates how carefully Abdülhamid controlled any competition in the beneficent arena from members of the new professional and middle classes, rightly judging that any philanthropic association they established could become a platform from which to organize politically. First organized in the mid-nineteenth century, the ORCS was repeatedly allowed to operate as a relief agent, in the wars of 1876, 1877–78, and 1897. However, with the end of each conflict Abdülhamid II withdrew imperial support and curtailed its activities, unwilling to risk the expansion of its peacetime activities into more overtly political realms.[63]

Following the Young Turk revolution, the government employed roughly the same tactics as Abdülhamid but in reverse: it incorporated Abdülhamid's showcase charity projects into the new Administration of Public Assistance in order to minimize the importance of his endeavors as well as to denigrate their uniqueness, portraying them rather as just "more of the same" compared with preceding sultans. Meanwhile, the ORCS was given a relatively free hand to organize throughout the empire. It became a thriving organization with an active Women's Auxiliary, providing both peacetime and wartime relief and support to the needy by distributing emergency medical care and convalescent aid, dealing with public health issues, and creating employment opportunities for

---

[63] Özbek, "Politics of Poor Relief"; Özbek, "Imperial Gifts"; Libal, "The Child Question," 263.

women and girls who were refugees, widows, or orphans. The ORCS also played an important role in the consolidation of the new elite that organized these activities and through them stepped into the public sphere.[64] Politically, therefore, charity (or welfare agencies) remained a viable means of expressing and legitimizing power, whether the donors were rulers or subjects.

Organizations like the Ottoman Red Crescent Society were an important new form of social welfare agent, that is, volunteer organizations formed by concerned subjects, with varying ties to government or other authorities. The ORCS represented one of three major trends in the Ottoman Empire and around the world: poor relief that sought greater control over the poor; the growth of state-sponsored institutions; and the emergence of independent philanthropic organizations. None was entirely successful in its aims nor one hundred percent efficient, for a host of reasons that began with a lack of resources and included flawed planning, a misapprehension of the efficacy of certain measures, the changing reasons for and nature of poverty, the continuation of traditional forms of poor relief including reliance on family support and begging, and the ongoing impact of informal individual efforts. One cultural factor that worked counter to state efforts was what has been called "a religious ethos of care for the poor," which motivated individuals to look after the poor and tolerate their presence, even counter to official policy. Thus together with government initiatives to manage the poor, the formation of modern welfare institutions has been shown to be the product both of the demands of the needy and of the activities of individual philanthropists and non-governmental organizations.[65]

The proliferation of philanthropic associations beginning in the late nineteenth century was evidence of the dynamic role that both old and newly emerging elites took on in shaping and reshaping Islamic societies, often within the framework of nation-building, but equally influenced by identities based in confession, gender, or locale. The projects focused on recurring themes of providing medical care, education, job training, food, clothing, and shelter to poor people. However, the associations themselves differed in their approaches, their scope, and in the factors that drew together and motivated their members. An association like the Children's Protection Society in Turkey exemplifies this. Founded in the late Ottoman period by professionals and notables, it focused on the needs of orphans and homeless children. The large numbers of children displaced by the wars of the early twentieth century took most of its energies and funds until the 1920s, at which time it became more engaged in the project of caring for children in the context of raising the young generation in the new Turkish Republic. Minimal government contributions flowed to the Society; it was mostly funded by private contributions and volunteer efforts. Always insufficient for the

---

[64] Özbek, "Politics of Poor Relief," 17, 27–29.   [65] Ener, *Managing Egypt's Poor*, 19.

task, the funding situation generated an ongoing debate about whose responsibility it was to care for the nation's children.[66] Thus a careful study of such associations also brings out the lines of disagreement and competition between elite groups, between the elite and the government, and between elites and the emerging middle class. Governments, most often holding the upper hand, might alternately seek to cooperate with, control, or disband associations, partly based on perceptions about the potential political influence or ambitions of any group.

Another example is the Egyptian King Farouk (1936–52): unlike his father, who chose to contribute to and tolerate a variety of philanthropic associations, the government of Farouk took over the associations in 1939 and established the Ministry of Social Affairs in the same year. The ministry followed and sometimes subsidized the activities of the associations, but it also aimed to create its own projects for similar purposes. Some years later, the Minister of Social Affairs reflected on the decision:

[i]t was felt at the time that it was no longer wise to leave the various social problems to be dealt with by haphazard efforts curtailed by opposing currents and conflicting opinions. It was a supreme duty of the State to observe and record social conditions and their development, to diagnose social diseases and defects and to study the methods of treatment; to plan, in light of these observations and studies, a comprehensive and permanent policy of social rehabilitation with a view to uplifting the poor classes, raising the standard of living of the individual as well as the family, and finally assuring the biggest share of social justice to the people.[67]

Only a few short years after these words appeared, private philanthropy in Egypt sustained a jolt as the 1952 revolution directed by Gamal Abdul Nasser took over and shut down most independent associations and organizations, replacing them with state welfare agencies, eventually on a socialist model. The balance in the mixed economy of charity in Egypt was forcefully altered.

National and local civil society associations and non-governmental organizations have proliferated throughout Muslim societies in the twentieth century, whether they are located in majority or minority Muslim cultures. The impetus for founding such associations came partly from economic and political changes that allowed for the growth of a middle class and a certain freedom of action for it, together with a rise of self-consciously Islamic activism in the twentieth century that is probably best typified by the Muslim Brotherhood in Egypt. The strength and style of Islamic identity in these organizations varies from country to country, but also depends on the goals of each organization and the policies of the local

---

[66] Kathryn Libal, "The Children's Protection Society: Nationalizing Child Welfare in Early Republican Turkey," *New Perspectives on Turkey* 23 (2000): 53–78; Libal, "The Child Question."

[67] As quoted from the "Foreword" to *Social Welfare in Egypt* (Cairo: Royal Government of Egypt Ministry of Social Affairs, 1950), presented by Dr Ahmed Hussein, Minister of Social Affairs, October 3, 1950, in Ener, *Managing Egypt's Poor*, 130.

government. The organizations were founded to serve the needs of their members, mostly the middle classes, as well as the needs they identified among poorer people. At the same time, they embody the conflict between secular and religious organizations.[68] As the few examples discussed above indicate, these organizations sometimes have links to governments and sometimes seek to operate entirely independently of any official sponsorship or guidance. Whether they are able to do so depends on the character of local political regimes and the extent to which any government is willing to allow such associations. The legal guidelines and restrictions for associations also differ widely, though they are probably nowhere as extensive as in the United States and Great Britain.

There remains room to say only a few words about the proliferation of international Islamic associations in the late twentieth century. This is, however, a topic which has been discussed much more extensively in accessible publications than the charity of earlier Islamic societies. The catalyst for the formation of transnational Islamic relief organizations seems to have been the war in Afghanistan against the Soviet invasion of 1979, although the call for Islamic solidarity was much broader in both geographical and practical scope. The activities of these organizations were of three main types: *da'wa* (preaching or call) which focused on religion and education, sometimes conceived of as spiritual relief and aimed at both Muslims and non-Muslims; *jihad* (military action) on behalf of Muslims in a large number of conflict regions (Bosnia, Chechnya, the Sudan); and *ighatha* (relief), which comprised humanitarian aid directed mostly, but not exclusively, to Muslims suffering from poverty, natural disasters, and military conflicts. As in the broader world of humanitarian agencies, the Islamic organizations differ with respect to wealth and the focus of their efforts, and there are some dynamic disagreements between them about how their resources should be spent for the greatest impact. Moreover, the organizations are shaped by and respond to the demands of their sponsors, governments, beneficiaries, and circumstances, so that they are not static. Some organizations are adamantly political and engaged in overlapping campaigns of da'wa, jihad, and ighatha; some specialize exclusively in humanitarian aid. Others are firmly rooted in their development projects, like the Aga Khan Development Network which is the umbrella organization for a group of agencies and funds concentrating on education, health, culture, relief, and micro-finance.[69]

---

[68] See the discussion of specific organizations and their activities in Clark, *Islam, Charity, and Activism.*

[69] One recent book on charity in the Muslim world is Benthall and Bellion-Jourdan, *The Charitable Crescent*, which situates the topic in the context of contemporary aid organizations. Another portrait of Islamic charity in the 1990s and early twenty-first century, largely pessimistic in its focus on the nexus of charity and violent political activism, can be found in Burr and Collins, *Alms for Jihad.* On the Aga Khan's activities, see http://www.akdn.org/ (accessed September 12, 2007). See also ISIM Review 20 (Autumn 2007): 5–19, a special section of articles on Muslim NGOs.

"Kimse Yok Mu" ("Isn't there anyone?") is an example of one local Turkish organization with a transnational vision. The text in its half-page newspaper advertisement (Fig. 17) from 6 Ramadan 1427 (September 29, 2006) reads:

"Mother, will we have an *iftar* meal to break the fast this evening?" We are bringing the blessing of Ramadan to Palestine, Lebanon, Indonesia, and Pakistan. [Contribute] a one-person iftar meal for 4 ytl [new Turkish lira]; a package of provisions for 50 ytl. You can also contribute to this effort by telling your friends about the campaign.

The advertisement provides details on how contributions can be made by direct bank deposit, by sending a text message to a particular number belonging to either of two Turkish mobile phone service providers, or by visiting the organization's website. While all the banks listed in the advertisement are Turkish and located in Turkey, the only beneficiaries mentioned are foreign. The organization's website, however, lists a large number of projects both in Turkey and abroad, for disaster relief as well as ongoing support to needy families, young people, and hospital patients.[70] This is only one example of a contemporary aid association that identifies itself and its beneficiaries as Muslims. If the Muslim community, the umma, has always been imagined as a global community, in the early twenty-first century it is possible, even simple, for Muslims actually to reach out to Muslims anywhere. The worldwide potential of all contemporary aid organizations is by now a commonplace.

National and transnational Islamic organizations alike may have uneasy relationships with governments, which, on the one hand, applaud the relief and development efforts of citizens' associations, while on the other, may view with suspicion the resources and support that some of these organizations can marshal. Like Sultan Abdülhamid II and the early efforts of the Ottoman Red Crescent Society, today's governments are wary of the possibility that social projects may turn into political ones.

The composition of the mixed economy of charity changed noticeably in the nineteenth and twentieth centuries in response to the needs of benefactors and beneficiaries alike, introducing new forms of donors and donations, and altering some definitions of beneficiaries. The relative impact of imperial and elite charity lessened as governments slowly took on some of what had previously been left largely in private hands. Individual rulers continued to play a role as prominent benefactors of the subject population, especially in those Muslim countries where dynastic rule survived, and in this way the importance of individual giving by rulers continued in many places as an integral component of their office and status. Scholars of Islamic history have mostly argued that until the reforms of the nineteenth century changed the conceptualization of the role of government and

---

[70] Http://www.kimseyokmu.org.tr/en (accessed September 10, 2007).

Fig. 17. Newspaper advertisement in Turkey's *Radikal* newspaper, September 29, 2006, for the organization "Kimse Yok Mu" suggesting different ways for people to pay zakat al-fitr by sponsoring individual iftar meals or larger packages. "Kimse Yok Mu" means "Isn't there anyone?" and was the phrase used by rescuers when looking for survivors after the devastating 1999 earthquake in Turkey. In 2006, the organization was specifically targeting needy people in Palestine, Lebanon, Indonesia, and Pakistan. Courtesy of Kimse Yok Mu.

the nature of the state, the actions of rulers can be understood only as those of individuals.[71] The Islamic laws relevant to charitable giving recognize only individuals as benefactors. However, it seems difficult to maintain this neat separation between the individual ruler and the office of ruler when it comes to charitable action. Ottoman sultans, Byzantine emperors, and Russian tsars alike, as well as the English and Jordanian monarchs of the present, have often been active benefactors. While their actions are essentially those of individuals, they are also part of their obligations as rulers, as defined by the traditions of sovereignty they inherited. One can disentangle only with great difficulty the ruling office from the individual occupant and this is particularly true when one tries to assess to what extent a sovereign was free to decide about acts of charity, with regard to either size, character, place, or timing. Ultimately, too, the distinctions between the sovereign and the office may not have been firm in the public mind until the modern era when the apparatus of government became, at least in some places, more ideologically, structurally and functionally distinguished from its serving head. The fact that no clear line existed at all times between the Ottoman privy purse and a state treasury only reinforced the identification of ruler and state. Although rulers gave sadaqa as individuals, there was also an element of obligation inherent in their giving, and it is perhaps this obligation of office that constitutes a link between the long-familiar personal, individual charity of rulers and the impersonal, bureaucratic welfare of modern states.

Over the course of the nineteenth century, waqfs played a dwindling role in the general provision of social services and in the distribution of assistance to the poor. As more and more waqf revenues flowed into the coffers of the Ottoman treasury, with the budget of the Ministry of Waqfs gradually shrinking, state mechanisms emerged to fill the place formerly held by the endowments as well as by private efforts. Eventually, too, various kinds of private trusts and endowments modified by modern law also joined the mixed economy. The reorganizations of poor relief that continued throughout the nineteenth and twentieth centuries included opening state-sponsored shelters and hospitals to which admission could be voluntary or imposed, as well as the founding of private, voluntary associations and organizations to provide relief. While poor relief continued to be inspired by religious precepts and motivations, there emerged a new politics of poverty that was thoroughly entangled in the processes of modernization, the activities of missionaries, merchants, diplomats, and foreign travelers, the creation of centralized bureaucratic states, the imposition of colonial regimes, the struggle for nationhood and independence, and the emergence of an educated, professional middle class. The interests and identities that bound people together and elicited a charitable response stretched

---

[71] Stillman, "Charity and Social Service in Medieval Islam," 105.

beyond political boundaries, even as they did in the past. However, by the late twentieth century, technological innovation had made possible global communication and movement such that transnational communities became a reality. International aid became as feasible as local or national assistance.

Voluntary associations and non-governmental organizations worldwide have gradually become important contributors to social welfare and economic development. Islamic countries and Muslim minority communities alike have witnessed the dynamic growth of independent associations created by individuals and groups motivated by everything from single local goals like assistance for widows or responding immediately to emergencies such as earthquakes, to broad long-term issues like healthcare, literacy, environmental protection, and human development. Associations provided elite groups and then the middle class a means to claim some measure of public presence and even authority in the context of different authoritarian regimes, at least in the few Middle Eastern examples we have discussed. Their inclusion in the mixed economy also highlights further the competitive aspects of charity as well as the potential threat posed, for example, by citizens' associations to autocratic governments or by governments to individual liberties. Competition and risk are today an important aspect of the dynamics informing charitable action and the negotiation of the charitable sphere between sovereigns and subjects, states and citizens.

More donors became visible as people from the growing middle class joined associations and combined their resources for common goals. Historically, they perhaps gave similar amounts of charity, but their collective impact became more noticeable. As in most of the cases discussed throughout this book, the missing or invisible agents remained the poorer households whose charitable giving was largely personal and small. Missing, too, are the people who straddled the line between poverty and sufficiency throughout their lives, falling now to this side, now to the other. The baker Abu Illya hinted to Lalla Fatiha of the day when he would no longer be able to work and might rely on the zakat of Lalla Fatiha's children to support him. Abu Illya and Lalla Fatiha's story continues to offer a rare window into a middle-class version of zakat paying where no official system exists. While the example of Abu Illya has provided much food for thought, one can only speculate whether he and his family were typical of a broader phenomenon. It leaves unanswered the question of whether there were state-funded agencies to which Lalla Fatiha might have turned, whether she did so, and what factors might have colored her decision.

The emergence of the welfare state and its addition to the mixed economy of charity did not alter the fact that Islamic societies are essentially welfare societies. The new welfare services provided by states may have displaced private giving to different targets than those under government responsibility, but the spiritual importance of zakat and sadaqa have remained undiminished. In theory, states were involved in zakat collection and distribution from the earliest Muslim era. In practice, as we have seen, many apparently abandoned this function, or else considered it to be incorporated into broader taxation policies. By the second half of the twentieth century, more governments with a self-consciously Islamic identity were implementing official or quasi-official zakat collection and distribution systems. It will be interesting to observe their fate in light of what seems to be the limited success of such systems in the past. The advantages for governments imposing centralized zakat today are several, including the ability of governments to tap into income at source in much the same way that social security, health insurance, and other payments may be deducted from individuals' paychecks. It seems clear, as well, that a well-run national system ultimately would be more effective at delivering aid to individual needy people, particularly with the tools of modern communication and transport. On the other hand, it is not certain that central governments are generally more effective at constructing development projects that contribute to the overall reduction of poverty and create capacity for self-sustenance among those in need.

Fig. 18. Complex at Divriği (northeast Anatolia), including a mosque built by the Mangujukid ruler Ahmad Shah and an adjoining hospital built by his wife Turan Malik in 1228–41. Author's photo.

Conclusion: re-orienting charity

> The ancient Moslem tradition of tossing a coin to the leprous beggar in the square was brought up to date by the Aga Khan in huge endowments to hospitals and schools.
>
> From the obituary of Sir Sultan Mahomed Shah Aga Khan,
> *Time* magazine (July 22, 1957)

With these words, *Time* magazine offered what was presumed to be an irreproachable encomium to describe the late Aga Khan (1877–1957). Yet while the sentence was obviously a sincere tribute to his impressive philanthropic endeavor, it reflected utter ignorance of the charity ethos that is an inseparable part of Muslim belief and practice, as well as of the obvious evidence of centuries of monumental charitable endeavors (Fig. 18). It is the intentions and accomplishments of charity in Islamic societies that this book has sought to understand by studying Muslim religious teachings and specific historical examples. The focus on Islamic societies has also suggested the extent to which Muslim acts of charity share in more universal traits of philanthropy and how studying them contributes to a subtler appreciation of philanthropy throughout history.

This book has set out to do a number of things. First, to raise the question of whether there is something identifiably Islamic in the ideologies and practices of charity in Islamic societies. Second, to demystify the nature and practice of Islamic charity for scholars, students, and interested readers at the beginning of the twenty-first century. Third, to confirm that the prism of charity is a fruitful one through which to examine the historical record of human activity and the engines of historical change. If this book began with the proposal that it was in part the seeming transparency of charity in Islamic societies that had heretofore deflected attention from it as a topic of study, the intervening chapters have, I hope, problematized the topic in a convincing manner. Fourth, the book aimed to illustrate that the comparative study of charity contributes to exploring the differences and similarities between societies and their historical experiences. Fifth, this study has sought to attract students and scholars to the historical study of charity as a fruitful field of inquiry in the history of Islamic societies. The examples discussed throughout the book represent only a starting point, and they illustrate the extent and variety of source materials available for research.

The answer to the question of whether it is possible to talk about Islamic charity and not simply charity in Islamic societies is "yes". Charitable acts, both as zakat and as sadaqa, play a key role in the religious beliefs of Muslims, and are the especially close companions to prayer: without them, faith is incomplete. They are an integral aspect of the relationship between God and human beings during their lives and with reference to an afterlife, and they are a key expression of religious belief in the interactions between human beings. Yet the charity practices of Muslims are also shaped by the individual personality of each benefactor and the immediate circumstances of each act, as well as its larger historical context. These factors determine that Muslim charity also belongs inseparably to human beneficence in general.

Throughout history, charitable giving had enormous symbolic significance and its practical impact seems to have been felt almost universally, if not equally or necessarily equitably. Normative Islamic texts and the interpretations of Muslim jurists defined a charity ethos and prescribed the form, amount, circumstances, duration, and manner that charitable giving would take. They proposed principles and rules to govern the giving and acceptance of charity in order to guide people and to mitigate some of the less positive human responses – pride, condescension, shame, greed – that might be inspired by acts of charity. Yet at the same time, enormous scope remained for the translation of principles into concrete actions.[1] It bears remembering that any event was an occasion to praise God, recognizing God's omniscience. Praising God is a form of prayer, and prayer and charity are closely and repeatedly linked in the Qur'an, such that any occasion for prayer could equally become one for a material donation, recalling the Qur'anic exhortations to pray and give alms.

Why is it the case that an emphasis on charitable giving permeates the Qur'an, hadith, juristic, and literary texts produced in Islamic contexts? Theologically, charity was God's divine command as revealed to his prophet Muhammad. Historically and sociologically, it was a legacy from the predecessors and a characteristic shared with contemporaries of the Muslims. Culturally, politically, and economically it became inseparably embedded in most vertical relationships. Muslims chose to preserve and highlight charity, or rather the authors of the texts we read did so. One important project is to study the authors of Muslim texts to understand their own relationships to the ideals and practices of the charitable giving they discussed. Did they recognize in charitable giving an important factor binding people to God and to each other? The authors discussed here belonged mostly to the large class of literate and learned people who were spiritual leaders and teachers. Donations of all sizes from the community of believers made an important contribution to their

---

[1]   See, for example, Bird, "Comparative Study," 145.

support, and they thus had a clear interest in maintaining, indeed nurturing, an attitude that contributed to their sustenance. In this they resembled the priests of the Catholic and Orthodox churches, the men and women belonging to Christian monastic orders, the Jewish rabbis and scholars, and other religious leaders. Yet it is important to explore further why the frame of charity was chosen to accomplish certain projects beyond the distribution of assistance to the needy and support for a learned class of Muslim scholars. An enormous spectrum of social and cultural projects was created and sustained by charitable contributions, many of them endowments. These all came under the heading of promoting maslaha, public good. Any investment that furthered maslaha was considered an acceptable use of wealth. Public good included the notion of social justice and just relations between people in society.

The impact and message of charity were continually on display in the form of buildings, fountains, paintings, textiles, and calligraphed inscriptions worked into wood, ceramic, and metal. Reminders to be generous took different forms. Key phrases and maxims not only were learned by heart, but could be written out as decorative reminders, as on the doors of the Beyhekim mosque (see Fig. 1). Among other places, these phrases appeared written on bowls produced in medieval Iran and Central Asia. One such inscription read: "Generosity (*jud*) is the guardian of honor and property," while another said: "Generosity does not consume wealth before it is exhausted, and greed will not increase a miser's wealth" (Fig. 19). The sayings were a visual reminder that a feast or an everyday meal was an occasion for practicing generosity and suggested that generosity has the capacity to increase and preserve material and social standing. These were ideas drawn from the broader cultural values defined by *adab*, moral and intellectual ideals and habits instilled by education.[2] Several centuries later and a continent away, Evliya Çelebi copied down a verse he read inscribed on the reception halls of Balkan mansions where he was a guest. Its words echoed the sentiment and expectations found on the Samanid bowls: "The honor of the house depends on its owner, and the honor of its owner depends on his generosity" (*Şerefü'l-beyti bi-ehlihi ve şerefü ehlihi bi-sehā'ihi*). Evliya claimed that it was considered shameful to eat alone and that the homes of the wealthy were always open to guests and wayfarers.[3]

The proverb found on another Samanid bowl – "Generosity is not just giving money from excess, but rather sharing with the poor" – articulates the link between generosity and one aspect of charity, that is, giving to the poor.[4] This

[2] Oya Pancaroğlu, "Serving Wisdom: The Contents of Samanid Epigraphic Pottery," in *Studies in Islamic and Later Indian Art from the Arthur M. Sackler Museum* (Cambridge, MA: Harvard University Art Museums, 2002), 61–62.
[3] Robert Dankoff and Robert Elsie, trans. and eds., *Evliyā Çelebi in Albania (Kosovo, Montenegro, Ohrid)* (Leiden: Brill, 2000), 167–69.
[4] Pancaroğlu, "Serving Wisdom," 61–62.

Fig. 19. Earthenware bowl from Nishapur, Iran, *c.* 850–1000, with inscription around the interior, reading: "Generosity does not consume wealth before it is exhausted, and greed will not increase a miser's wealth" *(lā'l-jūdu yufnī'l-māla qabla fanā'ihi wa lā'l-bukhlu fī māli'l-shaḥīḥi yuzīdu).* With the permission of Harvard University Art Museums, Arthur M. Sackler Museum, Gift of John Goelet, 1958.22.#15979.

brings our discussion back to the unresolved matter of how to draw boundaries between the ideas of charity, hospitality, generosity, welfare, and patronage, and the question of whether there are actually clear distinctions between them. The generosity celebrated on the Samanid bowls and the walls of notable Ottoman houses was the hospitality implied by sharing meals and welcoming guests. Yet the same notable houses, according to Evliya or the description of the impoverished Enis Pasha, also provided meals to indigent people. Meanwhile, when a powerful person fed his own retainers or promoted their welfare, it was called patronage. The same act of feeding people became imperial charity in an endowed imaret. When modern state ministries eventually took over the effort, it would be as part of the functions of welfare services. Is it possible that these different words all describe the same action, and that the label changes depending on who takes the action and the context of the act? Are they alternative linguistic choices meant to hide or cushion the fact of vertical relationships? Do they signal different expectations regarding recompense or return, and the presence or absence of reciprocity? Do they imply different motivations for making distributions? And how is it possible to judge motivations in the absence (or even in the presence) of first-person accounts?

The Qur'an suggests answers to some of these questions by reminding believers that only God truly knows the intentions of a single person and a person's true intentions cannot be hidden from God. Historians and social scientists, on the other hand, examine evidence of all types to understand human behavior and its impact on society. We might make the case that distributing food is really an example of altruistic beneficence. And yet, with respect to each of the examples listed above, the benefactors may also have expectations from the beneficiaries. The poor are (in theory) calmed by having their bellies filled, and so less likely to be discontent in ways that can be exploited for political purposes. Most scholars, receiving support to continue their study and research, upheld and reproduced systems of law and learning that strengthened government and a social order that maintained Muslim rulers in power. For the sultan or any person distributing food, the presence of guests served to reinforce the standing of the host in the eyes of his subordinates and his peers. Under the Ottomans, patronage and hospitality met in the distribution of meals. The philanthropy at work in the public kitchens of the Ottoman Empire was part of an extensive and ongong project of beneficence inextricably linked to the Muslim identity of the dynasty. However, it was a wide-ranging philanthropy, extending to include practically every part of society as its beneficiaries. Like much philanthropy, its goals were not radical but conservative, aiming to reproduce or bolster social or cultural norms and in so doing to strengthen vertical economic and social relationships, including those determined by profession, class, age, and gender.

Philanthropy is a complete language, with a lexicon of actions that acquire meaning through a grammar of social order and a syntax of significations. This language becomes part of religion, law, social practice, economic exchange, and cultural expectations. To understand the implications of philanthropy requires decoding the meaning of each act in order to discover which relationship is being created or invoked, and the expectations implied. The preceding attempt to thread our way through a collection of terms highlights how far the discussion of actions described as sadaqa has stretched the meaning of charity, and it is now time to confront this and its implications. Charity, which we have used in this book along with the words philanthropy and beneficence as synonyms, is perhaps too restrictive a term to express the relationships described by actions that come under the headings of zakat and sadaqa. Seeing charity only as a response to poverty produces a distorted perspective of its role and impact on Islamic societies, in fact on any society.

Rather, charity is only one way of framing the relationships formed by human obligations and entitlements. Obligations exist throughout human society, while the idea of entitlement opens up a vast number of possibilities for whom we might find on the receiving end of beneficent distributions, shattering our initial expectations. As discussed in chapter 1, the idea of entitlement is inherent in the Qur'anic term *haqq* (right, just claim). In this context, it is less surprising to find that commanders, ministers, scholars, and indigent people would all receive distributions from a sultan on the same occasion. Eating at an imaret, for example, was a privilege claimed by deserving people of status as rightfully theirs, not something that compromised their status or seemed shameful. Distinctions between different forms of entitlements or the status of the recipients were signaled in the imarets by different kinds and varying amounts of food, the order in which people ate, the place where they ate, and the dishes from which they ate. The Süleymaniye imaret in Damascus hosted its high-ranking guests in individual rooms where they were served around spaces especially set for meals, two groups of five in each room. Compare this with the eight hundred others who dined in two common refectories. In Istanbul, descriptions of food distributions from the imperial palace do not neglect to mention in detail the containers in which the food was given out; it was not necessarily the contents, but the beautifully crafted vessels made from costly materials and wrapped in finely embroidered fabrics which marked the rank of the recipients.[5] However, for some, even economic need was not a sufficient qualification to receive something from the institutionalized distributions. These, rather, had to depend on more haphazard and spontaneous distributions or ones that more often escape the historians' eyes.

There is a general tendency to look at charity/philanthropy as the province of the rich and powerful as givers, and the recipients as poor. Studying charity in Islamic societies suggests that this assumption needs to be reconsidered to understand how charity works as a social process. The charity relationship exists at all levels of society, defining vertical hierarchies and power gradients even between those who have relatively little, all of which were reinforced,

---

[5] Tülay Artan, "Aspects of the Ottoman Elite's Food Consumption: Looking for 'Staples,' 'Luxuries,' and 'Delicacies,' in a Changing Century," in *Consumption Studies and the History of the Ottoman Empire, 1550–1922: An Introduction*, ed. Donald Quataert (Albany: State University of New York Press, 2000), 107–200.

much as Mauss proposed, by gifts. Donations affected the texture of inter-personal relations and charitable giving created bonds of dependence and obligation, gratitude and subservience. These were a form of social glue. At the same time, the ability to give at a particular level is an important indicator of horizontal divisions in society, enabling people to identify their peers as those who give in similar ways and comparable amounts.

We must acknowledge that charitable giving may be the product of sincere religious belief. The fact that belief is (for most people other than the saints and some holy figures) inseparable from some measure of self-interest (the desire to attain Paradise, for example) or self-promotion (seeking status within the community) has been acknowledged as a deeply human trait in religious texts, even as it is seen as a weakness. Qur'anic passages and hadith about proper ways to give touch on some of the universal problems of charitable giving, issues which find their echoes in Judaism and Christianity, in the present as well as in the past, in contemporary secular philanthropy and faith-based giving alike. Charity is not free of politics or propaganda, and it can be and is harnessed in the service of ideology. Just as people criticized the proselytizing agenda of Christian missionaries who provided education and health services, so do people criticize Islamic charity organizations and suspect the ulterior motives of their social welfare projects. However, it is not sufficient to examine only the propagandistic, unfamiliar, or even destructive aspects of charitable activities; one must understand the social context in which they exist, how they serve interests associated with class, confession, gender, or national identity, and why charity is the chosen medium for acting.

It is perhaps time to re-orient charity-philanthropy studies. Even the current nascent state of charity-philanthropy studies in Islamic societies is sufficient to challenge the long-held perception that western (Judeo-Christian), and most especially the US charitable traditions and practices, constitute the most power-ful charity-philanthropy paradigm in history.[6] It is useful to reconsider Alexis de Tocqueville's oft-cited description of philanthropy as he observed it on his visit to the United States in the early nineteenth century.

Americans of all ages, all conditions, and all dispositions constantly form associations. They have not only commercial and manufacturing companies, in which all take part, but associations of a thousand other kinds, religious, moral, serious, futile, general or restricted, enormous or diminutive. The Americans make associations to give entertain-ments, to found seminaries, to build inns, to construct churches, to diffuse books, to send missionaries to the antipodes; in this manner they found hospitals, prisons, and schools.

---

[6] A recent collection of essays has questioned the long-standing, ahistorical presentation of US charity which has seen American philanthropy as unique, distinctive, and perhaps even morally superior. See Lawrence J. Friedman, "Philanthropy in America: Historicism and its Discontents," in *Charity, Philanthropy, and Civility in American History*, ed. Lawrence J. Friedman and Mark D. McGarvie (Cambridge, UK: Cambridge University Press, 2003), 16–17.

If it is proposed to inculcate some truth or to foster some feeling by the encouragement of a great example, they form a society. Wherever at the head of some new undertaking you see the government in France, or a man of rank in England, in the United States you will be sure to find an association.[7]

De Tocqueville identified associations in the United States as a key aspect in the development of democracy, but his description has also been cited to point to the extraordinary force of US philanthropy. Yet the power and achievements of philanthropy in Islamic societies are equally notable. They were largely the accomplishment of individuals until the early twentieth century, but since that time include associations of all types as well. The ability of individuals and associations to act has been and continues to be circumscribed by political constraints in many places and there are also those with destructive and violent agendas. However, the presence of these latter is not a sufficient reason to discredit the phenomenon or to ignore the long-standing tradition on which it is based.

The building achievements of Muslim philanthropists might also be reconsidered in the light of US industrialist and philanthropist Andrew Carnegie's (1835–1919) prescriptions for establishing institutions for the public good as the best way to use wealth. In his famous essay "The Gospel of Wealth," Carnegie assigned to the super-wealthy few the duty of improving society wisely through the administration of their wealth, as custodians of the fortunes of society at large. He defined the best uses of philanthropy as being the founding of universities, libraries, hospitals, public parks, meeting halls, swimming pools, and churches. According to Carnegie, each of these institutions could improve the lives of the poor and working classes, and also contribute to the rest of society.[8] Carnegie's philosophy evolved within the context of his own Christian background and his rags-to-riches American immigrant life history. In the same way, wealthy Muslim men and women made their endowments to promote public welfare, with reference to Islamic traditions, personal achievements, and local expectations. What is curious is that their efforts over hundreds of years for the most part produced a list of buildings similar to the one compiled by Carnegie (except for the swimming pools). It is unlikely that Carnegie knew about philanthropic practices in Islamic societies. Rather, powerful elites have long recognized the diverse benefits of creating institutions to provide education, health, religious ritual, and leisure facilities. The study of charity in Islamic societies offers new ways of understanding the role of charity in human history.

---

[7] De Tocqueville, *Democracy in America*, 595.
[8] Carnegie, "The Gospel of Wealth."

Select bibliography

Abbott, Nabia. *Two Queens of Baghdad: Mother and Wife of Hārūn al-Rashīd*. Chicago: University of Chicago Press, 1946.

Abedi, Mehdi, and Michael M. J. Fischer. "An Iranian Village Boyhood." In *Struggle and Survival in the Modern Middle East*, edited by Edmund Burke III, 320–35. Berkeley: University of California Press, 1993.

Abu Zayd, Nasr Hamid. "Intention." In *Encyclopaedia of the Qur'ān*, vol. II, edited by Jane Dammen McAuliffe, 549–51. Leiden: Brill, 2002.

Alshech, Eli. "Islamic Law, Practice, and Legal Doctrine: Exempting the Poor from the Jizya under the Ayyubids (1171–1250)." *Islamic Law and Society* 10 (2003): 348–76.

Amin, Muḥammad M. *Al-Awqāf wa'l-ḥayāt al-ijtimā'iyya wa'l-iqtiṣādiyya fī Miṣr: 648–923 (1250–1517)*. Cairo: Dār al-Nahḍa al-'Arabiyya, 1980.

Catalogue des documents d'archives du Caire de 239/853 à 922/1516. Cairo: Institut Français d'Archéologie Orientale, 1981.

Arberry, Arthur J., trans. *The Koran Interpreted*. New York: Macmillan, 1955.

Arjomand, Said Amir. "Philanthropy, the Law and Public Policy in the Islamic World before the Modern Era." In *Philanthropy in the World's Traditions*, edited by W. Ilchman, S. N. Katz, and E. L. Queen, 109–32. Bloomington: Indiana University Press, 1998.

Artan, Tülay. "Aspects of the Ottoman Elite's Food Consumption: Looking for 'Staples,' 'Luxuries,' and 'Delicacies,' in a Changing Century." In *Consumption Studies and the History of the Ottoman Empire, 1550–1922: An Introduction*, edited by Donald Quataert, 107–200. Albany: State University of New York Press, 2000.

Atasoy, Nurhan. *1582 Surname-i Hümayun: An Imperial Celebration*. Istanbul: Koçbank, 1997.

Atil, Esin. *Levni and the Surname: The Story of an Eighteenth-Century Ottoman Festival*. Seattle: University of Washington Press, 2000.

Baer, G. "Jerusalem's Families of Notables and the Waḳf in the Early 19th Century." In *Palestine in the Late Ottoman Period*, edited by David Kushner, 109–22. Jerusalem: Yad Izhak Ben-Zvi, 1986.

"The Dismemberment of *Awqāf* in Early Nineteenth-Century Jerusalem." In *Ottoman Palestine, 1800–1914: Studies in Economic and Social History*, edited by Gad G. Gilbar, 299–319. Leiden: E. J. Brill, 1990.

"The Waqf as a Prop for the Social System, 16th–20th Centuries." *Islamic Law and Society* 4 (1997): 264–97.

"Women and Waqf: An Analysis of the Istanbul Tahrîr of 1546." *Asian and African Studies* 17 (1983): 9–27.

Barkan, O. L. "Osmanlı İmparatorluğunda bir İskân ve Kolonizasyon metodu olarak Vakıflar ve Temlikler: I. İstila Devirlerinin Kolonizatör Türk Dervişleri ve Zaviyeler." *Vakıflar Dergisi* 2 (1942): 279–386.

Barkan, O. L., and Ekrem Hakki Ayverdi, eds. *İstanbul Vakıflar Tahrîr Defteri, 953 (1546) Tarîhlî*. Istanbul: Fetih Cemiyeti, 1970.

Barnes, John Robert. *An Introduction to Religious Foundations in the Ottoman Empire*. Leiden: E. J. Brill, 1987.

Baron, Beth. "Islam, Philanthropy, and Political Culture in Interwar Egypt: The Activism of Labiba Ahmad." In *Poverty and Charity in Middle Eastern Contexts*, edited by Michael Bonner, Mine Ener, and Amy Singer, 239–54. Albany: State University of New York Press, 2003.

The Women's Awakening in Egypt: Culture, Society, and the Press. New Haven: Yale University Press, 1994.

Bashear, Suliman. "On the Origins and Development of the Meaning of Zakāt in Early Islam." *Arabica* 40 (1993): 84–113.

Beach, M. C., and E. Koch. *King of the World: The Padshahnama*. London: Thames and Hudson, 1997.

Behar, Cem. *A Neighborhood in Ottoman Istanbul: Fruit Vendors and Civil Servants in the Kasap İlyas Mahalle*. Albany: State University of New York Press, 2003.

Ben Shemesh, A., trans. and ed. *Qudāma b. Ja'far's Kitāb al-Kharāj*. Vol. II of *Taxation in Islam*. Leiden: E. J. Brill, 1965.

Benthall, Jonathan, and Jérôme Bellion-Jourdan. *The Charitable Crescent: Politics of Aid in the Muslim World*. London: I. B. Tauris, 2003.

Berkey, Jonathan P. *The Formation of Islam: Religion and Society in the Near East, 600–1800*. Cambridge, UK: Cambridge University Press, 2003.

The Transmission of Knowledge in Medieval Cairo: A Social History of Islamic Education. Princeton: Princeton University Press, 1992.

Bilici, Faruk. "Les *waqf*s monétaires à la fin de l'empire Ottoman et au début de l'époque republicaine en Turquie: des caisses de solidarité vers un système bancaire moderne." In *Le waqf dans le monde musulman contemporain (XIXe–XXe siècles): fonctions sociales, économiques et politiques*, edited by Faruk Bilici, 51–59. Istanbul: Institut Français d'Études Anatoliennes, 1994.

ed. *Le waqf dans le monde musulman contemporain (XIXe–XXe siècles): fonctions sociales, économiques et politiques*. Istanbul: Institut Français d'Études Anatoliennes, 1994.

Bird, Frederick B. "Comparative Study of the Works of Charity in Christianity and Judaism." *Journal of Religious Ethics* 10 (1982): 144–69.

Bonner, Michael. "Definitions of Poverty and the Rise of the Muslim Urban Poor." *Journal of the Royal Asiatic Society* 6, 3rd series (1996): 335–44.

"The *Kitāb al-Kasb* Attributed to al-Shaybānī: Poverty, Surplus, and the Circulation of Wealth." *Journal of the American Oriental Society* 121 (2001): 410–27.

"Poverty and Charity in the Rise of Islam." In *Poverty and Charity in Middle Eastern Contexts*, edited by Michael Bonner, Mine Ener, and Amy Singer, 13–30. Albany: State University of New York Press, 2003.

"Poverty and Economics in the Quran." *The Journal of Interdisciplinary History* 35, no. 3 (2005): 391–406.

Bonner, Michael, Mine Ener and Amy Singer, eds. *Poverty and Charity in Middle Eastern Contexts*. Albany: State University of New York Press, 2003.

Bosworth, C. E. *The Mediaeval Islamic Underworld: The Banū Sāsān in Arabic Society and Literature. Part One: The Banū Sāsān in Arabic Life and Lore*. Leiden: E. J. Brill, 1976.

Bowen, Donna Lee. "Abu Illya and Zakat." In *Everyday Life in the Muslim Middle East*, edited by Donna Lee Bowen and Evelyn A. Early, 218–21. Bloomington: Indiana University Press, 1993.

Briggs, Asa. "Welfare State." In *Dictionary of the History of Ideas*, vol. IV, edited by Philip P. Wiener, 508–15. New York: Charles Scribner's Sons, 1973.

Brown, Peter. *Poverty and Leadership in the Later Roman Empire*. Hanover, NH: University Press of New England, 2002.

al-Bukhari, Muhammad b. Isma'il. *Sahih al-Bukhari*. 8 vols. in 4. Istanbul: Al-Maktaba al-Islami, 1979.

Burr, J. Millard, and Robert O. Collins. *Alms for Jihad: Charity and Terrorism in the Islamic World*. Cambridge, UK: Cambridge University Press, 2006.

Ca'fer Efendi. *Risāle-i Mi'māriyye. An Early-Seventeenth-Century Ottoman Treatise on Architecture*. Facsimile with translation and notes. Edited by Howard Crane. Leiden: E. J. Brill, 1987.

Calder, Norman. "Khums in Imami Shi'i Jurisprudence, from the Tenth to the Sixteenth Century." *Bulletin of the School of Oriental and African Studies* 45, no. 1 (1982): 39–47.

Calder, Norman, Jawid Mojaddedi, and Andrew Rippin, eds. and trans. *Classical Islam: A Sourcebook of Religious Literature*. London: Routledge, 2003.

Carnegie, Andrew. "The Gospel of Wealth." *North American Review* 148 and 149 (June–December 1889): 1–36.

Cavallo, Sandra. "The Motivations of Benefactors: An Overview of Approaches to the Study of Charity." In *Medicine and Charity before the Welfare State*, edited by J. Barry and C. Jones, 46–62. London: Routledge, 1991.

Charity and Power in Early Modern Italy: Benefactors and their Motives in Turin, 1541–1789. Cambridge, UK: Cambridge University Press, 1995.

Chaumont, Eric. "Pauvreté et richesse dans le Coran et dans les sciences religieuses musulmanes." In *Pauvreté et richesse dans le monde musulman méditerranéen/ Poverty and Wealth in the Muslim Mediterranean World*, edited by Jean-Paul Pascual, 17–26. Paris: Maisonneuve et Larose, 2003.

Çizakça, Murat. "Cash Waqfs in Bursa, 1555–1823." *Journal of the Economic and Social History of the Orient* 38 (1995): 313–54.

A History of Philanthropic Foundations. Istanbul: Boğaziçi University Press, 2000.

Clark, Grace. "Pakistan's Zakat and 'Ushr as a Welfare System." In *Islamic Reassertion in Pakistan: The Application of Islamic Laws in a Modern State*, edited by Anita M. Weiss. Syracuse: Syracuse University Press, 1986.

Clark, Janine A. *Islam, Charity, and Activism: Middle-Class Networks and Social Welfare in Egypt, Jordan, and Yemen*. Bloomington: Indiana University Press, 2003.

Cohen, Amnon. *Jewish Life under Islam*. Cambridge, MA: Harvard University Press, 1984.

Cohen, Mark R. "The Foreign Jewish Poor in Medieval Egypt." In *Poverty and Charity in Middle Eastern Contexts*, edited by Michael Bonner, Mine Ener, and Amy Singer, 53–72. Albany: State University of New York Press, 2003.

"Maimonides and Charity in the Light of the Geniza Documents." In *The Trias of Maimonides: Jewish, Arabic and Ancient Culture of Knowledge*, edited by Georges Tamer, 65–81. Berlin: Walter de Gruyter, 2005.

Poverty and Charity in the Jewish Community of Medieval Egypt. Princeton: Princeton University Press, 2005.

The Voice of the Poor in the Middle Ages: An Anthology of Documents from the Cairo Geniza. Princeton: Princeton University Press, 2005.

Cole, Juan R. I. "Al-Tahtawi on Poverty and Welfare." In *Poverty and Charity in Middle Eastern Contexts*, edited by Michael Bonner, Mine Ener, and Amy Singer, 223–38. Albany: State University of New York Press, 2003.

Conniff, Richard. "Why We Take Risks." *Discover* 22 (2001): 62–67.

Constable, Olivia Remie. *Housing the Stranger in the Mediterranean World: Lodging, Trade, and Travel in Late Antiquity and the Middle Ages.* Cambridge, UK: Cambridge University Press, 2003.

Constantelos, Demetrios J. *Byzantine Philanthropy and Social Welfare.* New Brunswick: Rutgers University Press, 1968.

Cook, Michael. *Commanding Right and Forbidding Wrong in Islamic Thought.* Cambridge, UK: Cambridge University Press, 2001.

Cornell, Vincent. "Fruit of the Tree of Knowledge: The Relationship between Faith and Practice in Islam." In *The Oxford History of Islam*, edited by John L. Esposito, 63–107. Oxford: Oxford University Press, 1999.

Crecelius, Daniel. *Fihris waqfiyyat al-ʿasr al-ʿuthmani al-mahfuzah bi-wizarat al-awqaf wa-dar al-watha'iq al-tarikhiyyah al-qawmiyyah bi-al-Qahirah.* Cairo: Dar al-Nahdah al-ʿArabiyyah, 1992.

"The Organization of *Waqf* Documents in Cairo." *International Journal of Middle Eastern Studies* 2 (1971): 266–77.

"The Waqf of Muḥammad Bey Abū al-Dhahab in Historical Perspective." *International Journal of Middle East Studies* 23 (1991): 57–81.

"The *Waqfiyah* of Muḥammad Bey Abū al-Dhahab, I." *Journal of the Arab Research Center in Egypt* 15 (1978): 83–105.

Cronbach, Abraham. "The Gradations of Benevolence." *Hebrew Union College Annual* 16 (1941): 163–86.

"The Maimonidean Code of Benevolence." *Hebrew Union College Annual* 20 (1947): 471–540.

Daftary, Farhad. *The Ismāʿīlīs: Their History and their Doctrines.* Cambridge, UK: Cambridge University Press, 1990.

Dankoff, Robert, and Robert Elsie, trans. and eds. *Evliyā Çelebi in Albania (Kosovo, Montenegro, Ohrid).* Leiden: E. J. Brill, 2000.

Davis, Natalie Zemon. *The Gift in Sixteenth-Century France.* Madison: University of Wisconsin Press, 2000.

"Poor Relief, Humanism and Heresy." In *Society and Culture in Early Modern France*, 17–64. Stanford: Stanford University Press, 1968; repr. 1975.

de Tocqueville, Alexis. *Democracy in America.* Edited by Gertrude Himmelfarb. Translated by Arthur Goldhammer. New York: Library of America, 2004.

Deguilhem, Randi. "Gender Blindness and Societal Influence in Late Ottoman Damascus: Women as the Creators and Managers of Endowments." *Hawwa* 1 (2003): 329–50.

ed. *Le waqf dans l'espace islamique: outil de pouvoir socio-politique*. With a preface by André Raymond. Damas: Institut Français de Damas, 1995.

Deguilhem, Randi, and Abdelhamid Hénia, eds. *Les fondations pieuses (waqf) en Méditerranée: enjeux de société, enjeux de pouvoir*. Safat, Kuwait: Kuwait Awqaf Public Foundation, 2004.

Denny, Frederick Mathewson. *An Introduction to Islam*. 2nd edn. New York: Macmillan, 1994.

Deringil, Selim. *The Well-Protected Domains: Ideology and the Legitimation of Power in the Ottoman Empire 1876–1909*. London: I. B. Tauris, 1997.

Deshayes de Courmenin, Louis. *Voiage de Levant Fait par le Commandement du Roy en Lannée 1621 par Le Sr. D.C.* Paris: Adrian Taupinart, 1624.

Dols, Michael. *Majnūn: The Madman in Medieval Islamic Society*. Oxford: Clarendon Press, 1992.

Donner, Fred M. *The Early Islamic Conquests*. Princeton: Princeton University Press, 1981.

Doubleday, Veronica. *Three Women of Herat*. Austin: University of Texas Press, 1990.

Dunn, Ross E. *The Adventures of Ibn Battuta: A Muslim Traveler of the 14th Century*. Berkeley: University of California Press, 1986.

Düzdağ, M. Ertuğrul. *Şeyhülislâm Ebussuûd Efendi Fetvaları Işığında 16. Asır Türk Hayatı*. Istanbul: Enderun Kitabevi, 1983.

Edip, Halide. *The Memoirs of Halide Edip*. London: John Murray, 1926.

Ener, Mine. *Managing Egypt's Poor and the Politics of Benevolence, 1800–1952*. Princeton: Princeton University Press, 2003.

Erdem, Y. Hakan. *Slavery in the Ottoman Empire and its Demise, 1800–1906*. Basingstoke, Hampshire: Macmillan, 1996.

Ergin, Nina. "Taking Care of Imarets: Repairs and Renovations to the Atik Valide İmareti, Istanbul, circa 1600–1700." In *Feeding People, Feeding Power: Imarets in the Ottoman Empire*, edited by Nina Ergin, Christoph K. Neumann, and Amy Singer. Istanbul: Eren, 2007.

Ergin, Nina, Christoph K. Neumann, and Amy Singer, eds. *Feeding People, Feeding Power: Imarets in the Ottoman Empire*. Istanbul: Eren, 2007.

Ergut, Ferdan. "Policing the Poor in the Late Ottoman Empire." *Middle Eastern Studies* 38 (2002): 149–64.

Evliya Çelebi. *The Intimate Life of an Ottoman Statesman: Melek Ahmed Pasha (1588–1662)*. Translated and edited by Robert Dankoff. Albany: State University of New York Press, 1991.

Fahmy, Khaled. "The Police and the People in Nineteenth-Century Egypt." *Die Welt des Islams* 39 (1999): 340–77.

Faris, Nabih Amin. *The Mysteries of Almsgiving: A Translation from the Arabic with Notes of the Kitāb Asrār al-Zakāh of Al-Ghazzālī's Iḥyā 'Ulūm al-Dīn*. Beirut: Centennial Publications, American University of Beirut, 1966.

Faruki, Kemal A. "Pakistan: Islamic Government and Society." In *Islam in Asia: Religion, Politics, Society*, edited by John L. Esposito, 53–78. Oxford: Oxford University Press, 1987.

Fay, Mary Ann. "Women and Waqf: Toward a Reconsideration of Women's Place in the Mamluk Household." *International Journal of Middle Eastern Studies* 29 (1997): 33–51.

Findly, Ellison Banks. "Women's Wealth and Styles of Giving: Perspectives from Buddhist, Jain, and Mughal Sites." In *Women, Patronage, and Self-Representation in Islamic Societies*, edited by D. Fairchild Ruggles, 91–121. Albany: State University of New York Press, 2000.

Flynn, Maureen. *Sacred Charity: Confraternities and Social Welfare in Spain, 1400–1700*. Ithaca: Cornell University Press, 1989.

Foucault, Michel. *Discipline and Punish: The Birth of the Prison*. Translated by Alan Sheridan. New York: Random House, 1975.

Madness and Civilization: A History of Insanity in the Age of Reason. Translated by Richard Howard. New York: Vintage Books, 1965.

Friedman, Lawrence J. "Philanthropy in America: Historicism and its Discontents." In *Charity, Philanthropy, and Civility in American History*, edited by Lawrence J. Friedman and Mark D. McGarvie, 1–21. Cambridge, UK: Cambridge University Press, 2003.

Friedman, Lawrence J., and Mark D. McGarvie, ed. *Charity, Philanthropy, and Civility in American History*. Cambridge, UK: Cambridge University Press, 2003.

Frisch, Ephraim. *An Historical Survey of Jewish Philanthropy*. New York: The Macmillan Company, 1924.

Fück, J. W. "Ibn Khallikān." In *EI²*. III:832–33.

Gallagher, Nancy Elizabeth. *Approaches to the History of the Middle East: Interviews with Leading Middle East Historians*. Reading, UK: Ithaca Press, 1994.

Gerber, Haim. "The Waqf Institution in Early Ottoman Edirne." *Asian and African Studies* 17 (1983): 29–45.

Geremek, Bronislaw. *Poverty: A History*. Cambridge, MA: Blackwell, 1994.

al-Ghazālī, Muḥammad b. Muḥammad. *Iḥyā 'Ulūm al-Dīn: Kitāb Asrār al-Zakāt*, 274–303. Cairo: Mu'assassat al-Ḥalabī, 1387/1967–68.

Gibb, H. A. R., trans. and ed. *The Travels of Ibn Baṭṭūṭa AD 1325–1354*, vols. I–III. Cambridge, UK: Cambridge University Press, 1958–71.

trans. and ed. *The Travels of Ibn Baṭṭūṭa AD 1325–1354*, vol. IV. London: The Hakluyt Society, 1994.

Gil, Moshe. *Documents of the Jewish Pious Foundations from the Cairo Geniza*. Leiden: E. J. Brill, 1976.

Gimaret, D. "shirk." In *EI²*, IX:484–86.

Ginio, Eyal. "Living on the Margins of Charity: Coping with Poverty in an Ottoman Provincial City." In *Poverty and Charity in Middle Eastern Contexts*, edited by Michael Bonner, Mine Ener, and Amy Singer, 165–84. Albany: State University of New York Press, 2003.

Ginzberg, Lori D. *Women and the Work of Benevolence: Morality, Politics, and Class in the Nineteenth-Century United States*. New Haven: Yale University Press, 1990.

Gleave, R. "khums." In *EI²*, Supplement, 531–34.

Goitein, S. D. *A Mediterranean Society, volume I: Economic Foundations*. Berkeley: University of California Press, 1967.

Goodwin, Godfrey. *A History of Ottoman Architecture*. Baltimore: The Johns Hopkins University Press, 1971.

Gross, Robert A. "Giving in America: From Charity to Philanthropy." In *Charity, Philanthropy, and Civility in American History*, edited by Lawrence J. Friedman, and Mark D. McGarvie, 29–48. Cambridge, UK: Cambridge University Press, 2003.

Haarmann, U. "Islamic Duties in History." *Muslim World* 68 (1978): 1–24.

Hands, A. R. *Charities and Social Aid in Greece and Rome*. Ithaca: Cornell University Press, 1968.

Hathaway, Jane. *The Politics of Households in Ottoman Egypt: The Rise of the Qazdağlıs*. Cambridge, UK: Cambridge University Press, 1997.

Hennigan, Peter Charles. *The Birth of a Legal Institution: The Formation of the Waqf in the Third Century AH Hanafī Legal Discourse*. Leiden: E. J. Brill, 2004.

Herrin, Judith. "Ideals of Charity, Realities of Welfare: The Philanthropic Activity of the Byzantine Church." In *Church and People in Byzantium*, edited by Rosemary Morris, 151–64. Birmingham: Center for Byzantine, Ottoman and Modern Greek Studies, University of Birmingham, 1990.

Hess, A. "The Battle of Lepanto and its Place in Mediterranean History." *Past and Present* 57 (1972): 53–73.

Hillenbrand, Robert. *Islamic Architecture: Form, Function, and Meaning*. New York: Columbia University Press, 1994.

Himmelfarb, Gertrude. *The Idea of Poverty: England in the Early Industrial Age*. New York: Alfred A. Knopf, 1984.

Poverty and Compassion: The Moral Imagination of the Late Victorians. New York: Alfred A. Knopf, 1991.

Hodgson, Marshall G. S. *The Venture of Islam*. 3 vols. Chicago: University of Chicago Press, 1974.

Hoexter, Miriam. "Charity, the Poor, and Distributions of Alms in Ottoman Algiers." In *Poverty and Charity in Middle Eastern Contexts*, edited by Michael Bonner, Mine Ener, and Amy Singer, 145–62. Albany: State University of New York Press, 2003.

Endowments, Rulers and Community: Waqf al-Ḥaramayn in Ottoman Algiers. Leiden: E. J. Brill, 1998.

"*Waqf* Studies in the Twentieth Century: The State of the Art." *Journal of the Economic and Social History of the Orient* 41, no. 4 (1998): 474–95.

Hoexter, Miriam, Shmuel N. Eiserstadt, and Nehemia Levtzion, eds. *The Public Sphere in Muslim Societies*. Albany: State University of New York Press, 2002.

Hoffmann, Birgitt. *Waqf im Mongolischen Iran: Rashiduddins Sorge um Nachruhm und Seelenheil*. Stuttgart: Steiner, 2000.

Horden, Peregrine, and Richard Smith, eds. *The Locus of Care: Families, Communities, Institutions, and the Provision of Welfare since Antiquity*. New York: Routledge, 1998.

Hourani, Albert. "Islam in European Thought," 1990. www.tannerlectures.utah.edu/lectures/hourani90.pdf.

Humphreys, R. Stephen. *Islamic History: A Framework for Inquiry*. rev. edn. Princeton: Princeton University Press, 1991.

"Women as Patrons of Religious Architecture in Ayyubid Damascus." *Muqarnas* 11 (1994): 35–54.

Hurgronje, C. Snouck. "La zakāt." In *Oeuvres choisies*, edited by G.-H. Bousquet and J. Schacht, 150–70. Leiden: E. J. Brill, 1957.

Hurvitz, Nimrod. "Biographies and Mild Asceticism: A Study of Islamic Moral Imagination." *Studia Islamica* 85 (1997): 41–65.

Ibn Khāllikān. *Ibn Khallikan's Biographical Dictionary*. 4 vols. Translated by Mac Guckin de Slane. 1961. Paris: Printed for the Oriental Translation Fund of Great Britain and Ireland, 1842–71.

Ilchman, W., S. N. Katz, and E. L. Queen, eds. *Philanthropy in the World's Traditions.* Bloomington: Indiana University Press, 1998.

Iliffe, John. *The African Poor: A History.* Cambridge, UK: Cambridge University Press, 1987.

Imber, Colin. *Ebus's-Su'ud: The Islamic Legal Tradition.* Stanford: Stanford University Press, 1997.

Inalcik, Halil. "Istanbul: An Islamic City." *Journal of Islamic Studies* 1 (1990): 1–23.

Inalcik, Halil, and Donald Quataert, eds. *An Economic and Social History of the Ottoman Empire, 1300–1914.* Cambridge, UK: Cambridge University Press, 1994.

al-Jāḥiẓ, Abū 'Uthmān ibn Baḥr. *Book of Misers (al-Bukhalāʾ).* Translated by R. B. Serjeant. Reading: Garnet Publishing, 1997.

Jordan, W. K. *The Charities of London, 1480–1660.* London: Allen and Unwin, 1960.

The Charities of Rural England, 1480–1660. New York: The Russell Sage Foundation, 1961.

Philanthropy in England, 1480–1660: A Study of the Changing Pattern of English Social Aspirations. New York: Allen and Unwin, 1959.

Jütte, Robert. *Poverty and Deviance in Early Modern Europe.* Cambridge, UK: Cambridge University Press, 1994.

Juynboll, Th. W., and J. Pedersen. "'aḳīḳa." In *EI²*, I:337.

Kahraman, Seyit Ali. *Evkâf-Hümâyûn Nezâreti.* Istanbul: Kitabevi, 2006.

Katz, Michael B. *In the Shadow of the Poorhouse: A Social History of Welfare in America.* New York: Basic Books, 1986.

Katz, Michael B., and Christoph Sachsse. *The Mixed Economy of Social Welfare: Public/Private Relations in England, Germany and the United States, the 1870s to the 1930s.* Baden-Baden: Nomos Verlagsgesellschaft, 1996.

Kermeli, Eugenia. "Ebū Su'ūd's Definitions of Church *Vaḳfs*: Theory and Practice in Ottoman Law." In *Islamic Law: Theory and Practice*, edited by Robert Gleave and Eugenia Kermeli, 141–56. London: I. B. Tauris, 1997.

Khadduri, Madjid. "maṣlaḥa." In *EI²*, VI:738–40.

Koch, Ebba. *The Complete Taj Mahal and the Riverfront Gardens of Agra.* London: Thames and Hudson, 2006.

Konyalı, İbrahim Hakkı. *Âbideleri ve Kitabeleri ile Konya Tarihi.* Konya: Yeni Kitap Basımevi, 1964.

Köprülü, M. Fuad. *The Origins of the Ottoman Empire.* Translated and edited by Gary Leiser. Albany: State University of New York Press, 1992.

"Vakıf Müessesesinin Hukuki Mahiyeti ve Tarihi Tekâmülü." *Vakıflar Dergisi* 2 (1942): 1–36. (Published in French as "L'institution du vukouf, sa nature jurisdique et son évolution historique." *Vakıflar Dergisi, Partie Française* 2 (1942): 3–48.)

Koven, Seth, and Sonya Michel. "Womanly Duties: Maternalist Politics and the Origins of Welfare States in Germany, Great Britain, France and the United States, 1880–1920." *American Historical Review* 95 (1990): 1076–108.

Kozlowski, Gregory C. "Private Lives and Public Piety: Women and the Practice of Islam in Mughal India." In *Women in the Medieval Islamic World: Power, Patronage and Piety*, edited by Gavin R. G. Hambly, 469–88. New York: St. Martin's Press, 1998.

"Religious Authority, Reform, and Philanthropy in the Contemporary Muslim World." In *Philanthropy in the World's Traditions*, edited by W. Ilchman, S. N. Katz, and E.L. Queen, 279–308. Bloomington: Indiana University Press, 1998.

Kozma, Liat. "Women on the Margins and Legal Reform in Late Nineteenth-Century Egypt, 1850–1882." Ph.D. dissertation, New York University, 2006.

Kunt, I. Metin. *The Sultan's Servants: The Transformation of Ottoman Provincial Government, 1550–1650*. New York: Columbia University Press, 1983.

Kuran, Timur. "Islamic Redistribution through Zakat: Medieval Roots of Contemporary Problems." In *Poverty and Charity in Middle Eastern Contexts*, edited by Michael Bonner, Mine Ener, and Amy Singer, 275–94. Albany: State University of New York Press, 2003.

"On the Notion of Economic Justice in Contemporary Islamic Thought." *International Journal of Middle East Studies* 21 (1989): 171–91.

"The Provision of Public Goods under Islamic Law: Origins, Impact, and Limitations of the Waqf System." *Law and Society Review* 35 (2001): 841–98.

Kürkçüoğlu, Kemal Edib. *Süleymaniye Vakfiyesi*. Ankara: Resimli Posta Matbaası, 1962.

Lambton, A. K. S. "Awqaf in Persia: 6th–8th/12th–14th Centuries." *Islamic Law and Society* 4 (1997): 298–351.

Lane, Edward W. *An Account of the Manners and Customs of the Modern Egyptians*. London, 1836. Repr. London: East–West Publications, 1978.

An Arabic–English Lexicon. London: Williams and Norgate, 1863–93.

Lapidus, Ira M. *A History of Islamic Societies*. Cambridge: Cambridge University Press, 1988.

Muslim Cities in the Later Middle Ages. Rev. edn. Cambridge, UK: Cambridge University Press, 1984.

Lev, Yaacov. *Charity, Endowments, and Charitable Institutions in Medieval Islam*. Gainesville, FL: University Press of Florida, 2005.

"Charity and Social Practice: Egypt and Syria in the Ninth–Twelfth Centuries." *Jerusalem Studies in Arabic and Islam* 24 (2000): 472–507.

Lewis, Bernard. *Race and Slavery in the Middle East: An Historical Enquiry*. New York: Oxford University Press, 1990.

Libal, Kathryn. "'The Child Question.' The Politics of Child Welfare in Early Republican Turkey." In *Poverty and Charity in Middle Eastern Contexts*, edited by Michael Bonner, Mine Ener, Amy Singer, 255–72. Albany: State University of New York Press, 2003.

"The Children's Protection Society: Nationalizing Child Welfare in Early Republican Turkey." *New Perspectives on Turkey* 23 (2000): 53–78.

Lindenmeyr, Adele. *Poverty is not a Vice: Charity, Society, and the State in Imperial Russia*. Princeton: Princeton University Press, 1996.

Lis, C., and H. Soly. *Poverty and Capitalism in Pre-Industrial Europe*. London: Humanities Press, 1973.

Little, Donald P. *A Catalogue of the Islamic Documents from al-Ḥaram Aš-Šarīf in Jerusalem*. Beirut and Wiesbaden: Franz Steiner Verlag, 1984.

Litvak, Meir. *Shiʻi Scholars of Nineteenth-Century Iraq: The 'Ulama' of Najaf and Karbala'*. Cambridge, UK: Cambridge University Press, 1993.

Løkkegaard, Frede. *Islamic Taxation in the Classic Period, with Special Reference to Circumstances in Iraq*. Copenhagen: Branner and Korch, 1950.

McCarthy, Kathleen, ed. *Lady Bountiful Revisited: Women, Philanthropy, and Power*. New Brunswick: Rutgers University Press, 1990.

ed. *Women, Philanthropy, and Civil Society.* Bloomington: Indiana University Press, 2001.

McChesney, Robert D. *Charity and Philanthropy in Islam: Institutionalizing the Call to Do Good.* Indianapolis: Indiana University Center on Philanthropy, 1995.

Waqf in Central Asia: Four Hundred Years in the History of a Muslim Shrine, 1480–1889. Princeton: Princeton University Press, 1991.

MacFarlane, Charles. *Turkey and its Destiny: The Result of Journeys Made in 1847 and 1848 to Examine into the State of that Country.* London: John Murray, 1850.

Madelung, W. "Shī'a." In *EI²*, IX: 420–24.

Makdisi, George. *The Rise of Colleges.* Edinburgh: Edinburgh University Press, 1981.

Mandaville, J. "Usurious Piety: The Cash Waqf Controversy in the Ottoman Empire." *International Journal of Middle East Studies* 10 (1979): 289–308.

Marcus, Abraham. *The Middle East on the Eve of Modernity.* New York: Columbia University Press, 1989.

"Poverty and Poor Relief in Eighteenth Century Aleppo." *Revue du Monde Musulman et de la Mediterranée* 55–56 (1990): 171–80.

Marmon, Shaun. *Eunuchs and Sacred Boundaries in Islamic Society.* New York: Oxford University Press, 1995.

"The Quality of Mercy: Intercession in Mamluk Society." *Studia Islamica* 87 (1998): 125–39.

Masters, Bruce. *Christians and Jews in the Ottoman Arab World: The Shifting Boundaries of Political Communities 1516–1918.* Cambridge, UK: Cambridge University Press, 2001.

Mattson, Ingrid. "Status-Based Definitions of Need in Early Islamic *Zakat* and Maintenance Laws." In *Poverty and Charity in Middle Eastern Contexts*, edited by Michael Bonner, Mine Ener, and Amy Singer, 31–52. Albany: State University of New York Press, 2003.

Mauss, Marcel. *The Gift: The Form and Reason for Exchange in Archaic Societies.* Translated by W. D. Halls, with a foreword by Mary Douglas. London: Routledge, 1990.

Meier, Fritz. "The Mystic Path." In *The World of Islam*, edited by Bernard Lewis, 117–40. London: Thames and Hudson, 1976.

Meisami, Julie Scott. trans. from the Persian, ed. and annotated. *The Sea of Precious Virtues* (Baḥr al-Favā'id): *A Medieval Islamic Mirror for Princes.* Salt Lake City: University of Utah Press, 1991.

Melikian-Chirvani, A. S. "From the Royal Boat to the Beggar's Bowl." *Islamic Art* 4 (1991): 3–111.

Meriwether, Margaret L. "Women and *Waqf* Revisited: The Case of Aleppo, 1770–1840." In *Women in the Ottoman Empire: Middle Eastern Women in the Early Modern Era*, edited by Madeline C. Zilfi, 128–52. Leiden: E. J. Brill, 1997.

Mollat, Michel. *The Poor in the Middle Ages: An Essay in Social History.* New Haven: Yale University Press, 1986 (originally published in French, 1978).

Mottahedeh, Roy P. *Loyalty and Leadership in an Early Islamic Society.* Princeton: Princeton University Press, 1980.

Muslim b. al-Ḥajjāj al-Nisābūrī. *Al-Jāmi' al-Ṣaḥīḥ.* Beirut: Al-Matkab al-Tijārī, n.d.

Ṣaḥīḥ Muslim. Translated and edited by 'Abdul Ḥamīd Ṣiddīqī. Lahore: Sh. Muhammad Ashraf, 1973.

Nanji, Azim. "Almsgiving." In *Encyclopaedia of the Qur'ān*, vol. I, edited by Jane Dammen McAuliffe, 64–70. Leiden: E. J. Brill, 2001.

Natsheh, Yusuf. "Al-ʿImara al-ʿAmira: The Charitable Foundation of Khassaki Sultan (959/1552)." In *Ottoman Jerusalem: The Living City, 1517–1917*, edited by S. Auld and R. Hillenbrand, 749–90. London: Altajir World of Islam Trust, 2000.

Necipoğlu, Gülru. *The Age of Sinan: Architectural Culture in the Ottoman Empire.* Photographs and drawings by Arben N. Arapi and Reha Günay. Princeton: Princeton University Press, 2005.

"A *Kânûn* for the State, a Canon for the Arts: Conceptualizing the Classical Synthesis of Ottoman Arts and Architecture." In *Soliman le Magnifique et son temps*, edited by Gilles Veinstein, 195–216. Paris: La Documentation Française, 1992.

Niẓām al-Mulk. *The Book of Government, or Rules for Kings. The Siyar al-Muluk or Siyasat-Nama of Nizam al-Mulk.* Translated from Persian by Hubert Darke. London: Routledge and Kegan Paul, 1960.

Nizami, K. A. "faḳīr." In *EI²*, II:757–58.

Novossyolov, D. "The Islamization of Welfare in Pakistan." In *Russia's Muslim Frontiers*, edited by D. F. Eickelman, 160–74. Bloomington: Indiana University Press, 1993.

Ormsby, Eric. *Ghazali.* Makers of the Muslim World. Oxford: Oneworld Publications, 2007.

Ostrower, Francie. *Why the Wealthy Give: The Culture of Elite Philanthropy.* Princeton: Princeton University Press, 1996.

Owen, David. *British Philanthropy, 1660–1960.* Cambridge, MA: Harvard University Press, 1964.

Özbek, Nadir. "Imperial Gifts and Sultanic Legislation in the Late Ottoman Empire, 1876–1909." In *Poverty and Charity in Middle Eastern Contexts*, edited by Michael Bonner, Mine Ener, and Amy Singer, 203–20. Albany: State University of New York Press, 2003.

Osmanlı İmparatorluğu'nda Sosyal Devlet: Siyaset, İktidar ve Meşruiyet 1876–1914. Istanbul: İletişim, 2002.

"Osmanli İmparatorluğu'nda 'Sosyal Yardim' Uygulamaları: 1839–1918." *Toplum ve Bilim*, no. 83 (winter 1999/2000): 111–32.

"Philanthropic Activity, Ottoman Patriotism, and the Hamidian Regime, 1876–1909." *International Journal of Middle East Studies* 37 (2005): 59–81.

"The Politics of Poor Relief in the Late Ottoman Empire 1876–1914." *New Perspectives on Turkey* 21 (Fall 1999): 1–33.

"The Politics of Welfare: Philanthropy, Voluntarism and Legitimacy in the Ottoman Empire, 1876–1914." Ph.D. thesis, Binghamton University, State University of New York, 2001.

Öztürk, Nazif. "Osmanlılar'da Vakıfların Merkezi Otoriteye Bağlanması ve Sonuçları." In *Le waqf dans le monde musulman contemporain (XIXe–XXe siècles): fonctions sociales, économiques et politiques*, edited by Faruk Bilici, 19–41. Istanbul: Institut Français d'Études Anatoliennes, 1994.

Türk Yenileşme Tarihi Çerçevesinde Vakıf Müessesesi. Ankara: Türkiye Diyanet Vakfı Yayınları, 1995.

Pancaroğlu, Oya. "Serving Wisdom: The Contents of Samanid Epigraphic Pottery." In *Studies in Islamic and Later Indian Art from the Arthur M. Sackler Museum*, 59–75. Cambridge, MA: Harvard University Art Museums, 2002.

Patlagean, Evelyne. *Pauvreté économique et pauvreté sociale à Byzance 4e–7e siècles.* Paris: Mouton, 1977.

Pedersen, J., G. Makdisi *et al.* "madrasa." In *EI²*, V:1123–54.

Peirce, Leslie P. "The Family as Faction: Dynastic Politics in the Reign of Süleyman." In *Soliman le Magnifique et son temps,* edited by Gilles Veinstein, 105–16. Paris: La Documentation Française, 1992.

   The Imperial Harem: Women and Sovereignty in the Ottoman Empire. New York: Oxford University Press, 1993.

   Morality Tales: Law and Gender in the Ottoman Court of Aintab. Berkeley: University of California Press, 2003.

Peri, Oded. "The Muslim *Waqf* and the Collection of *Jizya* in Late Eighteenth-Century Jerusalem." In *Ottoman Palestine 1800–1914: Studies in Economic and Social History,* edited by Gad G. Gilbar, 287–97. Leiden: E. J. Brill, 1990.

   "The Waqf as an Instrument to Increase and Consolidate Political Power: The Case of the Khassekî Sultân Waqf in Late 18th Century Jerusalem." *Asian and African Studies* 17 (1983): 47–62.

   "Waqf and Ottoman Welfare Policy." *Journal of the Economic and Social History of the Orient* 35 (1992): 167–86.

Peters, Rudolph, *et al.* "wakf." In *EI²*, XI:59–99.

   "nafaqa." In *EI².* Supplement, 643–44.

Postel, Guillaume. *Des Histoires Orientales et principalement des Turks ou Turchikes et Schitiques ou Tartaresques et aultres qui en sont descendus, oeuvre pour la troisième fois augmenté.* Paris: Imprimerie de Marnef, 1575. Edited with an introduction and notes by Jacques Rollet. Istanbul: Isis, 1999.

   De la République des Turcs, là ou l'occasion s'offrera, des meurs & ly de tous muhamedistes. Poitiers: Enguilbert de Marnef, 1560.

Powers, D. S. "Orientalism, Colonialism and Legal History: The Attack on Muslim Family Endowments in Algeria and India." *Comparative Studies in Society and History* 31 (1989): 535–71.

Quataert, Jean. *Staging Philanthropy: Patriotic Women and the National Imagination in Dynastic Germany, 1813–1916.* Ann Arbor: University of Michigan Press, 2001.

The Qur'an. Hebrew version. Translated and edited by Uri Rubin. Tel Aviv: Tel Aviv University Press, 2005.

Rabie, H. *The Financial System of Egypt AH 576–741/AD 1169–1341.* London: Oxford University Press, 1972.

Rafeq, Abdul-Karim. "The Poor in Ottoman Damascus: A Socioeconomic and Political Study." In *Pauvreté et richesse dans le monde musulman méditerranéen/Poverty and Wealth in the Muslim Mediterranean World,* edited by Jean-Paul Pascual, 217–26. Paris: Maisonneuve et Larose, 2003.

Rahman, Fazlur. "Some Key Ethical Concepts of the Qur'ān." *Journal of Religious Ethics* 11, no. 2 (1983): 170–85.

Raymond, A. "The Ottoman Conquest and the Development of the Great Arab Towns." *International Journal of Turkish Studies* 1, no. 1 (1979–80): 84–101.

Riis, Thomas, ed. *Aspects of Poverty in Early Modern Europe.* Vol. I, Stuttgart: Klett-Cotta; vols. II–III, Odense, Odense University press, 1981–90.

Rizvi, Kishwar. "Gendered Patronage: Women and Benevolence during the Early Safavid Empire." In *Women, Patronage, and Self-Representation in Islamic*

Societies, edited by D. Fairchild Ruggles, 123–53. Albany: State University of New York Press, 2000.

Robbins, Kevin C. "Philanthropy." In *New Dictionary of the History of Ideas*, vol. IV, edited by Maryanne Cline Horowitz, 1757–61. New York: Charles Scribner's Sons, 2005.

Rodinson, Maxime. *Europe and the Mystique of Islam*. Translated by Roger Veinus. London: I. B. Tauris, 1987.

Rodriguez-Mañas, Francisco. "Supplanting the Ruler: The Levying of Taxes by Sūfī Zāwiyas in the Maghrib." *Islamic Quarterly* 40 (1996): 188–99.

Rosenthal, Franz. "Ṣedaḳa, Charity." *Hebrew Union College Annual* 23 (1950–51): 411–30.

"The Stranger in Medieval Islam." *Arabica* 44 (1997): 35–75.

Ruggles, D. Fairchild, ed. *Women, Patronage, and Self-Representation in Islamic Societies*. Albany: State University of New York Press, 2000.

Sabev, Orlin (Orhan Salih). "Tales of Ottoman Book Theft (19th Century)." *Journal of Ottoman Studies/Osmanlı Araştırmaları* 29 (2007): 173–201.

Sabra, Adam. *Poverty and Charity in Medieval Islam: Mamluk Egypt 1250–1517*. Cambridge, UK: Cambridge University Press, 2000.

"'Prices are in God's Hands': The Theory and Practice of Price Control in the Medieval Islamic World." In *Poverty and Charity in Middle Eastern Contexts*, edited by Michael Bonner, Mine Ener, and Amy Singer, 73–91. Albany: State University of New York Press, 2003.

Salama, O., and Y. Zilberman. "Aspakat ha-mayim li-yerushalayim ba-meot ha-16 ve-ha-17" [Water Supply to Jerusalem in the 16th and 17th Centuries]. *Cathedra* 41 (1986): 91–106.

Sanders, Paula. *Ritual, Politics, and the City in Fatimid Cairo*. Albany: State University of New York Press, 1994.

Sayyid Qutb. *Social Justice in Islam*. Translated by John D. Hardie, rev. trans. and intro. Hamid Algar. Oneonta, NY: Islamic Publications International, 2000.

Schacht, J. *An Introduction to Islamic Law*. Oxford: Oxford University Press, 1964.

Scott, James C. "Resistance without Protest and without Organization: Peasant Opposition to the Islamic *Zakat* and the Christian Tithe." *Contemporary Studies in Society and History* 29 (1987): 417–52.

Sells, Michael. *Approaching the Qur'ān: The Early Revelations*. Ashland, OR: White Cloud Press, 1999.

Shefer, Miri. *Living with Death: Medicine and Society in the Early Modern Middle East*. Albany: State University of New York Press, forthcoming.

Shoshan, Boaz. *Popular Culture in Medieval Cairo*. Cambridge, UK: Cambridge University Press, 1993.

Simonsen, Jørgen Baek. *Studies in the Genesis and Early Development of the Caliphal Taxation System*. Copenhagen: Akademisk Forlag, 1988.

Singer, Amy. "Charity's Legacies: A Reconsideration of Ottoman Imperial Endowment Making." In *Poverty and Charity in Middle Eastern Contexts*, edited by Michael Bonner, Mine Ener, and Amy Singer, 295–314. Albany: State University of New York Press, 2003.

Constructing Ottoman Beneficence: An Imperial Soup Kitchen in Jerusalem. Albany: State University of New York Press, 2002.

"Imarets." In *The Turks*, vol. III, edited by Hasan Celâl Güzel, C. Cem Oğuz, and Osman Karatay, 657–64. Ankara: Yeni Türkiye Publications, 2002.

Palestinian Peasants and Ottoman Officials: Rural Administration around Sixteenth-Century Jerusalem. Cambridge, UK: Cambridge University Press, 1994.

"The Privileged Poor of Ottoman Jerusalem." In *Pauvreté et richesse dans le monde musulman méditerranéen/Poverty and Wealth in the Muslim Mediterranean World*, edited by Jean-Paul Pascual, 257–69. Paris: Maisonneuve et Larose, 2003.

"What's so Charitable about Ottoman Charity? [Hebrew]." *Jama'a* 15 (2006): 9–30.

Slack, Paul. *The English Poor Law, 1531–1782*. Cambridge, UK: Cambridge University Press, 1995.

Smith, Grace Martin. "'Ashure and, in Particular, the 'Ashure of Muharrem." *Journal of Turkish Studies* 8 (1984): 229–31.

Sonbol, Amira al-Azhary. "Adoption in Islamic Society: A Historical Survey." In *Children in the Muslim Middle East*, edited by Elizabeth Warnock Fernea, 45–67. Austin: University of Texas Press, 1995.

Stephan, St. H. "An Endowment Deed of Khâsseki Sultân, Dated 24th May 1552." *Quarterly of the Department of Antiquities in Palestine* 10 (1944): 170–94.

Stillman, Norman A. "Charity and Social Service in Medieval Islam." *Societas* 5 (1975): 105–15.

Tabbaa, Yasser. "The Functional Aspects of Medieval Islamic Hospitals." In *Poverty and Charity in Middle Eastern Contexts*, edited by Michael Bonner, Mine Ener, and Amy Singer, 95–120. Albany: State University of New York Press, 2003.

Taylor, Christopher S. *In the Vicinity of the Righteous: Ziyāra and the Veneration of Muslim Saints in Late Medieval Egypt*. Leiden: E. J. Brill, 1999.

Terzioğlu, Derin. "The Imperial Circumcision Festival of 1582: An Interpretation." *Muqarnas* 12 (1995): 84–100.

Tezcan, Semih. *Bir Ziyafet Defteri*. Istanbul: Simurg Yayıncılık, 1998.

Thompson, E. P. "The Moral Economy of the English Crowd in the Eighteenth Century." *Past and Present* 50 (1971): 76–136.

Thys-Şenocak, Lucienne. "The Yeni Valide Mosque Complex at Eminönü." *Muqarnas* 15 (1998): 58–70.

Tietze, Andreas, ed., trans., and notes. *Muṣṭafā 'Ālī's Counsel for Sultans of 1581*. 2 vols. Vienna: Verlag der Österreichischen Akademie der Wissenschaften, 1979 and 1982.

Toledano, Ehud. "The Emergence of Ottoman-Local Elites (1700–1800): A Framework for Research." In *Middle Eastern Politics and Ideas: A History from Within*, edited by I. Pappe and M. Ma'oz, 145–62. London: IB. Tauris, 1997.

Tolmacheva, Marina. "Female Piety and Patronage in the Medieval 'Ḥajj.'" In *Women in the Medieval Islamic World: Power, Patronage and Piety*, edited by Gavin R. G. Hambly, 161–79. New York: St. Martin's Press, 1998.

Trimingham, J. S. *The Sufi Orders in Islam*. Oxford: Clarendon Press, 1971.

Tripp, Charles. *Islam and the Moral Economy: The Challenge of Capitalism*. Cambridge, UK: Cambridge University Press, 2006.

Uçuk, Cahit. *Bir İmparatorluk Çökerken*. Istanbul: Yapı Kredi Yayınları, 1995.

Ünver, A. Süheyl. *Fâtih Aşhânesi Tevzî'nâmesi*. Ankara: Istanbul Fethi Derneği Yayınları, 1953.

van Leeuwen, Richard. "The Maronite Waqf of Dayr Sayyidat Bkirkī in Mount Lebanon during the 18th Century." In *Le waqf dans l'espace islamique: outil de pouvoir socio-politique*, edited by Randi Deguilhem, 259–75. Damas: Institut Français de Damas, 1995.

Vaux, Tony. *The Selfish Altruist: Relief Work in Famine and War.* London: Earthscan, 2001.

Veyne, Paul. *Bread and Circuses: Historical Sociology and Political Pluralism.* With an introduction by Oswyn Murray, translated by Brian Pearce. London: Allen Lane, 1976.

Waines, David. *An Introduction to Islam.* 2nd edn. Cambridge, UK: Cambridge University Press, 2003.

Watt, W. Montgomery. "Al-Ghazālī." In *EI²*, II:1038–41.

Muhammad at Medina. Oxford: Oxford University Press, 1956.

Weir, T. H., and A. Zysow. "ṣadaḳa." In *EI²*, VIII:708–16.

Weiss, Holger. "Attempts to Establish an Islamic Economy: A Survey on Zakāt in Some Nineteenth-Century Muslim States of the Bilād as-Sūdān," Helsinki, 2000. Http://www.valt.helsinki.fi/kmi/Tutkimus/Sal/Weiss%20accrapaper.htm (accessed December 27, 2006).

"*Zakât* in Pre-Colonial Sub-Saharan Africa. A Tentative Survey. Part One." Helsinki, 2000. Http://www.valt.helsinki.fi/kmi/Julkais/WPt/2000/WP100HW.HTM (accessed July 5, 2007).

"*Zakât* in Pre-Colonial Sub-Saharan Africa. A Tentative Survey. Part Two." Helsinki, 2000. Http://www.valt.helsinki.fi/kmi/Julkais/WPt/2000/WP2004.HTM (accessed July 5, 2007).

Wensinck, A. J. "khitān." In *EI²*, V:20–22.

"niyya." In *EI²*, VIII:66–67.

Wensinck, A. J., and P. Marçais. "'Āshūrā'." In *EI²*, I:705–6.

Wolper, Ethel Sara. "The Politics of Patronage: Political Change and the Construction of Dervish Lodges in Sivas." *Muqarnas* 12 (1995): 39–47.

Yediyıldız, Bahaeddin. *Institution du vaqf au XVIIIe siècle en Turquie – étude socio-historique.* Ankara: Imprimerie de la Société d'Histoire Turque, 1985.

"Vakıf." In *İA*, XIII:153–72.

Yerasimos, S. "Les waqfs dans l'aménagement urbain d'Istanbul au XIXe siècle." In *Le waqf dans le monde musulman contemporain (XIXe–XXe siècles): fonctions sociales, économiques et politiques*, edited by F. Bilici, 43–49. Istanbul: Institut Français d'Études Anatoliennes, 1994.

Zarinebaf, Fariba. "Feeding the Poor: The Rabʿ-i Rashidi ʿImaret in Il-Khanid Tabriz." In *Feeding People, Feeding Power: Imarets in the Ottoman Empire*, edited by Nina Ergin, Christoph K. Neumann, and Amy Singer. Istanbul: Eren Yayınları, 2007.

Ze'evi, Dror. "The Use of Ottoman Sharīʿa Court Records as a Source for Middle Eastern Social History: A Reappraisal." *Islamic Law and Society* 5, no. 1 (1998): 35–56.

Zilfi, Madeline C. "The Kadizadelis: Discordant Revivalism in Seventeenth-Century Istanbul." *Journal of Near Eastern Studies* 45 (1986): 251–69.

The Politics of Piety: The Ottoman Ulema of the Postclassical Age (1600–1800). Minneapolis: Bibliotheca Islamica, 1989.

Zysow, A. "zakāt." In *EI²*, XI:406–22.

Index

240